POWERHOUSE

Arrington from Illinois

Taylor Pensoneau

Heritage Special Edition
American Literary Press

Powerhouse: *Arrington From Illinois*

Copyright © 2006 The Arrington Foundation

Library of Congress
Cataloging-in-Publication Data
ISBN-10: 1-56167-955-0
ISBN-13: 978-1-56167-955-3

Library of Congress Card Catalog Number:
2006908109

Published by

Heritage Special Edition
American Literary Press

8019 Belair Road, Suite 10
Baltimore, Maryland 21236
www.americanliterarypress.com

Manufactured in the United States of America

Contents

the legislature had refused to approve a boost in funding for the financially strapped mass transit authority in Chicago. Seeing he was downcast, I tried to comfort him by pointing out a possible upside: some of the anger within the Republican caucus over his support of the increase might now abate. But he said to me, "That's not the point, Jim. We're here to solve problems, and we didn't solve the problem."

He fascinated me from the first time I saw him in action at a meeting of the Illinois Legislative Council. I had prepared for my initial interaction by studying his official photo, unaware that he used a decades-old picture. So, I did not immediately recognize him. However, my attention soon fixed on a fairly short, bushy-haired man wearing an expensive silk suit and a French-cuffed shirt. He essentially commanded the agenda even though he was not the chairman. Over and over again during the next several years, I watched this mastery. His intellect, his preparation, his keen sense of purpose and a presence that summoned both respect and fear—all made him the dominant force in the General Assembly and arguably allowed him to emerge as a larger figure than the governor, Otto Kerner, in the Statehouse of the 1960s.

Senator Arrington was not possessed by a need to be liked, which gave him an advantage over colleagues who were concerned about offending others. Politicians generally do not want to make anyone mad, and Senate Republicans definitely did not want to anger this self-made millionaire attorney who was smarter, better informed, more intense, more resolute, more aggressive, more abrasive and brassier than any of them. He also, by the way, could help them fend off strong reelection challenges with an infusion of campaign cash. So, he laid out his game plan, puffed on his cigar while listening to occasional dissents from his caucus and then proceeded to follow the course he had charted with their sometimes reluctant votes amassing behind him. I remember one occasion when I was instructed to tell a former Senate Republican leader that Senator Arrington wanted him to vote against a particular piece of legislation. "Do you know why?" he asked. I told him I had been given no reason. The senator shrugged his shoulders and obeyed the directive.

Foreword

❧

I still remember how tough it was to make that phone call in 1979, even though it was more than a quarter of a century ago. I dreaded telling Senator Arrington I had decided to resign as a member of the Illinois House of Representatives. He and Abner Mikva, who went on to serve as a congressman, federal appellate judge and White House counsel, had established the legislative internship program that brought me into the Statehouse in 1968, shortly after I graduated from Eastern Illinois University. Senator Arrington had mentored me. I had observed him while he served as the Senate Republican leader during the General Assembly's 1969 session, which may have been the most momentous session in Illinois history. Moreover, W. Russell Arrington not only had dominated the legislature, but he had championed it as a coequal branch of state government. He and Jesse Unruh, then speaker of the California House of Representatives, had stood as giants on the national landscape in developing the professional staffs and information-gathering capability to deal effectively with the challenges and demands of a rapidly urbanizing, increasingly diverse Space Age society. W. Russell Arrington had been the brilliant, visionary, committed architect and engineer of the modern Illinois General Assembly, a body I now was leaving to join the executive branch as the governor's chief legislative advisor.

To my relief, the phone call went well. The stroke that had hastened his departure from the Senate years earlier left him mellow. Besides, I think he knew—at least I hope he knew—that he had made a profound impact on my approach to public service, an impact that would guide me during my days as secretary of state and governor. Often, I found myself recalling a conversation in his office after

Senator W. Russell Arrington

It raised few eyebrows when a man who built a fortune as a lawyer for businesses and by helping to launch companies like Combined Insurance and Alberto-Culver did battle for the corporate world. It also followed that a suburban Republican targeted election fraud most closely associated with the Chicago Democratic organization. However, Senator Arrington also championed laws outlawing discrimination in employment and housing. He spearheaded the effort to require that firearm owners registered with the state. He played a pivotal role in creating the Illinois Department of Children and Family Services and in development of the Department of Mental Health. Ultimately, he unsettled many Republicans and perhaps even himself by helping Governor Richard Ogilvie enact the state income tax. Indeed, he was the Senate sponsor of the income tax bill, even though he had been a longtime foe of raising revenue in that fashion. But, Arrington joined the Republican governor in recognizing there was a severe budgetary problem that required a bold solution. Furthermore, in that 1969 legislative session that earned historic status with its astonishing productivity, he aided Ogilvie in funding a massive road building program and in establishing new agencies that included ones on corrections and law enforcement, the latter of which encompassed a controversial Illinois Bureau of Investigation.

W. Russell Arrington came from modest beginnings. He was born in the downstate mining town of Gillespie and raised for the most part in East St. Louis at a time when his father worked for a railroad. He went on to wealth and a life among the affluent of Chicago. Yet, he was an advocate of civil rights legislation and of the creation of government agencies to serve the needy. He was an often intractable foe of one governor and an invaluable ally of another. His strong Republican majority in the Senate during much of his reign let him lord over Democrats; still, he enjoyed socializing with Democratic legislators in the Springfield night spots. He could be ruthless one moment and sensitive the next.

Busy in his office one day, he sent me to the Senate floor to relay a message to Cecil Partee, a Chicago Democrat destined to become the first black Senate president. Partee was struggling to win approval of then controversial legislation to commemorate the birthday of Martin Luther King Jr. with a state holiday. I told him Arrington would leave his office and come to the floor if his vote would make a difference. Partee appreciated the offer, but said he still was not near the threshold of mustering the required majority and that the Republican leader need not aggravate his conservative members. It was a revealing insight into their mutual respect, and a kind of civility we saw too little of in politics later on. There were many engaging lessons in those days for a young man interested in taking a leadership role himself in the years ahead.

Taylor Pensoneau is a gifted storyteller and he has a riveting tale to tell in this book. As readers will discover, Russell Arrington had his imperfections, like all of us. Those who enjoy alliteration found the adjective "arrogant" and the name Arrington to be a convenient and accurate tandem. He loved to wield power and often did so without regard for the feelings of others. However, he also used that power to move our state forward in many vital ways.

Senator Arrington was an amazing legislator. He also was an inspiring teacher.

Governor Jim Edgar
March 2005

Acknowledgments

❧

I had been a general assignment reporter for the *St. Louis Post-Dispatch* for a little more than three years when the editors asked me to cover the Illinois Statehouse, beginning in the fall of 1965. It was a terrific opportunity for a reporter still shy of his twenty-fifth birthday since it meant that I would have my own bureau from which to cover the world of Illinois politics.

It would be challenging. Although I was a Belleville, Illinois, native, I was a greenhorn on my state's politics and really only familiar with its biggest names at the time—Governor Otto Kerner and Chicago Mayor Richard J. Daley, along with the political headliners from my neck of the woods, mainly Alan Dixon and Paul Simon.

In trying to bone up on state government action in 1965, prior to my arrival in Springfield, I repeatedly read another name in news coverage of the capital. It was W. Russell Arrington, a Republican from Evanston who was the leader of the Illinois Senate and seemingly a major figure in every issue, legislative or otherwise.

Inquiring about Arrington, I was told that he was a rich lawyer, smart and uppity—a man who'd forcefully captured the state governmental spotlight through sheer will and determination. Not all liked him, but few did not respect him. Veteran reporters in the Capitol pressroom viewed him as a big picture guy, an individual driven to radically upgrade the General Assembly. Beyond that, he had strong ideas on where he wanted to take Illinois government—which happened to be in directions favored by many reformers.

I certainly had no quarrel with this portrait of Arrington after getting to know and cover him in the last five years of his stewardship of the Senate. His legislative prowess easily separated him from most of his peers, as did his obvious independence and forthrightness. However, frankness in the case of Arrington frequently meant tongue-lashings for those who didn't measure up in the senator's eyes. Nothing triggered Arrington's volatile temper more than incompetence. Reporters sometimes sympathized with those incurring Arrington's displeasure, but his verbal chastisements surely made—in the lingo of print journalists—darn good copy.

In the twelve years overall that I chronicled Illinois government for the *Post-Dispatch*, I found Arrington to be one of the four or five figures making the greatest impression. I wrote books on two of the others, governors Dan Walker and Richard B. Ogilvie. At the same time, I always believed that Arrington's extraordinary journey through life certainly merited recording in Illinois' political annals.

To bring this book into reality, the cooperation of many individuals was necessary. The most significant was Michael Arrington, the senator's son. From the day of the memorial service following his father's death in 1979, Michael never wavered from a determination to see that a book was written on his father and the many accomplishments in his life. But, twenty-three years transpired before Michael decided that I was the ideal person to pen the biography. He contacted me in 2002 after his daughter Jennifer saw in reading my Ogilvie book that I'd given major play to the great contributions by Senator Arrington to the success of Ogilvie's governorship.

I found Michael's assistance invaluable in providing personal and professional documents and records tied to his father. In addition, arrangements for a number of interviews important for the narrative were facilitated by Michael.

I also appreciated the ample time for the book afforded by Senator Arrington's daughter, Patricia Smythe, and Jennifer Arrington. Too, the story was strengthened by information on the family history of Ruth Browne Arrington, the senator's wife, supplied by Linda Relias, a niece of Arrington.

In addition to Arrington family members, a number of other persons were helpful in contributing background for the book or aiding in other ways.

They included Michael Lawrence, director of the Paul Simon Public Policy Institute at Southern Illinois University; Kay Harris, a

W. Russell Arrington (on right)

historical researcher in Springfield; W. Robert Blair, a former speaker of the Illinois House of Representatives; Dick L. Williams, an attorney in East Peoria; Jerry Owens, a political columnist for the old *Illinois State Register* in Springfield; Wallace (Wally) Gair, an aide to former Illinois Secretary of State Paul Powell; Rosa Escareno, assistant press secretary for Mayor Richard M. Daley of Chicago; Brian Whalen, deputy governor under former Governor Richard B. Ogilvie; and Jerome Mileur, a retired political science professor at the University of Massachusetts at Amherst.

Written sources of information for the book were extensive. I was provided with the transcript of memoirs that Senator Arrington himself dictated into a recorder in 1978 as part of his therapy in recovering from a stroke seven years earlier. The account covered his life experiences from boyhood into the year of the recording. The bulk of the quotes by Arrington in the book referring to his upbringing, his professional life and early political career was taken from the memoirs.

I also was loaned a series of scrapbooks, compiled by Arrington associates, that contained newspaper clippings, pictures and miscellaneous items related to Arrington from the 1950s through the end of his life. Transcripts of oral histories dictated by a number of Arrington's political contemporaries—through a program at the former Sangamon State University (now the University of Illinois at Springfield)—added to the input.

Furthermore, I had the use of my own *Post-Dispatch* articles, interview notes and collection of state reports during the five years that I followed the activities of Arrington.

More than fifty men and women were interviewed for this undertaking, most of whom are included in a list at the back of the book.

Of course, gratitude goes to former Governor Jim Edgar for taking the time to write the foreword about Arrington, a man the governor considered his mentor in public life.

And finally, this project would not have come to fruition without the editing and forbearance of my wife Elizabeth.

The story of W. Russell Arrington is both appealing and intriguing. I have written it in the style of a journalist. If it does not flow in an interesting manner, the responsibility lies solely with the author.

Taylor Pensoneau
April 2005

Chapter 1

℃

Born on the
Fourth of July

The Fourth of July in 1906 was an ideal day in the Illinois coal mining county of Macoupin, not many miles south of the Prairie State's capital, Springfield. Thousands of people, many of them carrying American flags and sporting red, white and blue colors, flocked to Carlinville, the seat of Macoupin, for a day of star-spangled revelry befitting the most cherished of American holidays.

They came from all parts of the county, in horse-drawn wagons, newfangled automobiles and by foot, to laugh at the troupes of black-faced and Irish comedians and compete for prizes in the wheelbarrow, three-legged, sack and foot races—all open to both "professional and amateur runners." *The Macoupin County Enquirer* also noted that the competition extended to men scurrying to snare one or more of the dozen turkeys tossed down from one of the higher buildings in Carlinville.

Enthusiastic ovations greeted the patriotic oratory of the politicians on the Macoupin County Courthouse lawn, and the assembled throng oohed and aahed at the nearly two-hour display of fireworks—an extravaganza illuminating the Carlinville town square, said the *Enquirer*, with "lights of the most delicate color."

The day's biggest thrill was the daring parachute jump from a gas-filled balloon by one Professor Cowan, an intrepid aeronaut from East St. Louis. It almost didn't happen. While the balloon was being inflated, it toppled over onto the balloon's furnace, causing burn damage. Extensive repairs on the spot saved the day, though, and the balloon finally ascended to permit Cowan's leap. As he floated back to earth, the crowd cheered wildly, according to the *Enquirer*.

After the fireworks brought the curtain down on the exciting day, spirits were soaring as many of those on hand wound their way back to their homes in other parts of the county. As always, the Fourth of July was a counterpoint to the more sobering happenings coloring the temperament in the still young nation. For instance, only several months earlier the country was shocked by the devastating earthquake and fire that left more than 450 dead in the collapsed ruins in much of San Francisco.

As for those residents of Gillespie who journeyed twelve miles north to Carlinville for the Independence Day festivities, relief may have been sought from a tragedy of their own. Just the year before, a wind-swept blaze had wiped out virtually the entire business section of the growing mining village of 2,000 or so individuals. Most traced the fire to a carelessly discarded cigar or cigarette at the windup of a board meeting in a room above a prominent store. A few simply laid the blame on rats or mice gnawing on matches. The rebirth of downtown Gillespie already was under way; tastefully constructed brick structures were rising in place of the mainly frame buildings that perished. It was a lot to handle, though, and the Fourth of July offered a welcome respite for many Gillespians.

Among the persons in Gillespie not making it to Carlinville that holiday were those who stayed home to watch Gillespie split a baseball doubleheader with one of its strongest foes in the Trolley League, a team known as the White Seals. Two other individuals not straying from Gillespie that warm day were a young married couple, William Parnell Arrington and the former Ethel Louise Fanning. Although they lived in the Mississippi River town of Alton, Illinois, twenty-five miles away, they had come to Gillespie—to the home of Ethel's parents— for the delivery of their first child. Giving birth in hospitals was not common back then, and Ethel's mother, who bore fourteen children (eight of whom survived) was well schooled in midwifery.

The big event for the Arringtons coincided with the Fourth of July. Before the day was out, twenty-one-year-old Ethel gave birth

W. Russell Arrington at twelve years old

prematurely to a three-pound boy who would live in a precarious state of health for quite a while. Born without eyebrows and finger-nails, the infant had to suffer through numerous bouts with pneumonia in his first three years.

But he survived, and by the time William Russell started school, he was a strong and scrappy if still diminutive lad.

Little Arrington would have no brothers or sisters. Complications surrounding his birth made it impossible for his mother to have another child. Ethel, a beautiful woman with a will of iron, would encounter health problems the rest of her life. After Arrington's birth, his father, a railroad employee, returned to Alton. Ethel and the baby remained in Gillespie for much of the rest of the summer.

And so life began inauspiciously for William Russell Arrington.

Such a beginning offered little portent of the path to be trod by a man who before his death seventy-three years later would leave an indelible mark on the public life of his native state.

Arrington never was elected governor and did nothing to bring shame upon himself during his many years as a state representative and then state senator. Therefore, he did not become a household name in Illinois. But to those who knew him, dealt with him and sometimes locked horns with him, whether in the ornate chambers of the Statehouse in Springfield or in the private world of business, Arrington was a giant. Foremost in the legacy left by Arrington was a revolutionized state legislature. In making the General Assembly his personal domain, in pushing it to reach its full potential, he impacted the well-being of every Illinoisan, whether they knew him or not.

Among his peers, and they included many of the best known names in Illinois in the twentieth century, Arrington earned utmost respect. This was not to say he'd have won a popularity contest because his personality was a complex mix. Crossing his path meant meeting a man who could be gracious, charming, pugnacious, force-ful, brilliant, profane, insightful, impetuous, compassionate and, not least of all by any stretch, downright arrogant. Few adjectives were out of bounds in thinking of Arrington.

In the end, Arrington's story was a classic American one. Maybe not exactly Horatio Alger stuff, but close enough. A kid of very modest means from downstate Illinois grows up to capture success in Chicago, genteel Evanston and political mecca Springfield.

When Arrington was riding high in Springfield, not many on the scene were aware of his downstate roots. Few had ever a clue that the Arrington tale originated there, and on a day of such great importance for Americans.

Arrington himself got right to it, as he was wont to do, when he undertook dictating his memoirs in a Chicago condominium in 1978 during the final struggle of his life.

His first words, plainspoken and unadorned, were vintage Arrington: "My birth was on July 4, 1906. It was a hell of a long time ago."

Chapter 2

𝒯

Getting His Feet Wet

*T*he early life of William Russell Arrington was steeped in a world of coal, railroads and one very tough town. In fact, none was more rough and tumble than East St. Louis.

Before he arrived there, though, there were other stops. For the first five years following his birth, his parents continued to live in Alton, the hometown of his father and a community where the Arrington name was well known. Louis Arrington, his grandfather, was by most accounts a popular figure in Alton, a man instrumental in the growth of the glassblowers' union in the United States.

A Virginia native born in 1837, Louis Arrington found his way to Alton in the period following the Civil War after serving with a West Virginia regiment in the Union Army. Settling in Alton made sense for Arrington because it housed a growing glassblowing industry, and Arrington was an expert in the art of shaping glass. Besides knowing his trade, he was also a skilled labor organizer. He reached his peak in this role when he was elected in 1890 as president of the United Green Glass Workers Association of the United States and Canada. He held the office for four years before retiring to enter the shoe business in Alton.

In 1897, Arrington, a Republican, was appointed Illinois state factory inspector by Governor John Tanner, a fellow Republican. Arrington also happened to be a personal friend of President William McKinley, whose support for protectionism coincided with Arrington's advocacy of the doctrine of tariff protection. Arrington

*Louis Arrington – carved stone memorial at Greenwood Cemetery,
Alton, Illinois – W. Russell Arrington's grandfather*

had a big hand in the wording of the glass schedule in McKinley's tariff bill.

Whatever his position in life, Arrington never seemed to be far from the hearts of his fellow glassblowers—to whom he was fondly known as "Old Lew." When he died in 1911 of liver cancer, the *Alton Telegraph* pointed out that "a number of years ago when the glass-blowers throughout the country learned that their beloved former chief had lost heavily in a business venture and was in need of some assistance, they raised a handsome testimonial which they hoped would be enough to make him comfortable the remainder of his life. Honest, plainspoken, faithful…he…carried to the grave with him the undying respect and esteem of the men he had helped…." A history of Madison County, published after his death, praised him for exercising in his union stewardship "a balance of judgment and integrity of motive that was invaluable in his relations to business and the community."

Old Lew's funeral was quite an event. After the service in his home, a line of more than 250 men followed the body to Greenwood Cemetery near Alton. Afterward, his union placed an elaborately carved stone memorial over his grave.

Arrington and his first wife, Mary Hughes, whom he married in 1871 at Jerseyville, Illinois, had three children who reached adulthood. The youngest, William Parnell, was born at Alton in 1883.

Decades later, William Russell Arrington by then long known to the world as W. Russell Arrington—remembered his grandfather Louis as a strong, stern individual very proud of his Irish ancestry. The grandson also recollected that his father did not share the warm relationship that Louis Arrington had with his fellow unionists. For one thing, the grandson recalled that his father objected to Louis' remarriage after the death of Louis' wife, Mary, in 1893. The second wife, Mary Raymon, was a nurse who had tended to Mary Arrington during an illness preceding her death.

William Russell recalled meeting his grandfather Arrington only once. Although noting that "my father and grandfather had had some quarrels, and were not friendly," Arrington said that he and his father visited Louis shortly before his death. "I remember the event very well because it stuck in my mind so vividly," said Arrington. "He

(Louis) embraced my father, and then pulled me up to the bed and gave me a kiss."

The dying man then murmured to his grandson that there was not "an ounce of English blood" in the older man's body. "He was saying in other words," said Arrington, "he was an Irishman and not English."

As for William Parnell, he was graduated from high school in Alton in 1901. After that, he went to work in his hometown for the Chicago, Peoria & St. Louis Railroad, first as a yard clerk, then a billing clerk and finally as the line's freight agent at Alton. When his marriage to Ethel Louise took place in Alton in 1905, a future in that town looked fairly secure for the pair. They were active in a Catholic parish, and when their son reached school age they sent him to kindergarten at a Catholic school in the city. Ethel was not raised as a Catholic, but converted to the religion of her husband when their son was christened as a Catholic.

However, when William Russell was ready to enter the first grade, the family's stay in Alton ended. The tot's father, although only in his late twenties, had become burned out working for the railroad, so much so that his health was threatened. An alternative was needed. It was provided by his father-in-law, John Albert Fanning.

Like Louis Arrington, Fanning was a highly respected person. He and his wife, Jennie Gilmore Fanning, had been living in St. Louis when Ethel, their oldest child, was born in 1884. Fanning had been employed as a teacher, among other things, while living on the Missouri side of the Mississippi, but became a recognized figure in coal mining after moving his family to Illinois and establishing roots in Gillespie and the surrounding area.

By the time his son-in-law, William Parnell Arrington, desired to leave Alton, Fanning was a top boss, a man of influence, for the Superior Coal Company, a major mine operator in the rapidly growing coal industry in south central Illinois. Under the wing of Fanning, Arrington went to work for Superior, starting as a blacksmith and then as a weigh master. Fanning not only got William new employment, but also provided the Arringtons with living space in a house maintained by Fanning in Sawyerville, a hamlet a bit south of Gillespie.

The Arringtons lived in Sawyerville long enough for their son to finish the first grade. After that, the couple moved to Gillespie, where they resided until their son was in the sixth grade. Those were years in which William Russell's impressionability was governed by his exposure to the heartaches, triumphs and stark contrasts often found among families in mining communities.

When his father joined Superior Coal, the company was producing coal from three large mines at small towns around Gillespie—Sawyerville, Eagarville and Mount Clare. (A fourth Superior mine later was sunk by nearby Wilsonville during World War I.) The tons of coal produced by these operations were used almost exclusively to stoke the steam engines of the Chicago and Northwestern Railroad, which owned Superior. And, the wide breadth of Superior's small mining empire was mainly responsible for the stoking of the robust economy in that part of the state back then.

Of course, life was not a bed of roses for many families. The Superior collieries were almost solely responsible for drawing a diverse ethnic mix to the area. Italian, English, Croatian, Welsh and Scottish immigrants flooded Gillespie and other towns south of Springfield to work the underground mines and lend color and vitality to the scene. William Russell later remembered perceiving Sawyerville to be heavily Italian, leaving his immediate family members as "about the only…Americans." Historically, Macoupin County, mainly in the years after the Arringtons were gone, would become a principal battleground in organized labor history. Union miners confronted the operators in sometimes violent strikes. The conflicts also pitted the insurgent Progressive Miners of America union, which was organized in Gillespie, against the established United Mine Workers of America run by the autocratic and legendary John L. Lewis.

When William Parnell entered the coal industry, he was a company man like his father-in-law. His toil in the beginning as a blacksmith, though rugged, was a cure for the maladies he was beginning to suffer in his previous job. Impressing the hierarchy at Superior with his work ethic, he was relieved of the iron forging and made a weigh master. This assignment, which required him to weigh coal coming out of a mine to authenticate the tonnage being produced, permitted him to again use his office skills.

But, the job entailed some uneasiness. While he didn't go under-ground and encounter the dangers there, he had to position himself in a small office high up in the tipple of a mine, the aboveground, shed-like structure through which coal railcars were loaded. William Parnell was skittish about working so high above the surface, and he was especially uncomfortable with the ladder he had to climb to reach the post.

When W. Russell Arrington was asked many years later by a reporter if he, himself, ever considered mining as a career, he replied without hesitation, "I never intended to do that if I could walk or breathe." Yet, he evinced pride in telling questioners that he was a son of a coal miner, not the offspring of a railroader. He also was not hesitant to rekindle memories of Gillespie with those who were interested, such as Hugh Hill.

Hill, who in his days as a widely watched Chicago television political reporter covered the legislative activities of Arrington, grew up in Gillespie, a son of an Irish miner working for Superior. For Arrington and Hill, there was more than Illinois politics to talk about. Arrington sought to keep track of his mother's numerous brothers and sisters and their families, and Hill could be helpful. As Hill put it in a 2003 interview in his Naperville, Illinois, home, the Fannings constituted "a large, well-known and likable family." Arrington never kept as close a tab on those in the smaller Arrington side of his family.

Looking back on Arrington and his tie to Gillespie, Hill opined years after Arrington's death that it was hard to pinpoint anybody with a link to Gillespie more successful in life than Arrington. Or at least, Hill felt that Arrington was "right up there" with Howard Keel, a leading man in a number of Hollywood musicals who came out of Gillespie.

The world of young Arrington broadened greatly after his parents left Gillespie and moved to East St. Louis in 1917. This triggered the most formative period of his early life. East St. Louis provided an instructive crucible for Arrington's progression from a wet-behind-the-ears kid to a young man with an early appreciation of, and con-siderable insight into, the way things worked.

The Arringtons' move to East St. Louis was prompted by William Parnell's departure from Superior Coal to accept employment with the St. Louis & O'Fallon Railroad. It was another railway tied to the highly productive Illinois coal industry during World War I. While his duties took him to and fro in St. Clair County and then eventually to an office in St. Louis, East St. Louis would remain the home for William Parnell and Ethel into the late 1920s. As for their son, he lived there seven years before leaving to attend college, after which he never returned to East St. Louis for anything more than brief periods.

Long before the arrival of the Arringtons, East St. Louis was afflicted with the stained reputation that it bore throughout the twentieth century. Scribes struggled to find adequate adjectives for East St. Louis. Some went overboard, like one crime writer who characterized the town as "a grimy, bawdy suburb of Hell." To the thousands of upright individuals living in East St. Louis during the attention-getting stages of its history, comparing the place to hades was not fair. Nevertheless, by no account was East St. Louis ever equated with gentility, starting with the hardy souls who labored tirelessly to construct the city on the swampland of the Great American Bottom.

For a balanced view of East St. Louis during the period the Arringtons lived there, one could draw upon an article in *St. Louis Commerce* magazine in 1982 written by Carl R. Baldwin, a highly regarded *St. Louis Post-Dispatch* reporter who knew the East Side (highbrow St. Louisans' moniker for East St. Louis) like the back of his hand.

"East St. Louis," wrote Baldwin, "seemed to be sitting on top of the industrial world in 1920. It ranked No. 1 in the sale of horses and mules, and was near the top in hog sales. It was the world's largest aluminum processing center, the second largest railroad center (behind Chicago), and led the country in the manufacture of roofing material, baking powder and paint pigments. It was the third largest primary grain market and had the cheapest coal in the world. Its population was over 75,000." After Chicago, East St. Louis was one of the biggest cities in Illinois.

Still, Baldwin did not ignore East St. Louis' chronic problems— most notably the blatantly corrupt politicians and the railroads, their tracks seemingly everywhere, choking the city. When the Arringtons came to town, more than twenty lines of railroads made East St. Louis their center or terminal point. The city was encircled by belt lines connecting all of the railroads. Visitors couldn't decide which was more aggravating, the tracks that stymied movement through East St. Louis or acrid memories of a place smothered by smoke and the putrid smells from the stockyards and factories.

East St. Louis also suffered in those years from the shock waves emanating from a violent race riot in the city in 1917, the year the Arringtons arrived. It was one of the worst in United States history. A congressional investigating committee found that at least thirty-nine blacks and eight whites were killed. Other sources put the figures higher.

Just as in the mining towns of Macoupin County, the Arringtons found East St. Louis to be a melting pot, one in which few ethnic groups were not counted. To one historian, the city was "a rich tapestry, woven with the lives of those simple folk who migrated here from all over the globe to earn a living and to make a life for their families." Even before its severe economic decline in the latter part of the twentieth century, many neighborhoods in the city were not much to look at. Nevertheless, most residents took pride in their parts of town, sections with names like Goose Hill, Whiskey Chute and Pearl Harbor.

The failure of East St. Louis to shed its wicked underbelly took on deeper meaning during the Arrington years in the community. The start of Prohibition in 1920 ushered in a new era of lawlessness as the city became the headquarters for the notorious Shelton brothers' gang and its far-flung bootlegging empire. As the Roaring Twenties ensued, corrupt officeholders, ladies of the night, gamblers and mobsters flourished with impunity in the town. The "Valley" alone kept East St. Louis on the map. An internationally known vice district, the Valley was a particularly dark world of brothels, gaming joints and saloons crammed together a short walk from city hall. Because of it, mothers in the surrounding area tried to forbid their sons from setting foot in the city.

Yet, many from East St. Louis scoffed at suggestions that the image of the city created unusual challenges during their upbringing.

In the case of William Russell Arrington, his school days there appeared to be typical of those of most American kids.

The first item of business facing Arrington upon entering public school in East St. Louis as a sixth grader was to slug the hardest in the inevitable fights confronting the new boy in class. Those viewing him as a pit bull later in life wouldn't have been surprised to learn that Arrington did not back down in his school day encounters. Having weathered fisticuffs with classmates at Gillespie and even as far back as Sawyerville, Arrington knew what to expect at Slade and then Park, the schools he attended before entering East St. Louis High School.

Once he'd earned his stripes battling with his fellow public schoolers, he joined their ranks in the almost ritualistic scuffles in after-school hours with the boys from a nearby Catholic school. Here was Arrington, a Catholic, lining up with his mostly Protestant schoolmates to go toe to toe against the Catholic kids. Awkward as it may have been for Arrington, he felt he had no choice but "to fight against the Catholics."

Arrington was no slouch in class work either. But, he also was a self-described "smarty." On the one hand, he won a spelling bee at Slade. However, he could not resist being a smarty-pants about it and other doings in class. When he once went too far in mouthing off, he remembered vividly that his teacher, a woman, "gave me hell…and she had a cane, a wooden cane, and she spanked me. It happened that I had some rubber boots, and she beat me at my legs, and it didn't bother me at all."

Not until he reached high school did Arrington begin, in his words, "to amount to somebody." By the time he finished his secondary school studies in three and a half years and graduated with his class in 1923, Arrington was a well-liked and astute student, one whose intellectual curiosity was stirred by teachers for whom he'd have lifelong respect. He was president of the school's literature club, a standout in the debating society and the elected president of his senior class. (However, a classmate, Robert Smith, ended up serving as president because of Arrington's early completion of his high school courses and abbreviated attendance his final year.)

A lasting attachment to Latin was nourished in high school by one of his favorite teachers, Ruth Davis. Her special assignments for him in the ancient language "formed a basis," he later emphasized, "which I have used all my life." He was even able "to speak Latin—not fluently at all—but passably." Although Arrington was to drift away from Catholicism, he still got special satisfaction in his high school years from "going to Mass and reading the Latin rather than the English version."

Latin also helped trigger in Arrington an enduring love for William Shakespeare. In addition to the writings of the bard, Arrington was introduced in high school to the classics of other literary giants by one Mr. Finley, an English teacher regarded by Arrington as the biggest influence on him throughout his education, college days included. Finley also tutored Arrington in the sharper tactics of debate, perhaps to the later chagrin of Illinois legislators and even a governor or two unable to match the fiery discourse of Arrington on issues.

It was not likely that Finley ever suspected that he'd be lionized years afterward by Arrington as "probably the most important teacher I've had."

Added Arrington: "I was just fascinated by that man…I was just agog about how he would give me ideas about things which I would think about afterward. He was just a real teacher; he made me want to learn. I loved it. A teacher can be a great influence with a student…."

Ethel Flanagan was another high school teacher impacting Arrington, but in a different vein. Heeding advice from his father to mix in commercial courses in event he never made it to college, Arrington signed on with Flanagan to learn shorthand and typing, skills that served him well. Flanagan was an older woman, a demanding taskmistress with an intimidating air. Nevertheless, she took, said Arrington, a "fancy" to him. She also made Arrington a test case in her desire to set up a program through which her students found jobs before leaving high school.

Working after school hours was nothing new for Arrington. Although he was small, Arrington was a good, tough athlete who had made the East St. Louis football team as a halfback in his initial year at the school. However, he had landed a job with a florist, his first employment, and the hours the job required forced him to drop football, much to his regret. He had little choice in the matter. The income from his job, though meager, was important because his mother's declining health was necessitating her hospitalization. As a result, Arrington had to help his father, himself working day and night, to pay the bills.

In addition to finding Arrington to be a productive student, Ethel Flanagan was aware of his mother's ills and the family's tight finances. For all these reasons, Arrington surmised, he was the first she picked for an employment program for high school students she had arranged with the nearby stockyards. This occurred during his senior year. From three o'clock in the afternoon to nearly midnight each weekday, Arrington labored as a typist in a packinghouse amid the piercing screeches and smells of blood from the livestock being slaughtered. The working atmosphere was hard, but he earned what he considered a good wage. And besides, Flanagan excused him from most of his homework since he was working at night.

Interestingly, Arrington's time in the stockyards came several years after another young Irish lad, this one from Chicago's Bridgeport neighborhood, went to work at a stockyards commission house not far from his home. This person, like Arrington, also had clerical duties. But he also spent time out of the office herding cattle off trucks. Down the line, long after each had departed the stock-yards, Arrington and the other individual became well acquainted — when Arrington was the monarch of the Illinois Senate and Richard J. Daley was mayor of Chicago.

Arrington's career in the yards didn't last long. Shortly after graduating from high school, he exited the packinghouse to follow in the footsteps of his father by going to work for one of the seeming-ly innumerable rail lines traversing East St. Louis. His employer was the Mobile and Ohio Railroad, a line operating in the South that used the East Side as a northern terminus.

Assigned to billing duties in the railroad's freight yard office, Arrington worked days and, whenever he had the chance, followed up his regular hours by filling in on the second shift for anyone who was sick. That suited him because his second shift pay was one and a half times his normal rate. Consequently, it didn't matter to him that working beyond his scheduled hours often tied him up Saturdays and Sundays, and sometimes until three o'clock in the morning. He could not believe the money he was making. His dollar intake became so high that for a spell he was pulling down more than the chief clerk in his area. When that individual caught on to this, his embarrassment led to a forced reduction in Arrington's hours. Still, Arrington was pocketing enough to permit him to begin thinking about college.

Besides real dough, Arrington was exposed to other things while rubbing shoulders with fellow clerks in the sprawling rail yards. He learned a lot, got to run a bit with some hard-driving guys, all because he was a crackerjack typist. Their adeptness at typing impressed him, as did the dedication of many to boisterous behavior in off-hours.

"They were quite a group," Arrington recalled. "Some would drink, everybody smoked and they were all hell-benders."

From time to time, there'd be typing contests among the different railroad clerk teams to determine the most rapid. The Mobile and Ohio gang seldom had to settle for second place.

Arrington distinctly remembered one in his crew named Pete who was unbelievably fast even though he typed with just two fingers. Arrington also took note that Pete, an unabashed party animal, "loved the girls—thought about them all the time." Women were of course enmeshed in a period of life-style liberation in the Roaring Twenties, the convention-flouting Jazz Age, and the fun-loving railroad clerks, especially those on the second shift, encountered little difficulty in finding female companions when setting out after work to "raise hell." Whether or not the mainly young men might end up in the naughty Valley in the wee hours Arrington did not say.

In looking back, Arrington did admit to escaping during day shift noon breaks to an out-of-the-way place to read, while others in his crew lolled in the sun. Once, the freight agent, his boss, approached him and asked what he was reading. When the recent high school graduate replied that he was boning up on stocks and bonds, the older man's jaw dropped.

As the months in the employ of the railroad mounted, Arrington made up his mind that he was going to head for college. Although part of his wages still was used to help keep his family's finances from sinking, Arrington was saving enough to convince himself that higher education was within his reach. Moving quietly, he enrolled at St. Louis University, a Jesuit institution, without telling his parents. Then, at just about the time he'd decided to inform his folks of this step, the three of them attended a performance at East St. Louis High School by the University of Illinois glee club. Ethel and William Parnell were quite taken with the show and the high quality of the students putting it on. So, when their son disclosed his intent to attend St. Louis University, they did not object but suggested that he consider the University of Illinois.

Arrington had no problem with that. One reason he'd selected St. Louis University was his concern that his parents would oppose him going to college far from home. This turned out to be unfounded. He realized that he had failed to keep in mind one of his mother's favorite sayings.

"When the birds are weaned," she'd relate, "it's time to shut them out and let them go on their own."

Elated, Arrington switched gears and soon was accepted for admittance to the University of Illinois. He held onto his Mobile and Ohio job until the time he departed for Champaign-Urbana in September 1924. He'd need every cent he could save because his parents could not help him financially.

Nevertheless, he had their blessing, which was important to him, to take off on his own to build a foundation for a new life that would open up, he was confident, greatly expanded opportunities. He neither asked for nor expected anything more in departing East St. Louis than his parents' final reminder that "the only thing they could give me was my health—and I was in splendid health."

And, oh yes, he was told one other thing as he took off. It was imperative, he recalled, that he not forget that his mother "would mail my laundry every week."

Chapter 3

ៃ

A Young Lawyer,
Chicago and Ruth

rrington entered college as the country was kicking up its heels in the flamboyant 1920s. Dramatic change was visible everywhere, propelled by a tidal wave of economic, social and intellectual energy. The economy took off at the start of the decade on an unfettered flight, with the gross national product and wages ballooning, working hours declining and inflation hardly anything to worry about. All revolved around an upwardly mobile consumer society that glorified business and democratized a growing middle class. People freed from past bondages suddenly had time and sufficient income for self-indulgence, self-improvement and invidious consumption.

No question, as economic prospects drew folks to the cities, urban living increasingly became the dominant life-style in America. Bigger and better office and apartment buildings went up, including splendid art deco structures, leading to the breathtaking skylines of Chicago and other megalopolises.

Having a car became an achievable dream, and, as a result of massive road paving programs in Illinois and elsewhere, even the look of the countryside—with gas stations and motels popping up— was transformed.

When Arrington entered the University of Illinois, he joined about 11,000 undergraduate and graduate students at the Urbana campus— which already was a mainstay of higher education in the United States. He was as wide-eyed as other students about all the possibilities out there, but he did think that once he finished the work for a law degree, he'd probably start out as a small town Illinois attorney.

Even the University of Illinois, primarily an agricultural school in its early years, was in the business swing of things during Arrington's time there. Had he taken business courses, which he did not, he'd have been exposed to the university's upgrading of the study of commercial ins and outs by trying to inject scientific principles into a field benefiting from the country's new fascination with the culture of profit-making.

Of course, two of the most talked-about businesses in the Roaring Twenties, bootlegging and speakeasies, sprouted in response to Prohibition. Although a "noble experiment" aimed at moral improvement, Prohibition was as widely ignored on college campuses as in many other places. Because of Prohibition, or in defiance of it, many Americans for the first time openly and knowingly patronized crime. For eighteen-year-old Arrington, who came from East St. Louis and the highly publicized world of the Shelton gang, youthful worldliness at his campus offered him nothing he'd not already seen.

The school's reputation was enhanced at the time by its success in athletics. Arrington's period at the university, six years in all, saw some golden days for Fighting Illini athletes.

In fact, Arrington had been on campus only a few weeks when an ultimate day of glory erupted for Illinois football fans. It was October 18, 1924, the day of the formal dedication of the university's Memorial Stadium. It also was the day that Illinois routed mighty Michigan, 39 to 14, on the unbelievable running legs of Wheaton's Harold (Red) Grange. The Galloping Ghost, as sportswriting dean Grantland Rice called Grange, romped for four touchdowns in the first twelve minutes of the game, and he ran for a fifth in the second half before passing for another.

Arrington also happened to be matriculating when the university's legendary, and sometimes controversial, symbol, Chief Illiniwek, debuted. Although Arrington did not make the acquaintance of the second chief while on campus, the lanky lad from Decatur who danced in American Indian regalia and roused Illini fans to a frenzy, Arrington encountered him forty years later. The fellow, Webber

Borchers, went on to win a seat in the Illinois House of Representatives in 1968 while Arrington still was a state senator.

As was often the case with an individual who had tasted the "real working world" between high school and college, Arrington was determined to make the most of his shot at higher education. Social activities were not ignored if they could be squeezed into his tight budget. But, his spare-time priority was work, and he never turned his back on a chance at any campus job that might reap a few bucks. Not all panned out, though, like a stint at waiting tables at a sorority house. He was abruptly fired after a few days for dropping a tray of dishes. He fared better with a secretarial position in the office of the university president, a slot made possible by his extraordinary typing skills.

First and foremost, he was a student with his nose to the grindstone. Staying focused, he made a grade of A or B in every course prior to his senior year, with the lone exception of a C grade in hygiene the first semester of his freshman year. No explanation for the lower grade was given on his college transcript; however, he took hygiene again the next semester, upping the grade to a B. His diligence was rewarded with election to membership in the national honor society Phi Beta Kappa.

Overall, Arrington received almost straight A's in rhetoric, composition, history and political science classes enroute to receiving a Bachelor of Arts degree in 1928. He slipped a bit in courses tied to the field of mathematics. On the other hand, he was graded top notch in artillery drill and tactics, and in two rather unlikely courses, wrestling and boxing. No record of Arrington the college pugilist is known to exist, assuming he even engaged in formal bouts. However, his schoolboy fisticuff days back in East St. Louis may have served him well in whatever the boxing class entailed.

In the summer prior to his initial classes at the University of Illinois College of Law, Arrington worked for tire manufacturer Goodyear in Akron, Ohio. He was among some 2,500 college students hired by the firm to comprise a "flying squadron" of individuals to fill in for vacationing or ill employees in the middle of the year. Besides providing more workplace experience, the job put badly needed money into Arrington's pocket.

The dawn of the summer of 1929, following the completion of his first year of law studies, found Arrington back with the college squadron at Goodyear. However, by mid summer, Arrington and the other collegians were let go, a result of Goodyear losing a major contract with Sears, Roebuck & Co. Desperate for funds, Arrington returned to Illinois with the hope that the mother of Ruth Browne, his steady girlfriend, could use her contacts in Chicago to help find him a job. Although that didn't pan out, he was successful in returning briefly to railroad employment in East St. Louis. He made the most of the dollars he earned there to help him get through his final year of legal courses. By the time he was graduated from law school on June 11, 1930, he was the pride of his family. And, as always, hard pressed for cash.

His tight finances only added to the tension surrounding the next step in his progression—studying for and taking the Illinois bar examination. It was a brief but Spartan chapter in his life, made more tolerable by his determination to spare a few moments each evening for Ruth, the woman he was by now intent on marrying.

Home for Arrington during his month-long preparation for the exam was a Young Men's Christian Association building in Chicago's south side neighborhood of Hyde Park, not far from Ruth's home. His daily regimen was repetitious and demanding. He later described it as follows:

"We were required to take this course (for the bar) during the morning and then study during the afternoon and evening, which I did. I think the class started at 9 o'clock and lasted until noon. Then I would have lunch and work until 4 or 4:30, go to the gym and exercise, then get ready to have dinner with Ruth. She would always walk to the Y, and we'd have dinner nearby, and I'd go back to studying until 11 or 12. That was my routine for the whole month. I remember the only time (day) Ruth and I could see each other was on Sundays, but during the week we'd just have dinner and I would go back to work. By the way, the price of dinner was 35 cents each. Sometimes on Saturdays, we would splurge and get a seven-course dinner for 50 cents (each). The only time I didn't work was on my birthday…and Ruth and I took a day out and just relaxed."

Senator W. Russell Arrington and Ruth Browne Arrington

The exam, which took two and a half days to complete, was given on the downtown Chicago campus of Northwestern University. Arrington found the questions quite taxing, but he was confident that he passed, especially after learning at the end of the second day that his grade for the first morning session was higher than required.

Unfortunately, he became ill while awaiting the results of the bar exam, necessitating him to spend several weeks with his parents, who by that time had moved to St. Louis. When he finally received the official word that he passed, he had little chance to celebrate because he knew he had to find a job right away.

Law degree in hand, he decided to pass on a tentative job offer from an attorney who represented farmers in the rural town of Paxton in Ford County. Admittedly he once had felt destined to practice law in a small town, but by the time of his graduation from law school, he realized he would not be happy practicing in a sparsely populated area. As he put it, "I would have fossilized in…Paxton." Besides, if he was to hold on to his girl, he had no choice in the matter. "Ruth made it clear," he said, "that she expected me to try to get a job in Chicago."

He was not daunted by the fact that he knew virtually nobody in Chicago besides Ruth and her family. The boom period of the 1920s had ended, giving way to the Great Depression with its stagnant economy and soaring unemployment. Still, to Arrington, Chicago was vibrant compared to the places in his own background. It was exciting, pure and simple. Depression or not, he'd find a way.

In tackling Chicago, Arrington was engaging the country's most significant city away from the East Coast. Its population was both increasing—it had risen to about 3,375,000 residents by 1930—and undergoing major changes in character. Older Protestant families were leaving in droves for the developing suburbs. Taking their place were incoming Catholic and Jewish families and the growing number of blacks migrating to the city. By the time of Arrington's arrival, more than 50 percent of Chicagoans had been born abroad or were children of immigrants.

The population upheaval contributed greatly to a rapidly changing political atmosphere. Arrington hit town in time to catch the final months of the administration of Chicago's last Republican mayor in the twentieth century, the often contradictory William Hale (Big Bill) Thompson. When Democrat Anton Cermak swept Thompson out of office in the 1931 mayoral election, the coalition of diverse Chicago ethnic groups carefully constructed by Bohemian immigrant Cermak cemented the foundation of the Democratic machine that would maintain a stranglehold on the politics of the city. That machine would be the eternal nemesis of Republicans from the Chicago suburbs and downstate, GOPers whose shaky political standing some thirty years later would be rescued largely by the iron will of Arrington.

In 1930, though, Arrington had his hands full trying to fathom Chicago as much as any other new arrival. Yet, unlike many, he was somewhat prepared for the undertaking. He'd witnessed as he grew up extremes between haves and have-nots, although certainly not to the extent visible in Chicago. The city's great railroad network was a subject about which he hardly was inexperienced. The world-beating stockyards and slaughterhouses presented a scene with which he had more than a little familiarity. Even the incredible mix of people from all over the world was something he'd gotten a taste of in the southern Illinois mining towns and East St. Louis. And, in speaking of East St. Louis, its crime and attendant violence had surely primed him to a certain degree for the lawless image affixed to Chicago by its 1920s-bred gangsterism.

The immediate challenge facing Arrington was to find a job. The first door he knocked on was that of a highly regarded attorney who was a brother of Arrington's old high school teacher, Ethel Flanagan. He was courteous, but had nothing for Arrington. On the heels of that, though, lightning struck. Arrington never would look back.

Little more than two months out of law school, he was interviewed and in short order hired by a well-respected LaSalle Street firm, D'Ancona, Pflaum & Kohlsaat. The hiring left Arrington grateful but surprised, especially since his law school grades were only slightly above average. However, he was informed by principals at the firm that they were impressed by his self-sufficiency since high school and by his earning Phi Beta Kappa as an undergraduate. Also, concluded Arrington, "I think they hired me because they wanted to have a gentile because the firm was so heavily Jewish...."

Besides being fortunate to get on with the firm, Arrington benefited in another way too. D'Ancona had a policy, or at least a reputation, of never employing a young lawyer for less than $100 a month. Since Arrington figured that he needed $65 monthly to live on, he was ecstatic. He felt he'd "died and gone to heaven." Subsequently, he learned that, of the members of his law school class, he and Albert E. Jenner Jr., who would eventually become one of the biggest names practicing law in Chicago, received the highest starting salaries. Actually, a good number of Arrington's classmates found no job at all, or had to settle for employment removed from the field of law, such as waiting on restaurant tables.

The D'Ancona firm wasted no time putting young Arrington to work, and on very sensitive subjects, namely bank failures, bankruptcies and mortgage foreclosures triggered by the Depression. Too, Arrington moved immediately and successfully to latch onto the coattails of Harry N. Wyatt, one of the prominent lawyers at the firm. Wyatt, who was Jewish and a University of Chicago graduate, was a brilliant writer and speaker in addition to being an expert on taxes and related matters. He would have a profound influence on Arrington. Like a beginning reporter at a newspaper, Arrington did leg work for Wyatt and other older hands, handling research and information gathering in regard to their cases or clients. He treated every assignment as a learning experience, absorbing something new every day or night about financial intricacies, including investments. The stock market had bombed, but that did not prevent Arrington from gaining insight into the world of securities that might serve him well if and when the market rebounded.

The plummet into monetary ruin by so many individuals, businesses and institutions was devastating many lives, but numerous law firms serving as receivers or mitigating the losses of others were realizing substantial profits. Resentment flared in the cases of some closed banks, where depositors were left with next to nothing while law firms reaped huge fees as attorneys for the receiverships.

As for Arrington's firm, it was counsel for the Foreman bank and trust group that folded and was absorbed by the First National Bank in 1931. Arrington was brought into this situation when he was asked to determine whether a bank and its directors could rescind a dividend declaration. Soon, he was doing research for many of the questions growing out of the Foreman downfall. Eventually, he was assigned the task of keeping the members of the Foreman bank family out of bankruptcy—a task he did well.

Sparked by his Foreman experience, and based on his "hunch that there was going to be a lot more trouble with banks than there had been before," Arrington took it upon himself to brief every foreclosure case in Illinois that he could find. Drawing from this, he became very knowledgeable about successful strategies for both plaintiffs and the defense in foreclosure proceedings. His growing expertise on the subject was a factor, he believed, when he was not included among the newer lawyers at D'Ancona who were let go in the early 1930s because of hard times affecting even successful law firms.

Along with his competency on foreclosure law, another reason for keeping his job, he reasoned, was that he was a workhorse, toiling day and night, often into early morning hours. Perhaps more than anything, he later contended, his often laboring alone during evening hours, doing "any kind of work I could find for the firm," assured his retention. He not only held onto his job, but got a raise in 1932 that put him at $230 a month.

Now, at last, he and Ruth could think about marriage.

Trim and dark-haired Ruth Marian Browne may not have known it, but Arrington told friends he'd met the girl he was going to marry after the two were paired on a blind date in 1928 following an Illinois-Northwestern football game. Never wavering from this goal, his four-year courtship ended on October 8, 1932, when the two were wed in a small ceremony in the Kenwood Evangelical Church, a south side Chicago Protestant church not far from Ruth's home. Dorothy Browne, a sister of Ruth, was maid of honor, and Howard Pontious, a friend of Arrington and future husband of Dorothy, was best man. The marriage would last for the remaining forty-one years of Ruth's life.

Born June 1, 1907, not quite a year after the birth of Arrington, Ruth was the oldest of the four children of Albert Farrar Browne and Anna Belle Hazelhurst, a widow Albert married in 1905. Both were interesting individuals.

For a man who lived only into his mid forties, Albert Browne packed a lot into his life. He was born in 1871 in the Illinois River town of Ottawa, the place where his Irish immigrant parents, Patrick and Mary Prindiville Brown, settled. Albert was the second of the couple's nine children. Seeking to somewhat camouflage his Irish identity, Albert dropped Patrick from his original name, assumed the middle name Farrar and added the letter e to his last name.

Albert, a robust fellow, spent a few years teaching in Ottawa, then headed for Chicago to study law. Following classes at the John Marshall Law School and time spent clerking for an attorney, he passed the bar exam. He also was on the Northwestern football team in the mid 1890s as a "gypsy player," meaning he was on the squad roster even though he was not a student at the university. Evidence suggests that, in the years after his college grid days, Albert served his country in uniform during the Spanish-American War.

Based in the Hyde Park and South Shore neighborhoods of Chicago, Albert utilized his law practice in the making of a number of successful business investments. Along with a brother, he acquired a horse farm in Saskatchewan, Canada, and spent some time living in that country. Back in Chicago in the last years of his life, he immersed himself in real estate transactions.

The parents of Ruth's mother also were immigrants. Samuel and Mary Hazelhurst migrated to the United States from England in 1870. Anna Belle was born in St. Louis, as was Arrington's mother, but the family moved afterward to Chicago, where Samuel continued to pursue the invention and manufacture of mechanical parts for engines. As a young woman in Chicago, Anna Belle displayed considerable talent as a vocalist, so much so that she sang in local concerts. Her daughter Ruth's lifelong love for singing may have been inherited from Anna Belle.

The first marriage of Anna Belle to a manufacturer named Noble Higgie occurred early in her life. It ended with the death of Higgie as a result of an explosion and fire in his factory.

Her second marriage, the one to Albert in 1905, took place in Milwaukee. The birth of Ruth two years later, in a hospital in the Cook County village of Maywood, was followed by the birth of Dorothy, another daughter, Hazel, and a son, Albert Farrar Browne Jr. Ruth and the other children were baptized as Protestants in the Church of the Redeemer in Hyde Park. Albert had been raised Catholic, but he left the faith at the time of his union with Anna Belle, a Protestant.

In 1915, two years after young Albert was born, tragedy struck Anna Belle for the second time. Husband Albert died suddenly in a hotel in Joliet, where he was taken to recuperate from an injury suffered in a train wreck that occurred as he was riding, accompanied by his little daughter Ruth, from Chicago to Lincoln, Illinois. His death was unexpected because his injury, sustained when the Alton "Hummer" derailed near Elwood, was not thought to be serious. However, several weeks earlier, Browne had suffered another injury in an automobile accident that may have been a contributing factor to his death.

Widowed again, and in spite of Browne's business and legal acumen, Anna Belle found herself in difficult circumstances with four children eight years old or younger and minimal resources.

Linda Relias, a teacher from Wilmette and the daughter of

Dorothy Browne Pontious, recalled years later that her grandmother, Anna Belle, was left with "no family or business umbrella" after her husband's death. Her efforts to support her family took various turns, including years spent working as a truant officer for the Chicago public schools. She also served as a Republican precinct captain in Hyde Park, doing so in years when the GOP was still a respectable political organization in Chicago.

Anna Belle's involvement in politics led, in turn, to the first real political activity for the young attorney who would become the husband of her oldest daughter. Upon settling in Chicago in 1930 after law school, Arrington's only family life was provided by Mrs. Browne and her children. Arrington reciprocated by putting aside time to assist Anna Belle with canvassing and other political tasks in her south side precinct.

Ruth also joined in these efforts, as did her sisters and brother. This gave her an intimate view of the time demands imposed upon those who participate seriously in politics. This insight would make her more attuned to some of the exigencies she'd face as a political wife during most of her married years. Whatever personal aspirations Ruth might have had were put on hold in deference to the man whose public and private accomplishments would dominate their life together. Although she had attended Northwestern University after graduating from Hyde Park High School, she dropped out and did not graduate. If Arrington ever encouraged her to return to college or to seek a career apart from the housewifery role so standard at the time, there was little sign of it.

Working the precinct with Anna Belle cemented a budding interest in politics brewing inside Arrington. Yet, as he and Ruth embarked on married life, he maintained that he "never planned on running for office." In his words, it was just that "I thought it was important for a young lawyer to take part in politics." Sticking to this notion, he wasted little time wading into Republican politics in Evanston, the suburb north of Chicago where the pair moved after the start of their marriage.

Still, making more money and establishing a foothold in Chicago's legal world—any base usable for advancement—remained

Arrington's priorities. Continuing to toil at the feet of Wyatt, Arrington was a key operative in D'Ancona's handling of quite likely the largest practice in foreclosures of any Chicago firm. Dealing with or closing in advance problem loans made by or transferred to the First National Bank was a full-time job alone for the firm. Arrington grew so adept on federal income tax matters that D'Ancona clients with troubles in this area began to seek him out specifically. Gaining confidence in this complicated arena, Arrington took to calling himself "some pumpkin" in tax law.

Not too far along in 1933, the management at D'Ancona recognized the increasing productivity of Arrington by raising his monthly salary to $300, retroactive to the beginning of the year, and declaring that he had become entitled to a two-week vacation annually. Arrington was so delighted he allowed himself to dream, for a while, that he was on easy street.

The extra money permitted him to finally pay off in installments a $200 debt that he still owed the University of Illinois. He was able to put his mind at ease on the subject when he received a short note in August 1933 from H. B. Ingalls, the university's bursar.

Ingalls wrote, "Thank you for your remittance of $12.50, which completes the payment of your student loan obligation, with the exception of a small accrual of interest amounting to 26 cents, for which we would appreciate your prompt remittance."

Arrington could handle that. Yes, indeed, financial independence was within his grasp. More than that, he was going to be in high clover.

As the direction of his life in Chicago would eventually show, he never shied away from a promising business venture and never lacked the gumption to try to make big bucks, even when he had very few dollars of his own. These traits stamped him as a true son of the 1920s, golden years for a speculative spirit bolstered by a conviction that nothing was unobtainable.

Chapter 4

ℰ

Spreading His Wings

A spectacular production engineered to bring dollars into the local economy during the Depression, the Century of Progress World's Fair in Chicago opened in 1933, the anniversary of the city's one hundredth birthday. Set along Lake Michigan and on Northerly Island, the fair attracted nearly 40 million visitors who gazed at dazzling exhibits depicting wonders of the world. There was something for everybody, including the swarms of men who flocked to catch the exotic fan dance of Sally Rand. Showing up in nothing but carefully arranged feathers, she was the biggest attention-getter of the exposition.

The lives of few Chicagoans remained untouched by the fair, whether it was through lasting memories or one of the numerous opportunities to make a few extra bucks. For instance, take one particular Irish chap, Thomas Arthur McGloon. Law student McGloon got a piece of the action by pushing visitors up and down the fairground in a cart for a small fee and tips. This was the same fellow who would be the Democratic minority leader in the Illinois Senate years later when Arrington was running the chamber.

As for Arrington, one of the things at the fair that intrigued him was a successful concession located near Soldier Field that featured ice skating in the summer. He had no idea that an individual tied to that exhibit, Chicagoan Robert J. Sipchen, would go on to spearhead an updated version of it at the New York World's Fair at the end of the 1930s, nor that he himself would be hired as an attorney for the undertaking. It was to be an assignment that would necessitate his frequent presence in New York, and would be just one of the out-of-the-ordinary ventures in which Arrington immersed himself as a young lawyer spreading his wings.

For example, before the New York World's Fair, there was the Soybean Products Company.

With Arrington's know-how on tax matters drawing increasing numbers of persons to his office, some clients proceeded to solicit his services in other areas. Assenting to one such request, he handled the legalities for the 1935 formation of a company designed to use soybeans to develop a low-priced substitute for albumen, the white of an egg. Even though the firm was headed by a wealthy young man whose wife was from a prominent family, Soybean Products Company, itself, had little money. Consequently, the firm (D'Ancona) was to be paid for Arrington's services with stock in the fledgling business.

When Arrington informed Harry Wyatt that the stock was being offered in place of a fee payment, Wyatt replied that the stock was so inconsequential that Arrington should keep it for himself. He did, and the company became his first exclusive client. Arrington soon went further and became involved in the management of the venture.

Needing to determine whether the egg white substitute product could be manufactured in a commercially feasible way, Arrington and others behind the undertaking arranged for a test run in a plant made available to them in Ottawa, Kansas. The experiment was a runaway success—literally.

The albumen substitute was described by Arrington as very nourishing and possessive of all the properties of egg white. It also was considerably more "sudsy." Consequently, he recalled, several hours after the start of the test run, the three-story plant in Kansas was filled with suds. When a befuddled Arrington and his cohorts were forced to open the facility's windows, suds "came pouring out."

"We were up to our ass (in suds). They went up to the second floor, the third floor, and we had suds you couldn't believe."

The good news was that the test proved the product could be produced.

Returning to Chicago, the group secured a plant in Indiana and undertook the successful manufacturing of the product. Arrington remained an active part of the company's management and accumulated more of its stock accordingly. When World War II came around, and the head of the company was drafted into the armed services, Arrington served as president during the duration of the conflict. By that time, the firm's product had cornered a large share of its market. However, because of constraints imposed by tax codes and the absence of sufficient funds to fully export its product, Arrington and others in the company sold out to giant food producer Borden in 1945. The sale reaped $25,000 for Arrington. Never before, he noted, did he have "a hand on that kind of money."

His involvement in the New York World's Fair was not as lucrative. It was a heck of an experience, though. And, as he said, "quite a lot of fun." But, it certainly had some trying moments.

Arrington's work for an amusement concession began in 1939, the year of the fair's opening, and occurred at the same time he was ending his affiliation with the D'Ancona firm to go out on his own. His duties at the fair required him to stay in New York during most of the summer and early fall, which created a double-edged situation for him. On the one hand, he learned his way around New York, made many new acquaintances and garnered even more insights into the law and business world. The downside was that he wasn't in Chicago often enough to take on and spend time with a number of the new clients needed to build his private practice.

To put it mildly, Arrington's stint with the world's fair had few dull moments. As he was leaving D'Ancona, he became the attorney for the Sun Valley Amusement Company, which staged, under a contract, a "winter wonderland" exhibit in the fair's amusement area. It featured an Alpine village, ski and toboggan slides, a forty-foot waterfall and a daily snowstorm. Allotted an acre and a quarter near the center of the amusement section, the concession also included a stork tower, featuring real storks, and a cuckoo clock tower, out of which the cuckoo made a personal appearance each quarter hour. The construction cost for all of this was $800,000—a sizable sum at the time. Sun Valley expected to recover the investment and then realize a profit from the concession's 25-cent admission price.

Looking to be most impressive about the concession were the shows of professional ice performers. However, lining up a headliner proved to be one of the first challenges faced by Arrington as he worked closely with Robert Sipchen, the Chicago world's fair veteran who was now general manager of the Sun Valley concession. Out to seek a star attraction, Sipchen and Arrington went for the best in attempting to negotiate with none other than the glamorous Sonja Henie, the world skating champion from Norway. However, they couldn't compete with the allure of Hollywood, which also wanted to employ the talents of Henie. So, they set their sights on Erna Andersen, another Norwegian who might have been the best female skater in the world if not for always losing to Henie. This time, Arrington and Sipchen got their woman.

A petite blonde, twenty-four-year-old Andersen certainly gave the exhibit its star quality. Arrington was quite impressed with her looks, claiming she was "much more beautiful than Sonja," but he also lamented that Andersen "was more selfish than you could imagine." She also caused him considerable grief. She needed a visa to stay in the United States, and it fell to Arrington to get her one. He had, as he put it, "a hell of a time" getting it done, even having to go to Washington to enlist the aid of his congressman. World War II was erupting in Europe, Arrington recalled, and "it was very hard for anyone to get into this country on a permanent basis." But, she got her visa.

Not long after the fair opened, Andersen was injured in a fall while performing and had to be carried off the ice. This gave Arrington and Sipchen cold chills. Luckily, she did return.

If it wasn't one thing it seemed to be another. Right from the start, lousy weather plagued the early days of the fair. In fact, it was so cold at the opening that Arrington took pity on horse-riding girls in a nearby show. Wearing nothing but "thin pants and brassieres," he remembered, "they almost froze." With fair attendance smaller than expected at the start, and not picking up—at least not in the amusement area—many of the performers at Sun Valley and in the other concessions "had nothing to do but play games, drink and raise hell, and the police were there almost every day," Arrington said.

In thinking back on the repeated employment of his legal skills to resolve many of these scrapes, he concluded: "It was just a mess."

A big problem for Sun Valley and others in the amusement area was that their section was too far from the fair's main admission point. Instead of putting the amusement center at the end of the fair's grounds, Arrington felt, it should have been placed in between the famous, streamlined exhibits that glorified the miracles of laboratories and the mind-boggling benefits of a mechanized future. Portending a technological utopia, these exhibits—reflecting the profound impact of technology on 1930s culture—constituted the thematic heart of the fair.

Arrington lamented that after first exploring these futuristic exhibits, fair goers usually did not wander to Sun Valley's neighborhood until late in the afternoon or night. This prompted the cancellation of two of the three shows planned daily at Sun Valley and the firing of many of the performers.

The amusement area also had several other monkeys on its back.

A Cuban village concession, a short hike from Sun Valley's, was supposed to showcase the rhumba and the traditional Yanego rite in a Cuban setting. Fetching senoritas were available to teach willing visitors native dance steps. However, a month after the fair opened, the Cuban village folks went a few steps further by allowing their leading dancer and certain women from other amusement area concessions to compete in a contest to select "Miss Nude of the World's Fair 1939." This prompted howls of protest from upstanding New Yorkers and a sheriff's raid at the Cuban village only a few minutes after the start of the competition taking place before 300 excited onlookers. The incident left the amusement area mired in ignominy.

An embarrassed Southern Rhodesia reacted by removing its name, flag and crest from its Victoria Falls exhibit in the amusement area—an exhibit that featured a huge model of the legendary African waterfall. A Rhodesian commissioner explained that his country did not want to be officially associated with an event as "depraved and obscene" as the nudity contest.

The indignant commissioner said, "The placing of the Victoria Falls model in the amusement area in the first place was against my better judgment, and I endeavored to obtain a site more in keeping with the government's dignity, but I yielded to assurances that the area in question would be restricted to shows of a high-class nature."

There was more monkey business besides naked women in the amusement area, which Arrington may have found quite amusing or quite irritating, or both.

Down the way from Sun Valley was wild beast captor Frank Buck's Jungleland concession housing an incredible array of animals. A highlight was Monkey Mountain, where umpteen monkeys were encouraged to live, as a *New York Times* writer phrased it, "their usual merry lives." No fence, only a moat, surrounded the mountain. Sure enough, a batch of the merry critters eventually escaped, adding unscheduled excitement to the amusement area.

Buck, of "bring 'em back alive" fame, dispatched safaris to recapture the escapees, but no dice. Several of the creatures found safe refuge under a bridge spanning a nearby creek and came out at night to either beg for sugar and scraps from waitresses and patrons at the Heineken Tavern or to swim out in the lagoon and shin up and down the rigging of a Dutch fishing lugger. One never knew where they might turn up.

No doubt, some visitors to the amusement area got more than they bargained for.

On the whole, though, there were not enough visitors to the amusement section to make ends meet, forcing some of the concessions to fold their tents after the fair's first month. Unwilling to close Sun Valley, Arrington bargained personally with Grover A. Whalen, the dapper, glad-handing promoter who was president of the fair's governing corporation, to alter admission prices and take other steps that might help prevent the concessionaires from losing their shirts. Whalen tried to be accommodating, even to the point of doling out dollars to Sun Valley and other concessions fighting to keep shows open. Nevertheless, as 1939 rolled on, Arrington said the Sun Valley venture remained "a financial disaster."

Besides squeezing Sun Valley, the money nightmare also threatened Arrington. He wasn't getting paid for his services, which was very problematic since he was devoting so much time to the concession at the expense of his new law office in Chicago. Consequently, he devised a rather drastic maneuver to force payment of the roughly $7,000 in fees he was owed by Sipchen and various contractors at Sun Valley.

Sipchen had given Arrington a note payable on demand for the fees. With this in hand, Arrington retained a shrewd New York lawyer to lay groundwork in court for a levying on the note by attaching (taking by legal authority) the electricity needed to power a huge ice-making mechanism for the concession. Without the daily manufacture of the ice, Sun Valley couldn't operate. The scheme called for the New York attorney to execute the plan by filing suit on the Friday before the Labor Day weekend, thereby turning off the electricity for Sun Valley prior to a time of anticipated heavy attendance.

Although he told Sipchen he was sorry it had come to this, Arrington insisted that he was "resolute that unless you guys pay me my note by early Friday, I'm going to levy on my note and attach the electricity."

"Well," he added, "that was quite horrendous, and at first they didn't believe me. But, when they got their lawyers and found out I was able to do this (and they knew I would do it), they…said they would give me a check for the whole amount." Shortly after noon that Friday, Arrington had his money in the demanded form—a certified check.

Although several of those who anted up were not pleased with Arrington, he continued to represent the concession and most of its contractors. Some even became long-term clients of his, including one who labeled Arrington one of the most determined persons he'd ever worked with.

"Any son of a bitch as hard as Arrington, and as honest," this individual said, "I want as my lawyer."

Arrington had to play hardball to get the money due him at the fair because fees were only trickling in at his new law practice in Chicago. No doubt, for a while at least, he gained renewed appreciation for the monthly salary checks he'd received from the D'Ancona firm.

Finding space for his law office was no snap either. His first office location after striking out on his own March 16, 1939, was in a downtown Chicago building at Dearborn and Madison streets, where he paid $15 a week to share space with another attorney. After a month, Arrington asked the other fellow if he, Arrington, could use the entire office. The individual obliged, moved elsewhere, and left Arrington with rental payments of $30 weekly and sole responsibility for paying a secretary and buying all office supplies. Quickly seeing this as less than satisfactory, Arrington moved in May or June of 1939 to an open office in a complex housing a group of lawyers at 29 South LaSalle Street. However, he found little comfort there since his specialty was tax preparation and most of the others were patent lawyers, specialists in a field of little or no interest to Arrington.

The place "wasn't the kind of dish for me," lamented Arrington, adding that the other attorneys "weren't doing well at all because of the awful economy."

Several months later, he was looking for new office space again—in between his fair visits to New York. He only imposed one condition on his quest. He wanted to stay on LaSalle Street, an urban canyon sided by steep buildings traditionally filled with lawyers, banks and brokerage houses. He succeeded.

Before the end of November 1939, Arrington hung out his shingle at a ninth-floor office in the Field Building, an edifice of note at 135 South LaSalle. The building would house his activities for the remainder of his law career.

There was another new wrinkle. This time, at least on the surface, Arrington was a principal in a legal firm, Watson, Healy and Arrington. Both of his associates, Deneen Watson and Allan Healy, had more widely recognized names in some circles and appeared to be good affiliates for the thirty-three-year-old Arrington, who had yet to pass his first decade of law practice in Chicago.

In truth, though, his new firm wasn't structured in the traditional fashion. "The three of us each had our practices," said Arrington, "and we had no real firm at all—just by name. None of us practiced for the others…all we were doing was sharing offices, electricity, typing and secretarial responsibilities." Still, this was not an arrangement that Arrington found objectionable.

Deneen Watson was a namesake of Charles S. Deneen, a reform-minded Republican attorney who served two terms as Illinois governor, the first beginning in 1905. Watson, who came from a family with close social ties to Governor Deneen, was an avid Republican with acquaintances throughout the state. Knowing Watson's infatuation with politics, Arrington was hardly surprised when Watson endeavored to run for a United States Senate seat from Illinois on the ballot in 1940. Watson had his eye on the GOP nomination for the seat held by Chicago Democrat James M. Slattery, who had been named to the post by Governor Henry Horner following the death of incumbent James Hamilton Lewis in 1939. However, Watson's bid was short-circuited prior to the state primary election in April 1940, when the Republican nomination was captured by Chicago lawyer C. Wayland Brooks in a contest with Congressman Ralph E. Church of Evanston. Brooks went on in the fall general election to defeat Slattery.

Although unsuccessful, Watson's brief campaign was spirited and hectic. Arrington had a front row seat for much of it, and he wasn't pleased. In spite of the fact that his own initial try for public office would be in the near future, Arrington was annoyed that Watson's effort brought "all kinds of politicians to my office," causing difficulty for Arrington in "squeezing in my little clients."

"I suggested to Deneen that he really ought to have his own office so that he could conduct his political activities," said Arrington, "and so the rest of us could get our work done. Deneen bought the idea, and he moved to an office at 11 South LaSalle to conduct his campaign." After the primary, Watson still spent part of his time in the separate office, from which he pursued a variety of interests largely unrelated to law.

Much more agreeable to Arrington was the presence in his law office of John J. Healy, a well-heeled estate lawyer and father of Allan Healy. To Arrington, John Healy "was a prince of a man who everyone revered and held in the highest esteem." Interestingly, Healy also had ties to Governor Deneen.

Prior to Deneen's first successful race for the governorship, he was elected to two terms as state's attorney of Cook County. John Healy was a successor to Deneen in the prosecutor's post. But, Healy's popularity in the office waned considerably when he insisted on enforcing a law at the time not permitting saloons to open on Sunday. Later on, Healy practiced law with Deneen, whose candidacy for a third term as governor fell short in the election of 1912. (Before his death in 1940, Deneen held elective office one more time, as a member of the United States Senate from 1925 to 1931.)

As the early 1940s unfolded, Arrington was upbeat about the way things were falling into place. He had new clients at his law office, the New York fair had become history and several of his business ventures were looking profitable. He was driving a sleek, four-door, black Packard sedan, equipped with white sidewalls, trunk lid guards and a deluxe radiator emblem, that he purchased for $496. It was a forerunner of the many large black cars that were to become an Arrington trademark.

Said Arrington, "I worked very hard, but the business was there, and I was making enough money to get along all right."

By then, Arrington and Ruth were active participants in the life of their adopted home city of Evanston, and the first of their two children, Patricia, had been born. If Arrington had a lingering regret, it was the minimal time he'd been able to spend with his father after he moved to Chicago following law school.

Years of financial strain for William Arrington, spurred in large measure by the costs incurred in combating his wife's ill health, ended with the death of Ethel Arrington in 1931. Although her passing permitted William to finally see some daylight money-wise, he remained heartbroken over the loss of the love of his life.

Although he continued to live in St. Louis after the death of his wife, William's emotional attachment during the rest of his years was reserved for his son's family 300 miles to the north. According to his son, William had lady friends because he "was an attractive man and the ladies liked him." However, Russell added, "father never thought of getting married again...he loved my mother so much."

As an outgrowth of William's devotion to his son's welfare, William loaned him $10,000 to $11,000 in the early days of his independent law practice to help cover office expenses, as well as household necessities.

"I would have had to go to the bank for it," said the younger Arrington, "but father wouldn't think of having me borrow when he had a little money himself. He was not a wealthy man, and when he gave me a loan of $10,000 or $11,000, it probably represented his net

*Arrington with parents William Parnell Arrington
and Ethel Louise (Fanning) Arrington*

worth, or very close to it. But, he did it without hesitation. He encouraged me in every way anyone could."

As a result of his desire to share more of his life with his father, Arrington jumped into yet another of the business undertakings that absorbed so much of his time. Keeping an eye open for an opportunity to bring his father to Chicago, Arrington came across a magazine advertisement for a small computing device, selling for $2.95, with the name Baby Calculator. Arrington was intrigued. He had a notion that here was something that might interest his father. Therefore, in typical Arrington fashion, he wasted no time in tracking down the owner of the business, and, as luck had it, discovered the individual was willing to sell out.

After negotiating briefly, Arrington agreed to buy Baby Calculator for $4,000. The deal called for a $1,000 down payment June 1, 1940, and the rest to be paid ten days later. Arrington didn't have the other $3,000 on hand, but he borrowed it from one of the more interesting persons in his life, W. Clement Stone. Arrington and Stone had met through young Republican activities in Evanston, and Arrington subsequently had helped Stone organize an insurance firm that appeared to be an up-and-comer.

Getting the cash to purchase Baby Calculator was one thing; operating the business was another. Yet, while acknowledging he was not "mechanically inclined," Arrington quickly covered the bases needed to take over production of the calculators. To him, it wasn't complicated.

The calculator, he related, "very simply...consisted of a dish, a stylus and a tin condenser. I had a manufacturer who would give me the tin and shape the machine. I had another manufacturer make the stylus, and another who would put on some device that used the stylus to figure. Then, I also had a manufacturer who made a leatherette case. And that was it." He intended to market the product through the same magazine ad that first caught his eye.

As the purchase was being consummated, and as Arrington was projecting the role his father would play, he received bad news. His father, suffering from a serious staph infection, had become gravely ill and was hospitalized in St. Louis. Arrington rushed to his father's bedside, but nothing could be done to save him. He passed away at the age of fifty-seven. A downcast Arrington watched as his father joined his mother in burial at Calvary, a Catholic cemetery in St. Louis. Afterward, he tended to his father's affairs before returning to Chicago.

Instead of backing out of the Baby Calculator undertaking, Arrington forged ahead with it for what he termed "emotional" reasons. He said he wanted to show that, had his father lived, "I would have been able to let him sell the Baby Calculator and make a business out of it."

In short order, Arrington knew he had a winner. As orders poured in for the little calculators, they were assembled at a machine shop and then mailed to Arrington's law office. There, working at night, and aided by a young woman, Marion Belland, who'd eventually become his girl Friday, he, himself, finished the assemblage by applying the glue for the leatherette case. The devices were mailed out in small boxes stored at the law office.

The orders, some of which originated outside the United States, were almost more than he could handle. Arrington did not conceal his astonishment at the success of the venture, especially the dollars produced. In no time at all, he repaid the $3,000 loan from Clement Stone. All in all, an annual average net of $6,000 was realized during the four years he operated the business—not bad for one of his sidelines to the law practice. When he sold the business in 1944 for $10,000, he allowed himself to sit back for a moment and reflect that he'd netted $34,000 overall from Baby Calculator. His many irons in the fire—including increased political involvement—had necessitated the sale of Baby Calculator. Still, he could not help but lament the giving up, in his words, of a "gold mine."

One had to remember that Arrington had a hand in various other enterprises during the World War II years, including not only the running of the Soybean Products Company, but also involvement with a group operating under the business name of Swain Nelson that had hastily set up a war plant to develop prisms for glasses and lenses for binoculars.

He even dabbled in teaching. Seeking to capitalize on his tax expertise, he proceeded, in 1942, to set up what he called his own tax institute. With tax codes becoming ever more complicated, Arrington offered a course, for lawyers only, on income tax complexities. This was another demanding chore time-wise; he'd sometimes take sixteen hours to prepare one lecture. The response was positive, though. Enrollment was sizable enough to force him to rent a large room in the Field Building to accommodate all of the attendees.

Orchestrating all of his activities out of his law office obviously generated considerable to-and-fro. However, in the case of Baby Calculator, Arrington took special care to do his part of the assembling and packing for shipping during evening hours so as not to upset John Healy. As the World War II years progressed, Healy was the only other lawyer remaining full-time in the office with Arrington—although Deneen Watson was in and out on an irregular basis. Since John's son Allan had joined one or two of his brothers in the armed services, it led to poignant moments when John Healy joined Arrington in his office to listen to radio accounts of battles in the war.

Arrington himself, who was thirty-five years old when his country entered World War II, was registered with his local draft board under the President's Selective Service Proclamation. But, he was exempted from the draft, primarily for reasons of his age and involvement with business activities considered important to the home front war effort.

With the continued growth of his practice and bevy of side businesses dictating a need for more operating space, Arrington moved in 1942 to a more accommodating office area on the eighth floor of the Field Building. The descent down one floor occurred in the same time frame that Arrington asked John Healy to join him in a new firm to be called Arrington and Healy.

"I told him (Healy) that I wanted to have my name first in the firm," Arrington said, "and, he was just so great, he said he was honored to have the firm known as Arrington and Healy."

Arrington made it clear that Allan Healy would be welcomed as a partner in the firm after his return from military duty. However, Allan's life revolved around teaching and other pursuits after World War II. Nevertheless, even after the death of John Healy in the years following the war, the firm remained known, as it had been except for one brief interlude (when the firm included attorney George Fiedler and was known as Arrington, Fiedler and Healy), as Arrington and Healy. When Healy died, Arrington informed his family that he, Arrington, still desired to keep the name Healy with the firm. In case the family didn't want this, Arrington said he'd delete the name. It was the wish of Healy's family that his name be retained.

For one thing, the relationship between John Healy and Arrington was a warm one. Furthermore, association with Arrington, even if in name only, was no longer insignificant. Arrington's name was gaining respect in the legal and business worlds.

Another thing. There was yet one more new side to Arrington. In 1944, a watershed year for the man, he was elected to a seat in the Illinois House of Representatives. This was an outgrowth of his deep interest and resultant activism in local politics. It was the first step toward a stellar political career at the state level.

Before too many more years, Arrington's public persona would overshadow much of everything else in his life.

Chapter 5

❦

At Home in Evanston— Land of the GOP

*A*rrington and Ruth never intended, after their marriage, to live in Chicago. They wanted a fresh start in the social life of a suburban community and a public school education for their children, but not in Chicago's system. Yet, they needed to be close to the big city, with ready access to Arrington's law office and to the attractions offered only by Chicago.

Evanston, the first city north of Chicago, the gateway to the North Shore, was the perfect fit.

Although it had many facets, none was more basic to Evanston than its self-proclaimed reputation as a "city of homes." Many of them were large, long-standing houses on tree-shaded streets—picturesque settings perfect for Norman Rockwell paintings. Ruth expressed a desire to someday get her hands on one of these structures, but her husband didn't encourage it. An older house, he feared, "would give us a lot of troubles I wouldn't be able to handle." But Arrington certainly shared Ruth's wish to eventually have a house on Lake Michigan. It was their goal from the start in Evanston even though finances dictated a more modest beginning in their new hometown—a comfortable flat in an old brick apartment building in the 1100 block of Maple Avenue.

The Lake Michigan shoreline, with its generous offering of both residential and recreational opportunities, was one of the amenities of life in Evanston. But there was much more—things that separated Evanston, not only from its sister North Shore communities above

Chicago, but also from the maze of often colorless, homogeneous suburbs surrounding Chicago to the west and south.

First off, Evanston was no small burg. When the Arringtons moved there in 1932, Evanston's population of 63,000 made it the eighth largest city in the state and the third biggest among Chicago's suburbs (behind only Cicero and Oak Park). Even for its size, Evanston was heavily endowed with arts and cultural attractions. Some simply identified the city with its venerable Grosse Point Lighthouse, a landmark near a sandy Evanston beach built to help safeguard lake navigation after the loss of nearly 300 people in the wreck of the passenger steamer Lady Elgin near the shores of Grosse Point in 1860.

Evanston was a special place in the minds of historians. The town had been the home base of Frances Willard, a tireless reformer and feminist who made the Woman's Christian Temperance Union a dynamic force after becoming its president in 1879. And prominent banker and Evanston resident Charles Gates Dawes was very much alive when Arrington surfaced in the city. Dawes, a Nobel Peace Prize laureate who lived in a French Provincial mansion on Greenwood Street, had been a brigadier general in World War I, United States Vice President under Calvin Coolidge and ambassador to Great Britain. Evanston also had been the home of Republican lawyer John Beveridge, who served as Illinois governor from 1873 to 1877.

Above all, Evanston was a college town. Northwestern University, which Ruth had attended, was more or less a parent of Evanston. The community was named for Dr. John Evans, a physician, philanthropist and member of a group of Methodist leaders in Chicago who founded the university in 1851. It was Evans who signed a mortgage to purchase, for $25,000, a lakeshore farm to house the campus. Evans also was among the individuals who platted for the town that would grow around the university, and eventually become the city of Evanston.

Imbued by an atmosphere of higher learning, Evanston became a magnet community for authors, professors, pastors and well-known figures in finance and business. Evanston also was somewhat unique in that the Northwestern trustees saw to it in the 1850s that the school's charter prohibited the sale of liquor within four miles of the campus, one reason for the WCTU's prominence in the city's history. Evanston remained "dry" until 1971.

Evanston stood out in another regard. Devout Republicanism. In deciding against Chicago in favor of Evanston for a place to live, Arrington settled in territory much more in line with his political persuasion. With little delay after he hit town, Arrington immersed himself in local Republican activities—pretty much a norm for a newcomer seeking integration into Evanston's flow of things.

Arrington jumped into his new political activism during a particularly low period for his chosen party. Stuck with the political blame for the Depression and the resulting economic stagnation, the GOP was on its heels nationally and in many states, including Illinois.

The 1932 election left Illinois Democrats in control of every elective statewide office, except one, and with majorities in both houses of the General Assembly. After the 1930s, such Democratic dominance would be rare in Illinois until the 1960s. During the middle of the '60s, just about all major statewide officers were Democrats and the Illinois House was controlled by their party. However, voters still left the state senate with a Republican majority. And, led by a strong leader, the Senate Republicans managed to exercise a decisive voice in the direction of Illinois government. The leader was none other than Arrington.

The likelihood of a scenario like that occurring hardly could have been envisioned by the young lawyer Arrington while getting his feet wet in Evanston politics. He did not even have his sight set on elective office when he became politically active.

As he saw it at the time, "I was very interested in politics, but I never planned on running for office. I was a lawyer, but I thought it was important for a young lawyer to take part in politics."

The Evanston Young Republican Club was being born when Arrington came through the door to assist in its founding. William Fetridge, long identified in his lifetime as the guiding spirit of the United Republican Fund, a leading money-raiser for the party, was a principal in the club's origin. He recognized Arrington right away as a soul mate in the defining of the main purpose for the club. Some joining the organization were doing so for mainly social or business reasons, considerations from which Arrington was not entirely divorced. On the whole, though, Fetridge and Arrington wanted to see the club count for something in public life. They combined their considerable energies to make that happen.

Arrington was elected president of the club in 1934 and held the office for four or five years. When Arrington secured his post, Fetridge was chairman of the organization's board of directors. Several years into his presidency, Arrington was in the vanguard of a rebellious group of Young Turks—individuals impatient with the stodginess of the old-line Republicans holding the upper hand in Evanston—who captured the GOP reins in Evanston Township. The upstarts, as Arrington and his cohorts were branded, would not relinquish this hold, even though friction with the older establishment Republicans, dubbed conservatives, would simmer for years in the lower part of the North Shore.

As the twentieth century progressed, rapidly growing DuPage County and its environs more and more became the GOP heartland, not only for the Chicago area but also from a statewide perspective. Concurrently, demographic changes significantly watered down the once almighty Republican influence in Evanston and certain other sections of the North Shore. Nevertheless, the Evanston Young Republican Club, operating from a base that Arrington helped build, remained a potent resource for the party for many decades.

John E. Porter, like many, regarded the club as nothing less than "a political powerhouse." Besides Arrington and onetime Illinois Attorney General William J. Scott, Porter was probably the best-known political figure affiliated with Evanston. A son of Harry H. Porter, a long-standing chief judge of the Evanston Municipal Court and later a Cook County circuit judge, John Porter, an attorney, served in the Illinois House in the 1970s before representing the North Shore in Congress for twenty-one years. Before all that, he was president of the Evanston Young Republican Club in 1968 and 1969.

In those days, the club had more than 450 members and maintained offices on the second floor of a building on Davis Street in downtown Evanston. The importance of the organization was underscored by the fact that even gubernatorial aspirants deemed it important to seek the club's backing. Take 1968 for example. In their fight for the Republican nomination for governor that year, both former Cook County sheriff Richard Ogilvie and Peoria businessman John Altorfer zealously sought the club's endorsement.

Later in his life, after he'd retired from Congress and was a partner in the Washington, D.C., law firm of Hogan and Hartson, Porter still remembered vividly the annual chicken barbeque staged by the club in an Evanston city park on the lakefront. "Thousands of people, many of them Republican workers from around the whole area, came to the event," Porter recalled in a telephone interview. "It was certainly a testimony to the club's vitality." He also retained warm memories of young Republican gatherings at Arrington's home.

"Back then, Russ Arrington was the towering figure of Illinois legislative politics," said Porter. "He was just a big deal to the young Republicans."

Events like the chicken barbeque, opportunities to mix fun with politics, were a staple of the young Republican club from its early years. Arrington certainly was a factor in the early doings along this line. One such occasion, orchestrated by Arrington not long after he became the club president, was especially memorable.

Arrington noticed that many in the organization loved to dance. So, he decided to throw a club dinner dance, a fancy affair, not ragtag. To pull it off, he named as event chairman W. Clement Stone, a young insurance man in the club that Arrington had taken a liking to and who, moreover, displayed quick feet on a dance floor. This was, of course, a few years before the two men established a business relationship.

At first, Stone pussyfooted on planning for the dance, but, after being warned by Arrington that continued inaction meant the event was "going to fizzle," Stone "really went to town," according to Arrington, to get the job done. Arrington, not easy to please even back then, was impressed. For one thing, Arrington didn't know an appropriate place for the dance, but Stone came up with a private club in Wilmette that he deemed perfect. However, Stone was told by club officers that one had to be a member to use the facility. Consequently, Stone immediately bought a membership in the club, and within hours thereafter, noted Arrington, "was on his way to organizing the dance."

The event was a success, a credit to Arrington's club leadership. A cute twist to the occasion was the presence of a six or seven-foot-tall robot that Stone had gotten his hands on. To say the robot was a smash was an understatement. Nobody had ever seen one whose movements included the smoking of cigars. Quite a while passed before Arrington discovered that Stone had stationed a cigar-puffing midget inside the robot. That left Arrington even more amused by the mechanical apparatus, as well as increasingly fascinated by the free-spirited Stone.

Humor never may have been identified as an Arrington strong suit, but he did not ignore the lighter side of life or shy away from sometimes divulging a self-awareness of comic undertones or improbable occurrences in his own experiences that others might not admit to. He also wasn't above playing a trick or two on others.

The night of the birth of his daughter, Patricia Lee, was climaxed by an episode that, bone chilling as it was, evoked sympathy and laughter, mostly the latter, as Arrington told it through the years. February 8, 1936, was a bitterly cold and windy Saturday, and the temperature had plunged to well below zero by the time Arrington left Chicago's old Passavant Hospital where Ruth had given birth in the evening to the first of their two children.

Arrington was ecstatic. Even as he turned numb in the icy night air, his head swirled with the warm thoughts of the first squeals from his daughter and of his undisguised pride while holding the baby on the edge of Ruth's bed. His night simply was going "beautifully" as he hailed a taxi to ferry him to his latest residence in Evanston, a spacious apartment occupying the whole third floor of a brick building at 137 Custer Avenue, just a few steps north of the Chicago city line.

Images of little Patricia faded quickly inside the cab, though, as Arrington realized to his horror that the driver was intoxicated. As the taxi swerved wildly on the slick streets, an alarmed Arrington demanded to be let out. When his words fell on deaf ears, he jerked open a cab door and jumped to the street while the vehicle was precariously sliding.

Finding another taxi took a bit, but Arrington finally managed to thumb one down. Arriving at his apartment building, he was frozen but at least safe and secure. Or so he assumed. Reaching the third

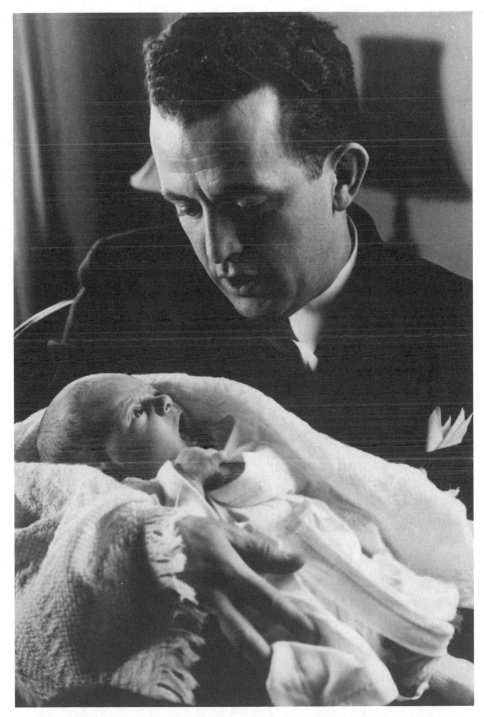

Arrington with daughter Patricia Lee Arrington in 1936

floor, he was hit with another rude discovery. Peering through a slit in the front door curtain, he saw enough to realize that a window obviously had blown open, leaving in a frigid wind that had broken open a pair of French doors in the living room. Dumbfounded, he sought his key. He didn't have it. Damn it, he'd left it at the hospital.

Nearing desperation, he retreated to the second floor and awakened the family in its apartment. The couple living under him earned his everlasting gratitude by brewing him hot coffee, loaning him a screwdriver and accompanying him back upstairs. Boosted upward by his neighbors, Arrington unscrewed part of a transom high above his front door so the transom would open. Then, with a renewed burst of energy, the couple shoved Arrington up and into the narrow void. After a clumsy mix of squeezing and acrobatics, he landed on the floor of his apartment—which was colder than an icebox. The wind gushing in had made a mess of more than the French doors. While straightening things as best he could, he tried to warm the place. But, overcoming the cold took so long he was forced to end up in bed with his clothes on.

Yet, as he lay under every cover he could find, he remembered telling himself that he was "very happy."

"I had a new child," he said later. "Ruth was fine...everybody was healthy."

The years in the apartment on Custer, which was considerably larger than the Arringtons' first apartment on Maple, were happy ones for the small family. Details of her first home remained vividly sketched in the mind of Patricia Arrington Smythe, including the long hallway where she practiced ballet. Lighter moments in the place were highlighted by a Christmas tree incident. The apartment had a fireplace, and Patricia's father gave it a stern test one year by trying to burn the family's yuletide tree in it (the Arringtons always had real Christmas trees). This backfired, leaving the apartment drenched in smoke for a spell.

Arrington doted on Patricia, his and Ruth's only child for seven years. To her father, Patricia was a "very smart little girl—just as sweet as could be." Patricia was young during the era before Arrington's sustained involvement in Springfield, and he was determined—in spite of his widely dispersed law and business interests—to be an attentive father. There were normal, inevitable occurrences as well as poignant memories. Once, Patricia was so sick for a period in 1940 that Arrington could hardly see her for four or five weeks and Ruth couldn't leave her unattended (thereby preventing Ruth from accompanying Arrington to St. Louis for his father's funeral). And Arrington never forgot that on Sunday, December 7, 1941, a few months after Patricia started attending Oakton elementary school in Evanston, she was sleeping peacefully in his arms in their living room when he and the rest of the country learned that the Japanese had attacked Pearl Harbor.

When Michael Browne, the Arringtons' son, was born March 24, 1943, the family still was living in the Custer apartment. This time, Arrington did not find himself locked out of his residence after Ruth gave birth. Yet, tardiness by Arrington in getting to Passavant prior to Michael's birth left Ruth a little miffed and Arrington unusually sheepish. To begin with, Arrington asked the wife of a friend to drive Ruth to the hospital the day of Michael's birth. The reason was that he believed he had no choice but to attend an important business meeting tied to his work for Swain Nelson. To his chagrin, the gathering dragged on and on while Ruth was in labor, but he didn't think he could leave "no matter what." When he finally was free and able to rush to the hospital well into the night, he arrived just in time for the birth of his son.

Ruminating back on the occasion, he felt regret that "it was very hard for Ruth to understand why this would have to happen." He could only add that "when she needed me desperately, I couldn't do much of anything about it."

With the arrival of Michael, Arrington had what he described as a "strong...and handsome kid." Arrington also had a son to carry on the family name. Moreover, the son right away showed signs of his father's scrappiness. Actually, Arrington saw Michael as a "little devil in so many ways—which was bad for us at that time." Years later, though, Arrington said he "loved to think about it."

Michael had so much get-up-and-go as a toddler that his parents were forced to strap him down in his crib to make him fall asleep. Imagine their surprise the night they were relaxing in the living room, assuming he was sleeping, when they suddenly looked over and saw him sitting in the hall.

"He had broken the straps, and they were flowing in all directions," related Arrington. "He was so pleased that he was able to get out of the crib, which involved his climbing over the side and getting down. His room was the farthest from the living room, and he thought he was quite a little hero. He was a little scamp. At that time, we could have smacked him or spanked him. But, we didn't. He was just quite a little devil."

Michael was not even two years old when Arrington became a member of the Illinois House. When this role was tacked on to everything else to which Arrington was devoting his talents, time with his family would be harder to come by.

As Patricia observed in an interview in her Evanston home in 2003, "Dad was able to be home a lot more when I was a young child and growing up. This was not as true with Mike." As Arrington himself later rationalized it, "Ruth was a fine mother for both of them. Even though I was working almost night and day, she took care of the kids in splendid fashion."

The considerable time that Arrington committed to politics in his early years in Evanston was designed to further the standing of his party and to encourage others to seek public office—but not to necessarily promote himself.

As Arrington and his fellow upstarts maneuvered to take command of as much local Republican Party machinery as they could, he also urged runs for public office by young Republicans he considered to be attractive candidates. One of his first successful ventures in this regard turned out to be quite important to Arrington's own future.

Early in his presidency of the Evanston Young Republican Club, Arrington took favorable notice of Alan E. Ashcraft Jr., a Wisconsin native and Republican lawyer living in Evanston who was the same age as Arrington. Although saying no at first, Ashcraft finally acquiesced to imploring by Arrington to run for an aldermanic seat in Evanston in 1935. With Arrington as his campaign manager, Ashcraft won. After that, Ashcraft's political career became a personal project of Arrington.

Although it didn't take long after his victory for Ashcraft to turn into what Arrington viewed as an "avid politician," Arrington kept a firm hand on, in his words, the "steering of Alan's political destiny."

Even though Ashcraft was an astute attorney, Arrington recognized that Ashcraft "didn't have to work as hard as I did because he had some money, and he liked a social life and was very well known." At the same time, added Arrington, Ashcraft "was very cold and had no facility to let people warm up to him or love him." Yet, although not liked by everybody, "Alan was a good man, and stood for good government," Arrington held.

In the election year of 1940, during Ashcraft's sixth year on the Evanston City Council, he and Arrington set their minds to getting Ashcraft elected to the Illinois House. There was plenty of skepticism about their chance for success; however, with Arrington's organizing talent in high gear, Ashcraft successfully emerged from the primary election as a Republican candidate for one of the three House seats to be filled from the legislature's Sixth District. This meant that Ashcraft stood a strong chance of victory in the fall general election since the district, which encompassed voters from Evanston and some north side Chicago wards, was not lacking in Republican voters.

Sure enough, the district's voters sent Ashcraft and another Republican lawyer from Evanston, James J. Barbour, to the Illinois House chamber. They also elected a Republican senator from the district, William G. Knox, a Chicago manufacturer. The third House seat from the Sixth was retained by Democrat Charles H. Weber, another businessman and his party's committeeman of Chicago's Forty-fifth Ward. Under a cumulative voting procedure for House members decreed by the Illinois Constitution of 1870, then in effect, the weaker party in each district was virtually assured of winning one of the three House seats in each district. That was accomplished by providing that each district voter could cast one vote for each of three candidates, one and a half for each of two, or three votes for any one candidate. The last option—casting all three votes for one, called "plumping"—was designed to guarantee a minority representation system in the lower chamber, where all members served two-year terms.

After Ashcraft was seated in Springfield, he encouraged Arrington to finally throw his own hat in the ring for public office. Arrington obliged, launching a campaign for alderman from Evanston's Eighth Ward in the April 1, 1941, municipal election. His candidacy soon became a point of great interest. The south side ward was dominated by political figures still among those viewing Arrington as a Republican insurgent who stubbornly refused to toe the line with the city's long ingrained political hierarchy. They fielded one of their own to seek the seat being vacated by the retiring incumbent, Hugo A. Pape. Without question, Arrington faced an uphill fight.

He did receive a boost when—to the surprise of many—Pape endorsed Arrington for the seat. Pointing out in a written statement that he'd "withdrawn in favor of Mr. Arrington...a candidate admirably qualified for public office," Pape declared that Arrington's "many years' activity in Evanston civic affairs have revealed him to be a man of character, ability and notably high ideals...."

Arrington himself, besides citing his legal and business interests, reminded folks that he had initiated a drive for civil service reform in Evanston back in 1934. Too, he stressed that in 1940 he served as spokesman for several civic groups in their battle against a city council-passed ordinance that would have hiked cab fares in the city. That fight was won with the repealing of the ordinance.

Aided by a vigorous mobilization of Arrington workers by his fellow young Republicans, Arrington waged what he considered "a hell of a campaign." As Arrington and his backers canvassed residential blocks night after night for votes, some observers began to suspect Arrington just might pull it off. But, he fell short. Just barely. In garnering some 48 percent of the vote, though, he stunned his opposition. It was certainly a moral victory for Arrington, and the atmosphere was anything but gloomy at a gathering afterward of his supporters.

"After the returns were in," recalled Arrington, "we had a hell of a party with hundreds of people at my apartment. You'd have thought we'd won instead of losing."

Later, Arrington realized that his defeat, the only loss voters ever dealt him, "was the best thing that had ever happened to me. It changed my whole life. Otherwise, I would have been part of the Evanston aldermanic group, and probably would have stayed there for some time. It would have altered the course of my career. But, fortunately, I didn't win."

After the bid for alderman, Arrington rechanneled his political energy toward the nuts and bolts of grass roots Republican activity in his home area. He stayed especially close to Ashcraft, even visiting him a few times in Springfield when the General Assembly was in session. Arrington served again as Ashcraft's campaign director when he ran in 1944 for a third term in the House. Ashcraft cruised through the primary and looked to be a sure bet for victory in the fall general election. Then things changed.

A coveted position of master in chancery in the Cook County judicial system became open in the middle of 1944 with the death of its incumbent. Ashcraft was interested in the post and, moreover, had the political clout to get it. But, Ashcraft, by then the elected Republican committeeman of Evanston Township, also made it clear that he could secure the slot for Arrington and that, if Arrington wanted it, Ashcraft would defer to his friend and political ally.

"Alan told me that he and I were going to own the two offices (master in chancery and state representative)," said Arrington. "But, I told him, 'Well, really, Alan, I'm not interested in either one.' He told me not to make up my mind right away, but to think it over."

"Well," Arrington continued, "I thought about it. I didn't want to be the master in chancery because I was trying to develop my law firm and didn't want to take the path of becoming a judge. I wanted to be more active in my practice." Nevertheless, after further deliberation, Arrington decided that "it would be great for a lawyer to have some experience in the legislature." He advised Ashcraft of his revised thinking, and the two successfully collaborated in, number one, getting Ashcraft off the ballot for state representative and on his way to becoming a master in chancery and, secondly, in sliding Arrington into the House nomination spot vacated by Ashcraft.

This time, Arrington was not to be denied. Although more than a couple of the older Republicans in the Sixth District still turned up their noses at him, Arrington's backers had substantially increased their immersion into the GOP machinery in Evanston since 1941. Furthermore, Republican voters in the Chicago wards in the district were not averse to Arrington. As a result, the celebration by Arrington people in the aftermath of the November 7, 1944, general election was for real, meaning they had a true winner this round.

Of the four candidates on the ballot for the House from the Sixth, Arrington and the other Republican, Chicagoan Stanley C. Armstrong, were elected, along with one of the two Democrats. Armstrong, a former assistant corporation counsel for the city of Chicago and another attorney with an office on LaSalle Street, received 147,219 votes. Arrington was next with 143,151. Finishing in third with 137,730 was Democratic incumbent Weber.

Arrington had taken a first major step toward a successful career. But, he had it in his mind that he would serve just one term, stay there just long enough, as he phrased it, "to get the hang of things and get some idea about the legislature." This was a man who, in the waning weeks of 1944, had much else on his plate that still needed attention. But then, holding a seat in those years in the General Assembly, which met in regular session for only six months every other year, was hardly considered full-time employment.

As it turned out, whether Arrington realized it or not, his victory in November 1944, his initial success at the ballot box, switched on the ignition of a new level of political involvement that would most define him the rest of his years. He was only thirty-eight as he entered this new world that was about to become his oyster. It was an orbit of the high and mighty of public life—a galaxy of first-rate individuals, veritable characters and a hard to pinpoint number of crooks. Most of those who'd interact dramatically with Arrington were not yet there when he arrived. But, they'd be coming—names such as Richard B. Ogilvie, Clyde L. Choate, William C. Harris and Robert E. Coulson.

Ogilvie, Choate, Harris and Coulson would share center stage with Arrington in the 1969 spring session of the General Assembly, the heavyweight of all Illinois lawmaker gatherings in the second half of the twentieth century. In late 1944, though, these men were unknown to each other. And all were many miles away from Arrington.

Take Ogilvie. He was Sergeant Ogilvie, a twenty-one-year-old Sherman tank commander in action in France, who had part of his face demolished by an exploding German shell on December 13, 1944.

Choate was another young American army sergeant late in 1944, one who in October of that year single-handedly blunted an attack by a German Mark IV tank and a company of Nazi soldiers on an

American infantry position in France. For his valor, Choate was awarded the Congressional Medal of Honor.

And then Harris. The last days of 1944 found Harris, twenty-three, a native of Pontiac, Illinois, and an enlistee in the navy, stationed on a combat zone island in the South Pacific, loading planes with ordnance for bombing raids on Japanese-held territory.

As for Coulson, from Waukegan, Illinois, he was an army legal officer, thirty-two years old, assigned to Fort Lewis in Washington state near the end of 1944. While Arrington was gearing up for his entrance into the Illinois House, Coulson was defense counsel for an officer charged with improper conduct for drinking booze with a black enlisted soldier in an alley. The defendant was adjudged guilty, but Coulson heard later that the conviction was reversed. By that time, Coulson was an army captain serving on emergency missions in China with the Office of Strategic Services.

Except for Choate, who was elected to the Illlinois House in 1946, Arrington didn't meet the rest for some time. But there were certainly other interesting folks he'd get to know fairly quickly after taking his seat in the lower chamber at the start of 1945. He lost no time getting his feet wet in his new world.

Chapter 6

℃

A New Face in the House

*N*othing in 1945 was more important than the end of World War II, starting with the allied armies' victory in Europe followed by the surrender of Japan. That was also the last year in the twentieth century that the Chicago Cubs, to the chagrin of their ever loyal fans, won the National League pennant and advanced to the World Series—where they lost to the Detroit Tigers. The Cubs' Phil Cavaretta was the league's most valuable player that season.

It's those sorts of things many Illinoisans remember most about 1945.

But to those who follow the state's legislative lore, 1945 was memorable because it saw the arrival in Springfield of the Sixty-fourth General Assembly. When it convened in regular session on January 3, a fresh face taking a seat in the Capitol's cavernous House chamber was Russell Arrington, a self-described "greenhorn."

Most freshman lawmakers are greenhorns since they are not acquainted with the manners and customs peculiar to legislative bodies. Of course, Arrington also started out as a backbencher, the word in American political parlance for a legislator lacking seniority. As in many walks of life, a safe course for beginning legislators was to be seen and not heard. This may have been too much to expect of Arrington, never a shrinking violet, but he did come down on the side of caution in his early days in Springfield.

A bit of lying low, not a customarily Arrington trait, was employed even before the House convened. Arrington and the other Republicans outnumbered Democrats in the House, 79 to 74, meaning that the GOP was sure to elect the speaker, the presiding officer in the lower chamber. A spirited contest for the speakership was in progress as Arrington arrived in the capital city on a train from Chicago. The GOP aspirants were two downstate lawyers, Hugh Green of Jacksonville and Reed F. Cutler of Lewistown. Arrington really didn't care which man won, just that he would know enough to vote for the winner. So, he decided to follow the suggestion received on the train from an advisor to Governor Dwight Green, a Republican.

If Arrington were smart, the governor's aide suggested, he'd go straight to the room awaiting him in the Abraham Lincoln Hotel and stay there until the advisor could determine the likely winner for speaker. When that happened, he'd give Arrington a call and tell him which way to vote. Arrington followed the advice to a tee, and even fell asleep in his room while waiting for the call. It did come, tipping off Arrington that Hugh Green was going to prevail.

Subsequently, the General Assembly session opened, Arrington and the other House members took the oath of office—an affirmation in which they pledged not to accept bribes for their upcoming votes—and Arrington went for winner Green in the race for speaker. Above all else, Arrington didn't want to begin his stay in the House on the wrong foot.

Compared to the hectic pace of the General Assembly in later decades, the legislature at the time of Arrington's first term was almost low-key. It was really only a part-time undertaking, which fit the then still traditional concept that the members of the two chambers were not full-time government people, but "citizen-legislators." The lawmakers met in a regular six-month session just every other year (in the odd numbered ones). This situation afforded them plenty of time to make money in other pursuits, which was appropriate because in the period of Arrington's emergence in the Capitol the legislative salary was increasing from just $5,000 to $6,000 each biennium. Legislators had no staffing or Springfield offices, and very few were known outside their districts. In a few parts of the state, election to the General Assembly was simply no big deal. Later on, Arrington would aggressively address these matters, which he came to see as shortcomings. But not at first.

Many of the eventual earmarks of Arrington in his legislative career, such as brusqueness and temper flare-ups, were under wraps in the beginning. As a new kid on the block, he intended to make friends, to size up for himself the numerous seatmates he'd never heard of. He didn't know at the start if he'd run for another term anyway. Thus, there was little reason for being antagonistic. No, whether he'd run for reelection or not, he wanted to at least analyze the place and its players, study the legislative process and get more than an inkling of the ways business really got done.

Arrington also saw that, if he stayed around, he'd have to wrestle with the eternal question facing lawmakers: Should one be a true legislator or a representative? As the latter, a lawmaker goes to Springfield to be a representative of his constituency, an advocate for the special needs of the folks back home and an enforcer making certain that his or her district gets its "share," or even more than its share of the largesse dished out by the state. On the other hand, a true legislator considers his priority duty to be the passage of laws that benefit the entire state. More than the representative, the true legislator concentrates on pushing policies not necessarily influenced by one party, region or interest. The true legislator delves deeply into the substance of subjects to ascertain, in his mind, the best direction for the populace, not what more obviously suits just the lawmaker and his district.

In the long run, Arrington would be both a true legislator and a representative. Unlike many, he realized the two roles did not have to conflict. However, to facilitate having it both ways, one had to master the nuts and bolts of legislative workings in order to lay a firm foundation from which it was possible to have a voice on statewide issues while still protecting one's backside—meaning the accommodation of the sometimes narrow concerns of his own constituents.

To achieve these ends, Arrington needed insight and friends.

As a Republican, Arrington found many doors automatically open to him as he entered the state government scene. The GOP's low standing in Springfield during the Depression-dominated 1930s was history. Arrington arrived to find his party in control of the

W. Russell Arrington as a member of the Illinois House of Representatives

Senate as well as the House. With the exception of Secretary of State Edward J. Barrett, a Democrat, all elected statewide officials were Republicans. Governor Dwight Green presided over a far-flung state political organization, fueled by GOP-controlled patronage, that in Chicago was called a machine.

Arrington lost no time meeting Governor Green, and was favorably impressed. He found the state's chief executive to be handsome, seemingly popular and still regarded as an astute lawyer, always a plus in Arrington's eyes. Arrington was hardly content, though, to court only legislators and others in the Republican mainstream.

He was quite interested in exploring the ins and outs of his new world with what he termed "old-line politicians...the real politicians." This required him to reach beyond the other North Shore and suburban Chicago Republicans, with whom he had much in common. It called for him to extend himself to Democrats and, even more, to specific groupings mainly within Democratic ranks, such as blacks and Italians. He also made a point of cultivating members of the so-called West Side bloc, a gang of Chicago legislators (mainly pseudo Republicans) with intriguing connections.

Alan Ashcraft had shunned these types, Arrington noted, asserting that his predecessor was "very aloof and a do-gooder." For his part, Arrington openly sought their friendship, saying that in not looking down his nose at their drinking and gambling, he "began to know and like them...and they came to like me as a person." Arrington could easily persuade himself to partake in these activities since he was trying mightily to illustrate he was not a snob.

In those days, the legislative work load was relatively light until the final weeks of the session, giving the solons ample time for other pursuits when in Springfield. Some days, Arrington spent as many hours in the Lincoln hotel as in the Statehouse. A lot of those hours were in a certain fifth floor room, where legislators had to be pulled away from a card table.

"They started playing gin, my primary game, for money the minute we'd get to the hotel," he recalled. "The game went on all day and night, continuously." Even when the House was in session for much of the day, Arrington sometimes headed for that fifth floor room after dinner. In his mind, it was just a great path for "learning about the people."

One of his more poignant recollections of the 1945 session earned points in his mind for the so-called Italian bloc. The end of the fighting in Europe occurred when the legislators were in Springfield. Like everywhere else, spontaneous celebrations erupted throughout the town. This also happened during a week that Marion Belland, who by then was employed full-time as Arrington's Chicago office assistant, was in Springfield.

As the festivities gathered steam, Arrington observed that "everyone went on holiday," the restaurants closed and he and Marion became hard pressed to find a place to eat. Retreating to the Lincoln hotel, the guests of which he remembered as "staying awake the whole night," Arrington and Marion were rescued by Representative James Adduci, a Chicago Republican who had a room below Arrington's.

"Jim had sausage, onions and all kinds of things to eat...so we went to his room," said Arrington. Adduci and fellow Italian lawmakers, who were present, gave Marion and Arrington the royal treatment. "The Italian group," Arrington concluded, "was the best behaved in the hotel. They could not have been more gentlemanly."

Hanging around the old Abe, two blocks from the Statehouse, was also a way to pick up inside dope on what really was going on in the legislature. The major downtown hotels were as political as the town, and the old Abe, a Republican haven, was a caldron of lively fun, spirit and political shenanigans. The same was true over at the St. Nicholas Hotel on Jefferson Street, where Democrats filled rooms with thick smoke, strong booze, poker games and conspiratorial dealings.

Both hotels were safe for women chasing, a favorite sport of some legislators many miles from home and their wives. Things weren't much different at the GOP-leaning Leland Hotel, a nine-story hostelry at the corner of Sixth Street and Capitol Avenue, except that the action there appeared to be watered down somewhat because the place housed a lot of Springfield social events.

Congregating at the hotels were lobbyists, usually big spenders eager to open their wallets for just about anything the legislators wanted. Disclosure of lobbying expenditures, or for that matter the origins of campaign contributions, was unheard of in those days. A typical evening during the session might begin with a lobbyist treating one or more legislators to a good meal and drinks at the then newly opened night spot, the Lake Club, where top performers were booked and the right people admitted to a secret back room for illegal gambling with high stakes. Adjournment would follow to an upstairs room or bar at one of the hotels for serious discussion about a bill or other legislative matter important to the lobbyist's client.

Arrington may have had much to learn about the mechanics of the legislative game, but he could smell improprieties from the get-go. He was determined to avoid not only unethical conduct, but even the appearance of such. The operating scruples he maintained at his law firm accompanied him to Springfield. Besides, he didn't have the clout in his early legislative years to influence the outcome of big-ticket issues one way or the other.

Still, the exercise of caution to avoid unsavory relationships did not preclude Arrington from enjoying Springfield nightlife. Ruth seldom journeyed down to Springfield. She did not drive, and she was preoccupied in Evanston with the couple's two young children. Besides the pure enjoyment of it all, making the rounds in after hours was considered by many as an almost de rigueur component of the legislative experience.

Chicago Democrat Daniel Rostenkowski saw all sides of Arrington when he served with him in the House and then Senate before he, Rostenkowski, embarked on a long career in Congress.

"You must remember," Rostenkowski related in a telephone interview in 2003, "that a young kid, which I was when I arrived in the Illinois House, doesn't necessarily go to bed early at night. And neither did Russ Arrington. He was very active in the evening hours. I can say he enjoyed life tremendously."

Nevertheless, added Rostenkowski, "his (Arrington's) activity at night didn't detract from or curtail one bit his strong performance during the day. He was, from the days I was there and later on, just one of the more gifted members of the General Assembly.

"In looking back, the Russ Arrington I knew and remember was a man very young at heart."

For one thing, when Arrington began going to Springfield, his days of penny-pinching were long gone. By that time, he finally could afford to enjoy life. He was hardly dependent on the meager legislative paychecks. His was a far cry from the lot of some members, especially from southern Illinois, who were so poor at the start of their legislative careers that they were forced to sleep in the backseats of their cars in Springfield until they could find free lodging. Arrington had a steady income from the law practice, and his business interests were, or had been, remunerative. Plus, Ashcraft had maneuvered to obtain work for him with Chicago's sanitary district. The fees were quite lucrative, so much so that Arrington was able to hire an individual competent to handle some of the tasks assigned by the district.

Oftentimes, individuals awarded work from governing bodies are required to kick back some of the money received to the contract-letting officials. But, Arrington didn't play that game.

In accepting the work, he said he "made certain that in no case would anyone have a share of my fees. Alan was conspicuously honest. He never asked me for any portion of my fees—which I wouldn't have approved in that it would have been a clear conflict of interest since he was a master in chancery. He was the Republican leader in Evanston, and he just felt that I was entitled to have that business. That went on for three or four years. It was a sizable amount of fees. I was doing very well."

Decades later, in a time of reflection, Arrington characterized his first two-year term in the House as "nothing startling." Yet, while contending that he "got no (committee) appointments of any importance" and was little more than a bystander in the introduction of bills, he felt confident that he had accomplished his goals of "just looking around at what was going on" and gaining the friendship of the movers and shakers. He also sensed that some of those he cultivated "were beginning to understand" him.

Of the 1,507 bills introduced in the session, 691 ended up being passed and signed into law. Arrington was the sponsor or lead sponsor on four of them, measures increasing salaries of state's attorneys, permitting minors to accept aid under the federal GI Bill of Rights, providing for declaratory judgments in certain designated court cases and stipulating that a court order was not required to obtain issuance by a court clerk of a subpoena duces tecum to obtain records. He also was a cosponsor of a successful bill providing for assignment of additional state appellate court judges. All in all, it was a legislative scorecard more or less on par for a freshman lawmaker.

Perhaps more significantly, and in spite of his later contention that he received no important committee assignments, Speaker Hugh Green did name Arrington to membership on an impressive list of committees for a first-termer. They included the panels on education, elections, the judiciary, municipalities, parks, judicial practice, motor vehicles and insurance. As one of twenty-one lawyers in the 153-member House, Arrington landed seats on the panels traditionally most sought by jurists. His inclusion on the House Insurance Committee was also propitious in that Arrington was by then a leading figure in one of the fastest growing insurance firms in the country.

But, again, the acquaintanceships contributed heavily to Arrington's most salient memories of his maiden session. People, not legislation, left the most lasting impression, Democrats included. Especially several Democrats.

One that Arrington barely got to know at this juncture, but who captured his interest, was Democratic senator Richard J. Daley from Chicago, the upper chamber's minority leader. The name of Daley, ten years away from his election as mayor of Chicago, was on many of the measures enacted during the session. Because he was in a distinct minority, Daley impressed Arrington with his political adroitness.

In his own chamber, Arrington endeavored to better grasp the issues of most concern to the small number of African-American legislators. This led in particular to a bonding with Chicago Democrat Fred J. Smith, a native Tennessean who would enjoy a special relationship with Arrington throughout the rest of their days together in the House and, after that, in the Senate.

Then there was Paul Powell. For the middle fifty years of the twentieth century, historians could not find two more masterful practitioners of the Illinois legislative process than Democrat Powell and Arrington. Yet, for all the raw partisanship of which each was capable, they became friends almost from the day Arrington first strolled onto the House floor. Theirs was a curious association because Powell, from small Vienna in deep southern Illinois, had a folksy manner in sharp contrast to the bearing of Arrington. After all, while playing it down as much as he could in his first legislative go-around, the increasing urbanity of the man from Evanston could only be camouflaged so long.

Powell, who was four years older than Arrington, was elected to his first term in the House ten years before the arrival of Arrington. In that time, Powell had become the chief downstate operative for the Democratic State Central Committee and a man very wise in the ways of the legislature. The 1945 session was the one in which Powell earned his first leadership position, as his party's whip—even though he wasn't always in sync with the Chicagoans dominating the party.

Arrington followed Powell closely, especially Powell's skillful marshaling of forces to bring about the passage in 1945 of the Illinois Harness Racing Act, which established pari-mutuel betting for harness racing. This opened a door to an explosion of horse racing in the state because, up to then, harness racing, although popular at downstate county fairs and the state fair in Springfield, was conducted only for prizes. Pari-mutuel wagering was not authorized, and the prizes were minimal. As would be clearly revealed a quarter of a century later, the 1945 session was a watershed for a creeping entanglement of horse racing with legislators and other public officials—all played to a treacherous backdrop of hidden interests and big money.

Unlike Powell, Arrington never would be part of, or implicated in, the largely unethical, submerged dealings between leading Illinois politicians and the racing industry that would surface in rapid-fire fashion in the months after the death of Powell in 1970. That these things might come to light was not foreseen by many in 1945. At that stage, Arrington was just a serious student of the Powell-orchestrated maneuvering that led to the pari-mutuel legislation.

So it went for Arrington on his shakedown cruise in the House. Observe the Paul Powells, maybe probe gently here and there, hold his tongue when he was tempted to jump into this or that debate, sit for the time being on his expectations for himself and others.

As the session progressed, he made up his mind to seek election in 1946 to a second term in the lower body. It hadn't taken long for him to see in the General Assembly the potential to attain a great degree of self-fulfillment—a desire always smoldering inside Arrington.

Meeting challenges in the legal and business worlds rewarded him with personal success, self-esteem and more than respectable income. However, the legislature entailed more, he recognized. Responsible government required the participation of bright people. Government responsive to changing times and evolving issues needed periodic reenergizing with new blood, fresh faces dedicated to the resolution of problems. People just like Arrington.

For Arrington, the General Assembly was a perfect vehicle for doing good things for the benefit of many, something he couldn't accomplish nearly as much in his other venues. Too, as he proceeded on this path, he'd make a bigger name for himself, earn notice in the public eye. If one common thread united legislators, Democrats and Republicans, it was ego. Precious few suffered from a shortage of it.

Arrington had found a home in the House, and he wanted to stay there.

Chapter 7

₢

In the Midst of Things

After winning election to a second term in 1946, he went on to win reelection to three more terms before moving to the Illinois Senate. Unlike his first two years in the lower chamber, the last eight saw him—much more true to his character—right in the middle of things.

During that span, Arrington was a leading sponsor or strong backer of much legislation favored by good government groups and political reformers. He was on the ground floor of efforts, eventually successful, to bring about a convention to propose a modernization of the antiquated Illinois Constitution, which had been approved by voters in 1870. In the meantime, he had a hand in the successful submission to voters in 1950 of the Gateway Amendment to the constitution, which sought to make revision of the charter easier. The state's Little Hoover Commission, which fostered many bills for the streamlining of Illinois government, was set up pursuant to legislation first introduced by Arrington in 1949.

These were salient examples of big-ticket issues, the kind espoused by those representatives and senators striving to be "true" legislators. Having one's name associated with such initiatives caught the fancy of many reporters, editorial writers and political scientists—leading to favorable mention in newspapers and academic journals and, consequently, to an image as one of the good guys or gals.

At the same time, Arrington did not stray from the introduction and push to passage of numerous measures each year that lacked star quality, bills often so mundane that even the scribes in the House press boxes fell asleep when the measures were called.

For example, take the six-month session of the Sixty-fifth General Assembly, Arrington's second, which convened in January 1947 and adjourned "sine die" the last day of June, the normal practice then. (Ending a session sine die signified that no date was scheduled for a resumption of the session, meaning that the legislators would not meet again during the two-year life of each General Assembly unless called into special session by the governor—not a common occurrence.)

In the 1947 session, a review of Arrington's record showed that he was instrumental in the passage of legislation revising the pension systems for downstate police and firemen, increasing fees for filing land title documents, authorizing the creation of voting trusts by corporation shareholders, controlling depositing activities by treasurers of forest preserve districts, creating a highway working cash fund for Cook County, providing for the operation of a state office building in Chicago and creating a community property legislation commission to report to the next General Assembly. And, there were more and more Arrington bills of these types in each succeeding General Assembly.

Jumping to the 1951 legislative session, during Arrington's fourth term in the House, he alone introduced 118 measures (many of which became law), an extensive work load for one lawmaker. Granted, a sizable number were housekeeping bills, routine legislation requiring approval for the state's governing systems to function. A goodly number, though, were of significant import, even though they may have seemed pedestrian to some observers.

What exemplified those bills?

Some shifted the cost of hospitalizing relief patients in Cook County to the state, thereby enabling Chicago to pick up at least $4 million annually in new revenue without boosting property taxes. Another improved supervision of vocational schools in order to combat frauds being perpetrated against war veterans by phony career schools. One more provided a mechanism for restoring thousands of tax delinquent properties to the tax rolls, legislation roundly hailed by the Taxpayers' Federation of Illinois. Others further upgraded unemployment compensation laws, strengthened law enforcement's fight against drug trafficking, permitted public inspection of public assistance rolls and dictated improvements in insurance industry regulation.

Really, few subjects or issues escaped Arrington's attention during his decade in the House. His prolific pace was not impeded during the one time in that span when Democrats held a majority in the body or during the four years that Adlai Stevenson, a Democrat, was governor.

One measure of a legislator's true stranding, at least in the eyes of the lawmaker's legislative leadership, is through committee assignments. Arrington did well, thanks to his retention of a seat on and eventual chairmanship of the House Judiciary Committee.

Committees in the Illinois legislative process are important, or at least that was the case during Arrington's years in the General Assembly. Committees in Illinois may not have been as independent as they were in Congress, but the Illinois panels retained the power to recommend the passage, to kill or to amend (change) bills. When a committee heard a bill in the chamber of the measure's origin, it well may have been the most crucial stage for serious debate or consideration on the bill in the entire legislative proceeding. Moreover, nobody exercised more say over a committee's handling of a bill than the panel's chairman. The chairman, always a member of the chamber's majority party, orchestrated the calling of bills, governed the appearances of witnesses and allocated the time for testimony on the proposed legislation. Thus, the chairman did or should have dominated the work of the committee.

Along with the judiciary committee, Arrington's other main committee assignment during his House years was to the insurance panel. His occupation of a seat on it was extended through his second and third terms. During the second term, which covered 1947 and 1948, he was vice chairman of the insurance committee. He was not on the panel during his final two House terms. Nevertheless, his personal involvement in the insurance industry propelled him to continue to take a deep and abiding interest in insurance issues before the legislature.

Quite clearly, Arrington's chairmanship of the judiciary committee, a plum for an attorney in the legislature, defined his House tenure more than anything else. The panel's purview extended to all legislation affecting the administration of justice, including lifeblood matters in the branch of Illinois government in which judicial power is vested.

Arrington likely would have initially gained the judiciary chairmanship in the 1949 session, instead of two years later, if not for Democratic control of the House in the two years of the Sixty-sixth General Assembly, 1949 and 1950. Paul Powell presided over the lower body then in the first of his three stints as speaker. When the GOP recaptured control of the House in the 1950 election, the new speaker in the subsequent Sixty-seventh General Assembly, Republican farmer and insurance man Warren L. Wood of Plainfield, awarded the chairmanship to Arrington. He went on to retain it during his final term in the House, meaning he headed the committee from 1951 through 1954.

Arrington's stewardship of the committee was recollected with admiration by Alan J. Dixon, a Belleville attorney and a Democrat who was elected to the House in 1950. Dixon, who'd culminate a long and successful career in elective public office by serving as a United States senator, gained a seat on the committee at the start of his House days—just as Arrington did.

"Russ was the chairman when I came on, and, although we were on opposite sides politically, he quickly earned my respect by the way he ran the committee," Dixon recalled in an interview in 2003. "It was his show; he didn't allow any horseplay, any of the kind of looseness that you saw in some of the other committees. He was all business, which was good, since in my mind that was the top committee in the House.

"I framed my impression of Arrington right away, and it really never changed much in all the following years. The man was certainly a leader. Constantly. And, he was also a man seemingly always in a hurry. He was just a very bright man who had little time for small talk. He never stopped working, almost to the detriment of his health."

Echoing an assessment voiced by many in reflecting on Arrington, Dixon emphasized that "he did not suffer fools lightly." Too, when one further considered Arrington's "obvious lack of patience for slackers," added Dixon, "you could see in some cases why he could be noticeably abrupt with people."

Dixon, himself a House Judiciary Committee chairman before

getting elected to the Illinois Senate in 1962, was often the target of Arrington's sharp tongue when he was the Democratic minority's chief debater against Arrington and the Senate's Republican majority in the latter years of the 1960s.

Yet, Dixon remembered many pleasurable moments with Arrington when they were not on a public stage. There was a friendly, quite "charming," side to Arrington, Dixon noted, a person "given to good cigars and fine drinks." Even in the days when the two were political antagonists on the Senate floor, Dixon pointed out that they'd sometimes meet in the after hours at the bar in the Abe Lincoln or the Red Lion tavern at the Leland to "discuss our differences in a calmer setting.

"We'd share drinks for a half hour or so, and maybe continue our floor debates in a lighthearted vein. Or, we'd tone things down by talking about something apart from the issues of the day." Such as English political leader Winston Churchill. "We both were big fans of Churchill, had both read extensively about him. It was not unusual for us to share conversations about him."

Being political adversaries did not rule out cooperation on issues that Arrington and Dixon agreed on. Each was supportive of the other's efforts at bringing about judicial system reform, including Dixon's push for a resolution to amend the judicial article in the Illinois Constitution of 1870. The amendment, approved by voters in 1962, extensively realigned the court system, established an independent appellate court structure, gave the Illinois Supreme Court power to administer the entire judicial system and reformed provisions for the removal or suspension of judges for cause or disability. The pair also labored together to bring about a modern commercial code for Illinois as well as an upgrading of the criminal code.

Working with Democrats never was out of bounds for Arrington if common objectives were at stake. This was especially true in Arrington's early legislative years, when he did not have to be the aggressive partisan expected of one in leadership. For a Republican, Arrington had a very comfortable relationship with Adlai Stevenson after the Democrat became governor at the start of 1949. More than many of his fellow party members, Arrington was able to see bright spots in Stevenson's shake-up of Illinois government—a lot of which Arrington believed in his own mind to be overdue.

Of course, Arrington, as well as most others in the Illinois political world, did not think they'd be dealing with Stevenson when his party nominated him to run against Dwight Green in the 1948 election. At the onset of the gubernatorial campaign, Green appeared hard to beat in his bid for election to a third term as Illinois chief executive. There was his political army of Republicans in state jobs and plenty of dough, as well as an opposition party that seemed dispirited. However, a goodly amount of his political dollars came through payoffs from an illegal gambling industry that had grown rapidly in the state in the 1940s, spawning widespread graft and a deteriorating moral climate.

Dark clouds hinting at impropriety loomed over Illinois, but Green might have weathered the gathering storm if not for the assassination in July 1948 of gangster Bernie Shelton at his tavern on the outskirts of Peoria. Bernie was one of the infamous Shelton brothers who'd run the unlawful wagering and other rackets in downstate Illinois for decades. Early on, their headquarters was in East St. Louis, where they began wielding power when Arrington's family lived in the city and he was a student at East St. Louis High School.

The killing of Bernie Shelton, believed to have been ordered by an alliance of Chicago and St. Louis mobsters, triggered a tidal wave of newspaper disclosures about the illicit ties of gamblers, racketeers and other shady characters to numerous public officials at all levels. The great degree to which unfettered gaming and prostitution flourished in many counties was vividly spelled out. As the disclosures fueled public anger, ministerial and chamber of commerce groups sought investigations by grand juries and special prosecutors all over the landscape.

As if this was not enough to hamper numerous incumbents in the 1948 election, Green's candidacy also was saddled with other undesirable baggage—including allegations of state regulatory negligence in the Centralia coal mine disaster of 1947 (claiming 111 lives) and revelations that many newspaper reporters were on the state payroll without doing any work. To the surprise of some observers, Stevenson proved to be a quite effective campaigner in calling attention to these matters.

Although he was from an old political family, Stevenson was an aristocratic blue blood who, at the beginning of the campaign, was taken lightly by many old hands in both parties. The GOP endeavored to dismiss him as an egghead, unable to connect with the average Joe. Most in the party, as well as others, believed that Green stood to benefit from the shirttails of the seemingly strong Republican candidate for president in 1948, Governor Thomas E. Dewey of New York. Democrats themselves felt that Stevenson needed some unforeseen break to boost him into serious contention with Green. Perhaps a scandal stirring up public indignation would do. Their wish was largely granted by the Shelton murder and its aftermath. The final upshot was political disaster for Green and many other GOP candidates.

The balloting on November 2, 1948, produced one of the Democrats' greatest showings in Illinois history. Stevenson swamped Green, and Democrats won all the other statewide offices on the ballot. University of Chicago professor Paul H. Douglas, a Democrat, ousted Republican Wayland Brooks from his seat in the United States Senate and, in an eye-raiser to many, President Harry S Truman managed to edge Dewey in the presidential voting in Illinois by a thin margin. Without the strong showing of Stevenson, Democrat Truman most likely would not have carried Illinois, a state that turned out to be important for Truman in his upset victory over Dewey.

While Arrington held on to his Sixth District House seat, the election left Democrats in control of the chamber, 81 to 72. The Democratic landslide did not extend to the Illinois Senate, where the GOP retained the upper hand, 32 to 18. The ensuing biennium (1949-1950) of the Sixty-sixth General Assembly was the one, the only one during Arrington's House career, in which his party was not in the majority.

The amiable rapport between Arrington and Stevenson would not be repeated during the years in the 1960s when another Democrat, Otto Kerner, was governor and Arrington emerged as the leader of Senate Republicans. But that was another world far down the road when Stevenson took over the reins of state government.

In looking back, Arrington espoused nothing but respect for Stevenson, calling him "a great governor," one who "everybody knew" to be "unusually bright and intellectual and honest." Arrington's perception of Stevenson was based on an up-close view. Stevenson maintained an office in the basement or ground floor of the Governor's Mansion. He preferred to work there instead of in the spacious office reserved for the governor in the Statehouse. Many of those who supported his initiatives, or might be persuaded to be partly on board, such as Arrington, often were summoned to the Mansion.

It was important to remember that Stevenson took office with a call for a new era of nonpartisanship. He was hardly a strong organization Democrat to begin with, and, furthermore, he needed to try to reach out to the Republican-controlled Senate that he feared—accurately so—to be hostile. Having the House in Democratic hands when he became governor was not an assured luxury either because the new speaker, Powell, a rustic individual, had an almost automatic aversion to the urbane Stevenson.

Consequently, Stevenson had no choice but to forge working relationships apart from the normal course of things. Unconventionality was unavoidable—such as the hours spent by Arrington at the Mansion, especially during night hours. Besides being aware of Arrington's favorable response to some of his government reform endeavors, Stevenson surely took note of Arrington's inclusion in the Republican minority on the House Rules Committee during Stevenson's first two years in office.

The rules panel, chaired by Powell, exercised a decisive voice over the mechanics of running the House. Its members, few in number, were seen as insiders who had "arrived" in the minds of their peers. For that reason, it was worthy of mention that a GOP seatmate of Arrington on the committee was Orville Hodge, an amiable businessman from Granite City who at the time was only in his second term in the House. Hodge would generate a lot of headlines down the line.

Stevenson, a lawyer whose public career before running for governor was focused in Washington, knew little about state government. However, he threw himself headlong into the task of gaining command over his new domain, more so than ever after he and his socialite wife, the former Ellen Borden, were divorced early in his term.

According to Arrington, Stevenson became "a work demon...working all the time," even through the wee hours of the morning. "I came to know him through real close contact," Arrington said. "I'd sometimes be among those working at the Mansion in the after hours. It was good for me because it gave me new insight into how the state should be run."

By the time the second half of Stevenson's term began in 1951, Arrington concluded, he was primed for the national recognition that would propel him to his party's candidacy for the presidency in 1952 and again in 1956—both times without success.

A number of the undertakings or stands for which Stevenson became known had Arrington's backing openly or otherwise. They included a reorganization of the state police that put many officers under civil service, directing state police raids against illegal gambling, getting a major highway construction program through the legislature, support for a state constitutional convention and the push for Illinois' Little Hoover Commission—which commenced the first thorough survey of state government since its reform and restructuring under activist Governor Frank Lowden in 1917. The idea for the commission emanated from President Truman's naming of former President Herbert Hoover to direct an analysis of the operation of the federal government.

After moving vigorously and successfully for legislative sanction for the Little Hoover panel, Arrington closely monitored its proceedings under Walter V. Schaefer, a Northwestern University law professor who became Stevenson's chief legal advisor. Subsequently, Arrington had a big hand in garnering legislative support for some of the commission's recommendations for eliminating waste and inefficiency in Illinois government.

In those areas where he could cooperate with Stevenson, Arrington fashioned a working relationship with J. Edward Day, who had an office next to Stevenson's in the Mansion basement. Day, who joined Stevenson in Springfield after an affiliation with the same Chicago law firm as Stevenson, went on later to become postmaster general of the United States under President John F. Kennedy. Stevenson had a knack for tapping people for his administration

Ruth Arrington and Shirley Stratton (wife of Governor William G. Stratton) at reception in the Arrington home

who'd go on to bigger things. One, Richard J. Daley, no longer a state senator, was Stevenson's first revenue director. Another was Daniel Walker. A young aide in the latter part of Stevenson's governorship, Democrat Walker himself was elected Illinois governor in 1972.

With Stevenson running for the presidency instead of a second gubernatorial term in the 1952 election, the GOP recaptured the state's top office with the candidacy of Illinois Treasurer William G. Stratton. Stratton was only thirty-eight years old when he was sworn into office, but he was an authority on government, already having served twice as state treasurer and two times as Illinois' then congressman-at-large.

It took little time for Arrington to discern that Stratton "knew more about governing than any governor I had met up to that time." Since Arrington remained House Judiciary Committee chairman during Stratton's first two years in office, and was by then clearly recognized as a principal Republican player in the chamber, he and Stratton gravitated almost naturally to each other.

"We got together a lot, liked each other…and it was evident I was becoming someone who was one of his advisors," said Arrington.

The closeness of the two men was confirmed by Mrs. William Stratton when she was interviewed at her Chicago residence in 2003, two years after the death of her husband. Mrs. Stratton, the former Shirley Breckenridge, who married Stratton two years before he was elected governor, related that her husband "would refer to Russ as one of the most able legislators—a person, like Bill, whose word was his bond.

"Bill realized, of course, that cooperation of the legislature was essential to being a good governor. And, he saw quite quickly that Russ was confident about his own legislative capabilities and extremely knowledgeable about the (General Assembly) process."

Mrs. Stratton recalled her husband, who was eight years younger than Arrington, seeking to "bond" with Arrington by having him accompany the governor on drives between Chicago and Springfield.

In her words, "Bill would invite Russ to ride with him in the governor's limo because it was a great way for them to have private conversations, which might often be necessary on certain legislative issues. It was a four-hour drive either way, which made for quality time for both of them. The state trooper driving the car would be alone up front, and Bill, Russ and myself, when I was along, sat on jump seats in the back part of the limo. I can certainly say it was educational for me to listen to them talk."

Mrs. Stratton emphasized that Arrington was of great assistance to her husband in developing the toll highway system in the Chicago area. She also recalled Arrington helping to lay a foundation for Stratton-linked bond issues that assisted in the financing of major building programs for mental hospitals and universities. In addition, Stratton and Arrington were allies on the unending crusade for judicial reform.

To Arrington, Stratton was "a splendid governor." Beyond that, though, the Stratton era—he served two terms as governor—meant more to Arrington. At least the era's first part. The early years of the 1950s constituted a period in which Arrington found "things going along very nicely."

Those were years that left Arrington with a decided impression of "a country without turmoil, an economy doing well" and a populace that "seemed to be happy." Even government, he averred, "was enjoyable." The latter assessment, for Arrington, was really saying something.

In the eyes of many, the fifties were colored, more than anything, by uninterrupted economic prosperity for a great number of Americans, conservative politics and social conformity. Decades afterward, the fifties truly did seem to have been an unusually orderly time, years with little social dissent. The decade appeared to be the last chronicled in black and white, and the images portrayed were of people living tidy lives—from the patterned neatness of fast-growing suburbs to the prim and proper dress of men in suits and ties and their buttoned-down wives staying home to bear children at soaring numbers. Most younger folks were of no mind to challenge the given social mores. In a throwback to the 1920s, businessmen were back in vogue, and material success was the top priority. On the whole, government's role as an instigator of change, at least on the social front, was greatly if not totally restrained.

The tone for the decade was set by Dwight Eisenhower, who swamped Adlai Stevenson in the 1952 presidential election on a campaign to end the Korean War, combat Communism and improve the nation's moral fiber. Eisenhower aimed to steer his country down the middle, where things are not all black or white, where left and right extremists are shut out by middle Americans—the quintessential folks who pay most of the taxes, cast the majority of the votes and cling most closely to the time-cherished values of home, church and community. Atomic anxiety hovered overhead like a sword of Damocles, but the centrist, mainstream world offered a refuge, a cocoon in which so many, like Arrington, found "things going along very nicely."

In offering this assessment upon reflection, Arrington also had in mind his own life and that of his family.

On the home front, the Arringtons had departed the apartment life in 1948 with their purchase of a white brick, single family home at 606 Forest Avenue in the southeast section of Evanston. The house put them closer to Lake Michigan and the steady dream of Russell and Ruth to eventually settle their family along the lake.

Owning a home for the first time moved the family up the ladder on the Evanston social scale. At the same time, Arrington's sprouting reputation in public life thrust new responsibilities on the members of his family. Ruth increasingly was involved in activities of the town and her children's schools, but she had to keep in mind her husband's admonition against entering into random discussions of public issues. Caution was the byword. It applied to the kids too.

Patricia Arrington remembered "always being told as I was growing up to say 'I don't know' when teachers or others might ask what my father's view was on this or that. It was just the way it was. Everything had to stay at home."

Still, there was much about her family in the late 1940s and early 1950s that mirrored the idealized vision of American family life so accentuated at the time. "Mom and dad certainly weren't known for moderation in many things, but there was a lot of normalcy in our lives," said Patricia. "Mom and dad insisted on it, or tried to insist on it...dad as well as mom."

When Patricia ran for president of the eighth grade class at Nichols Junior High School at the end of the 1940s, her state representative father was as supportive as could be. Patricia and the other candidates for the office had to address their classmates to seek support, and Patricia could look out and see her father "sitting in the pupil audience."

The night before, she related, "he looked at my speech and suggested a line that he thought might add a lot to it. The line was, 'I'd rather be right than be class president.' I didn't use it, though. I also didn't win, but using his line, I was sure, would have made no difference."

Patricia sometimes accompanied her father to his law office on Saturdays. Before returning home, they might catch a movie in downtown Chicago or visit a secondhand bookstore. Arrington also took his daughter to Springfield now and then. On the trains, she played gin rummy with other legislators.

Come Sundays, Arrington drove Patricia for a while to Sunday school at a Presbyterian church and then, later on, to St. Mark's Episcopal Church in Evanston. Patricia and Michael were raised as Episcopalians, the church in which their mother eventually was confirmed. Arrington himself did not attend church, except for special occasions such as Christmas programs in which his children were participating.

Giving time to organized religion was not part of Arrington's regimen. His religious affiliation, if any, was largely unknown to those entering his life; the subject hardly ever came up. One time it did was at the midpoint of his decade in the House. Warren Barr Sr., a businessman, friend and client of Arrington from Oak Park, was to be president of Medinah Country Club and wanted Arrington to be on its board.

Medinah, with its exotic clubhouse of Byzantine and Italian architecture and revered golf courses, had become a very exclusive enclave since its development in the 1920s on prime farmland in north DuPage County purchased by members of the Ancient Order of Nobles of the Mystic Shrine. Although Shriners Club membership was waived as a requirement to join Medinah in 1938, Arrington's interest in Medinah had been negligible because of his Catholic background.

His upbringing as a Catholic, Arrington said, "had never seemed important to Warren or me. But, the club was made up of Masons, and I didn't know of anyone who was on the board or belonged to the club who was a Catholic."

Nevertheless, Arrington filled out the paperwork for joining Medinah, and was readily informed by Barr that he was going on the board. However, a small hitch had arisen.

"Warren came to my office and said there was just one little problem," related Arrington. "On the application, Warren said that I had replied, in response to a question, that I had no preference in religion. But, on a second question asking what would be my preference, I said 'Catholic.' Warren said that was 'quite embarrassing,' and asked if I'd change the application to say that I had no religious affiliation with anyone.

"Well, I told him, 'Warren, I'm not a religious man. But if I were going to be one, I would be a Catholic.' I was raised as a Catholic. My mother had not been a Catholic, but converted. I was baptized the same time my mother joined the Catholic church. My mother and father had some real conditions about religion. So, I couldn't say I was not anything. My answer to Warren was that I could not change my answer to the question…that I was going to leave it the way it is. If they throw me out for that reason, it would have to be that way because I would not change."

Consequently, concluded Arrington, "poor Warren had two or three meetings with various club members, and it took a couple of weeks before they decided I could be…on the board in spite of my answer to that one question."

A pleasurable relationship with Medinah ensued for Arrington and his family, even though he rarely partook of the golfing and the kids' time at swimming was limited because of the considerable distance from Evanston to Medinah. Actually, if Arrington's golf game seemed mediocre at Medinah, it went downhill even more after the Medinah years because of an increasingly hectic pace that left little or no time for the links.

All said, the Medinah experience was a plus in the coming of age for the Arrington family at the advent of the 1950s. It helped buttress his remembrance of the period as one in which he found "things going along very nicely."

He still had other reasons for feeling this way. As if becoming a potent state representative and successful family man were not enough, the man's private professional life was clicking on all cylinders. Arrington's alignment with Clement Stone years before had turned out to be fortuitous. They were a hell of a team.

Chapter 8

℃

Russ and Clem

hey started out as casual acquaintances in young Republican circles in Evanston. Then they began to have some business dealings, small stuff at first. As they got to know each other better, they saw they had things in common—a great ambition to succeed, certainly, but also a realization that neither one was born with a silver spoon in his mouth. With the insurance industry ventures of the one beginning to flourish, he increasingly sought legal assistance from the other. Soon, W. Clement Stone wanted Arrington to work with him full-time, but Arrington demurred. He committed himself enough to Stone, though, to become an indispensable figure in the hierarchy of Stone's insurance empire. Their bond, secured by strong friendship as well as professional collaboration, enriched both men.

Where their business partnership was concerned, Arrington was Mr. Inside and Stone was Mr. Outside. If they had been in a football backfield, Arrington would have been in the largely unheralded role of blocking back, helping to clear the path for the star ballcarrier, Stone. Arrington was no introvert, but in the business world of the flamboyant Stone the spotlight seldom shifted away from the short man with the pencil-thin mustache.

Stone was a demonstrative man par excellence, a person of unflagging energy and boundless confidence who exhorted those around him to follow his lead in reaching for the moon. He relished his reputation as an apostle for the self-made man, an image well deserved. He did, after all, parlay pennies in savings into a series of insurance endeavors eventually culminating in a vastly profitable network centering around the Combined Insurance Company of America, of which Stone was president.

Never one to stay put, Stone was always eyeing new opportunities, looking to acquire another insurance company or extend his other many interests into even more domains far flung from his Chicago base. In so doing, he had to satisfy, or, in many cases, negotiate with government regulators and their countless pages of legal dictates or restrictions affecting his operations. The handling of this task, usually done behind the scenes, was engineered by Arrington. It was a complicated challenge requiring insight into a plethora of overlapping state laws and federal as well as state bureaucracies. Tricky waters indeed.

The success by Arrington in meeting the challenge was evidenced by his positions of vice president, secretary and general counsel of Combined. However, Arrington's input went much further. He stood squarely enough with Stone to exercise or voice a sometimes moderating influence on Combined's top man, whose exuberant ideas or dreams of crossing new business frontiers could exceed the bounds of reality. Many days, Stone was not prone to even considering advice from anybody except Arrington or F. E. McCabe. An Iowan with Combined since its early days, the easygoing McCabe was the company's executive vice president for administration and, to some degree, a sort of father figure to the younger Stone.

One person with a close-up view of the interaction between Stone and Arrington was Arthur C. Niemann, an Arrington family friend and an individual who rose in a fifteen-year career with Combined from a mail boy to Stone's executive assistant.

Privy to the highest level decision-making at a firm that came to employ thousands of men and women, Niemann observed years after his departure from the company and Chicago that "Russ was the articulate brain behind Combined's success." What he meant, explained Niemann in an interview by phone from his home in Bend, Oregon, was that "Russ had the legal expertise to see that all the requirements attendant to our operations were met, to ensure that the ship stayed righted. And, I can say that he did a magnificent job of keeping Combined clean and out of trouble."

Senator W. Russell Arrington and W. Clement Stone

As the number-two person at the helm behind Stone, Arrington was depicted by Niemann as "the guiding force in the inner sanctum who took a conservative approach in trying to keep the dynamo Stone from sometimes going too fast.

"Put simply, Russ tried to harness Stone when he considered it necessary. And McCabe, also conservative minded, normally sided with Russ in trying to keep Stone within limits. At meetings of the board of directors, Russ was the lone individual often questioning Stone, urging Stone to always think things through. Quite often, though, Stone would just smile and twirl that cigar of his and tell Russ that he was going to do what he wanted."

Yet, Niemann emphasized, while Arrington refused to be a yes-man for Stone, the two remained "great friends." Furthermore, added Niemann, Arrington never wavered from crediting Stone with having "a real Midas touch. He (Arrington) just thought that Stone was the best salesman he'd ever seen."

A lot of others shared Arrington's view, including many of those who followed the fascinating life of Stone, which ended with his death in 2002 at the age of 100.

To encapsulate for those not familiar with William Clement

Stone, he was born on Chicago's south side in 1902, four years before Arrington. His father died when he was two or three years old, leaving Stone and his dressmaker mother impoverished because of his gambling losses. By age six, Stone was hawking newspapers to help his mom. Seven years later, he had his own newsstand. At sixteen, he embarked on an insurance career, selling policies for an agency his mother took over in Detroit. Going from door to door, he made "cold calls" to sell casualty insurance. Within a short time, he was bringing in $100 a week, enough to convince him that insurance was his ticket to "a poor boy makes good" ending.

In 1922, Stone established a Chicago-based insurance agency, the Combined Registry Company, with working capital of $100. The first day in this new role, when he sold fifty-four policies, buttressed his conviction that he was on the right track. Combined Registry, which acted as agent for some six insurers, grew steadily, employing 1,000 agents nationwide by 1930.

Stone originally had intended to be a lawyer and enter politics. He even had studied nights for a year at the Detroit College of Law. However, he put that ambition on hold when he married his Chicago sweetheart, Jessie Tarson, in 1923. Still, he had his mind set on selling enough insurance to retire at thirty and return to law school. By the time he reached thirty, though, his goals had changed and, as for his earlier desire to be a full-time politician, he'd decided to settle instead for influencing politics one day through the money channel.

During the Depression, Stone's business took a big hit and he was forced to reduce his number of agents to 135. But, he refused to buckle. To the contrary, by the end of 1939, Stone had acquired his first insurance company, the American Casualty Company of Dallas, known later as the Combined American Insurance Company of Dallas. It was in 1939 that he also organized the Combined Mutual Casualty Company of Chicago, followed by the Combined Casualty Company of Philadelphia. Out of these developments would come a new name for his undertakings, the Combined Insurance Company of America. By the time of this juncture, Arrington was heavily involved with Stone.

Looking back in tracing the friendship between Arrington and

Stone, it seemed clear that their relationship was one of the more interesting to come out of the Evanston Young Republican Club in the 1930s. Stone did not seek to befriend Arrington because he was an attorney or because he understood insurance law. Stone wasn't fond of lawyers, and Arrington was not well versed initially on the legalities of insurance. The reason, according to Arrington, was that Stone found him to appear politically astute.

"We met each other," said Arrington, "because he once had the idea that he wanted to have a part in government and, in reality, politics. He had thought he wanted to be a politician, and he still was very interested in that area."

At his end, Arrington was aware from day one that Stone already was recognized as a hotshot in his field, a man whose agency employed a great number of salespersons across the land. However, Stone gave little indication early on that his business needed or desired any of Arrington's legal services. Indeed, their first business interaction had nothing to do with Stone's agency.

It just happened that, in the mid 1930s, Stone's car was rammed into by another auto on Sheridan Road, causing slight injury to Jessie Stone. The accident "started my real association with Clem," recalled Arrington, "because he wanted to know if I would handle the insurance and damages involved."

Although admittedly lacking any "familiarity with insurance," Arrington said that he accepted the assignment and, without delay, invoked a rather direct technique in dealing with the claim adjuster.

"Adjusters used to haggle and argue, and I never liked that at all," Arrington related. "So, I talked to the claim agent and said, 'Now, I don't want to have a lot of trouble with you. I'd like to settle this case, and I don't know how badly Jessie was injured. But, I'm not going to haggle with you about this. I'll tell you what I'll do. I'll settle the claim for $3,000. You take it or leave it, but we're not going to spend a lot of time with it. If you don't agree, I'll file suit and we'll have a trial.'"

Consequently, the adjuster—described by Arrington as caught off guard by this approach—accepted the offer.

Noting that Jessie Stone's injury did not turn out to be serious,

Arrington was quite satisfied with the $3,000 settlement, a tidy sum of money in the 1930s. More importantly, "Clem was happy," Arrington added. He also pointed out that in resolving the matter without a trial he was entitled under a normal procedure to 25 percent, or $750, of the settlement figure. However, saying he didn't "know any better" at the time, Arrington took only $125 of the $3,000.

Soon afterward, Stone was hiring Arrington to handle minor legal issues arising out of his business. The fees he received were hardly substantial, but the insight Arrington was gaining into the makeup of the insurance industry was invaluable. Pleased with Arrington's prowess, Stone engaged him much more extensively by asking him to navigate the legal challenges involved in Stone's purchase of the American Casualty Company. The task consumed much of Arrington's limited time in Chicago in 1939, the year in which Arrington was most tied up with the New York World's Fair.

On the heels of the American Casualty acquisition, Stone moved quickly to organize the Combined Mutual Casualty Company of Chicago and take other steps to ensure a strong foundation for his new insurance network. Arrington was not involved at first with these endeavors, but he would be. Convinced of an imperative to get Combined Mutual off the ground before the end of 1939, and realizing the year was nearing an end, Stone turned away from an insurance law firm from which he'd sought assistance and, instead, appealed for overnight help from Arrington.

Getting Arrington on the phone in the first days of December of that year, Stone went further than ever with Arrington in flatly asking him whether he could handle the legal organization of an insurance company. Even though he still had much to learn about insurance firms, Arrington informed Stone that he was "a specialist in corporate law" and that he "could organize an insurance company in Illinois as well as anyone."

With that, Arrington rushed over to Stone's then nearby office on LaSalle Street, digesting on the way as much of the Illinois insurance code as possible. Already very familiar with "the actions needed to organize a corporation," Arrington proceeded to work through the night with Stone assembling the forms necessary to start an insurance corporation.

The next day, with no time to lose, Arrington headed by train for Springfield and the Illinois Department of Insurance, where he hoped to personally steer the incorporation paperwork through the bureaucracy. As luck would have it, he struck up a conversation at the train's bar with a fellow traveler, none other than Ernest Palmer. Palmer, another attorney from Evanston, also happened to be the director of the state insurance department.

"He (Palmer) had known of me, and I knew of him, but we'd never met," said Arrington. "Well, we had a couple of drinks together and got to know each other. I told him what I wanted to do, organize this insurance company, and made a date with him the following morning.

"He said it was all right for him; there was no reason why not. He knew that Clem and I were the organizers, and that we had good reputations. There was no reason at all why we couldn't start our own company."

But, when Arrington informed Palmer that the goal was to get the corporation organized to begin business before the end of the year, the director expressed reservation because of the time required for the necessary publication of the operating license application. Arrington countered that, with the assistance of Palmer in circumventing department red tape, publication could start immediately and be finished several days before the end of December.

"Palmer had never heard of anything like that before, had never heard of anyone starting an insurance company so quickly," remarked Arrington. "But he said to go ahead and we'll see. And, that's what we did. It turned out we got the license before the end of the month, which put us in the decade we wanted to be in. We were on our way."

Arrington's fait accompli was praised by Stone forty years later when he eulogized Arrington at a memorial service following his death. Pointing out that he had a problem many years earlier in wanting to incorporate a company in a very narrow time frame, Stone related that he gave Arrington "a challenge—namely that if he would do it within the time limit, that he would have the job. He got it done.

He was a man of action."

After the successful launching of Combined Mutual, Arrington was called upon frequently by Stone for legal assistance. Because of the state's insurance code, Arrington pointed out, "having a company was much more complex than Clem ever understood at that time. There were a lot of regulations which Clem didn't care to think about. But, as a lawyer, I had to find out those things. Even though Clem didn't care much for lawyers, he had come to understand me. So, I started to work more and more with Clem."

As Arrington became increasingly knowledgeable about insurance laws and regulations, Stone asked Arrington to surrender his own practice and work exclusively for Stone. However, Arrington declined, explaining that he wanted his practice to cover more than just one person or business. Stone then did find an attorney to serve him full-time. However, as Arrington remembered it, the new fellow did not have "the zip, style or quality needed." So, the replacement was let go, and Arrington returned to work for Stone on the same basis as before.

Arrington would spend part of many mornings at Stone's new headquarters, located in a two-story house he'd purchased on Sheridan Road in Chicago across from the Edgewater Beach Hotel. The home's living room became Stone's office, the dining room housed a secretarial pool, and another room was reserved for Arrington. Stone was often out of town, "selling everywhere," as Arrington phrased it. When Stone was in Chicago, the two conferred almost every day.

During the 1940s, Arrington paved the way for the licensing of Stone's operations in other states, a prime necessity for Stone's insatiable appetite for expansion. Eventually, Arrington also would oversee the negotiations needed to secure the authorization for Stone to sell insurance in numerous foreign countries. Arrington also began to attend national meetings of the state insurance commissioners, hooked up with the Illinois State Bar Association's insurance panel and, as noted earlier, served on the insurance committee of the Illinois House after his election to the body.

Arrington was at Stone's side during the acquisition in the mid 1940s that, more than anything else, cemented the nucleus of Stone's insurance empire. That particular development was Stone's purchase of the moribund Pennsylvania Casualty Company. After bringing it into his fold, he merged it in 1947 with Combined Mutual to form the Combined Insurance Company of America—the flagship of Stone's, and Arrington's, insurance endeavors the rest of their years together.

In no time at all, Combined Insurance was a conspicuous standout. Energized by the personal magnetism of Stone, an army of door-to-door salespeople carried Combined's accident, health insurance and hospitalization policies directly to homes and businesses. By the end of 1947 alone, Combined had assets of $2.2 million.

In 1949, Combined acquired the Boston Casualty Company, another accident and health insurer, and renamed it Hearthstone Insurance Company of Massachusetts. Five years later, Combined bought the First National Casualty Company of Fond du Lac, Wisconsin. And the pattern continued. Through it all, Combined continued to rely on direct sales of low-cost accident and health policies, a good risk. By the end of the 1950s, a boom decade for Combined and its subsidiaries, the assets of Stone's insurance empire reached more than $20 million. Along with Stone and Arrington, numerous other individuals serving the Combined network joined the ranks of the wealthy.

The images of Stone and Combined were synonymous. There was no other way to put it. Stone was simply a remarkable individual, a diminutive dynamo whose unbridled effervescence imbued every layer of his business empire. Stone's personal philosophy—always stick to a "positive mental attitude," or PMA—served as the foundation of Combined's day-to-day operations. His incantations resonated everywhere he popped up; his words supplied a daily invocation for the men and women under him. If the country had a greater adherent of self-help motivation, good luck in finding one. Combined's workers were urged to greet each day with his cheerful maxim, "I feel healthy. I feel happy. I feel terrific." His sales talks were memorized and recited by the company's grass roots representatives.

Few enterprises had a more visible pitchman at its top. His appearance alone, striking in comparison to the drab gray of most in corporate America, guaranteed it. Besides that ultra-thin mustache and those aromatic Havana cigars (plucked out of the vast stock he purchased before the Castro revolution), the earmarks of Stone included patterned vests, bright suspenders, colorful bow ties and, sometimes, spats. Writer William Braden thought Stone rather looked like Agatha Christie's detective, Hercule Poirot, when Braden interviewed Stone for the *Chicago Sun-Times* in 1969.

Stone was known to untold numbers, some of whom even became his disciples, through the self-help books and magazines he wrote or coauthored, edited and published. If any person could be said to have guaranteed personal success through his or her sheer will, it was Stone. Writer Braden certainly recognized this in his picturing of the man.

"Some men perhaps are the captains of their fate," wrote Braden. "Stone is the absolute dictator of his. By his own analogy, he is a sort of human computer who has programed himself to succeed—and his studies of motivation have convinced him he can train others to follow his example. His method, as he described it, is to condition people to believe that 'they're going to get what they want by doing what I want.'"

Of course, Arrington's compulsion to succeed in life was every bit as strong as Stone's. Too, Arrington had ways, emanating from his forceful personality, of getting people to bend to his will. He was not the showman that Stone was. Or, more accurately, Arrington's penchant for theatrics was limited to the confines of the Statehouse. Inside Combined, Arrington eschewed flamboyance, adhering strictly to what Niemann labeled "a dignified presence." Arrington received respect from the Combined crew for his surefootedness in playing his role, Niemann emphasized, just as Stone was esteemed for his extraordinary but winning portrayal of himself and his company. Each accommodated the ego of the other in recognizing that the strength of one complemented the strength of the other. They truly were a hell of a team.

The fact that Stone, not Arrington, was the master of pep talks at Combined (and also outside of the company) did not suggest that Arrington failed to impel those he encountered at Combined to strive for excellence. There were some in whom Arrington took a personal interest, just as he would do with the bright young legislative staffers he'd bring into Illinois government in the 1960s. One manifestation of his personal involvement was to help a number of these individuals, both at Combined and later in the legislative ranks, to move ahead financially.

At Combined, Arrington did not hesitate to use his position on the board of the Bank of Chicago to assist some company employees in obtaining loans from the bank to buy the lucrative stock in Combined. The bank was a few blocks away from the six-story building at 5050 North Broadway in uptown Chicago that Combined built and moved into in the early 1960s after outgrowing the Sheridan Road headquarters. Arrington was even a cosigner on many of the loans. One helped by Arrington in this manner was Niemann.

Niemann's relationship with Arrington was a story in itself. It started before Arrington ushered Niemann into Combined. It began on a sensitive note, but had a warm ending. It revolved around Arrington's son, Michael.

The story began in the late 1950s when native Chicagoan Niemann, a young science teacher at Evanston's Nichols Junior High School, was assigned a class of what he considered to be rowdies. A leader of the bunch was none other than Michael Arrington, whose father by then was a highly respected and quite potent state senator. Niemann wasn't aware of that when Michael first entered his world, but he did recognize that Michael presented a challenge.

"Mike was a little guy, but he was tough and arrogant…kind of a little hood type," Niemann said. "I sensed there might be a problem."

Niemann's premonition was right. The two clashed so sharply one day that Michael threw a punch at Niemann, and Niemann responded, in his words, "by roughing him (Michael) up." For his part in the encounter, Niemann was suspended.

After "the principal told me that Mike was Russ Arrington's son," related Niemann, the teacher went home on the day of his suspension to spend an uncomfortable evening in a very worrisome state of mind. Before the night was out, Niemann's unease heightened when there was a knock on the door of his small apartment in one of Evanston's big old homes. The caller was Russell Arrington.

"Here was the senator himself, dressed real spiffy, looking very dignified," Niemann stated. "First, he told me not to be upset. Then, he said, 'I'm giving you permission to hit, to stomp on that little shit anytime you want.' He then told me that my suspension already was over. He concluded by asking me to 'please take care of my son.'"

The following day, back at school, the younger Arrington noticeably showed Niemann respect. It was just the start. Michael also became a frequent visitor to Niemann's apartment, triggering a bond strong enough to give Niemann the feeling of "kind of having adopted Mike." His contribution, Niemann felt, was "to get Mike's life together."

Niemann believed that having minimal time to spend with his son during his teenage years was only one facet of the sometimes awkward relationship between Arrington and Michael. He also saw that "Russ was a very demanding parent, whose philosophy was that his kids, especially his son, had to earn everything. When Mike turned sixteen, Russ wouldn't even give him money to buy a car. It was a throwback to his (Arrington's) younger days, when he had to make his own way."

Niemann's friendship with Michael brought the teacher under the scrutiny of Michael's father, and he liked what he saw. Consequently, Arrington prevailed upon Stone to hire Niemann as a part-time mail worker at Combined in 1959. After five months on the job, Stone asked Niemann to leave teaching for full-time employment with Combined. The offer included a salary greater than Niemann was receiving as an educator. Acknowledging that "money talked," Niemann made the jump. By the time he left Combined in 1974 to set up a company to help small businesses get established, Niemann had handled top-drawer responsibilities at Combined, including years as Stone's executive aide and, for a spell, director of personnel. During the span at Combined, Niemann's rapport with the Arringtons further blossomed.

More than anything, Niemann was gratified to see Michael develop into a determined young man at Evanston Township High School. Niemann encouraged Michael to play football for the Evanston Wildkits, which he did at both fullback and middle linebacker. Michael, although of average size at one hundred and eighty pounds, exhibited incredible tenacity on a team in the 1960 season, the fall of his senior year, that sports analysts rated as the state champion. Niemann observed that Arrington could not disguise his pleasure when he accompanied Niemann to watch Michael play. Arrington, who liked football, took home movies of his son in action. In the years that followed, the closeness of Michael and Niemann endured—so much so that Niemann was best man at both of Michael's weddings.

Niemann was one slice of life in the Arrington world. The business orbit of Arrington and Stone touched or called upon the talents of plenty others. Two of the more luminous were Peer Pedersen and Leonard Lavin. More later on Lavin and his story, an incarnation of the American dream.

First, a look at Pedersen, a Chicago attorney who would become a member of Combined's board. Handsome and just as debonair, Pedersen incorporated all of the omniscience of a grand duke of Chicago's legal scene. Moving smoothly but succinctly through boardrooms and higher echelons of other walks in Chicago, Pedersen was a deft practitioner of the ancient art of knowing how things worked and, consequently, of being able to make things happen. His services were in demand—a situation still evident when this writer sat down with him several times in 2003 at the Deer Path Inn in Lake Forest, a property he owned.

To Pedersen, Arrington was a mentor, even a sort of father figure (Pedersen's own dad died when he was twelve years old). Joining Arrington two years after graduating from the University of Illinois law school in 1948, Pedersen soon became a partner and the number two attorney in the firm. During his eight years of practice with Arrington, it fell to Pedersen to keep the firm on course in Chicago when Arrington was in Springfield. Even after leaving Arrington and Healy to found his own law firm, Pedersen and Houpt, Peer remained an intimate of Arrington until his death.

Arrington's nurturing of Pedersen may have been spurred in part by Arrington's recognition of Pedersen as another individual capable of overcoming a modest beginning to achieve success.

Born in Denmark in 1925, Pedersen's parents emigrated to the United States before his first birthday. He grew up on the west side of Chicago, where his mother ran a boarding house after the death of his father. After graduation from Austin High School in 1942, he attended Carthage College in Wisconsin for a year and then

Newberry College in South Carolina for eight months before being commissioned as an ensign in the navy in 1944.

Active duty soon followed on what he described as a small and "totally unseaworthy" craft assigned to antisubmarine patrol in the Atlantic. Then came stationing in Panama for air and sea rescue missions and, finally, a hitch as executive officer on another patrol craft, this one in the Pacific. Although he did not encounter any overt hostilities in his days at sea, he recalled that "we did drop some depth charges in the Atlantic, but couldn't be sure that we ever hit anything."

He applied for law school at the University of Illinois while still in uniform, and was accepted for admission before leaving the navy. After receiving his degree, he landed with Arrington through a recommendation of Richard Faletti, a law school classmate of Pedersen who practiced with Arrington for a time before returning to the University of Illinois to teach law.

Following in the footsteps of Arrington in more ways than one, Pedersen lived in Evanston during his years with Arrington and Healy. Like Arrington and Stone, he was active in the young Republican club in the city, and served as its president in the mid 1950s. Pedersen's considerable insight into Stone and his insurance network was assured because Arrington and Healy, with its corporate tax and insurance law know-how, was the main legal firm for Combined.

Time and again, Pedersen was a turn-to guy for Arrington and Stone. Down the line, the two prevailed upon Pedersen to become active in the Robert R. McCormick Chicago Boys and Girls Club, which grew out of undertakings by Stone and Arrington as part of their ever expanding civic leadership activities through the years. Eventually, Pedersen would be president of the McCormick club, as well as vice chairman of the Boys and Girls Clubs of Chicago.

When Arrington and Ruth finally realized their dream of purchasing a home on Lake Michigan, Pedersen was called upon to help negotiate the transaction. It was 1955, the year that Arrington entered the Illinois Senate and the capstone year of that period in the 1950s that Arrington later remembered as among the most satisfying and rewarding of his life.

It was Stone who tipped off Arrington that a very nice house on the lake was for sale, much like the Evanston lakefront home near the Northwestern campus that Stone had purchased in the recent past. Arrington and Ruth moved quickly to get a look at the place, a three-story stone residence of French provincial architecture facing Edgemere Court, a short, private street in Evanston less than a mile from Chicago's north boundary. The house, with a large back yard running out to the lake, was only a few steps away from the Edgemere residence of business magnate Henry Crown.

Right off, the Arringtons recognized the house was what they wanted. "We loved it," said Arrington. "It was large with a beautiful lawn. It was right on the lake." However, he remembered years later, "I still didn't feel I could afford a big house. I talked to the judge, who I think was asking $90,000 for it. That was too much for me."

The judge to whom Arrington referred—the seller of the house—was Floyd E. Thompson, who at that time was an attorney associated in practice with Albert Jenner, Arrington's law school classmate. Earlier in his life, Thompson had been chief justice of the Illinois Supreme Court and the unsuccessful Democratic candidate for Illinois governor in 1928 against Republican Louis L. Emmerson.

Desiring the house, but not willing to pay the asking price, Arrington engaged in a bout, in his phraseology, of "horsing around with the judge." Thompson was, said Arrington, "a splendid man, even though he was a Democrat, who apparently wanted us to have that house. He and I knew of each other, so we talked and talked. I offered under $70,000, and he finally lowered a little. I eventually upped my offer a little, and the end result was that I bought the house for $75,000."

In the end, Arrington noted, he gambled in his bargaining that Thompson was not paying lip service in indicating a preference for Arrington "to have the house." And, added Arrington, Thompson showed that he really did favor the Arringtons because Thompson and his wife "had an affection for the house...and knew that we would take care of it." Correspondingly, the Arringtons sold their smaller home on Forest Avenue for $38,000 (Arrington had bought it, he said, for $32,000).

For the rest of their years together, the Edgemere residence was a focal point of Ruth and Arrington's social life. Although Arrington was away more and more with his increasingly encompassing political career, the home and its spacious landscape became almost a private preserve for Ruth. When Arrington was there, and the couple entertained, guests came away with warm memories.

Pedersen included.

One occasion still brought a sly smile to his face years afterward. And why not? It was a setup if Pedersen had ever seen one. He had in mind a gorgeous Sunday afternoon when some 150 folks gathered on Edgemere's rear lawn for a party of Arrington law office personnel and clients. To add further zest to the day, Arrington asked Pedersen to show off his swimming skills in a 250-yard race in Lake Michigan off the Arrington property.

This seemed okay with Pedersen because he was a darn fine swimmer, having competed for Austin High and also lifeguarded at the Foster Avenue beach on Lake Michigan. Here was a chance to display the versatility of one leading light in the law firm. Of course, Pedersen assumed Arrington, wanting him to look good, would find a patsy to oppose him in the race. But no, Arrington didn't exactly have that in mind. Pedersen's opponent, he soon discovered, was Novart Tavitian, the law firm's switchboard operator.

"When I found this out, it dawned on me that she had almost made the U.S. Olympic swimming team a few years back," recalled Pedersen. "I knew I was in trouble."

"I talked to her ahead of time, and tried to get her to let me win," he related. "But, she said, 'I can't do that, Mr. Pedersen.'" As might be expected, he finished second.

Other moments of levity erupted, planned or not, in Pedersen's days with Arrington. Some mighty big doings, too. Pedersen, an eyewitness to a lot, often was called upon to lend a hand. One of the most significant happenings occurred in 1955, the same year Arrington got the Edgemere house, and involved Arrington, Stone and Leonard Lavin. It proved to be a dandy.

Chapter 9

༄

Alberto-Culver

*A*rrington and Stone were not accustomed to investing in losers, but it happened at least once. On that occasion, their money was spent on lipstick of all things.

Never ones to turn their backs on a possibly promising financial venture, the two men put considerable dollars into a firm called Lipmate, which intended to revolutionize the application of cosmetics to the lips of American women. Unlike most of their activities, this undertaking filled them with anxiety—even as they plunked currency into it. So, they decided an outside evaluation was needed by an expert in the cosmetics field. It just happened that F. E. McCabe, Combined's administrative chief, knew one, and he put Stone and Arrington in touch with him. His name was Leonard H. Lavin.

Lavin was a Chicago entrepreneur who, as a manufacturer's rep, had developed great insight in the marketing of various items, including beauty aids. He recalled clearly the time Arrington and Stone approached him about Lipmate when he was interviewed nearly a half century later, on a cold February day in 2003, in his stately home on Lake Michigan in Glencoe.

"Stone and Russ came to my office to ask my opinion about this lipstick venture they'd put money into," related Lavin. "They didn't feel it was going well."

Lavin told the pair he'd analyze the endeavor, would seek to assess the likelihood of its acceptance. During the interim, he advised against the investment of more money in Lipmate. "I told them," he said, "I'd see what I could do." Three months later, Lavin delivered his verdict. He informed them that Lipmate was likely to fail. Although Arrington and Stone's outpouring of dough to Lipmate didn't end there, they eventually liquidated their holding. Arrington ended up sticking around $100,000 into the venture and Stone nearly twice as much. At least for Arrington, he acknowledged it was "a huge loss."

However, one thing endured out of Lipmate. Both Arrington and Stone grew to like and also respect Lavin. In Lavin's view, "Russ recognized and admired my being honest with them in the matter."

As a result, Arrington and Stone went to bat for Lavin when a unique investment opportunity opened up for Lavin while he was visiting the West Coast in 1955.

"I was out there, having lunch with the president of a drugstore chain," explained Lavin. "I asked him what was new, what might be available. He told me about a product, Alberto VO5 hairdressing and conditioner, that women were coming into his stores and wanting. Yet, he'd never noticed a salesman or any advertising for the product, even though it was selling quite well."

Wanting to know more, Lavin learned that Alberto VO5 was manufactured by a Los Angeles area beauty supply firm known as the Alberto-Culver Company. The product, named after the chemist who invented it, was developed at the request of Hollywood folks who wanted something to combat the drying of stars' hair under the harsh lights of movie studios. Soon, VO5—made from a water-free, five-oil formula—also was being sold to beauty salons in southern California. It was so well received that ladies, after leaving the salons, began requesting it in drugstores so that they could use it in between visits to the parlors.

Lavin's ears really perked up that first day, though, when the drugstore executive concluded by telling him that the owner of Alberto-Culver (a person apart from the VO5 inventor) had suffered a stroke and was trying to sell the business. Putting it mildly, Lavin found that "very interesting."

Foregoing any hesitation, the thirty-five-year-old Lavin asked for the name and telephone number of the company and its owner. Calling the owner immediately, Lavin found himself invited to the

Left to right: Peer Pedersen, Professor Cleary of the University of Illinois, Senator Arrington, (unknown), Bert Jenner, Dick Faletti, (unknown)

man's home that same day. That night Lavin and the owner "shook hands" on Lavin buying the company. Next, Lavin had to get his fingers on the money needed to consummate the purchase of the firm.

Enter Arrington, Stone and McCabe. In spite of their disappointment with Lipmate, Arrington and Stone held to a belief that the beauty products industry still was ripe for investment. The challenge lay in finding the right opportunity. When they learned of Lavin's action, and became further aware of his search for financing, they jumped in. They were impressed that Lavin felt so strongly about the latent potential for Alberto-Culver. They trusted his judgment and did not doubt that he had the marketing skills and overall drive to bring home the bacon.

Lavin needed $400,000 for the acquisition, and Stone, Arrington and McCabe reached an agreement with him to ensure that the money would be available. Under the conditions or terms of the purchase arrangement, there was a time deadline for the provision of the money. In return, Stone, Arrington and McCabe were to receive healthy shares of Lavin's new enterprise.

To secure the financing, Arrington and the other two entered negotiations to guarantee a $500,000 loan ($400,000 to buy the business and $100,000 to give Lavin working capital) from American National Bank of Chicago. Peer Pedersen was enlisted to work with all involved, including Lavin, in both structuring and finessing many of the technical components of the transaction.

At the start, Arrington later recounted, the bank dragged its feet on the loan, prompting him to observe that "we were having a hell of a time getting the bank to extend our credit to come up with the money." With time running out for obtaining the funds necessary for the purchase, Arrington lined up a make-or-break lunch with a senior vice president of American in a private room at Chicago's Union League Club, a favorite place of Arrington. At exactly the same time, Lavin and Pedersen were in California, negotiating final details of the transaction—all of which were dependent on securing the loan without any more delay.

It is not unusual for the course of a major business development to revolve around a particular encounter or happening. Such an occasion in Lavin's acquisition of Alberto-Culver was the Arrington lunch at the Union League Club. To Pedersen and other insiders, it became "that famous lunch." Lavin remembered being reliably informed that vodka martinis flowed freely during the five-hour lunch, a definite inducement to dissolution of the stalemate on the loan negotiations.

Arrington himself emphasized in looking back that he spent much of the time convincing the banker of the project's worthiness before the loan itself was broached.

"Little by little he (the banker) got interested, and then, by George, he said he would help," said Arrington. "I told him that was great. Then he asked how much money we were talking about. I told him, and said we needed the whole amount (from the bank). I told him we were extended, and couldn't raise any portion of the $500,000. So we wanted the bank to finance the deal."

The banker's initial reaction to the amount requested by Arrington was incredulity. "He told me," continued Arrington, "it was incredible to think a bank could approve that kind of money when you have nothing in it but your word."

To that comment, Arrington said he replied: "I told him that wasn't true, that we had some assets but not the collateral we would need. We didn't have any ready cash, and the contract (purchase agreement) was expiring within four or five days. So, if the bank couldn't do it, we were in some real trouble."

Well, continued Arrington, the banker rejoined that he did not "know how you can do that to me." To which, Arrington answered that he was "sorry, too, but that was the way it was."

With the afternoon getting late and the outcome of the lunch still up in the air, Arrington reached deep for his utmost skills of persuasiveness—while martinis continued to be poured. He sensed the banker was about to capitulate, but then the man held out for a final request. He himself wanted a word with Lavin. Minutes later, Arrington had the financier on the phone with Lavin in California. Lavin remembered it well.

"He asked me, in words that were slurred, whether I was really sure about this," Lavin related. "I told him that, yes, I felt very sure about what was occurring."

Finally, the banker ended the marathon lunch by telling Arrington that he'd move to convince American National to make the loan with a five-year repayment schedule. And he did. Said Arrington, "I don't know how he was able to do it, but the bank made that loan." Years afterward, looking back on that day, Lavin would say, "We were lucky." However, Lavin also would point out with pride that the note was paid off.

After gaining ownership of the company, Lavin moved Alberto-Culver to Chicago. There, he proceeded with the help of his wife, Bernice, to guide his acquisition into a global, multi-billion dollar company that stood out among the success stories of family-controlled enterprises.

Furthermore, Lavin was able to say, with complete accuracy, that "the interesting thing is we built this business without putting a penny of our money into it."

By the same token, neither Arrington, Stone nor McCabe had any financial regrets about sticking out their necks to help Lavin get his hands on Alberto-Culver.

As explained by Pedersen, who had a hand in establishing the arrangement between the trio and Lavin, the $400,000 segment of

the loan secured by Arrington and the other two went to a corporation, set up by Pedersen and headed by Lavin, that used the money
to buy the business assets under the name of Alberto-Culver. In
exchange for the loan guarantee, Lavin gave a 25 percent share of the
stock in the corporation to Arrington, Stone and McCabe. This share
was split evenly among the three. As Alberto-Culver prospered, the
stock turned into a big-ticket holding. This time, Stone and Arrington
would not find the beauty products business unprofitable.

Both Arrington and Stone would go on to serve on Alberto's
board of directors. Anything but a passive director, Arrington was
often at Lavin's side when the company encountered challenges that
required the sorts of legal strategies at which Arrington excelled. For
a time, biographical information on Arrington identified him as a
vice president of the firm. In looking back at Arrington's contributions to Alberto, Lavin resurrected an image of Arrington as "a tough
guy…our tough guy."

Moreover, the Lavin-Arrington relationship extended into the
social scene, where Lavin saw a different Arrington, a man "who
liked to have a good time, liked to drink." Arrington spurred the interest of Lavin and his wife in the Chicago Symphony Orchestra, where
Lavin recollected Saturday night performances at which Arrington
"just closed his eyes and listened to the music." Obviously, Lavin
observed, the symphony "provided a form of relaxation for him."

For his part, Arrington categorized Lavin as "without doubt the best
businessman I've ever known." Labeling Lavin "sharp, a good thinker
and ingenious," Arrington credited him with "keeping the company
prosperous" as it doggedly expanded through the years in a field of big
and strong competitors—outfits with names like Procter & Gamble.

At Alberto's start in Chicago, Lavin concentrated almost exclusively on the marketing of VO5 hairdressing. One of his key strata-
gems was to pour every spare dollar into the still relatively new
arena of television advertising. By 1958, three years after Lavin's
acquisition, Alberto VO5 was the number-one selling brand in its
class. Sticking to TV ads, VO5 was an initial sponsor of early shows
such as "What's My Line?" and the popular program of the Smothers
Brothers. Overcoming opposition from the networks, Alberto-Culver

became a first advertiser in the early 1970s to win the right to use 30-second spots instead of the then standard 60-second commercials. Such a victory helped alter the face of television for all advertisers, viewers, networks and stations.

The 1960s were years of great growth for Alberto. The decade began with the company opening a new plant and corporate offices in the Chicago suburb of Melrose Park and with the establishment of a plant in Canada. By the mid 1960s, annual sales were exceeding $100 million, and the company's stock was listed on the New York Stock Exchange. Many more products were introduced in the 1960s, and other firms were acquired, including Sally Beauty Company. Before the end of the 1960s, Alberto had more than 2,000 employees and was selling products in at least sixty-five countries.

Sally Beauty turned into a success story of its own. Like Combined Insurance, the first major American business entity involving Arrington, Alberto always was on the lookout for acquisitions. The purchase of Sally Beauty in 1969 brought into Alberto's fold a largely untapped concept with a lot of promise—the same thing Lavin recognized fourteen years earlier in California with Alberto VO5.

When acquired, Sally Beauty consisted of one store and nine independent franchises that sold professional products for hair stylists and barbers. The franchises were closed, and Alberto set up a new merchandising program. It eventually bloomed into more than 1,000 company-owned and operated outlets, mainly in the expanding world of shopping centers. The stores supplied thousands of salon products and appliances to retail customers as well as professionals. The day would come when Sally Beauty alone would be the largest international beauty supply company in the world.

As the reach of Alberto-Culver extended further and further, the fellow that Lavin called "our tough guy," Arrington, was usually in the wings, readily available to Lavin. A big crisis wasn't always necessary for Arrington to surface.

One of his firm's annual meetings in Chicago came to mind when Lavin thought back on the many ways in which Arrington counted.

On that occasion, a pesty woman was threatening to disrupt the meeting. Finally, an annoyed Lavin asked her what he "needed to do to get her off my back."

"Buy my book," she replied.

"How much?" asked Lavin.

Her asking price was $200. Lavin didn't have that much money on him at the time.

"However, Russ was standing there, taking this in," Lavin said. "He just fished me the money. I paid her, and that was the last I saw of her." Afterward, looking to see exactly what kind of book apparently had been purchased for the Alberto library, the two men observed a tome on "corporate governance."

Arrington's participation in Lavin's acquisition of Alberto-Culver in 1955, a seminal action providing the seeds for part of the wealth to be accumulated by Arrington, was one more reason for him to reflect on the first half of the 1950s as a period of relatively smooth sailing in his life.

It didn't take long for the second half of the decade to present some troubled waters, though. For Arrington personally and for his party.

Chapter 10

❦

Orville Hodge—A Dark Cloud

*I*f the General Assembly had been a town, the Senate would have stood for the neighborhood on one side of the tracks—the section with the big homes—and the House of Representatives would have occupied the other side. Not that the House was a shantytown or anything like that. But it couldn't match the genteel image, the aristocratic tenor of the Senate, which was, after all, labeled the upper chamber.

Putting it another way, House members were cast as more proletarian, more blue-collar than their Senate brethren. The number of lower chamber members alone, thrice the Senate membership in 1954, abetted the unruliness often marking the House. It may have been couched delicately, if openly discussed at all, but the clubby realm of the Senate just exuded more prestige. Going from the House to the Senate, with an exception here and there, signified political advancement. When an opportunity to make the jump arose, it seldom was squandered.

In looking ahead to the election year of 1954, Arrington planned to run for another term in the House. His reelection was considered a certainty. However, his political destiny was altered notably by the death of William G. Knox, the Republican industrialist occupying the Senate seat from Arrington's Sixth legislative district during Arrington's years in the House. GOP leaders in the district, who were instrumental in getting a replacement for Knox on the ballot, realized they needed a strong candidate to ensure the seat remained in

Republican hands for the unexpired two years of Knox's term. Arrington was the logical choice, and he'd decided he wanted the nod. He got it.

Evanston provided the core of the GOP vote in the district, and Arrington was firmly established as a Republican strongman on his own turf. The importance of having a potent Republican candidate from Evanston was even more underscored by the likelihood of a substantial Democratic turnout in 1954 in the north side Chicago wards that were located in the Sixth.

As proven by the balloting to fill the vacant seat, Arrington needed the huge plurality he received in Evanston to offset the strong showing by his Democrat opponent, Wilbert M. Foley, in the Chicago part of the district. Although Arrington's 7,477-vote margin of victory was substantial (he received 23,334 votes to 15,857 for Foley), Arrington realized that his future security in the Senate seat required either a shoring up of his standing in the Chicago wards or elimination of those wards from his district through legislative district reapportionment. The latter was the preferable course for him. And, that was exactly what was going to transpire.

After building considerable stature during his years in the House, Arrington found himself sitting in an awkward position when the Sixty-ninth General Assembly convened January 5, 1955. Republicans heavily outnumbered Democrats in the Senate, 32 to 19, which was certainly to Arrington's liking. However, not enough seats were available on the GOP side of the chamber for all the Republicans. As a result, the Senate GOP leader, Arthur J. Bidwill from River Forest, relegated freshman senator Arrington to a seat on the Democratic side.

Starting out in his new legislative arena as a real backbencher, Arrington recollected that he couldn't help but be "puzzled" by his stationing in the last row among the Democrats, three seats away from the chamber's middle aisle. "Everyone knew I was a Republican," Arrington said, "and there I was on the Democratic side. I didn't like it."

At first, Arrington resented what he perceived to be unusually brusque treatment by Democratic leaders in the body, Chicago lawyers William J. Lynch and Donald J. O'Brien. This was especially hard for Arrington to stomach since he had proven himself to be a top-notch lawmaker in the House.

Following a particularly heated exchange with the pair on a certain issue, Arrington confronted them directly on the "hard time" they were giving him. To his surprise, he related, "it came out that they thought I was English." Consequently, in no uncertain words, he told the two: "You know, you guys, I'm just as Irish as both of you. So don't give me that crap about the English." It must have worked.

"Strangely enough, that did something for us that substantially changed our relationship and helped quite a bit in that session," Arrington added.

Arrington also detected, in the early going, a bit of wariness toward him by some Republican senators, probably stemming, he assumed, from his reputation as a hard charger in the House. He sensed that the cautionary ones included his fellow Chicago suburbanite Bidwill, who as the majority leader held the official title of president pro tempore of the Senate. A University of Notre Dame law school graduate and businessman, the fifty-one-year-old Bidwill, a member of the Senate since 1935, was a genial individual who led with a live and let live demeanor.

However, if Bidwill had any notion of sitting on Arrington, it was not evident in the standing committee assignments he engineered for the new senator. One of twenty-four lawyers in the upper chamber, Arrington was named to the Judiciary Committee for a start. In another sign that he missed few beats in leaping from the House to the Senate, he secured a seat on the Insurance Committee. Moreover, he was the panel's vice chairman, its second in command under the chairman, fellow Republican Marvin F. Burt, a Freeport attorney. Landing seats on these two committees alone was sufficient to permit Arrington to continue in the Senate the comfortable melding of his political and professional lives that had begun in the House.

There was more. Arrington also was placed on the committees dealing with industrial affairs, municipalities, public utilities and railroads. And, he joined Bidwill and other GOP stalwarts on the influential Executive Committee. Finally, he was included on the Committee on Apportionment and Elections, a truly choice spot for him. With legislative redistricting definitely on the session's agenda, the jurisdiction of this committee especially hit home with Arrington.

General Assembly districts had not been redrawn in more than half a century. However, that status quo was about to end as a result of voter approval in 1954 of a state constitutional amendment mandating a realignment of legislative districts in 1955 that could not have been more advantageous for Arrington.

The amendment dictated a reapportionment creating fifty-eight senatorial districts and fifty-nine separate representative districts. They were to replace the fifty-one legislative districts each electing one senator and three representatives. Under the remap, the fifty-eight senators were to be elected from districts with boundaries different from the boundaries outlining the new House districts. So, with each House district still to elect three representatives, the reapportionment would hike the total number of General Assembly members to 235 from 204.

The part of the amendment most appealing to Arrington, without question, was the stipulation that the twenty-four new state senatorial districts mandated for Cook County included eighteen within the Chicago city limits and six covering the territory in Cook outside Chicago. There would be no overlap between the city and suburban Cook districts, thereby automatically eliminating the troublesome Chicago wards from the new district to be carved out for Arrington.

The principal challenge for Arrington, as the legislators tackled redistricting in 1955, was to keep his hand in the maneuvering to ensure strict adherence to the amendatory language, which if met to the letter could make him just about politically invulnerable. The townships in his part of Cook County, as in much of the county, were solidly Republican. It was only a question of which ones would join Evanston in his district.

Capitalizing on his seat on the reapportionment committee, Arrington zeroed in on the always sensitive, and often contentious, give and take of redistricting as the issue moved through the chambers. He riveted his attention on the excruciating detail work entailed in the remapping process, alert to any proposals or insertions that might undercut his own position as well as that of many Republican senators more exposed to political danger than himself in the redistricting. As the session moved on, his capable watchdogging on this subject propelled him almost overnight from any early freshman novice image to standing as a full-fledged player.

His successful insertion of himself into the redistricting issue—which ended with legislation reflecting the amendment's mandated guidelines—earned Arrington recognition both within and outside the Senate.

In lauding Arrington the following year as "a legislator of exceptional ability," the *Chicago American* depicted the man from Evanston as "a leader in writing the Reapportionment Bill which created the new districts, and in the fight for its passage." Arrington himself insisted that much of the credit for the approval of new districts should go to Governor Stratton, who made it clear that the will of voters in approving the amendment would be met, irrespective of the legislative winners and losers in the matter.

One of the clear winners in the remap measure that finally emerged from the legislature and was signed by Stratton on June 28, 1955, was Arrington. The new Fourth Senatorial District, Arrington's, was comprised of Evanston, New Trier, Niles, Northfield and Wheeling townships. In reflecting, he said, "I now had a beautiful territory," one "quite nice because I never had any trouble afterward in being elected in the district."

Aside from his undying attention to redistricting, Arrington was a workhorse on many other issues during his inaugural Senate session. As senators on both sides of the chamber watched with a touch of wonderment, Arrington introduced 110 measures, an extraordinary number for a freshman member. Many ended up being enacted into law. While a certain number covered fundamental government housekeeping, more than a few wrought statutory improvements in regard to crime prevention, judicial practices, county and other local governmental administration and state responsibilities in public education.

He was a chief sponsor of a bill providing a major rewrite of the

Governor William G. Stratton and Senator W. Russell Arrington

state's banking law, a revision designed to trigger tighter state regulation of the Illinois banking industry. The legislation passed the
Senate without a dissenting vote, and then made it through the House
without one negative vote. The measure was signed by Stratton on
May 11, 1955. The new Illinois Banking Act went into effect after it
was ratified by voters in the 1956 general election.

Arrington also was a main backer of another major item for submission to voters in 1956—a proposed amendment to the Revenue
Article of the Illinois Constitution. Endorsed by numerous civic
organizations, the proposed change was designed to combat widespread tax evasion in the state by authorizing the classification of
personal property so as to bring about more equitable taxation rates
and easier collections. However, voters would refuse to approve the
amendment.

The volume of Arrington's legislative agenda in 1955 was one
thing. More eye-catching was his frenetic pace and attention to
details as he immersed himself in the deliberations of his numerous
committees and in the less visible legislative mechanisms leading to
actions on the Senate floor. Predictably, he was viewed as brash by

some old Senate hands who felt new members, for a start, should be seen and not heard.

Too, it was noted, sometimes with a snicker, that Arrington lost no time in establishing a say-so on insurance matters coming before the Senate. As vice chairman of the committee on insurance, Arrington was able to continue in the Senate what he did in the House. The unchanging role found him supportive of regulatory restraints on the insurance industry's fly-by-nighters but opposed to new restrictions on core members of the industry—such as his own Combined Insurance Company of America.

Nevertheless, to many of those monitoring the General Assembly, such as newspaper scribes, Arrington continued to receive the same high marks he'd gotten in his House years. And, the Chicago-based Better Government Association, an effective watchdog group that liked much of what it saw in Arrington, labeled him for the record a "highly capable legislator."

Satisfaction with his first session as a senator was a key reason for Arrington to look back on 1955 as a landmark year for him personally. Of course, it also was the initial year of his fortuitous involvement with Alberto-Culver, a year in which his insurance partnership with Clement Stone was going great guns and the year in which his family secured Edgemere, its home on Lake Michigan. Furthermore, the new maps for General Assembly seats made him an odds-on favorite to retain his Senate slot in the 1956 election.

No question, life looked rosy for Arrington, and for his fellow Republicans too, going into 1956. But, dark clouds were to loom, threatening the GOP's days in the sun.

Scandal, a major one, hit the party squarely between the eyes.

The political history of Illinois has been deflowered again and again by the raising of the ugly head of governmental corruption with seemingly unfailing regularity. Being one of the more populous states, and certainly one of the most conspicuous politically, scandalous conduct by Illinois public officials often has generated national attention. As a state with a truly bipartisan political landscape throughout the twentieth century, Illinois' shady dealings were never limited to just one party. A backlash from voters, though, often awaited the party of an individual or individuals caught off base or perceived to have fallen on the job.

In Arrington's early years on the scene, he'd witnessed the downfall of Republican Governor Dwight Green in the 1948 election following damage to his image for a variety of reasons. They included his permissive attitude toward illegal gambling, allegedly lax enforcement of the state's coal mine safety program and the fact that numerous newspaper people were discovered to be on the state payroll while he was governor without doing any work.

The administration of Green's successor, Adlai Stevenson, was not entirely free of scandal. His campaign manager and executive secretary stepped down after a revelation that he used his insider status to purchase Chicago Downs racing stock at 5 cents a share. The superintendent of foods and dairies in the Department of Agriculture was fined for accepting a $3,500 bribe to allow the sale of horse meat as beef. However, as was shown, these sorts of episodes were hardly sufficient to dull the political reputation of Stevenson and disrupt his march to national prominence.

More ominous, much more so, was the eruption in 1956 of one of the most sordid chapters in the state's political annals. It had few rivals, before or afterward, in regard to a gross violation of the public trust. The Hodge scandal, as everybody came to call it, well may have entailed the greatest embezzlement of public dollars in the history of Illinois.

Although Orville Hodge had entered the House two years after Arrington's arrival, the insurance and real estate businessman from Granite City quickly became a rival of Arrington for prominence among the chamber's Republicans. Hodge proved to be an effective and likable legislator at the same time, a person regarded more warmly by Republicans, and many Democrats, than the highly proficient but hard driving and sometimes taut Arrington. Nevertheless, Hodge's affability, buttressing a penchant for glad-handing and backslapping, masked a well-honed knack for getting others to do his bidding.

Arrington never said he disliked Hodge, although animosity was visible between Hodge and other House Republicans loyal to Reed Cutler and those, like Arrington, favoring the alternative GOP leadership of Warren Wood. Arrington did allow, later on, that he "began to like" Hodge much more, even to the point of calling him a "seemingly pretty nice fellow" after Hodge capped a six-year career in the House by getting elected state auditor of public accounts in 1952.

Many others certainly shared this view. In ascending to statewide office, Hodge became, arguably, the most personally popular politician in Illinois. The good will for him even extended to the Statehouse pressroom, where he frequently was visible and never hesitant to offer to do favors. Hardly secretive about his goals, he felt he was destined for the governorship—an end result that many predicted to be almost preordained. He had announced an intent to campaign for governor in 1952, but was persuaded to run for state auditor. Talk surfaced in the ensuing years that he might challenge incumbent Governor Stratton for the GOP nomination for the state's top office in the 1956 primary election. If not then, he'd surely make his move for the top office the next time around.

Arrington's acceptance of Hodge was evidenced by a stay in 1955 by Arrington and his family at the Esquire Apartment Hotel in Fort Lauderdale, Florida, an establishment owned by Hodge.

About that, Arrington later had this to say: "Happily, I insisted on paying all my bills, although he wanted me to stay free. Many a legislator did take advantage of his offers, but I paid for everything because I didn't want anyone to say I was doing this for politics.

"It was fortunate I felt that way. Otherwise, I may have been included in his troubles."

Hodge's "troubles," when finally brought to light, did tarnish the reputations of numerous individuals in and out of politics who'd let themselves be tied to Hodge in fiscal or other matters.

The office from which Hodge ousted Democratic incumbent Benjamin O. Cooper in 1952 was central to the fiscal integrity of the state. Under the Illinois Constitution, money could be drawn from the state treasury only through an appropriation by the General Assembly followed by a warrant for the actual withdrawal—a check drawn on the treasury—issued by the state auditor. In this way, the auditor was supposed to be the watchdog for every penny received and spent by all branches of state government.

As Hodge himself put it in the 1953-1954 *Illinois Blue Book*, it was through his office that "the people of Illinois exercise controls over all expenditures of State money, over the accuracy of the financial records of State agencies, the inventory of State property, and the supervision of State-chartered financial institutions holding deposits of private funds."

The reality of it, though, was that, in the case of Hodge, the watchdog of the Illinois Treasury turned out to be a fox in the henhouse. After the eruption of the Hodge scandal, it was evident that there were signs beforehand that something may have been amiss in Hodge's office. His office had run out of operating funds before the end of the 1953-1954 biennium—Hodge's first two years as auditor—prompting the legislature to bail him out with a $525,000 emergency appropriation. His appropriation for the next biennium was several million dollars above the figure for the previous biennium, but for no apparent reason. It was true that he was living a lavish lifestyle. However, the man and his friends had successfully portrayed him as a person of means, a free spender who had it to dish out.

In the early months of 1956, the year in which Hodge was facing reelection as auditor, suspicions were being voiced quietly that he may not be on the up-and-up. Still, talk or speculation was one thing; proving or showing misconduct was quite another. Finally, the task of going beyond the rumors, and digging into Hodge's conduct of his office, fell to George Thiem, a Statehouse reporter for the *Chicago Daily News*.

Thiem later would confirm that a major impetus for getting him on Hodge's trail was a tip from Michael J. Howlett, Hodge's Democratic opponent for auditor in the 1956 election. Chicagoan Howlett was diligent in pointing out avenues begging for investigation in Hodge's running of his office. Charges by opposing candidates in election campaigns often are suspect, but Thiem knew that Howlett had a good reputation and was even known as a bit of a crusader. After World War II, while serving as a regional director of the United States Office of Price Stabilization during Stevenson's gubernatorial years, it was Howlett who tipped off newspapermen to the illegal sale in the state of ground horse meat as beef. So he had an established track record.

For his part, Thiem also had a track record. He worked with reporter Roy J. Harris of the *St. Louis Post-Dispatch* to expose the more than fifty Illinois newspaper editors and writers on the state payroll when Green was governor. The collaborative effort by Thiem and Harris won a Pulitzer Prize, the most coveted award in American journalism.

Nevertheless, Thiem still found it hard to believe at the start of his probe that Hodge would so openly display his prosperity if he were siphoning it off public funds. However, once the digging began in earnest—a quest employing techniques only familiar to a skilled and seasoned investigator like Thiem—pieces of a puzzle soon came together to reveal that Hodge had diverted huge amounts of taxpayer dollars under his wing into his and acquaintances' pockets.

Through illegal or unethical means, Hodge had used state money during his term of office to finance personal expenses for hotel suites, travel, meals, liquor and numerous other questionable things. With the complicity of certain aides in his office, and one or more outside bankers, Hodge had gone on a spree authorizing fraudulent state warrants that were cashed by or for him. He also padded his office payroll with persons doing little or no work. To pull off his plunder, he wove a web of deceit in which the phony checks were augmented by bogus contracts, fake expense accounts and other fabrications.

The exact amount tapped illegally from the state treasury remained anybody's guess. None of the auditors or investigators tracing the swindle put the sum at under $1 million. Press accounts eventually put the theft in the neighborhood of $1.5 million. Thiem himself, in his 1963 book, *The Hodge Scandal*, estimated that Hodge "stole or squandered" $2.5 million. Whatever, the case threw state government into an uproar.

Before getting into the aftermath of the Thiem-triggered disclosures of Hodge's escapades, it should be noted that Thiem's work won another Pulitzer Prize for the *Daily News* and further cemented his reputation as the most respected—or feared—Illinois Statehouse scribe in his time. As for Howlett, his candidacy for state auditor in 1956 was unsuccessful. However, in 1960 he went on to win the first of three four-year terms in that office. He was elected Illinois secretary of state in 1972. Four years later, his political career ended when he won his party's nomination for governor but lost the general election to Republican James R. Thompson. In each of his campaigns, he never hesitated to remind voters that he helped instigate the *Daily News* investigation of Hodge.

Back to 1956. One of the first concerns regarding the Hodge ignominy was that reaction from a stunned public would undercut Governor Stratton and other Republicans on the ballot that year. Still fresh on the minds of many was the unexpected defeat in 1948 of Green after the disclosures of questionable dealings by his administration opened a door to victory for Democrat Stevenson, originally an underdog in the gubernatorial race.

Having witnessed the Green-Stevenson situation, Arrington was among the concerned Republicans. Although unaware of Hodge's sham dealings, Arrington did recall the time that Paul Powell, still a Democratic leader in the House, pulled Arrington aside after the start of the almost daily newspaper disclosures on Hodge and his office. Powell was thought to have a close relationship with Hodge, and what Powell told Arrington did not subtract from that view.

According to Arrington, "Powell told me after the trouble for Orville was coming out that Orville had called him to come to one of his (Hodge's) hotel rooms. Powell saw a lot of checks spread out on the bed, a large number of them all in order, and was asked by Orville for advice. Paul told me he looked at the checks and talked to Orville about them. Then, Paul said that Orville asked, 'What's going to happen?' Paul said he replied, 'I'll tell you what's going to happen. You're going to prison.'"

In August 1956, about four months after newspaper articles began running on Hodge's misdeeds, he was sentenced in state circuit court to twelve to fifteen years imprisonment after pleading guilty to charges in an indictment accusing him of embezzlement, forgery and confidence game activity. He served more than six years at the Menard state prison at Chester, Illinois, before being released because of failing health.

At first, though, in the early weeks of the unfolding of the scandal, Hodge attempted to downplay the revelations while insisting that he had no intention of dropping his candidacy for reelection as auditor. The latter stance by Hodge was especially disquieting to Arrington and other Republicans who felt, more and more with each new disclosure of Hodge corruption, that the GOP state ticket might well be doomed unless Hodge was removed from the scene. But, they only saw that being brought about by Stratton.

Seeing this himself, and realizing that his own political future was perhaps the first to be at stake, Stratton injected himself forcefully into the Hodge mess even though Hodge, as an official elected separately from Stratton, did not have to accede to the governor's wishes. And, initially, Hodge rebuffed Stratton's urging not only to get off the ballot but also resign from office.

Stratton finally prevailed, though. Five weeks before he would be sentenced to prison, Hodge agreed to submit his resignation during an emotional meeting with Stratton and Illinois Attorney General Latham Castle, a Republican. Stratton later recalled that Hodge wept during the session, but regained control of himself over coffee and agreed not only to resign, but to face the music by getting "the story off his chest" to the office of the Sangamon County state's attorney. As he left Stratton's office that day, Hodge was quoted as saying, "I'm beat, but I feel better. At least I haven't killed anyone." However, two weeks afterward, one of his administrative assistants, a person who defended Hodge until finally realizing his boss really was a crook, drowned himself in Lake Springfield. It was one of the sorrier outgrowths of the Hodge affair.

On the heels of Hodge's departure from office, Stratton appointed Lloyd Morey, president emeritus of the University of Illinois, to the post of auditor to finish the remaining part of Hodge's term. Stratton also orchestrated the replacement of Hodge as the Republican candidate for auditor in the election with GOP state Senator Elbert S. Smith, a highly regarded Decatur attorney and decorated veteran of World War II. In addition, the governor wasted no time in asking the General Assembly's Budgetary Commission to investigate the Hodge fiasco and report back as soon as possible.

Impressed by Stratton's intervention, Arrington concluded that the governor "worked things out very well. He made no bones about it. He wanted Orville to resign, which he did. Bill then selected Elbert Smith to run in his place, and he won."

Along with Smith, who beat Howlett, all other members of the Republican state ticket also were victorious in the general election balloting November 6, 1956. Each won handily except for Stratton, who was reelected governor by the slim margin of 36,877 votes. The electorate also kept Republicans in control of both houses of the General Assembly. In the Senate alone, where Arrington was a big winner over Lincolnwood Democrat Jay Schiller in his new district, Republicans would enjoy a roughly two-to-one advantage over Democrats in the upcoming Seventieth General Assembly.

Because of all the hubbub over Hodge in the general election campaign, a serious turn of events for Arrington was largely submerged on the political radar screen. In the days leading up to the election, the fifty-year-old Arrington suffered a heart attack—the first of two in his lifetime—while at home. He was hospitalized for the remaining period in the campaign, and then was confined to bed at Edgemere for the rest of the year.

Arrington did what he could to divert attention from the attack. Although his affliction was not to be taken lightly, Arrington insisted on not making "any big fuss about it because I was going to win anyway in the election in November." Seeking to prevent any unnecessary boat rocking in his political world, Arrington said that he "just didn't let people know that I had a heart attack." He simply disappeared from the campaign scene, where he'd been spending most of his effort on the candidacies of Stratton and others on his party's state ticket. Particularly the campaign of Stratton, since he was likely to be the prime target of fallout from the Hodge brouhaha.

On the night of election day, nurses and doctors assembled in Arrington's room at Wesley Hospital to catch the returns on television. Although they had tried to dissuade him from watching preelection coverage the day before, they had capitulated to his demand that he be allowed to catch whatever results were available on the tube after the closing of the polls.

"When they (nurses) finally required me to go to bed after midnight," remembered Arrington, "Stratton was about 100,000 behind.

But, I told them, 'Don't worry. We're going to win.' I knew we'd get a big vote from downstate, which was still coming in, and, by George, that's what happened. I woke up at six in the morning and told them to put on the TV to see what the results were. And, sure enough, Stratton was running ahead. By eight o'clock, it was announced that Stratton had won, but not by much."

In the end, certain factors were thought to have benefited Stratton. At the top of the Illinois ballot, President Eisenhower easily carried Illinois in his bid for reelection by swamping his Democratic opponent, former Illinois governor Stevenson, in the state. Too, in the race for a United States Senate seat from Illinois, incumbent Republican Everett M. Dirksen topped his Democratic foe, Richard Stengel, by a respectable margin. Consequently, that may have bolstered Stratton, whose race was third on the ballot.

Furthermore, Democrats' efforts to saddle Stratton for the Hodge disgrace may have been diluted somewhat by troubles of their own.

The Democratic candidate for governor, Cook County Treasurer Herbert Paschen, withdrew from the contest in the summer after questions arose about the ethics of some key personnel in his office. It also became known that banks in which county funds were deposited had been "shaken down" for contributions to a "flower fund" for employees in Paschen's office. At the urging of the state's then newest Democratic power, Chicago Mayor Daley, the Democrats' state central committee slated Cook County Judge Richard B. Austin to replace Paschen as Stratton's opponent.

Austin was a respected jurist, but he was hardly known statewide. In addition, speculation persisted before and after the election that Daley might not really have his heart set on the election of a Democratic governor in 1956. That could have set up competition for Daley in his already visible drive to consolidate in his hands Democratic Party power in the state. Moreover, Daley had quickly developed a good working relationship with Stratton after becoming mayor in 1955. Political insiders knew the two had further plans for working together.

Post-election analyses insinuated that Stratton well may not have survived the election if not for Eisenhower's ballot strength, Paschen's unceremonious stepping down and suspicion that Daley's support for Austin was fleeting (although election results in Chicago indicated that Daley did exert a strong effort for Austin). Even after taking all of these matters into consideration, Stratton's slightly under 37,000-vote plurality still was meager. The main reason had to be that voters were not inclined to let him off the hook on Hodge, whether Stratton shared any responsibility for the scandal or not.

Nevertheless, in view of the magnitude of what Arrington called the "Hodge episode," he reasoned that the outcome of the 1956 election had to be "a good victory for Stratton" and the rest of the Republican slate. Arrington saw the survival of the GOP as a sign that Republicans had been given another chance to be the dominant, responsible party in state government.

He also recognized that the Hodge scandal required amends in the state's fiscal responsibility, and he intended to be one of the rescuers.

Chapter 11

ℰ

Keeping Track of the Money

*I*t did not take long to discredit the thought that the Illinois political world would see a less high-powered Arrington because of his heart attack and subsequent relegation to bed during the last stage of 1956. The man was not to be cooped up.

Members of the new Seventieth General Assembly, which opened for business January 9, 1957, hardly had gotten their seats warm before a fast-moving Arrington was smack-dab in the middle of the issues that would define the session.

His unrelenting push for reform of the Illinois judiciary led to legislative approval of a proposed state constitutional amendment that, if ratified by voters, would have greatly simplified the court structure. An exuberant Arrington declared the legislature's green light for the proposal "the outstanding accomplishment of the last century." Quite a claim. The senator from Evanston was even more in the news for spearheading an emotionally charged investigation by lawmakers into the state's skyrocketing public aid costs. However, the most lasting Arrington legacy from the session was the assertive watchdog commission he carved out in response to the Hodge affair.

The Illinois Legislative Audit Commission was Arrington's baby.

The session was marked early on by Republicans and Democrats almost stumbling over each other to bring about this or that corrective step to prevent another public dollar embezzlement of the Hodge magnitude. Just about everybody, including nonelected individuals, seemed to have ideas about what to do. Since better government was always the objective, Hodge's thievery actually sparked moves for stronger protection for taxpayers' dollars that otherwise might not have been.

The Illinois Budgetary Commission, the bipartisan legislative panel asked by Stratton to look into the Hodge matter and recommend remedial action, sought answers from a trio consisting of Lloyd Morey, the appointed state auditor after Hodge's resignation; Albert Jenner Jr., Arrington's law school classmate; and John S. Rendleman, a promising young lawyer from southern Illinois. From the commission's own analysis and the report it received from the Morey group, alterations in state auditing procedures and accounting were proposed as were major changes along the line of eliminating the office of auditor and having the state treasurer switched from an elected official to a gubernatorial-appointed one. Considerable support could be found for such treatment of the auditor and treasurer offices. However, getting rid of or making an elective state office appointive required constitutional change, and that did not happen in 1957.

The Morey report also backed the creation of a so-called legislative auditor to oversee post-audits of all state agency operations. This idea, or something close to it, set well with Arrington, who had definite goals in addressing the need for more safeguarding of public funds.

First, he wanted to make sure that whatever was done would restore public trust in the fiscal integrity of Illinois government. Secondly, he believed the General Assembly must have a much stronger hand in ensuring that tax dollars were spent as intended by legislative appropriations. Thirdly, he intended to endeavor as readily as he could to see that the GOP got as much credit as possible for the necessary fiscal reforms. He was under no illusion that voter resentment against his party for the Hodge transgressions had abated.

As he prepared to move full speed ahead on his agenda for the session, Arrington's standing had been buttressed significantly by his appointment as the new chairman of the Senate Revenue Committee, one of the chamber's most important panels. His other assignments included seats on the judiciary and insurance committees, both of which remained crucial to his public and private interests.

Although only in his second regular session as a senator, Arrington put himself in the legislative driver's seat in addressing the Hodge mess by heading a group of five GOP senators behind a bill to revamp state auditing along more effective and realistic lines. The measure would create the office of auditor general, an official appointed by and responsible to a new legislative audit commission Arrington wanted to create. The bill also called for professional staffing and beefed up powers for the budgetary commission, giving it more input in the drafting and procedures involved in putting together state operating budgets. Enlarging the commission's job would further increase the legislators' say-so in actually formulating the appropriations they were asked to approve.

Stratton, who did not want reaction to the Hodge scandal to become a vehicle for eroding the power of the executive branch of state government, was hostile to much of the proposal by his normal ally Arrington. He wanted the auditor general, who would function in many respects like the comptroller general in the federal government, to be appointed by and responsible to the governor. In essence, under Stratton's plan, the governor would be auditing his own administration.

With the potential for a rare public spat looming between Arrington and Stratton, mainly over the manner of naming an auditor general, newspapers and others weighed in. Arrington's approach impressed many as the way to go. As one Chicago paper editorialized, "The important thing…is that the auditor general be responsible to the General Assembly, as the Arrington bill provides. The Legislature appropriates the money and should act as a watchdog over the spending of the funds."

Arrington knew, though, that Stratton would not budge from his position that the Arrington bill constituted legislative encroachment on the executive branch. Arrington also did not doubt that Stratton would veto any measure that he viewed as doing that. Consequently, conceded Arrington, "In order to get the legislation through, we were required to have the auditor general appointed by the governor."

The upshot was legislative passage and subsequent enactment of a compromise fiscal reform program, largely fashioned by Arrington, that appeased Stratton and still gave the senator the increased legislative presence in policing state expenditures that he so desired.

Under the program, a new agency, the Department of Audits, was established and assigned a major portion of the auditing responsibilities formerly handled by the auditor of public accounts. The latter official remained a separately elected one, but with diminished authority. The new department was placed under the direction of an auditor general, whom at the insistence of Stratton was appointed to a six-year term by the governor. The appointee was subject to Senate confirmation. The revamping also included an upgrading of the budgetary commission and various other budgeting and auditing safeguards recommended in the Morey-Jenner-Rendleman report.

Finally, but hardly of least importance, the program included the permanent legislative audit commission so strongly advocated by Arrington. The mandate for the panel provided at last both clear-cut authority and the means for the General Assembly to require an accounting from state agencies on the legality and propriety of their expenditures. To do this, the commission was given considerable watchdog and review authority over many of the responsibilities of the auditor general.

To avoid the appearance of political bias in its proceedings, membership of the commission was bipartisan. To the surprise of nobody, Arrington, the panel's patriarch, was elected chairman. The initial membership was not lacking in potent Democrats, though. Three of them were Paul Powell, Fred Smith, the cordial Chicago senator often supportive of Arrington; and Representative George W. Dunne, a skilled politician from Chicago. However, without dispute, the commission's creation was the handiwork of Arrington. To repeat, it was his baby.

At first, Arrington recalled, many in Illinois government "didn't care much for the commission" because of a fear that "it could be made political." So, he said, "everybody was watching very carefully." For that reason, Arrington continued, "I arranged to get good people, both Democrats and Republicans, on the commission."

But, not too far down the road, Arrington went on, "a lot of the leery people came to have confidence in the commission." Noting that its members became "proud to be a part of that group," he pointed out that "we uncovered a lot of accounting errors, and found some scandalous situations. Almost always, we were able to work them out."

In reviewing the reports of the auditor general, the commission had multiple objectives—including assessments of the validity of the auditor's findings and, then, determining whether state agencies were complying with the auditor's recommendations with which the commission agreed. To facilitate the latter, top personnel of state agencies were summoned to appear before the commission at open hearings to discuss their compliance with the auditor's recommendations. When agencies failed to respond to negative audit findings to the satisfaction of the commission, the panel was bound to advise the governor— the official responsible for most of the agencies—of the situation. In event the governor failed to order corrective action, which was seldom, a political dispute might be in the offing. One result of that could be a commission request for legislative action to remedy any standoff—a last resort that all parties usually sought to avoid.

Primarily because of the public hearings that it conducted, the commission quickly gravitated to elite status in the eyes of Statehouse reporters and others interested in open government. The hearings, during which reluctant department directors and subordinates were called onto the carpet to explain the shortcomings of their operations and what they were doing to correct them, provided an unusual window into the inner workings of bureaucracies.

Moreover, the often heavily attended hearings were lively theater as Arrington, the presiding officer, and compatriots on the panel seldom tolerated stonewalling or feet dragging by uncooperative officials. More than one bureaucrat ignoring the auditor general's recommendations suddenly became receptive after a tongue-lashing from a member of the commission. Most often, Arrington was the one laying down the law, and he routinely did it in a blistering manner that could put the fear of God in a person.

Barbara Edwards, the commission's person for all seasons through the years, remembered with a wry smile that "he (Arrington) could easily scare the devil out of people—although I was not sure he always intended it to be that way. But, crossing him was not a pleasant experience."

The bottom line was that the audit commission definitely served its purpose, which was to give the General Assembly a strong voice in bringing about fiscal accountability by those entrusted with the expenditure of public dollars. After his legislative days were over, Arrington was justified in looking back and proudly proclaiming that the commission helped uncover and stop bureaucratic bungling or unlawful spending that had wasted many "millions and millions of dollars" in appropriated funds.

Because it dealt with inside fiscal stuff that even many government types found dry, the commission and its work remained largely anonymous in the eyes of the public. However, to those both aware of and concerned with government profligacy, the commission was a godsend.

As Statehouse columnist Joe Harris wrote in 1966, the "Legislative Audit Commission, since its creation…in the wake of the Hodge scandal, has been recognized as the most effective, most productive and most respected agency in state government." For Arrington personally, the commission gave him much broadened status in the Statehouse spotlight. In the hip vernacular of later years, it truly was his thing—his offspring from day one in 1957 and his personal showcase during the remainder of his legislative career.

One who got this message right off the bat was George Dunne, the savvy Chicago pol who was elected as the first secretary of the commission. After he was named to the panel, Dunne was approached by Arrington on the subject of the chairmanship. In an oral memoir years later, Dunne resurrected the occasion.

"Russ came to me, and he said, 'George, I see you're appointed to my commission,'" related Dunne. "I said, 'Your commission?' He said, 'Yes, that was my legislation.' I said, 'Oh, yes, I recall.' He said, 'That's the reason I've come to talk to you. I'd like to ask you for your vote as chairman of the commission.' I said, 'I wouldn't give it to you.' He said, 'What!' I said, 'No, Russ, I couldn't vote for you.' He said, 'I don't understand this. That's my legislation.' I said,

'Russ, you're Doctor Jekyll and Mr. Hyde. You're terrible with a gavel in your hand.' I added, 'You know (what I mean).'"

Dunne's comparison of Arrington to Doctor Jekyll—the good doctor in a Robert Louis Stevenson novel whose well-intended experiments on himself periodically turned him into the cruel Mr. Hyde—referred to Arrington's chairmanship during the 1957 session of a special joint Senate-House investigating committee on the state's soaring public assistance costs.

The committee's probe was triggered in part by concern over the Illinois Public Aid Commission's request for considerably more funds than the amount specified in Stratton's proposed budget for the 1957-1958 biennium. Heated debate, often along party lines, marked the committee's proceedings with Arrington-led Republicans charging that fraud in the relief programs was creating an unbridled fiscal quagmire for taxpayers. Democrats, like liberal Senator Marshall Korshak of Chicago, countered that cutting costs or stiffening the eligibility requirements for aid payments would impose great suffering on thousands of poor persons. Arrington, in particular, was singled out for criticism, with Democrats portraying him as "heartless" in running the committee—even to the point of saying he abused witnesses before the panel who objected to his cost control initiatives.

In his memoir, Dunne said he told Arrington after the legislative session that, in chairing a committee, "you don't chop up every head that comes along that has a different opinion."

Dunne jabbed ever harder, though, in voicing a contention that Arrington showed in his stewardship of the public aid inquiry that "he had ice water in his veins." Dunne, a son of Irish immigrant parents, further criticized Arrington as "a man that had lacked, in my opinion, compassion for the poor. And yet, he came from poverty, as I understand it. His family (members) were miners in southern Illinois."

Insinuations of this order dogged Arrington as his legislative stature increased. His toe-the-line demeanor, his espousal to a great extent of traditional Republican principles and his financial success in private business were pointed to (most often in private, but sometimes to his face) by Democrats and some other critics as things he ought to be ashamed of in view of where he came from. Certainly,

Secretary of State Paul Powell and Senator W. Russell Arrington

part of it was just political jargon, intended to prick his ego. But, the goading also reflected jealousy by some; envy of the consummate Arrington. In venting about what he was or had become, these critics maneuvered to convert Arrington's prowess into a political negativity. It was as if Arrington was to have a measure of vulnerability because of the changing stations of his life.

Years later, when Arrington was fighting the last battle of his journey, Dunne opined much more warmly about the man, saying that he had few equals in intelligence and knowledge of law and, furthermore, had turned out to be much more "human" than perceived earlier.

Getting back to the organization of the audit commission in late 1957, Dunne did follow through on his decision not to vote for Arrington for chairman. But, every other member did support Arrington for the post, trusting that he'd keep his word not to let the operation engage in any witch-hunts for purely partisan purposes. And, as observers soon discovered, it was remarkable in the usually polemic-charged atmosphere of the Capitol the way partisanship went by the wayside as the commission went to work.

Minor wrangling here and there, largely cosmetic, did not detract from the cooperation Arrington received from Democrats, including Dunne, in the commission's pursuit of a big picture role. The Democrat seen as most ensuring this situation during his time on the panel in its early days was Powell. The commission afforded another forum for the obvious affinity between Arrington and Powell, two men who persisted in not letting their party differences interrupt their harmonious working relationship.

Barbara Edwards, whose bird's-eye view of the inner functioning of the commission was unsurpassed, was privy to the Arrington-Powell rapport that got the commission off on the right path, the non-partisan course from which it never strayed. She was present more than once at evening dinners with Arrington and Powell—get-togethers at Herman Cohen's The Mill or some other Springfield restaurant where the two might check signals on the conduct of commission business or other matters.

"They did not really socialize that much," Barbara said, "but Russ and Powell both wanted an effective legislature, and each had great respect for the other's legislative capabilities.

"Russ knew that if he needed help on some difficult issue in the House or with the other party, he could go to Powell. And, Powell would say whether or not he could help. If he could help, his word was good. There'd be no pussyfooting around."

Barbara Edwards herself was very emblematic of the world that Arrington carved out under his hegemony in the Statehouse. It was a world, although within the bigger kingdom of Illinois government, that in Arrington's heyday governed the image and performance of the General Assembly, as well as the fate of public policy issues affecting the lives of every Illinoisan. Key ingredients of Arrington's world were its people—individuals, primarily young, brought onto the legislative landscape by Arrington to enrich the scene with new ideas and vigor. They were soldiers in Arrington's grand plan to reshape the legislature. Some went on to highly successful political careers; one succeeded in getting elected governor.

Quite noticeable about almost every one of these individuals was the unending loyalty to Arrington, a fealty quite different from the ever-shifting sands of routine political allegiances. Barbara Edwards, as the initial employee of the audit commission, well may have been the first of the Statehouse contingent that came to be identified as Arrington people.

When Roger E. Henn was hired away from the Taxpayers' Federation of Illinois, where he was a veteran research specialist, to be the first executive director of the commission, he found the logistical groundwork for its operation already set up by Edwards, who started off with the title of staff secretary. Subsequently, when the very competent Dick Viar served as executive director for several decades, Edwards was at his side as the agency's administrative secretary.

No mistake about it, staffers for the commission were not overly popular figures in the Statehouse because the panel's focus on fiscal irregularities did not put culpable officials in the best light. "Maybe we didn't make a lot of friends," Edwards said, "but we wanted to do a good job in what was an important area for the citizens of the state."

Still, where Edwards was concerned, discourtesy to her face was not advisable because of her closeness to Arrington. Besides discharging her duties with the commission, the woman that Fred Smith called "Little Lady" took care of, as she put it, "lots of loose ends in Springfield" for Arrington. She was his gal Friday in the capital, the counterpart of Marion Belland in Arrington's Chicago law office.

Edwards' enduring respect for Arrington was evident as she discussed the Springfield part of his life during an interview at her home in that city on a nippy fall day in 2003, eighteen years after her retirement from the commission.

She underscored a feeling that, above all else, "Russ did much more for this state than most people knew. He was just a great man." As to assertions that appreciation for his accomplishments was sometimes overshadowed by attention to his exacting personality, Edwards replied that "yes, he was a demanding taskmaster. But, to me, that was quite an asset. I liked the way he expected things to be done right the first time. I liked the way he wouldn't stand for foot-dragging. I admired those qualities in him." Pausing for emphasis, she added, "I can tell you, in spite of what some said, Russ could, and did, work very well with like-minded people."

Barbara was a young secretary—pert, quite attractive and heading for a divorce from her first husband—when she came to state government and, not long afterward, went under Arrington's wing.

A graduate of Springfield High School, she had worked as a secretary for Sangamon County State's Attorney George Coutrakon and then for a law firm in Springfield before agreeing to handle a relatively brief but new and interesting task. She was employed to do the secretarial duties tied to the investigation of the Hodge morass being conducted by Morey, Jenner and Rendleman at the request of the budgetary commission. After the Morey group's report was completed, she applied for and received the job of secretary for the Senate Judiciary Committee in 1957.

Arrington, a member of the committee, was impressed with her performance, which included work on the fiscal reform legislation that, among other things, established the audit commission. Consequently, Arrington asked Barbara in the months following the session to deal with the paperwork necessary for setting up the commission, a request that led to her becoming the first hire for the new panel.

As Edwards and others long associated with Arrington learned through the years, it was normal to expect the unexpected. One such episode for her occurred when Arrington invited her, in view of her stint with the Morey inquiry, to accompany him on a visit to Hodge at the Menard penitentiary.

"I told him (Arrington) that, sure, I'd like to go," she related. "I'd never been to a prison. I went, and got to talk to Hodge. It was very interesting for me to get a glimpse of what it was like in prison."

Being a member of Arrington's coterie usually meant more than the strict maintenance of an all-business image in public. In private, Arrington did not withhold personal advice to those around him if it was requested or deemed to be needed. With some, he became the most trusted figure in their lives. Barbara Edwards thought so highly of Arrington that he was the one who gave her away in 1970 at Westminster Presbyterian Church in Springfield when she exchanged vows with her second husband, William Mehlenbeck, then executive vice president of Central Illinois Builders of Associated General Contractors.

The General Assembly's hand in auditing, first fashioned by Arrington in 1957, was strengthened down the line in a change brought about by the Illinois Constitution of 1970. Through it, the legislature, and not the governor, appointed the auditor general, which was Arrington's original goal. Replacing the Department of Audits, the new auditor general—serving a ten instead of six-year term—was to work even more closely with the audit commission in scrutinizing the receipt and use of public funds by each state agency. The commission had the power to authorize the general to go further by making certain or special investigations if either the general or commission members smelled a major problem.

Arrington's drive in the 1957 session to bring about modernizing of the state's judiciary did not produce the happy ending for him that his fiscal reform campaign did. The proposed judicial amendment to the constitution that Arrington helped push through the legislature was not adopted because the electorate failed to give it a required vote for approval in the 1958 general election. The restructuring was heavily favored by those voting on it in Cook County, where Mayor Daley had joined Stratton, Arrington and other political leaders in its support. However, lukewarm backing outside of Cook doomed the amendment. For it to have passed, it needed to be ratified by a majority of the total number of voters in the election or by two-thirds of those voting on the amendment. The proposal met neither requirement.

However, Arrington eventually would taste victory on this issue in 1962 when voters finally did give a green light to an amendment of the constitution's judicial article that extensively revamped the state court system.

As the dust settled from the 1957 session, Arrington was flooded by plaudits for his aggressiveness on fiscal and judicial reform and for numerous stands intended to protect citizens from excesses by government at all levels. Maurice W. Scott, then executive secretary of the taxpayers' federation, wrote to Arrington that he deserved much of the credit for guaranteeing during the session that "local taxpayers will still have the right of referendum approval before new taxes or increases in property tax rate limits may be imposed."

Scott also applauded Arrington's immersion in the public aid funding controversy.

"Public and official awareness of the swollen relief and public assistance rolls resulted from your heading the special Legislative Commission to Investigate Public Assistance," wrote Scott. "Long term benefits will occur to Illinois taxpayers in future years as a result of this investigation."

Of course, some of those who saw Arrington in a different light on this issue sought to pummel him on the grounds that he was indifferent to the plight of the poor. Arrington did not deny that political blood, including some of his own, was spilled in the acrimonious debate on this subject, a fight which was only beginning.

Regardless of his won lost record, Arrington walked away from the 1957 session with the firm feeling that he had fully arrived as a senator—that he'd rather quickly become a major player in the upper chamber just as he had been in the House. He was certain that no senator had gotten more press coverage, the bulk of it positive. He realized he'd never win any popularity contest, but, by damn, his colleagues knew he was there.

He loved it.

Chapter 12

𝒞

Into the 1960s—
A New Ball Game

I n the winter of 1975-1976, on one of those Siberian cold
nights for which Chicago is famous, two heavily bundled up
men, moving slowly and gingerly, helped each other enter the
residence of a man viewed by many as Chicago's most important
white Protestant clergyman, Preston Bradley.

The gentlemen were invited to dinner by Bradley and his wife,
June. The occasion turned out to be an evening of rich conversation
as the two dinner guests resurrected events of years past when their
bonding on this night would have seemed unthinkable.

One of the guests, even though he had made a remarkable comeback from a serious stroke five years earlier, appeared frail. The man
was Arrington. Even with the use of a cane, he still needed assistance
from the other dinner guest to get out of his car and make it through
the snow to Bradley's door. The help was greatly appreciated by
Arrington because he knew that the other guest—released not too
long before from a federal prison—was suffering from cancer and
had little strength. He was Otto Kerner.

When Kerner, a Democrat, was governor of Illinois during much
of the 1960s, his major political antagonist was none other than
Arrington. Their relationship was often rancorous, with Kerner's
party riding high in state government and Arrington personifying the
loyal opposition.

But, on this cold night at Bradley's place the hostility was long
past. Kerner was very solicitous about Arrington's welfare, and

Arrington quietly questioned Kerner about his stamina.

"It was before the dinner," recalled Arrington, "that I asked Otto how he was getting along. And he said, 'Well, I'm a very sick man, but there's nothing you can do about it.' He just said it to me personally. So, I took him home that night. Then, some months later, he started to get sicker."

When Kerner entered a hospital for the final time, Arrington wrote to him and then, in a gesture of respect for Kerner, obtained a silver bookmark and had it inscribed: "To Otto Kerner with compliments of Senator Arrington."

While knowing Kerner to be an avid reader, Arrington felt the bookmark was "an attractive thing" that Kerner's family soon would receive and hopefully like because, said Arrington, "it was clear by that time Otto was not going to live too long." Arrington said he intended to visit Kerner in the hospital and give him the bookmark, but refrained from doing so because he said he "didn't want to interfere." Instead, Arrington had an aide drop off the bookmark to Kerner. Four days later (in May 1976), Kerner died.

The election of Kerner to the governorship in 1960 had signaled the beginning of a major sea change in Illinois politics. The electorate not only ended eight years of Republican occupation of the governor's office, but left Democrats in control of all statewide offices except for secretary of state, retained by East Moline's Charles F. Carpentier, and the minor post of Illinois Supreme Court clerk, held by Mrs. Earle Benjamin Searcy.

As for the General Assembly, the GOP did come out of the election with an 89 to 88-seat edge in the House. However, incredible as it may have seemed, Democrat Powell drew upon his considerable political acumen to get elected speaker in spite of his party being in the minority. Actually, it would be more accurate to say that Powell was reelected speaker since he held the presiding post in the Seventy-first General Assembly (covering 1959-1960), when the Democrats did hold a 91 to 86 majority in the chamber. For Powell to keep the post in the Seventy-second General Assembly, though, was a tribute to his political genius and a disgrace to the GOP. Since Powell, as speaker, ran proceedings and kept Democrats in control of committees, the party with the most members—the GOP—was relegated to minority status.

In view of the awkward if not downright weird political situation in the House, the lone bastion of Republican strength in Illinois government going into 1961 was the Senate. There, where Republicans outnumbered Democrats, 31 to 27, Bidwill remained the body's president pro tempore, and Arrington continued to chair the revenue committee and occupy a seat on other committees most important for him, most notably the judiciary and insurance panels.

If Republicans in Illinois and across the country didn't realize that the 1950s were largely halcyon years for them, the election of 1960 and its aftermath erased any doubt. Democratic Senator John F. Kennedy of Massachusetts defeated Vice President Richard M. Nixon in the race for president. Helping to ensure Nixon's defeat was Kennedy's very narrow victory in Illinois—an outcome that many Republicans swore to their dying day happened because of vote stealing by Democrats in Chicago.

Democrat Paul Douglas was reelected to his seat in the United States Senate in the November 8, 1960, balloting, defeating GOP attorney Samuel Witwer. The most crushing blow for Republicans was Kerner's victory over Stratton, who was seeking a third term as governor. Stratton, thought to still be saddled by negative residue from the Hodge scandal and carrying other political baggage, lost by the largest plurality of all the defeated GOP candidates for state office. (The only Republican winner for a state office on the ballot that year was Carpentier.)

Arrington himself did not have a free electoral path in 1960. Up for reelection to his Senate seat, he faced a challenge in the April 12 primary voting for his party's nomination for the seat. The challenger was Charles B. Marshall, twenty-nine years old, the alderman of Evanston's Eighth Ward. Marshall, a recent recipient of a law degree from Northwestern, captured wide notice in 1957 when he unseated a sixteen-year veteran of the Evanston City Council. Interestingly, the person Marshall beat was Fred Thoma, who defeated Arrington for alderman in 1941, the only election Arrington ever lost.

Marshall's bid to replace Arrington may have seemed like a Don

Quixote quest, but his effort was the kind that naturally attracted attention. *Chicago Sun-Times* writer Burnell Heinecke called Marshall a modern-day David shooting at a Senate Goliath. Other reporters took to walking with Marshall on his door-to-door campaign throughout the Fourth Senatorial District.

To prevail in the primary, Arrington banked on heavy support from Republican organization regulars and on the merits of his legislative record. Much emphasis was placed on his continued drive to channel or redirect state resources toward what many considered more responsible ends. In the legislature's 1959 session, for example, he was the chief sponsor of legislation providing an extra $100 million needed for the operation of elementary schools. At the same time, he remained on the warpath against excessive expenditures on public aid that he believed to be wasteful. Voters also were reminded of his many earlier legislative successes, especially his big hand in the state government fiscal accountability reforms in 1957.

A flood of endorsements for his reelection also bolstered Arrington. George E. Mahin, the executive director of the Better Government Association, notified Arrington that he was authorized to advertise that he was "recommended as outstanding" by the BGA, the highest rating given by the organization.

Among the numerous newspapers backing Arrington in the primary, the *Chicago Daily News* declared that "Marshall ought to have a future in public life, but it would not be appropriate to retire such an outstanding man as Arrington to make way for him in the 4th district." The *Sun-Times* endorsed him, but cautioned in a separate column that the "highly volatile Senator Arrington...might achieve reelection to the state Senate as long as his blood pressure stays down," an apparent suggestion that Arrington needed to better control his easily aroused temper.

As expected by most, Arrington won the primary going away, amassing more than twice as many votes as Marshall from those taking Republican ballots. The victory was, of course, tantamount to a win in the November general election because of the district's lopsided GOP tilt. To oppose Arrington in the fall balloting, the Democrats nominated Roman Domas, a plumbing contractor from

Wheeling. True to form, Domas was crushed by Arrington, 108,000 to 56,000.

Since he was considered a sure winner in November, Arrington, as in the past, had devoted much election year energy in the summer and fall to the support of GOP state office candidates, especially the contest of his friend, Stratton. Ruth Arrington was not on the sideline either. She and the wife of Cook County commissioner William Erickson were hosts of what the *Daily News* called "a big and handsome tea" for Shirley Stratton in "the big and handsome lakefront home" of Mrs. Arrington. More than 500 Republican women attended the event, intended to help invigorate Governor Stratton's campaign.

The Arringtons' strong push for Stratton had a touch of irony in that, had Stratton won, Arrington's political visibility would not have soared nearly as much as it did with the moving into office of the Kerner administration. It was more than the fact that the Senate provided the only meaningful GOP voice left in Illinois government. Arrington was clearly the Senate's most openly combatant Republican.

One outgrowth of the power switch in Springfield, Arrington recognized, was the likelihood of an enlarged, more aggressive role for government in meeting the challenges facing the state and its citizens. For one thing, he noted in a column he penned for his constituents that an economic recession appeared to be emerging in 1960, a factor contributing, in Arrington's mind, to the GOP's poor electoral showing at the national and state levels. He also was quick with a reminder that Democrats traditionally were more willing to address real or perceived problems in society with new or enlarged government programs and spending.

At the same time, Arrington acknowledged that the Seventy-second General Assembly, convening at the start of 1961, seemingly had no choice but to seek additional sources of revenue if the state was to adequately discharge its growing responsibilities in education, public assistance and other vital areas.

This was no small observation from the individual who was described in the fall of 1960 by one newspaper, *The Calumet Index*, as "a rare breed, indeed—a man in public office who is concerned with the

Left to right: Representative Harris Rowe, U.S. Senator Charles H. Percy of Illinois, Senator Arrington, future President Richard M. Nixon and Ray Page, State Superintendent of Public Instruction

welfare of the greatest scapegoat in history—the American taxpayer."

No question, Arrington looked to be walking a tightrope in the 1961 session, trying to strike a balance between his eagle eye for protecting taxpayer dollars with the imperative for responsible consideration of the state's pressing need for more money. The quandary was even more acute for Arrington because of his chairmanship of the Senate Revenue Committee.

The challenge for Arrington was indeed pretty much the way it was posed to him in a 1959 letter to the senator from one of Chicago's more mercurially successful business executives, Charles H. Percy.

Percy, the president of Bell & Howell Company and a Republican, wrote that he recognized the legislative difficulties faced by Arrington "in holding down expense levels in the face of ever-growing needs."

"It becomes a delicate balancing act," said Percy, "to hold back on certain desirable but not absolutely essential expenditures and, at the same time, not put us in the position of being a party opposed to providing for legitimate needs. But if we cannot maintain fiscal responsibility, we are also performing a disservice as a party."

Similar admonitions from others like Percy weighed heavily on Arrington as he carried the Republican flag onto the revamped battlefield of Illinois government in the 1960s. No, he was not the titular leader of Senate Republicans, and did not know if he ever would be. But, he comprehended that the gentlemanly Bidwill and certain other veteran Republican senators didn't have the fire in their bellies to go toe-to-toe with the reinvigorated Democrats. The Republicans had their backs to the wall now. No room was left for them to be cowed on the one island still held by the party in Illinois government. Arrington took it upon himself to ensure that, through the Senate, Republicans would stand their ground. It was a no-nonsense hour for his side. Gut-check time. A serious GOP presence demanded nothing less than a reversion to political hardball, which Republicans not always were used to. Arrington's day had arrived.

Beginning with the 1961 session and well into the decade, the GOP stake in state government issues largely revolved around Arrington—even though he didn't become the formal leader of Senate Republicans until the mid-1960s. With the departure of Powell from the House after getting elected secretary of state in 1964, the moving and shaking on so many public matters vital to Illinoisans involved essentially three individuals—Kerner, Mayor Daley and, although not a household name statewide, Arrington.

Kerner, a 1930 graduate of the Ivy League's Brown University, a World War II veteran and a onetime United States attorney in Chicago, was the county judge for Cook County when he was handpicked by Daley to run for governor in 1960. He first had to win a three-person primary contest to secure his party's nomination for the office before going on to whip Stratton in the general election. In putting Kerner into the state's top post, Illinois voters selected a man who was handsome, dignified in his bearing and socially adept.

Two years younger than Arrington, Kerner was a virtual stranger to state government when he arrived in Springfield. This was pointed out in the Kerner biography coauthored by Bill Barnhart and Gene Schlickman published in 1999 by the University of Illinois Press.

"Despite his lobbying efforts as Cook County judge on behalf of reforms in the state's adoption and election laws," wrote the authors, "Kerner knew almost nothing about how the legislature and the state bureaucracy worked."

Arrington took note of that inexperience years later when he declared, in sizing up Kerner, that "Otto, while he was a fine man, didn't know much about government." Although "Otto's heart was in the right place," averred Arrington, "he really wasn't a student of government."

Unlike Arrington, Kerner was a political blue blood. His father, Otto Kerner Sr., was a well regarded Illinois attorney general in the 1930s and then a federal appeals court judge. Although as attorney general the elder Kerner was not always in sync with the Chicago Democratic organization, he never escaped being labeled a political protégé of fellow Bohemian Anton Cermak, the principal architect of the Chicago Democratic machine that Daley later dominated. Governor Kerner's wife, Helena, was the youngest of Cermak's daughters.

Having never rubbed shoulders with the ward heelers and fixers so ingrained in the fabric of the Chicago machine, Kerner wouldn't have made it to the governor's chair without the express backing of Daley. Arrington concluded after many dealings with Kerner that "he really didn't know much about politics. He was naïve."

Nevertheless, once in Springfield, Kerner's polished, always correct manner set well with the Statehouse crowd and gained him acceptance into the city's society, something not always automatic for governors. Arrington acknowledged this in stating that Kerner was "very popular…everyone liked him."

In truth, Arrington held, "While I fought him (Kerner) on so many issues—and it got pretty spirited at times—we always respected each other." Arrington added that he was greatly saddened when Kerner went to prison after he was found guilty in a criminal trial of federal tax evasion and other charges stemming from scandalous racing stock deals while he was governor. Ironically, at the time of his indictment, Kerner was serving on the same federal appeals court bench as his father had years before.

"Otto was, I am sure, an honest man…and not really a crook," Arrington lamented. Arrington's thinking was that Kerner made "a huge mistake" in not distancing himself from a longtime confidant who engineered the stock manipulation that led to Kerner's downfall. "I don't think that Otto really knew that he was doing anything wrong," said Arrington, "but it turned out to be obvious that he was in the wrong. It was just a shame that he let himself get mixed up in it."

Arrington had not been as sympathetic to Kerner when they publicly confronted each other in the 1960s. A number of Kerner's goals as governor were shared by Arrington, but political bickering and posturing— seemingly unavoidable among political heavyweights in Illinois— oftentimes generated sharp antagonism before issues were resolved.

When this writer arrived in Springfield late in 1965 to cover the Statehouse for the *St. Louis Post-Dispatch*, Arrington was quickly mentioned by Kerner during the writer's initial introduction to the governor. Kerner made it clear that Arrington presented him with his biggest headache in trying to govern the state. In an off-the-cuff remark about his unending fights with Senate Republicans over the provision of sufficient revenue for the state, Kerner suggested facetiously that "Russ could really help solve the problem if he'd just let us use some of his millions."

By this time, the go-arounds between Kerner and Arrington on state finances were old hat in the Statehouse. As the smoke from each of the unending skirmishes settled, and while the two men collected their breaths for the next encounter, several old political truisms were always in play. Kerner was cast as the profligate Democrat, invariably hunting for more tax dollars to underwrite broadened government initiatives. On the other hand, Arrington was the parsimonious Republican, stridently insisting that government had to live within its existing means—and, furthermore, that it would be able to do so with more businesslike efficiency.

Looking back, the 1961 legislative session had been the first round for Arrington and Kerner. It didn't take long for them to be at loggerheads on the state budget, with Arrington soon changing his mind from his initial view that the session might be one in which the lawmakers would agree on a need for an infusion of additional dollars from taxpayers.

Kerner's drive for additional tax revenue during that session had both immediate and long-range goals. As for the latter, he called at one point for a revised constitutional Revenue Article that would give the General Assembly broad latitude to impose whatever taxes were deemed necessary for meeting the state's fiscal commitments. On the other side of the coin, Arrington had a proposed Revenue Article amendment of his own, one prohibiting graduated income taxes.

In pushing his plan, Arrington stated that the "people of Illinois are opposed to a state income tax. They have had experience with a federal income tax, initially imposed at low rates, but now having a staggering top rate of 91 percent. This should be ample warning against any such tax for state purposes. In addition, it must be remembered that such taxes would destroy the favorable business climate of Illinois."

Arrington's amendment also addressed the possibility of Illinoisans someday getting a flat-rate income tax.

He contended that under the then current constitution "it is usually agreed that the General Assembly may levy a uniform non-graduated tax on income." He stressed that under his proposed amendment "even a non-graduated income tax levied by the General Assembly must first be approved, both in principle and as to rate, by public referendum."

Neither Arrington's proposed amendment nor Kerner's was approved by the legislature for submission to voters. The wording of Arrington's proposal, so restrictive as to pretty much preclude any state income tax enactment, underscored his reputation as a strong opponent of a state income levy. His high profile on the matter would be ironic in view of his leading role in the later passage of a state income tax, a development with enormous political consequences.

As it was in 1961, Kerner had to settle for a half-cent increase in the state sales tax, along with a broadening of the base for the levy. Arrington was the most vocal foe of the sale tax hike. Although it did pass, Arrington on the other hand was successful in almost single-handedly forcing a reluctant Kerner administration to institute what Arrington labeled greater austerity in government spending. Arrington was especially dead set on bringing about cuts in Democratic appropriation requests for financing code department operations.

The Arrington-pushed reductions in state spending not only ticked off Democrats, but left some Republican senators uneasy—most notably those with big tax-supported entities in their districts. This was noted by *Sun-Times* political columnist John Dreiske, who kept close tabs on Arrington. "As a party unit," observed Dreiske, "the Republicans have not had their heart wholly in the…cut program." Dreiske added that Arrington, the "principal exponent of the cuts," did not by any means "have a devoted following in his own party."

"Many of his colleagues regard Arrington as a dangerous and fickle skyrocket to follow," he said.

Dreiske, who admired much about Arrington and would not hesitate to say so, pointed to the senator late in the session as a main factor in the Senate Republicans' roughshod run over the body's Democrats and, as a result, the stifling of much of what Kerner and his party desired in revenue raising and other areas.

As Dreiske saw it, "The incompleteness of high school and college civics courses is never more dramatically illustrated than in a committee meeting in which the gavel is wielded by Arrington." When presiding over the Revenue Committee, Arrington was said by Dreiske to have "only one attitude—angry. From the podium there emanates a thick atmosphere of contempt for all things and people Democratic."

Kerner and the legislature's Democrats became so bogged down in fighting to secure the sales levy hike in 1961 that they had to let other initiatives by the new governor pretty much fall to the wayside. Kerner did lay the groundwork for a major reorganization of the state's mental health program during his first two years in office, a nationally recognized effort that pulled the state's mental hospitals out of politics. He also was instrumental in the 1961 passage of the Illinois Fair Employment Practices Act and, in the words of authors Barnhart and Schlickman, "managed to squeeze enough money out of existing revenue sources" to pay the state's bills. But, they concluded, "Kerner's inability to control the game in Springfield led politicians and reporters to view him as a one-term governor…."

Tom Littlewood, the *Sun-Times* Statehouse reporter, wound up saying in a magazine piece late in 1962 that Kerner clearly was a disappointment in his first two years in office. Kerner's administration, wrote Littlewood, "has been content to coast through two years without anything resembling a 'crash program' to solve the state's financial problems or any other problems, save possibly the deplorable conditions of mental institutions."

Things might have been different, many Democrats felt, if not for the bullheaded refusal of Arrington during the 1961 session to let Kerner put his mark on Illinois government. Arrington's counter was that he was anything but an obstructionist to legitimate advances in governing. But, he minced no words in stating he was "damned determined" to do everything in his power to guarantee that the Senate GOP would not be a party to "unabridged spending and extravagant taxing proposals."

Again, one of the first to say amen to Arrington's fiscal posture was the well-thought-of Maurice Scott of the taxpayers' federation. In a letter to Arrington late in 1961, Scott assured the senator that taxpayers "of your district and Illinois appreciate your efforts to keep unnecessary taxes from being imposed upon them...." Furthermore, added Scott, "taxpayers appreciate your...work to cut non-essential expenditures from the state budget."

On the other hand, Arrington tried to point out in moments of calm that he was not an automatic roadblock to all things Democrats wanted. Kerner got considerable credit from civil rights leaders for the 1961 legislation establishing the Fair Employment Practices Commission to combat job discrimination. This cause was not favored by most Republicans, but Arrington stuck out his neck politically to help bring about passage of the legislation. He believed it was the responsible thing to do, but he received little praise for doing it—at least from other legislators and the increasingly vocal activists in restless minority groups.

In previous sessions, the House had passed legislation mandating fair employment procedures, but the measures died in the Senate. The bill that finally went to the governor in 1961 was a Senate one that was not as far reaching as a tougher FEPC measure passed by the House but facing defeat in the upper chamber. The Senate version was drafted by Arrington and Senator Arthur W. Sprague, a LaGrange Republican, and chiefly sponsored by Arrington, who never had supported FEPC proposals in the past.

An especially heated moment in the Senate's consideration of Arrington's bill occurred when a handful of Republicans joined minority Democrats on the Senate floor to discharge the bill from the body's Industrial Affairs Committee, where it was bottled up. This left most of the Republicans incensed since moves in the full Senate to usurp the deliberations of a committee hardly ever were successful. An angry Bidwill, no backer of the FEPC, warned that "complete chaos will prevail" if the Senate was going to make a practice of disregarding decisions of its committees.

Arrington was one of five Republicans to buck the majority of his GOP seatmates and join Democrats in voting to get the legislation out of the Senate. The others were Sprague, Robert McClory of Lake Bluff, John P. Meyer of Danville and Gordon E. Kerr of Brookport.

The ire aimed at Arrington by some FEPC opponents was not shared by a number of editorial writers. One, writing on the opinion page of *Paddock Publications*, attributed the Senate passage "in large part to the vigorous leadership" of Arrington.

"Sen. Arrington's courage and independence," said the editorial of June 1, 1961, "merits the gratitude of all citizens who will be guaranteed equal employment opportunities without regard to race, religion, color or national origin."

Arrington's emergence on the FEPC issue, a surprise to many, was recalled by Dawn Clark Netsch in a 2003 phone interview from her office at Northwestern University, where she was a law professor emeritus. Netsch, a point person for Kerner on many legislative issues, remembered "having dealings" with Arrington on the subject. After "some give and take," she said, "he was for it in the end."

Netsch, easily the most prominent woman in Illinois state government in the twentieth century, was an intelligent and chic attorney who, at the age of thirty-four, joined Kerner's staff after his inauguration. Given the unofficial title of deputy governor by Kerner, Netsch served as his legal advisor and had a hand in most other matters in the governor's office. Later on, she was an elected delegate to the Illinois Constitutional Convention of 1970, a state senator and the elected state comptroller. In 1994, as the Democratic candidate for governor, she made history by becoming the first woman to win a major party gubernatorial nomination in Illinois. She was defeated in the general election by Jim Edgar, the Republican incumbent in the office and a person whose governmental mentor happened to be Arrington.

While a number in Kerner's circle disliked Arrington, Netsch was not among them. Mutual respect governed their relationship. Arrington found her to be a worthy individual with whom to deal because of her legal acumen and deference to the legislative process. She found him, in her words, "so bright and confident...and arrogant at times."

Netsch acknowledged that Arrington "was often discussed in the governor's office because he could be quite challenging in engagements." Yet, she said, "we fully realized we had to deal with him. He dominated the Republicans, who dominated the Senate. He was a very strict disciplinarian. He was just a presence we couldn't ignore."

Nevertheless, Netsch believed that she came to have a special working relationship with Arrington. "Russ and I actually got along pretty well. Even though I probably could not help but be furious with him at times because of the difficulties in dealing with him, I still admired him."

Another subject on which Netsch made headway with Arrington was the so-called escheat law that the Kerner administration wanted, and got, in 1961. Under it, unclaimed deposits and other funds could be taken over by the state and used to meet monetary needs.

"Much work had to be done to bring this program about before property could be escheated to the state," Netsch recalled. Objections by banks and other private interests had to be addressed, she noted, and then there was the task of getting the escheat legislation through the Senate.

"Russ had to agree to our program for it to pass, because, once again, he was decisive in the Senate. He and I talked it out, and I got his approval. He really, in the end, didn't object to the idea or principal of the program."

However, Arrington projected that the program, once on the books, would bring in much more revenue for the state than anticipated by the Kerner folks. Under Arrington's thinking, the new money would help to blunt requests by Kerner for new or increased taxes. The Kerner camp countered that it was unrealistic to rely on the escheat initiative as a budget-balancing factor. As it turned out, the state's take under the program would neither meet the high expectations of some in the GOP, nor be as minimal as some Democrats predicted. The sparring was a blueprint for similar differences of opinion between the two sides during upcoming fights on other new sources of state dollars.

Kerner and Arrington remained at odds over the Illinois budget—its expenditures and the revenues for financing it—in succeeding years. For Capitol watchers, the standoffs became a soap opera, spiced by plenty of melodrama. Kerner seldom lost his cool as governor, but he sometimes could not restrain himself in trying to come to terms with Arrington on state finance altercations.

After their knockdown on budget making in 1965, Kerner lashed out at Arrington to Ralph Johnson, the legislative correspondent for the downstate *Lindsay-Schaub* newspapers, and other reporters.

Contending that the Arrington-led Senate Republicans forced upon him a budget with a huge hole in regard to adequate revenue, Kerner angrily remarked that he'd had "dealings with this man (Arrington) since 1961, and he has been proven wrong every time in his financial estimates. His is a planned program of deficiencies for the coming biennium. I picked up a bankrupt state four years ago, and we ran such a tight, efficient ship that we were able to put the state on a solvent basis. He (Arrington) would leave us without a red cent."

A decade later, on the night the two joined Preston Bradley at his home for dinner, the animosity between Arrington and Kerner was long past. Their get-together had the air of one of those occasions at which old wartime foes meet years afterward to reminisce respectfully about the way things had been at an earlier time and place.

Gone were the days when Arrington was a sharp burr under Kerner's saddle. Arrington was coming into his own then, and he was a real handful for the Democrats.

U.S. Senator Everett M. Dirksen of Illinois (left) and Senator Arrington

Chapter 13

T

Taking Command

*I*t was true. Arrington the legislator arrived in full dress in the 1960s. He reached his political zenith in a decade that was tailor-made for him. Two on-target descriptions of the 1960s—"supercharged and politically intense"—had Arrington written all over them.

The counterculturists, many of them young activists revolting against the establishment, may have been hard pressed to discern any kinship with Arrington. Their social and political idealism challenged the materialistic values of the fifties—exemplified so saliently by an affluent corporate America of which Arrington was a notably successful part. Their agenda seeking much greater governmental responsibility for social change met resistance from Arrington's party, if not so much from the senator himself. The long-haired youths driving the most active antiwar protest in American history never pegged Arrington as one of their number. He wasn't exactly what they had in mind.

He didn't expostulate on the Vietnam War. But, he did make a remark to his young staffers at dinner one night, at a time when college campuses were being torn asunder by student protesters, that caught Richard W. Carlson and the others by surprise.

"He said," related Carlson, "that 'if I was your age, I'd probably have hair down to my shoulders.' I took that to mean he was implying that there was room for protest. In truth, there were some on staff who did oppose the war."

If one of the recurrent themes of the 1960s was to bring about change, then Arrington was in the flow of things—inasmuch as his segment of the universe, Illinois government, was concerned. The forces led by Arrington were hardly apostles of change, but he, himself, was not content to live, governmentally speaking, with the status quo. The breakdown of the old order in so many walks of life in the 1960s created a ripe climate for Arrington. A door opened for him to forge ahead to reshape his world into the way it ought to be according to Arrington.

He was determined not to be sidetracked, even though it was tricky business since many of those he needed for support did not share his big picture view. However, once he became the clear-cut master of his domain—the Senate—he was darn near impossible to stop. That is, unless he got too far ahead of his troops, which he certainly did at least once.

A pretty obvious masquerade in the high level of Illinois politics was scrapped when the Republican majority in the Senate formally elected Arrington as its leader at the end of 1964—a few weeks after that year's election continued to leave the GOP with little power in the state outside of the Senate. Arrington's upstaging of Bidwill had become almost pro forma. Democrats from Kerner on down reserved their sharpest barbs for Arrington and not Bidwill, a testimony to the Dems' recognition of Arrington as their major headache.

It may or may not have been orchestrated, but certain Democratic senators almost seemed to be designated needlers of Arrington. Two were William L. Grindle, an insurance agency operator from the southern Illinois coal town of Herrin, and his close friend, William (Bill) Lyons of Gillespie. The pair, so tied together on and off the Senate floor that they were dubbed the "gold dust twins," often picked up on the old George Dunne refrain that Arrington was a person who'd forgotten his roots.

As Grindle recounted in a memoir, "We used to get up and gig him a lot, Bill Lyons and I, because the odd thing is that Bill is from Gillespie, and Russ Arrington was born in Gillespie. Although he (Arrington)…went to Chicago and became a big insurance executive up there and a lawyer, we used to always kid him.

"It was, you know, about, 'Here you are. You ought to be ashamed of yourself. Here you come from a coal mining town like the rest of us, and yet you've gone so high that you can't be bothered with helping the little people downstate.' Of course, this wouldn't set well with Russ."

Much of the political antagonism toward Arrington centered on the budget, where he utilized his continued hold on the chairmanship of the Senate Revenue Committee in 1963-1964 to throw cold water on Kerner's quests for more revenue for state operations. There were other areas in which Arrington prevailed by securing Democratic cooperation.

One quickly coming to mind was Arrington's reaching of a long-sought goal with the General Assembly's passage in 1963 of his legislation overhauling the administration of public assistance in the state. Sticking to his guns throughout a six-year effort to bring this about, Arrington maintained that prodigal spending could be cut without curtailing benefits to those most needy by making the governor directly responsible for the program. This was accomplished by his legislation's creation of the Illinois Department of Public Aid, a code agency under the governor, to take control of the program away from the embattled Illinois Public Aid Commission. In signing the legislation, Kerner named Harold (Hap) Swank, the executive secretary of the commission, to be director of the new department. Arrington, who was very high on Swank's capability, felt that Swank would have much more flexibility to implement necessary reforms in overseeing welfare by having to answer to the governor instead of the controversy-mired commission.

In another challenging area in Illinois society—the plight of abused, homeless and exploited children—the state was given broadened responsibilities for aiding victims through another new code agency created by 1963 legislation, the Department of Children and Family Services. Arrington was a cosponsor of the legislation.

Arrington also was a leading sponsor in 1963 of much of the legislation needed to implement the reforms authorized by the amendment to the Illinois Constitution's Judicial Article that state voters approved in 1962. Arrington had been chief sponsor of the Judicial

Article amendment that voters turned down in 1958 and, as noted earlier, a collaborator with fellow lawmaker Alan Dixon in getting a legislative green light for the judicial amendment successfully submitted to voters four years later.

The stewardship by Arrington of virtually all measures tied to the insurance and corporation laws of the state continued in 1963. One, Senate Bill 360, was dubbed the "Arrington Act" after the senator guided it through the legislature and Kerner signed it. Designed to broaden protection for prudent drivers against motorists driving without insurance, the bill required all automobile liability policies written or renewed in Illinois to offer the insurance buyer protection against death or injuries wrongfully caused by a financially irresponsible motorist. The casualty insurance industry asked Arrington to handle the measure.

Even on days when his bills were not the center of attention, Arrington still could be in the forefront of the news when the legislators were in session.

On April 23, 1963, Arrington collapsed at the Statehouse and was rushed by ambulance to Springfield's Memorial Hospital. He had suffered his second heart attack. Doctors expressed confidence that he again would recover, but insisted that he take a lengthy break from the legislative regimen. He reluctantly remained in the hospital until May 9, but he ignored advice that he was to do nothing but rest during the stay.

When George Hendrix, the administrator of Memorial, sought more than once to visit Arrington in his fifth floor room, he hesitated each time to interrupt the senator. As Hendrix explained in a letter to Arrington after his dismissal, "I did stop on the floor several times, but found that you were working at your job while at the same time you were a patient here."

Upon his return to the Senate, it immediately became clear that Arrington had used much of his time at Memorial to redraft his legislative package revamping public aid administration. Arrington later wrote, "It was a blessing to have the time to study the bills while in the hospital."

Arrington wasted no time getting back in the middle of the legislative grind. Paul Powell and some others in the General Assembly urged him to ease up, even offering to take over the guidance of some of his bills where politically possible. While appreciative of the overtures, Arrington was determined to show—just as he did in the wake of the recovery period after his late 1956 heart attack—that his perilous heart condition was not going to deter his pace one whit.

As the midpoint of the 1960s drew near, Arrington was a man on a mission. Actually, more than one. He clearly was emerging as the strongman of a party that had yet to regain the governmental supremacy in Illinois that it had enjoyed during most of the 1950s and a good part of the 1940s. At the same time, Arrington was establishing a beachhead for his drive to upgrade the General Assembly, to make it the hallmark of state government.

Arrington's fidelity to the legislature—his fervent commitment to its improvement—overshadowed everything else on his political radar screen. Arrington could have pushed, probably with success, for a GOP nomination for a statewide office or for a seat in Congress. Take the situation in 1962 when Republican Marguerite Stitt Church of Evanston did not seek reelection to the Thirteenth District seat in Congress. Arrington would have been tough to stop had he moved to be her replacement, which most of the time would have been a step-up according to conventional political thinking.

But, he demurred, opening the door for the election to the seat of Republican Donald H. Rumsfeld, a thirty-year-old Princeton University graduate and investment broker living in Glenview. Rumsfeld would stay in Congress for six years before departing for a series of top policy assignments under Presidents Richard M. Nixon and Gerald R. Ford. He didn't forget, though, the man who was the Republican wheelhorse back home on the North Shore during Rumsfeld's time in the United States House.

In October 2003, when Rumsfeld was secretary of defense under President George W. Bush and directing the United States' military overthrow of a brutal dictatorship in Iraq, Rumsfeld noted in written comments for this book that during his tenure in Congress, he "had the pleasure of working" with Arrington.

"Senator Arrington," said Rumsfeld, "was a dedicated public servant who applied himself with diligence, dedication and insight."

Rumsfeld's election to Congress was one of the bright spots for the Illinois GOP in the 1962 election. Republican Everett M. Dirksen was reelected to his United States Senate seat from Illinois, and GOP candidates were victorious in the statewide contests on the ballot that year. The victors included attorney William J. Scott of Evanston, who was elected state treasurer, and Ray Page, a teacher and successful basketball coach at Springfield High School, who won the race for state superintendent of public instruction. Besides retaining its control of the Illinois Senate, the GOP also held on to a slim majority in the House. However, as opposed to the previous two years, the Republican House majority stayed intact this time and elected a GOP speaker for the Seventy-third General Assembly being seated in 1963. He was John W. Lewis Jr., a farmer and auctioneer from Marshall.

Back to the 1962 balloting, one other outcome that would lead to bigger things in the future went unnoticed downstate while many Cook countians found it simply hard to believe. Richard B. Ogilvie, the facially wounded tank commander in World War II who'd gone on to become a crime-fighting federal prosecutor in Chicago, was elected sheriff of Cook. Since he beat an opponent backed by the Chicago Democratic machine, Ogilvie's victory was little short of extraordinary.

The GOP success in 1962 ignited cautious optimism that the party's comeback in Illinois would continue in the 1964 election, when the governorship and most other major state offices were on the ballot. The promising outlook faded, though, in the face of a variety of developments.

First off, the bound-for-defeat campaign of conservative United States Senator Barry M. Goldwater of Arizona, the Republican nominee for president, put an extra monkey on the back of top GOP candidates in many states, including Illinois. The uphill outlook for Illinois Republicans was exacerbated further by a hotly contested primary contest for the party's nomination for governor between Illinois Treasurer William Scott and Charles H. Percy, the Chicago industrialist who had not hesitated to impart to Arrington his views on legislative issues. Percy, a voice for a growing force of moderate (and even liberal) Republicans, defeated Scott, whose candidacy was favored by many party traditionalists and the *Chicago Tribune*, still a potent influence over Illinois Republicanism. Percy's victory left a serious split in GOP ranks that showed little signs of healing in time for a united effort by the party against a strong Democratic state ticket headed by Kerner in his bid for a second term as governor.

As if these matters were not problems enough for the GOP, the 177 members of the House were to be elected in 1964 in an unprecedented at-large election. This so-called "bed sheet ballot" was required because a state constitutional requirement for reapportionment of House districts prior to the 1964 election was not met.

A redistricting bill was passed in 1963, but Kerner vetoed it because it contained population variations he found unacceptable. The next step was the naming of a bipartisan commission, but it deadlocked when Democrats insisted that new districts overlap the Chicago city limits—a situation that would dilute Republican strength. The resulting at-large election was viewed favorably by some GOP county chairmen, who mistakenly thought the Goldwater candidacy would help the party's House nominees sweep the state.

But, Arrington and a number of political pundits had different vibes. They accurately saw Goldwater triggering an anti-Republican tide in Illinois portending ill for the party's House candidates. Unfortunately for the GOP, they were right. Democrats succeeded in electing their entire slate of 118 nominees, headed by lawyer Adlai E. Stevenson III. The Republicans were left occupying only one-third of the House seats in the Seventy-fourth General Assembly convening in 1965.

While voters did leave the Senate with a comfortable GOP majority, 33 to 25, the rest of the 1964 election went badly for Republicans at the state level. Boosted by the strong showing in Illinois of President Lyndon B. Johnson against Goldwater, Kerner and his fellow state ticket Democrats all were victorious. They included Paul Powell, the Dems' candidate for secretary of state.

Arrington himself had little trouble winning reelection in 1964 to his Fourth District Senate seat, readily dispatching the challenge of his Democratic opponent, David C. Baylor, a twenty-nine-year-old Chicago Loop attorney residing in Morton Grove. Arrington's focus in the weeks prior to the election was not as much on Baylor as on the overall GOP plight likely to result from the balloting. Accurately sensing that the electorate would leave the Senate as the sole base of Republican power in state government, Arrington was gearing in his own mind for an upcoming repeat of the 1961-1962 biennium when the Senate was the only meaningful GOP outlet in Illinois government.

This time, though, an emerging contingent of restless Republican senators felt that Arrington should be more than the de facto leader of the Senate GOP, that the time had come to formally anoint him as the chamber's president pro tempore. Their thinking was that the magnitude of the challenge for the GOP allowed no room for more of the placid leadership style of the routinely polite Bidwill.

Support for Arrington's rise to the formal leadership post was not unanimous among his GOP colleagues. Some newspapers characterized the push for Arrington as a "palace revolt" led by thirty-year-old Robert F. Hatch, a Chicago attorney and one of the newer faces among Senate Republicans. While Bidwill signaled that he would not fight to keep his job, a number of his veteran GOP Senate seatmates indicated a preference—if Bidwill was stepping aside—for the president pro tem to be even-mannered Senator George E. Drach of Springfield, a Bidwill ally who had served as majority whip. They were encouraged by Drach's stated willingness to be Bidwill's successor.

The Arrington-Drach contest, such as it was, had predictable political lines. On the one hand, noted John P. Dailey, who became an intern under Arrington late in 1964, "the Old Guard put up George Drach for leader. But, that was countered by Young Turks, led by Hatch, who worked to get together votes for Arrington."

Choosing between Arrington and Drach was the first significant political decision Chicago Republican John J. Lanigan had to make after getting elected to the Senate for the initial time in 1964. A few weeks after the election, recalled Lanigan, "Bob Hatch contacted me and said we needed to elect a new leader. He said we needed Russ.

"Hatch called a meeting of Arrington supporters at a downtown club in Chicago after the November election. Arrington was there. He said he wanted to be sure he had the votes before he'd run. Hatch had to show Russ the votes were there. Hatch was pushing Russ on this. We had to remember that Russ was not the most popular guy among the Senate Republican old-timers because he didn't play their games. I, of course, was a new guy, and I went along with Hatch on Russ from the start."

Arrington felt sufficiently comfortable with his backing to give a go-ahead for his nomination for the top job when the Senate Republicans caucused at Springfield's Sangamo Club in early December 1964 to formally elect their leader for the upcoming biennium. Arrington received 17 votes, a bare majority of the Senate's Republican number. Seven of the 33 Republicans to sit in the new Senate did not attend. Bidwill was one of those absent.

Seeing Arrington had enough votes to win, the Drach side moved at the caucus for Arrington's election to be unanimous. In Lanigan's words, "It really was pretty harmonious."

Afterward, in perhaps a mild dig at Arrington, Drach told newspersons that the election of Arrington showed that "perhaps they (Republican senators) want their leader to be a little more aggressive than I thought was desirable in the past."

His emergence as the official leader of the Senate erased any remaining doubt of Arrington being the undisputed centerpiece of the legislative spotlight. Really, little question of this had existed beforehand. John Dreiske, the *Chicago Sun-Times* political scribe whose pen seemed trained on Arrington, put the senator at the head of the class when the columnist delved in 1963 (a few weeks before Arrington's heart attack) into what Dreiske called "our inhibited" General Assembly.

The columnist contended that "the Legislature is deeply inhibited" by Arrington, whose "explosiveness sometimes exceeds his intelligence, but whose intelligence almost always eventually catches up." While Dreiske appeared to characterize an "inhibited" legislature as too restrained in its activity—something others might view as a virtue—he still pulled his punches in looking at Arrington.

"Arrington, actually, is pleasant and invigorating relief on the GOP side of the Senate," wrote Dreiske.

But, not much about the overall demeanor of the Senate impressed Dreiske at the time. In the main, he contended, members of the body were "characterized by a sort of smug lethargy which, if their eyes weren't open, you would think was sleeping sickness." He made an exception for one freshman Republican senator, Harris W. Fawell, a Naperville lawyer and middle-of-the-roader whom, according to Dreiske, "shows a somewhat disquieting tendency toward independent thinking and lively coherence."

As for the bulk of the other Republican senators, Dreiske lampooned them in saying that their "posteriors have been so closely associated with their red leather chairs that standing up to speak just about requires the services of a surgeon."

Dreiske's acerbity got no response from Arrington; he seldom ever openly commented one way or the other on what was being written about himself or his world. But, depictions of the Senate like Dreiske's stuck in Arrington's craw. Pride and vanity precluded Arrington from admitting that he was doing something in reaction to newspaper columns. Nevertheless, once he knew he'd be in complete command of the Senate, he signaled that change was coming—and right off the bat.

While he disdained hostile confrontations with reporters (even when pointing out what he considered inaccuracies in stories or columns), Arrington readily made himself available for interviews or even "backgrounders"—sessions with reporters or broadcasters in which he, not always for attribution, explained informally his or the GOP's side of things. Regular interviews were for the record, of course, and Arrington had gradually learned their usefulness in disseminating his positions and objectives to everybody, allies and foes alike. Thus, even before the Seventy-fourth General Assembly's convening on January 6, 1965, the new boss of the Senate had laid out his game plan through a series of interviews that he selectively granted. He couldn't have reaped better results through a press agent.

To wit:

"Arrington Clears Senate Decks for Action; Positive Image For GOP His Aim," blared a headline in *Paddock Publications*.

"Arrington to 'Crack Whip' As GOP's Senate Leader," warned the *Evanston Review*.

"Arrington Plans Senate Pace To Set House An Example," headlined the *Sun-Times* December 14, 1964, and "GOP State Senators Will Pursue Path of 'Affirmative Republicanism'" four days later. On December 25, 1964, *Sun-Times* readers were further greeted by the headline, "Arrington On The Move."

And on and on.

Arrington's takeover of the Senate helm seemed to be assuming a politically born-again cast. Some of those interviewing him, like Nancy Anderson of *Paddock*, said that his increasingly time-consuming devotion to the political world of Springfield meant that Arrington was pretty much retiring from practice at his Chicago law office. There were no quotes from Arrington denying this. The two GOP senators Arrington chose to serve as majority whips (assistant leaders), Robert Coulson and Joseph R. Peterson, both said they were putting their law practices on hold for the first six months of 1965, the length of the spring session, to devote their full time to legislative work.

"When we convene," predicted Coulson, "we intend to get to work, to work longer and to shame the (Democratic-controlled) House, if necessary, into meeting and working as long as we do."

Underscoring this intent, Arrington pledged in his interviews that for once the Senate would be organized for the start of business prior to its convening. In a break with tradition, he insisted on the naming before the opening gavel went down of the GOP members chairing committees. This contravened the routine practice of setting up committees in the weeks after the start of a session—a tradition that Arrington labeled a "bunch of bunk" because of its delaying effect on the consideration of legislation.

Tradition also was flouted by Arrington's serving of notice that major pieces of proposed legislation, primary planks of the Republican platform for the session, would be prepared for consideration at the beginning of the session instead of being allowed to surface only in the latter months. Indeed, his intent to have a comprehensive Republican legislative program was, in itself, a new wrinkle.

As Arrington noted to *Paddock's* Anderson, he viewed his election as Senate majority leader to be a mandate for coming up with an affirmative program for the GOP in state government.

"Unfortunately," said Arrington, "the way we've handled our affairs has given us a public image of nothing but dissension, as killers of legislation. My administration will be designed to change this." Yet, Arrington still cautioned in every sit-down with reporters that his troops would not sacrifice their responsibility for ensuring "every economy and efficiency in state government."

As for a linchpin of the Senate GOP's legislative initiatives, Arrington said that his bloc would push again for action leading to amendment of parts of the state constitution's Revenue Article that would ensure Illinoisans a more equitable basis for paying taxes. A tireless champion of past legislation proposing constitutional changes on revenue raising that voters failed to approve, Arrington vowed determination to win General Assembly approval in 1965 for placing before the electorate in the 1966 general election various alternatives for tax reform on which voters could say yes or no as a preface to Revenue Article amendment.

Arrington also pledged to focus energy on legislative passage of district reapportionment bills for the Senate as well as House. Going further, Arrington warned that Kerner could not expect Senate approval of any of the governor's new budget measures unless he had signed the remap legislation Arrington promised to get to his desk.

Arrington raised more eyebrows by revealing that Senate Republicans would entertain the passage of open occupancy legislation—as long as it did not become effective until ratified in a statewide referendum. In another sensitive area, Arrington made good on his intent to have key bills ready for immediate consideration by prefiling proposed measures for curbing conflicts of interest by state officials. In doing so, Arrington was stepping up his effort to have his party upstage Democrats in the public's mind as the main proponents of stronger ethics in government.

The Senate's new look in 1965 incorporated more than Arrington in the top post. On the Democratic minority side, Thomas A. McGloon, a fifty-three-year-old Chicago lawyer called Art by most folks, assumed the reins of leadership. Because McGloon was a genial person, quite easy to get along with, many wondered how one so amiable would stand up to the sharp-tongued, hard-driving Arrington. Fortunately for McGloon, the minority whip, Dixon, had the oratorical skills to go toe-to-toe with Arrington in floor debates. Furthermore, Dixon, then thirty-seven years old, was in the small club of senators who really knew in detail what was contained in all the bills being considered, which put him on a par with the equally astute Arrington.

Back on the GOP side, the erudite nature of the new leadership team was bolstered greatly by Arrington's elevation of Coulson to one of the two whip slots. The other whip, Joseph Peterson, a farm owner practicing law in the Bureau County seat of Princeton, came across as a crusty old salt, which he was. In selecting Peterson—a member of the Senate since 1956—to be an assistant leader, Arrington was seeking to accommodate the Republican Old Guard. Peterson was one of its number, albeit one loyal to Arrington.

The ascension of Coulson was another matter. A member of the Senate only two years when tabbed for leadership by Arrington, Coulson was a well-rounded person, a kind of Renaissance man with all the versatility that this implied. He brought competence, dignity and composure to the scene, qualities Arrington wanted to impart in striving to project a more positive picture of the Senate.

There certainly were things in Coulson's background that separated him from a number of others in the Senate—Democrats as well as Republicans.

His World War II experiences had the earmarks of a spy novel. After his stint as a Stateside army legal officer, Coulson went to China in 1945 as a captain volunteering for dangerous assignments with the Office of Strategic Services. For these missions, he'd received training, as he worded it, in "lock picking, explosives, special camera (techniques) and assassination and suicide methods."

Although the Japanese surrender coincided with his arrival in Asia, he became involved in negotiating the capitulation of numerous hostile Japanese troops in China and in securing the safe release of Bataan death march survivors as well as the rescue of American flyers who'd dropped into enemy territory in the Chinese back country.

This was ticklish business because China was awash with chaos from the postwar clashes of Mao Tse-tung's Red army, Chiang Kai-shek's Nationalist forces, local warlords, recalcitrant Japanese units and even well-armed bandits. Coulson escaped hostile gunfire on one mission to rescue downed American flyers held prisoner by bandits, but never erased from his memory the "ping-ping" of the bullets hitting his jeep. He also didn't forget that, while the bandits were detaining him and his men at gunpoint, the desperadoes "served us a 'meal' which included raw monkey brains, right out of the skull." After Communist soldiers reasoned with the bandits, Coulson's group and the captive flyers were released. Coulson was formally commended for the success of the mission.

Following the war, the University of Chicago law graduate was elected mayor of Waukegan, ousting an incumbent Democrat tied to corruption allegations in the working-class factory town. Taking office in 1949, Coulson established a reputation as a reform mayor, who, among other things, insisted on integrating the police and fire departments. He resigned as mayor after his election to the Illinois House in 1956.

Moving on to the Senate in the 1962 election, representing a district covering Boone, Lake and McHenry counties, Coulson marched to his own drumbeat, hardly liberal but still enough of the onetime Young Turk mayor not to be a Bidwill guy.

As Chicago attorney William R. Coulson phrased it in a 2003 interview, years after the death of his father, Robert Coulson, Arrington anointed his dad because "Arrington didn't want just 'yes' men."

"My father made a good number two guy because Arrington wasn't afraid to surround himself with capable people who might challenge him," said Coulson. "The things that Arrington did demand from those in his circle were honesty and integrity. He also wanted to have at his side people who talked only when they had something to say, and dad was that kind of person."

On a more personal note, William Coulson recollected his own firsthand contact with Arrington in the late 1960s, when Coulson was a law student at the University of Illinois. Noting that he "tried to spend as much time in Springfield with dad as I could," Coulson remembered "playing games with Arrington in which he'd show off his incredible memory by challenging me to test it on words and names and things."

"In those days," Coulson remarked, "people were in awe of Arrington. It was his self-assuredness and so much else, even down to the impeccably beautiful suits he wore. Yet, he never talked down to me. Quite the opposite, he made time in the day for young people who showed promise, who showed they wanted to make something of themselves."

Most certainly, Arrington's interest in young individuals eyeing roles in government became full-blown after he became boss of the Senate. His goals were at least twofold. One, he felt that state government would benefit overall from the structured nurturing of bright young men and women (mainly men at the start of this undertaking) who would commit to careers in public life—whether through key administrative roles or, in the cases of some, election to public office.

Secondly, Arrington believed that the quality of the General Assembly's performance was greatly impaired by the absence of competent, professional staffers. Actually, permanent staffing of any kind had been virtually nonexistent in the legislature itself (although some staffing was available in two General Assembly support operations—the Legislative Council and the Legislative Reference Bureau). Even secretarial help was lacking for rank and file members.

To Arrington, this was a void that had ballooned into a glaring deficiency in the legislative process—a ridiculous shortcoming that forced lawmakers to act on increasingly numerous and complex bills and issues with hardly any in-depth research or unbiased input available. Even decisions on matters approaching life and death seriousness frequently were made in an information vacuum.

Arrington was hell-bent on rectifying the situation. He had been a key catalyst for the start of an Illinois legislative internship program in the early 1960s. When he became Senate leader, he moved—darn near unilaterally—for greater emphasis on the program, which served both parties in the two chambers. Also, he was determined to bring professional staffing to the legislature, either by getting the interns to stay around after the end of their internships or through other avenues. He was determined to do this even if he had to foot the bill himself. And, in the early going, that is precisely what he did.

The first significant step in this direction came on the heels of his election as GOP leader when he revealed the appointment of William G. Simpson of Kenilworth as paid research director for Senate Republicans. Arrington said that he was hiring Simpson "at my expense" because the legislature provided no appropriation for such a position. Simpson's task was to come up with solid background and data for use by Senate Republicans in reaching policy decisions.

Simpson, a former lay director of the Catholic Archdiocese of Chicago and deputy administrator of the Small Business Administration in Washington, most recently had been a top aide in the unsuccessful Percy campaign for governor. In hiring Simpson, Arrington also was moving to help bridge a split in the Illinois GOP between backers of Percy and William Scott. Simpson had favored Scott in his primary battle with Percy for the gubernatorial nomination. However, Simpson joined the Percy campaign after the primary and would have spearheaded plans for Percy's takeover of state government in event he'd won the election.

Arrington also felt in retaining Simpson, a United States Military Academy graduate, that he was bringing on board a blue-ribbon guy, the kind that might engender more respect for the legislature. Building a favorable impression of the General Assembly was always an endgame for Arrington, and respect for the chambers was widely thought to be at a very low ebb at the end of 1964.

Many in Illinois, Arrington included, were especially stung by one episode in 1964 that cast an unusually dark shadow over the state's lawmakers. It was the publication during the year of an article in *Harper's* magazine entitled "The Illinois Legislature: A Study in Corruption." It was written by Al Balk, a feature writer for national magazines, and—most troublesome for Illinoisans—Paul Simon, a Democratic member of the Illinois Senate from the Madison County hamlet of Troy.

The piece ignited quite a storm in portraying the legislature as a cesspool of blatant corruption. Members were depicted as routinely taking payoffs for votes and accepting free trips and other gifts from individuals for whom the lawmakers granted favors. Simon suggested at one point that rumors held that one influential legislator averaged as much as $100,000 a session from bribes, which Simon admitted was a barely camouflaged reference to Powell. Certain columnists and others skeptical about legislative ethics had a field day with the article, jumping on it as confirmation of their long-held suspicions of legislators and boodle.

Although *Harper's* caught the Illinois political world by surprise, Simon's role was not as astonishing. In the years since his unexpected election to the House in 1954 and subsequent elevation to the Senate in 1962, Simon was a true political anomaly for Illinois. A small town newspaper publisher of scrupulous honesty, Simon was a breath of fresh air in the legislature to reformers and good government types. He never hesitated to openly question and vote against unsavory measures in which the public interest was sacrificed for the personal gains of some legislators. Simon was not alone among his colleagues in smelling bills that stunk to high heaven, but many of the others—although maybe not on the take— -were compromised to an extent that they did not oppose the nefarious stuff.

In his House years, Simon was perhaps the first among equals in a small Democratic band that functioned as a kind of "truth squad" or House "conscience" when political morality or ethics surfaced as issues in the chamber's proceedings. When something didn't smell right on a particular piece of legislation, these individuals no longer kowtowed to their own party's leadership—and certainly not to the GOP. They were not hesitant to go public when they smelled a rat, letting the chips fall where they might.

At one time or another, Simon's sidekicks in this gang were W. Richard Stengel of Rock Island, the refreshingly forthright Abner J. Mikva of Chicago and peppery Anthony Scariano of Park Forest. All

Lt. Governor Paul Simon with Senator Arrington

three were lawyers and World War II vets. The group also could often count on the comradeship of Dixon in his early Young Turk years in the House in the 1950s. Dixon and Simon, coming from neighboring St. Clair and Madison counties, were close throughout their long political careers (for a time, Dixon had ties to the business side of a chain of Downstate newspapers that Simon acquired).

Predictably, this little contingent enjoyed a ready rapport with many in the Statehouse press corps. Just as predictably, some in the House, representing both sides of the aisle, viewed the Simonites as conflictive or, to put it more bluntly, pains in the neck. To many old hands, Simon and the others were upstarts who failed to appreciate time-honored ways of conducting business in the House. They just came on as too sanctimonious, it was suggested, and none more so than Simon, a son of a Lutheran minister.

Thus, as for Simon, the *Harper's* feature was a last straw in the eyes of his detractors. Simon had grossly violated an unwritten but cardinal rule that incumbent legislators, in actions outside the chambers, don't say or do anything to impugn the character of colleagues. A code of silence was expected to be observed. It was hardly surprising that Senator Hudson Sours, a sharp-tongued Republican attorney from Peoria, prompted jeers and laughter when he stood up at a

Senate dinner after the appearance of the *Harper's* article and announced that Simon had won the "Benedict Arnold Award." Previous recipients, added Sours, were Judas Iscariot and Aaron Burr.

Arrington did not join in the open ostracism of Simon. He was among numerous legislators recognizing that Simon was calling attention to an undeniable cancer in the legislature. Yet, Arrington, along with virtually every other lawmaker with the exception of Simon, refrained from airing the legislature's dirty linen in public.

Incidentally, Simon went into this facet of Arrington when Simon was interviewed for this book a few months before his death near the end of 2003. Simon had things to say about Arrington, much of it laudatory about what Simon saw as Arrington's large impact on the governing of Illinois.

As for dealing with the dark side of legislative activities, though, Simon felt that Arrington could have done more.

"There was no question, ever, that Senator Arrington himself was personally honest through his legislative career," Simon noted. "There was also no question that he came to have great power (in the General Assembly), and that he knew what was going on aboveboard and otherwise. He was probably, at least certainly in his peak years, the one person in the legislature that could have forcefully addressed the shenanigans."

"Now," Simon continued, "I am not saying that he did not try to straighten some people out behind the scene. Maybe he did. But, I felt...I wished that he'd confronted out in the open some of the unsavory stuff he was aware of. If so, he was the one who probably couldn't have been ignored."

In the years before the *Harper's* piece came out, little interaction had occurred between Arrington and Simon. Arrington was leaving the House for the Senate at the time Simon entered the lower chamber. And, Simon had not been in the Senate for even two years when the article appeared. In years to follow, as Simon moved up the political ladder and Arrington guided the Senate, the two would get to know each other quite well. More on that to come.

Back to 1964 and *Harper's*, Arrington recognized that the story was another black eye for the General Assembly. He knew it steepened the grade he was determined to climb in order to make the legislature an institution to which people could point with pride. He had his work cut out for him.

Columnist Dreiske, the inveterate Arrington watcher, took wind of the challenge facing Arrington in writing, as Arrington became Senate captain, that the senator "is a showman, and showmanship is needed in the Senate leadership. Of course, it can be carried too far, and Arrington now and then probably will carry it too far."

Still, presaged Dreiske, while there was "nothing new about Arrington in the Senate…his new authority will automatically produce a new Arrington."

A variety of folks were waiting to see about that.

Chapter 14

℃

Arrington's Disciples

On June 17, 1996, when Jim Edgar was governor of Illinois, he hosted a reception and dinner at the Executive Mansion for a group of individuals with whom he'd shared a unique bond in earlier days. Each had served as a legislative intern or staff member—or both—under Russell Arrington. Nary a one would deny that it was a life-shaping experience.

In the decades following Arrington's era, interns and staffers flooded the Statehouse, becoming an indispensable part of the legislative process. It was hard to imagine that legislators, lobbyists, newsies and everybody else tied to the General Assembly once existed without them. How did the Capitol operate without their issue analyses, without their development of bills, without their tracking of measures in and out of committees, without their shepherding of the endless housekeeping tasks encumbering an increasingly complex legislature?

More than any other person, Arrington spawned and nursed the use of staff members. This was one of the reasons for Michael J. Madigan to call Arrington "the father of the modern General Assembly." Madigan, a Chicago Democrat whose first of numerous terms as House speaker began in 1983, himself exhibited many of Arrington's leadership characteristics in presiding with a firm hand over the lower chamber. Those traits included insistence on top-notch staff members.

One of the initial points made by Madigan in an interview for this book was that Arrington's generation of staff members turned out to be crucial "in terms of legislative services, the quality of the work and the product of the legislature." In Madigan's years as speaker, he also ensured that his staff was second to none.

However, back in the 1960s, it was the Arrington staff that stole the show—the crew that laid the foundation for cementing the importance of strong legislative staff work. Gene Callahan, another Democrat and a highly respected figure in and around Illinois government in the latter part of the twentieth century, echoed Madigan in saying that Arrington's push for staff was a key reason for Arrington becoming "the godfather" of the modern Illinois legislature.

Furthermore, Callahan declared in an interview, "No legislative staff ever worked harder than Russell Arrington's."

The mark left by those staffers remained indelible. They were called Arrington's army, his troops or, by some, his disciples. Arrington himself had a name for the ones who first came under his tutelage as interns. He called them "Gove's Guerrillas." The moniker referred to Samuel K. Gove, a University of Illinois political science professor who spearheaded the start of the General Assembly's legislative staff internship program in the early 1960s—an undertaking ensured of momentum because it enjoyed the supportive political muscle of Arrington buttressed by backing from a few other legislators, including Abner Mikva in the House.

A good number of these disciples or "guerrillas" were on hand for the Arrington gang reunion in 1996 at the behest of Edgar, who went the furthest of any of them politically.

More than any other person, Arrington molded Edgar for a successful career in public life that reached a zenith with his election in 1990 to the first of two successive terms as governor. When the former governor sat down with this writer at an Urbana, Illinois, restaurant on Saint Patrick's Day in 2003, he expressed regret that Arrington died before he (Edgar) won Illinois' highest office.

Yet, while Edgar wished that Arrington had lived to see him elected governor, he quickly added that Arrington "still might have been more proud of my election to the House."

Edgar, who grew up in Charleston, was elected to the lower chamber in the 1970s, but left his seat of his own volition to join the staff of then Governor James Thompson.

"When I quit the legislature and went to work for Thompson," recalled Edgar, "the toughest thing for me to handle was to call Arrington and tell him what I was doing. There was, remember, no greater advocate, even nationally, for the importance of state legislatures."

The Arrington chapter in the Jim Edgar story has similar touches to the stories of others whose roles in life were influenced greatly by Arrington.

The path that led Edgar to Arrington faced a juncture on a particular spring day in 1968, shortly before his graduation from Eastern Illinois University. The morning of that day, Edgar learned that he had been accepted for admission to the University of Illinois law school. However, later the same day, Edgar received a telegram from professor Gove informing him he'd been selected for the legislative staff internship program—for which he had interviewed.

Faced with a decision, the twenty-one-year-old Edgar could not ignore the fact that he was already married and that he and his wife Brenda had a son. Thus, for a person with, in his words, "a family to feed," the $600-a-month check coming with the internship weighed heavily. He said yes to Gove, a move that punched his ticket to the world of the Statehouse.

As he entered the internship, Edgar was not certain of his assignment. He considered himself a liberal Republican at the time, but wouldn't have minded working with a prominent House Democrat, Clyde Choate. Choate was from Brenda's hometown of Anna and was a friend of Brenda's father, Don Smith. Edgar hadn't met Arrington, but was aware that many referred to the senator as "Arrogant Arrington" behind his back.

On his fourth or fifth day in the program, though, Edgar was informed that he was assigned to Arrington. Coincidentally, that same day Edgar met Arrington, a first look that the future governor found very impressionable. The occasion was a meeting at Chicago's Bismarck Hotel of the Illinois Legislative Council. The panel of legislators and the lieutenant governor carried out research requested by lawmakers and supervised the internship program in conjunction with the University of Illinois Institute of Government and Public Affairs, which was directed by Gove. As the Senate's president pro tem, Arrington was an ex officio member of the council.

"I just shook hands with him that day," Edgar related. "I was scared to death of him. I'd been led to believe he was a forceful conservative obstructionist. He had been the last one I wanted to work with."

Nevertheless, Edgar couldn't ignore what he observed that first day. Although Republican Representative John Conolly of Waukegan was council chairman, Edgar watched Arrington "obviously running the show." Everyone, Democrats as well as Republicans, noted Edgar, "deferred to Arrington."

If Edgar still entertained any doubt about going with Arrington, it was erased, he noted, "when I learned quickly enough that his interns had the most influence." It was "not just that he was considered the father of the intern program," added Edgar, "but that interns got their best shot at playing meaningful roles with Arrington."

Edgar's internship ended shortly after the windup of the General Assembly's 1969 spring session, one of the most dynamic in state history. He then accepted an immediate invitation to join Arrington's permanent Senate GOP staff, a job that entailed a move to Chicago for the next year and a half to serve as a personal aide to the senator. Besides exercising a deft hand on legislative matters, Edgar emerged (along with fellow staffers Tom Corcoran and John Dailey) as an especially politically astute member of Arrington's young coterie.

"I became a political guy on the staff," said Edgar, adding that he had "to worry" about the standing of the Republican senators in their districts.

"The truth of the matter was that Arrington really didn't care about politics nearly as much as government substance. He had to be dragged to political dinners."

Like many others in Arrington's circle, Edgar never overcame "always being nervous around him." Just as others pointed out, Edgar remained conscious of an aura around Arrington, a nimbus surrounding his bearing that even extended to his "dressing so well, to his gray hair, to those distinguished sideburns."

"Believe me," stressed Edgar, "you just knew that you didn't want to screw up around the guy."

Edgar may have briefly jeopardized his relationship with his boss when he worked up the courage to ask Arrington for more than the $9,000-a-year salary he was to receive when he became a permanent member of Arrington's crew. Later on, Edgar said that Donald Tolva, a former intern who was Arrington's chief of staff at the time, "told me that Arrington said he was thinking of firing me when I requested more money." It didn't happen, and, moreover, Edgar added, "higher pay was coming in the end, but not much at first."

Arrington's influence over Edgar sometimes even worked in reverse. Edgar hated Arrington's early start of each workday during legislative sessions with a 7 a.m. breakfast at which attendance by staffers and interns was mandatory. This was still on Edgar's mind when, as governor, he refused—with few exceptions—to schedule early morning breakfast meetings.

However, back in his Arrington days, Edgar and his compatriots shook in their boots at the mere thought of failure to be on time for the breakfasts at the State House Inn, the hotel on Adams Street a block north of the Capitol where Arrington maintained a suite. To show up late was a cardinal sin—especially since Arrington himself was paying for the breakfasts.

More than once, recalled staffer Dick Buckley, "the lights in the breakfast room hadn't even been turned on at 7 a.m." On those occasions, he recounted, "Arrington would go and turn the lights on himself, and he'd yell to the hired hands to open up and get going because it was time for breakfast."

The breakfasts were crucial in Arrington's scheme of things because, before dismissing his charges, the agenda for the day in the Senate was mapped out. Even before other GOP senators, the staffers knew what bills were to be called on the Senate floor, which of those were likely to be passed and which ones were not. Every staff member or intern had a specific role to play in one or more aspects of the day's business. Each also was assigned issues or subjects on which they had better be up to snuff when Arrington peppered them for updates or additional information. This meant that, among other details to be covered, each aide was expected to have read the daily Chicago newspapers before the breakfasts so as to be aware of any breaking news on his assigned area.

There was still another direction of the breakfasts which reflected an intrinsic part of Arrington's leadership style. It was described by disciple Richard W. Carlson in the following words:

"When the General Assembly was in session, he (Arrington) would send out the young staff people to mingle in the bars and other gathering spots at night and listen to what the Republican senators were talking about. Their gripes, their concerns, things like that. We were his eyes and ears. Then, the next morning, we had to tell him at breakfast what we had heard. He wanted to know everything the guys were talking about. Of course, he had a photographic memory, which meant he recorded every tidbit he was told. Later, in caucus, our senators couldn't believe that Arrington knew all about their concerns. They didn't know we were reporting back to him on what we had heard in the bars the night before."

The breakfasts usually were followed by caucuses of the GOP senators in the Statehouse prior to the convening of the Senate or committee meetings. Traditionally, legislative caucuses were inviolably closed to all but elected members, but Arrington knocked down that wall by bringing one or two staffers with him to the caucuses. He also flouted convention by sometimes ushering an aide or two into top-level political summits on major issues. This was not kosher.

Once, during a critical confab in the 1965 session on the state budget, Arrington asked Buckley, who was concentrating on fiscal issues for the Senate GOP, to accompany him to a closed-door session with Mayor Richard J. Daley, Governor Kerner and James A. Ronan, the state finance director and Illinois Democratic chairman. The three Democrats appeared uncomfortable with Buckley's presence.

Finally, Daley looked at Arrington and said, "I didn't know staff would be here."

Buckley arose to leave, but was stopped by Arrington.

"Dick, just sit down," ordered Arrington in a terse tone.

Without question, Arrington's insertion of his staffers into situations once considered off-limits was known to irritate a lot of persons, including more than a few of the hidebound Republican senators. Years had to pass before some no longer viewed the young aides as smarty-pants upstarts intruding in a sacrosanct setting of elected lawmakers. The resentment toward Arrington over the new arrivals hardly could be contained as the staffers moved with boundless energy off and on the hallowed Senate floor, or hovered with impenetrable expressions behind Arrington's chair.

Even after the passage of time and the staffers' gradual acceptance, their image in many eyes never went beyond that of automatons. Most were, after all, or could be statistical machines and walking encyclopedias on the background of complex issues. When summoned, they might convey much more information than a legislator cared to know. If one of them seemed at times to be oblivious to political realities, it was because all but a few entered the scene with no knowledge of gut-level politics—of what some members had to do to get elected or remain in their seats.

As Buckley saw it, "Change can be a difficult thing, and our (the young staffers) coming on was a dramatic change. We had to proceed delicately since it was true that we weren't greeted with open arms. We did eventually overcome it, even though a few old-timers never stopped grousing about having to deal with kids."

The uneasiness also was flamed, added Buckley, "by a feeling of some on our side of the aisle that the staffers came between the Republican senators and Arrington, their leader."

This may not have been an unreasonable suspicion. Arrington did make the rounds at night with other members in his early General Assembly years, but as Senate Republican leader he seldom was seen dining or otherwise socializing with fellow GOP solons. Observing the evening dining companions of major officials in Springfield was good sport for those trying to detect nuances in political developments. But Arrington gave tracers little to go on. When he was spotted eating out, his table was shared more often than not by only one or more of his staffers.

Being an Arrington disciple enveloped one in an air of mystique that simply did not extend to staffers for other legislative leaders. If all of the young men and lesser numbered women assisting legislative leaders through the years were to have constituted an army, those assigned to Arrington would have been its elite unit.

The names of some who came to Arrington as interns were among those listed on a special plaque on a wall outside the fourth floor Senate bill room in the Statehouse. The names comprised the Samuel K. Gove Illinois Legislative Internship Hall of Fame, an undertaking of *Illinois Issues* magazine honoring onetime interns whose later careers were marked by outstanding public service. One of those named was Richard W. Carlson.

His story mirrored that of a number of the other disciples. Carlson described himself as a Swedish Lutheran Republican, which was apt in that his father, Hugo Carlson, was a first generation Swede who ran a corner grocery store in a suburb of Minneapolis, while his mother, Sylvia, a nurse, was a Norwegian immigrant who entered the United States through Ellis Island in 1922.

When he was working on a master's degree in political science at the University of Illinois in 1968, Carlson sought admission to the legislative internship program headed by one of his professors, Gove. Like other applicants, he had to clear two hurdles—maintenance of high academic standing and survival of an interview by the directors of the majority and minority staffs in each chamber. Carlson passed muster and joined eleven others for a nine-month internship beginning in the fall of 1969. He was one of three in the twelve (along with Richard M. Bird of Chicago and H. Thomas Schwertfeger of Litchfield) assigned to Arrington.

Carlson's introduction to Arrington came when he, Bird and Schwertfeger were ushered into Arrington's spacious Statehouse office only days before the start of a brief autumn session of the legislature. "He (Arrington) welcomed us with a pep talk, and told us how important we were," said Carlson. "He said we were going to be exposed to the entire legislative process, beginning right away."

Sure enough, before he could catch his breath, Carlson was writing bills and drafting amendments to others—measures that were going to be heard and passed. "It was," he remarked, "pretty heady stuff to be happening so quickly."

By the end of his internship in 1970, Carlson said, "the experience had shaped my work ethic for the rest of my career. Everything was traceable back to Arrington...his professional integrity, his attention to details, his insistence on getting things right, his demand for loyalty from those working with him."

Following the internship, Carlson became a regular Arrington staff member. Among his subsequent posts, he was superintendent of the Illinois State Lottery (Carlson wrote the legislation authorizing the lottery) and assistant director of the Illinois Department of Insurance. Many others who came out of Arrington's stable had parallel track records.

In the years after their Arrington staff or Senate Republican internship days, Richard J. Carlson (no relation to Richard W. Carlson) headed the Illinois Environmental Protection Agency; Tom Corcoran was elected to Congress from a north central Illinois district; John Alexander was a vice president of the Illinois Constitutional Convention of 1970; William S. Hanley served as Governor Richard B. Ogilvie's legislative counsel; Robert Cahill, Stephen Pacey and William DeCardy became judges in the Illinois court system; Richard E. Dunn filled major inspector roles for the Illinois State Police; Bruce D. Locher went on to be a prosecutor and respected Springfield attorney; and John Dailey became a bank president and the 1982 Republican candidate for Illinois treasurer. Edgar's ballot box success spoke for itself—state representative, secretary of state and the governorship.

Still other Arringtonites realized considerable accomplishments in the private business world. Attorney Donald Tolva became a real estate developer in the Chicago area. Martin Geraghty went on to be the founder and president of a commercial real estate firm in the windy city, and Timothy Campbell served as a top insurance industry official in New England.

And the list went on.

Because they were Illinois versions of the best and the brightest—always the cool bunch with ready answers on the issues for lawmakers and reporters alike—they probably couldn't be blamed for coming on as so darn cocksure of themselves. They never appeared to flinch or bat an eye in carrying out business. But then, they could afford to be imperturbable to all comers because they operated behind the shield of Arrington. If one survived the test of fire with Arrington himself, dealing with others could be kids' play.

Little could unsettle the disciples, except the man they called the boss. For many like Jim Edgar, even the first glimpse of or initial encounter with Arrington was an indelible occasion. Nothing about it was trivial, not even a handshake. Just ask Richard E. Dunn.

Before learning to which legislative leader he'd be assigned during his internship, Dunn was invited to a lunch with Arrington at Springfield's Leland Hotel. While Dunn wasn't quite sure what to expect, he was convinced that the inevitable shaking of hands with Arrington was of great importance. This was bred in him.

Dunn was a son of Richard T. Dunn, a Bloomington lawyer and a commanding general in the Illinois National Guard, and the grandson of Richard F. Dunn, also a Bloomington attorney and onetime GOP chairman of McLean County. It was grandfather Dunn who imbued upon young Richard the saliency of a handshake.

"Grandpa was famous for his vigorous handshakes," related Dunn. "I'd learned from him that the first handshake makes a big impression. So, I was really ready for it at that first meeting with Arrington. I'd had a summer construction job, and I was in great shape and very tan. When it came time to shake Arrington's hand, I saw that he, too, was very tan."

With his grandfather's words to the wise in mind, Dunn said he took Arrington's hand and "really squeezed it hard." In return, continued Dunn, "Arrington squeezed right back, and we became involved in an exchange of firm handshakes that became almost a standoff for several seconds. This ended when Arrington looked me in the eyes and said, 'Nice tan.'"

Later, surmised Dunn, "I actually thought that my strong handshake had something to do with it when Sam Gove told me I was being assigned to Arrington."

Taken lightly or not, Dunn's anecdote reflected the solicitousness accorded so much about Arrington. Inclusion in his orbit meant being constantly alert to his movements, his inclinations, his habits. Arrington commanded rapt attention from his charges. Where he was concerned, none dared to take anything for granted. Something could be discerned from everything he did, right down to the orchestration of his ever present cigars.

To digress for a moment, it must be noted that Arrington hardly ever was seen without a cigar in the 1960s. While he'd finally ditched cigarettes as a result of his heart problems, he apparently felt that his perilous condition could weather cigars. He preferred to smoke those elongated ones, expertly rolled in Havana, that he procured from Clem Stone's stock. When his supply of them ran out during long stays in Springfield, he'd resort to plan B. That's where a fellow like John Alexander came in.

Alexander, a lanky intern from Virden and a Monmouth College graduate, wasn't always called to the chief's office for matters of state. Frequently, it was to hear the words, "Johnnie, go get me some cigars." With that, Arrington always handed Alexander a $5 bill, and the young man was on his way down to the news-cigar stand off the Capitol's first-floor rotunda. The stand was manned by a blind individual, a nice gentleman whose first name was Carl.

"When I got to the stand," related Alexander, "Carl would immediately recognize my voice and know that I was buying more cigars for Senator Arrington. So, he'd automatically bring out the highest priced or best cigars he had available."

Cigars were, of course, a trademark for more Illinois politicians than Arrington. However, it was the way he manipulated his cigars and the extent to which they were smoked that were telltale signs of what was going on with the senator.

For instance, when Arrington appeared at the early morning breakfasts with his crew, some looked to see whether his cigar was freshly lit or burned down to a stub. If it was a stub, it was assumed Arrington had been up and about for some hours—probably pondering ahead of time an issue for which one or more of his team had better be prepared to thoroughly discuss.

More portentously, his cigars were an outlet for anger. During their internships, Alexander and Richard J. Carlson were permitted to accompany Arrington to another one of those budget summits involving the senator, Mayor Daley and Governor Kerner. Standing back in Kerner's office, the interns watched Arrington confront Daley on a point in dispute and angrily upbraid the mayor in a fashion to which the mayor surely was not accustomed. Arrington's cigar played a role.

"Daley said something that obviously ticked off Arrington," Alexander recalled. "Arrington turned beet red, and then his cigar started really twitching. That was a sure tip-off. The next thing, we heard Arrington snapping to Daley, 'You don't impress me one bit.' As Daley muttered something back in kind, Kerner looked horrified and seemed to wilt. He was trying to pretend he didn't hear the exchange."

The meeting soon came to an abrupt end, but not before Alexander watched Arrington and Daley try to stare each other down, a deadlock punctuated by Arrington forcefully tamping down his cigar for effect in an ashtray on the table between the senator and mayor.

It didn't take long for those around Arrington to run for cover—if they could—when he began to chomp on his cigar, sending it up and down out of his mouth like a seesaw. "When the vigorous chewing started," explained Buckley, "you knew he was agitated about something, and it was time to get out of his way."

Occasionally, the cigar shot up and down because of situations that were not a matter of great public importance. Take the day when Arrington was informed that John Dailey had rammed the senator's latest black Cadillac (Arrington purchased a new car about every year) into an older auto driven by an elderly fellow. The accident took place as Dailey was leaving a Springfield car wash during lunch hour.

Resurrecting the incident, which left him more than a tad red-faced, Dailey said he was "pulling out onto a one-way street, and happened to be looking in the wrong direction for traffic. The damage to Russ' car was minimal, but the other one was a total loss. Well, Russ just paid the poor old guy off so he could get a decent replacement car since his insurance would not have covered his loss."

When Dailey gingerly approached Arrington about the mishap, the young aide later confessed that "yes, he (Arrington) did chastise me. To put it nicely, he gave me a stern admonition to pay attention when I was driving his car."

Dailey's gaffe, in which he fortunately escaped injury, punctured the usually serious demeanor of Arrington's Statehouse world by generating some good-natured kidding—out of Arrington's earshot, of course. Other happenings here and there also brought levity to Arrington's inner sanctum.

An episode in point. One brainy young man, having been admitted to the internship program with his heart set on being assigned to Arrington, considered himself lucky to spy the senator at a Cubs' game at Wrigley Field. Seizing the moment, the chap boldly approached Arrington and introduced himself to the senator and a woman companion. Afterward, this individual penned a note to Arrington expressing delight at meeting the senator and his wife. The correspondence was sent to the Edgemere house, where Ruth Arrington opened it and read it. She found it enlightening in that she had not accompanied her husband to Wrigley Field that day. She was not amused.

The consequence was twofold. One, Arrington, the holy terror of Springfield, was sheepishly on the defensive as he explained in carefully chosen words the set of circumstances that placed him at the ballpark with another woman. Second, the new intern, although having been led to believe he'd make the Arrington team, suddenly found himself assigned without explanation to another legislative leader.

Was Arrington petty in obviously rejecting the well-meaning young fellow? Some thought so. More than a few also viewed Arrington as small-minded several years later when he hit the ceiling over a Senate Democratic intern's filing for election to the Senate while still in the intern program. The person was lawyer Terry L. Bruce of Olney. He was seeking a seat, being vacated by a retiring Republican, that represented a GOP-leaning district in southeastern Illinois. Arrington fumed that Democrat Bruce was unfairly exploiting his internship.

Injury was added to insult for Arrington when Bruce upset his Republican opponent in the election to become, at twenty-six years of age, an exceptionally young member of the Senate. Later on, Bruce's election to Congress from southern Illinois definitely stamped him as one of the intern program's most politically adept products.

While Arrington's piques received wide play, his gracious side—even magnanimous or certainly paternalistic at times—was readily visible to those under him. They assured doubters that Arrington evinced a very human dimension when he was out of the public spotlight.

Thomas Easterly was a bit of an anachronism when he was hired in 1968 as a Senate Republican committee staffer, mainly to focus on complex transportation issues. Easterly was forty-eight years old and the father of six children when he came to state government from Carbondale, where his father had been a businessman and mayor. Easterly was not a college graduate, another thing separating him from most others in the Arrington fold. Dubbed with the sobriquet "old man on staff" by some of the interns and even regarded by a few as "an old political hack," Easterly had to labor extra hard to earn his stripes. Arrington himself didn't make it any easier for Easterly at the start.

The first three times Easterly saw Arrington the senator could not remember his name. The third occasion was especially memorable. Asked to come to Arrington's Statehouse office for some long-forgotten reason, Easterly arrived to find none other than Richard M. Nixon standing there. Nixon had stopped to touch base with his friend Arrington while in Springfield during his successful campaign for the presidency in 1968.

"Arrington tried to introduce me to Nixon," Easterly related, "but the senator just couldn't remember my name. So, I quietly whispered who I was to Arrington, and then he identified me to Nixon. I then, on my own, told Nixon I was new on the staff."

A few days after that encounter, Easterly's self-confidence finally got a shot in the arm as he strode into the lobby of the Palmer House in Chicago to attend an Arrington-related function. Easterly spotted Arrington across the lobby and also observed that Arrington had noticed him. In a flash, said Easterly, Arrington "shot over the lobby to me and, before I could say a word, told me in a firm voice, 'Don't tell me your name...I know it.' He then went out of his way to introduce me to a number of people."

From then on, Easterly said he had "an ever growing feeling that Arrington kind of liked me, maybe in part because I too had come out of a coal field area." It also gratified Easterly to have Arrington periodically offer him one of the Havana cigars. This was a "person-al touch" in Easterly's mind, much appreciated in that, he contend-ed, the cigars were not handed out to the younger staffers.

As part of his march toward acceptance in the Arrington world, Easterly and his wife Billie hosted a staff party that unintentionally added more fodder to the Arrington lore.

Not long after Arrington showed up, Easterly's youngest child, Warren, entered the party scene with a complaint that a shoestring was broken. Arrington sought to come to the rescue by taking the string out of one of his own shoes. The senator was on the verge of being the hero of the hour.

"When Russ asked Warren to take off the shoe with the broken string and give it to him," Easterly recalled, "Warren said 'no.' Russ' string was black, and Warren insisted that he wanted a white shoestring. So, we had to stand and watch Russ lace his string back in his shoe."

"Boy," continued Easterly, "I was embarrassed. I tried to get Warren to at least thank Russ, but he wouldn't even do that. Russ was taken aback a little by this. He wasn't used to people saying no to him, not even governors. Russ didn't stay long after that. Of course, he wouldn't have stayed too long anyway."

Parties from which Arrington did not depart were the ones he himself threw for his crew after the windup of legislative sessions, either at Edgemere or a summer home of Marion Belland near the shore of Wisconsin's Lake Geneva. The long sloping yard of the Belland house was perfect for the interns to toss around a football, much like Kennedy family members did at Cape Cod's Hyannis Port or Paul Simon loved to do with reporters on the lawn of his big old home in Troy. The Arrington outings were restricted to his protégés in the government world—although Clem Stone or Leonard Lavin sometimes joined the staffers at Edgemere to enjoy the warm hospi-tality of Ruth Arrington.

At moments when the smoking lamps were lit—in the off-hours—Arrington was not hesitant to offer fatherly advice to any of his people requesting it. His paternalism surfaced in other ways too. He wanted everything connected with his world to have the best face possible. When Don Tolva married his sweetheart, nurse Beth Bryan, in 1969,

Left to right: Don Tolva, Marcia Marcusson, Mike Perry,
Senator Arrington, John Dailey, Michael B. Arrington, Tom Corcoran
and Dick Buckley, legislative interns and staff

the couple drove off from the ceremony at Saint Ita Catholic Church on Chicago's north side in Arrington's Cadillac. Arrington, who attended the wedding, gave the pair twelve place settings of china.

Arrington's largess was seen mostly in his determination to channel stocks, primarily certificates of Combined Insurance or Alberto-Culver, to his staffers. Some, like Easterly, received a nominal number of shares as gifts at Christmas. Others were encouraged to invest in the market rather heavily through loans from Arrington or facilitated by Arrington.

Not atypical was Arrington's arrangement at one point that made it possible for Buckley, Dailey and Corcoran to each buy thousands of dollars worth of Combined Insurance stock. Arrington's goal in doing this, explained Buckley, "was to help each of us, young guys still pretty much starting out, to become more financially sound."

For the trio to obtain money needed for the purchase, Buckley continued, "Arrington handled the mechanics of it, including cosigning on a Springfield bank loan that provided the funds for each of us to get the stock." As for his part, added Buckley, "I ended up paying Arrington himself back on my loan dollars. I never did send any payments to the bank involved." (As noted earlier, Arrington similarly was a cosigner on loans enabling a number of Combined Insurance employees in Chicago to buy company stock that often was escalating in value.)

A review of the ranks of the legislative interns in the 1960s showed only a handful of women going through the program—so few that it was not a misnomer to label the participants as members of a fraternity. Furthermore, in regard to the Arrington branch of the fraternity, it was easy to recognize that the housemother was a becoming woman simply called "Dee."

Dee was Denysia Bastas. She was Arrington's secretary and the gatekeeper to his office from the time of his election as Senate Republican leader until his departure from Springfield. She was privy to all the goings-on that seemed to make just about every day a hectic one in the Statehouse side of her boss' life. Nothing escaped her attention, a reality recognized immediately by the interns, staffers and others passing Arrington's way.

The capabilities of Dee were evident in the early 1960s when she served as secretary for George Drach, the veteran GOP Senate whip and the somewhat in name only opponent of Arrington for the top Republican leadership post at the end of 1964. After Arrington became president pro tem, Dee—a Valentine's Day birthday girl then in her late thirties—went to the senator's office and quickly established herself as an even more important Statehouse fixture.

Like Arrington and Easterly, she came out of Illinois coal country. In her case, Benton. However, a widely held assumption that her Greek immigrant father, Thomas Bastas, was a miner was not true. Her father and Arrington shared "a same sentiment," she said, "which was not to go down in a mine." Instead, her father was a candy maker. His place of business, the Metropolitan Café on Benton's square. was a popular hangout. It also served, Dee reminisced, "to make me the envy of everybody because I had all of that candy."

Sitting at the right hand of Arrington, Dee was a different person to different people. As the traffic cop at the entrance to the senator's office, she could be a straight-faced buffer for her boss on days he was too tied up to accommodate the steady stream of individuals seeking meetings. The interns and staffers saw another side, one in which she often confided her thoughts—mostly humorous but also at times caustic—about many of those interacting with Arrington's world.

She wasn't aware for a good while that her private observations were being duly recorded by several of the staffers in a document entitled, "The Sagacity of Dee Bastas." It was fun reading for the few permitted to scan it. In house, away from outside eyes, Dee displayed a penchant for injecting buoyancy into the atmosphere that helped uptight interns lighten up. Cheerful relief even was sought by the more devilish staffers at her expense.

All knew that Dee was definitely not among the women in the Statehouse, mainly younger gals, open to dalliances with philandering legislators or other officials. Consequently, it took considerable nerve for someone (suspected by Dee to be John Dailey) to once leave Arrington's black Cadillac with official Senate license plate Number 1 parked overnight on the street in front of her Springfield residence.

The occasional mischief, though, didn't subtract from Dee's steady equanimity with the interns, through which she guided them in their striving to make good with an unusually demanding boss.

"I got to watch," she reminded this writer, "the whole parade of these young men. The senator was a very hard working guy, and, as a result, a hard taskmaster. No question, he was tough on the kids. But, that was the reason they were so good. Even then, he still at times scared some of them to death."

In the same breath, she added, "Arrington didn't ask for more than he gave. And, when he got mad, he'd get over it. He really didn't carry a grudge."

One of her tips to those coming in was to keep a step ahead of Arrington. She herself tried, as she put it, "to keep four steps ahead of him." Arrington's lack of tolerance for mistakes even extended to misspelled words in things written to or for him. Pointing to Arrington's own meticulousness, Dee remembered that "he'd give me a list of big words that he'd want to use, and he'd have me look them up to verify if he'd be using them correctly."

Dee labored to avoid playing favorites among the interns. However, it was difficult for her and others to at first not conjure up memories of Dailey when thinking back on the program. Dailey was part of the intern class of 1964-1965, the first to call real attention to the program.

This was the contingent that included Dick Buckley. Raised in Springfield, a grandson of Frank Stoddard Dickson, the adjutant general of Illinois under three governors, Buckley was a Marine Corps veteran and Illinois State University graduate before entering his internship. He served it not with Arrington, but House Republicans. It was only after the end of his intern days, when he'd entered advanced political science studies in New York, that Buckley heeded a request by Arrington to become a professional Senate GOP staffer in Springfield.

According to Buckley, "He (Arrington) called me, and said, 'Why don't you come back where your roots are?' He said he was starting his own full-time legislative staff, and was going to pay myself and John Dailey, the first two on the staff, out of his own pocket since there was no appropriation for this. So, I did it. He moved me back to Springfield; he paid for my moving expenses."

The Dailey-Buckley class was the one that also included Senate GOP intern William Hanley, a successful Springfield attorney after his years with Governor Ogilvie, and James Ford, who became a leading executive with the Northeastern Illinois Planning Commission. The other two in the class were Douglas N. Kane, later a Democratic state representative from Springfield, and Michael P. Duncan. Democrat Duncan, a standout as an intern assigned to House Speaker John P. Touhy in 1965, went on to wear several important hats in the administration of Democratic Governor Dan Walker before becoming a top official for Allstate Insurance.

However, it was Dailey—always Dailey—who was talked about out of this group. Certainly among the Arrington interns, he was the golden boy—the individual that most predicted would go the farthest in life. If one of them was to become governor, the money was on Dailey.

"It was true...John was everything," agreed Dee Bastas. "He did it all for Senator Arrington, even his cleaning and, of course, washing his car. He had that boundless energy, and he was always walking right behind the senator. John didn't have an office at first, not even a chair. His files on legislation and other things were piled on top of a filing cabinet. Honestly, there were times I thought he just slept in our office. I really thought he did."

John Paul Dailey appeared to epitomize what Arrington wanted in the intern project. His intelligence, good looks, unreticent personality and political know-how beforehand made him a perfect mold for the program.

Born in Minneapolis in 1942, the youngest of five children of a bond salesman, his family moved to Elmhurst, Illinois, when he was eight years old. There, he was graduated in 1959 from York High School in a class one year ahead of his friend, Lee Daniels, a future leader of Illinois House Republicans. While in high school, Dailey was introduced to Springfield when he was elected youth governor of Illinois in a statewide program of the Young Men's Christian Association.

Moving on to DePauw University in Greencastle, Indiana, Dailey was a young man bitten by a political bug as he interspersed his political science studies with Republican activism. While at DePauw, he became the leader of the college young Republicans of Indiana. He went to the Republican National Convention in Chicago in 1960 to plug unsuccessfully for the nomination for vice president of Barry Goldwater. Four years later, at his party's national convention in San Francisco, Dailey demonstrated on the convention floor for the nomination of Goldwater for president, which did happen.

Dailey spent the summer of 1962 working on GOP congressional campaigns in Pennsylvania, Connecticut and Rhode Island. In Pennsylvania, he spent a month working for the successful bid for reelection of Republican incumbent Willard S. Curtin against a widely known Democratic challenger, author James Michener. While assisting Curtin in campaign organization in his suburban Philadelphia district, which included fabled Bucks County, Dailey met and came to respect the idealistic Michener.

Dailey too was idealistic back then, as a young conservative. Those were the days, said Dailey, that he and other young persons he met on the campaign trails "were saving the world." To himself and the others, he stressed, "government did matter. If you cared, you participated. We did care." He added that on his part this conscious-ness continued to motivate him in his later years with Arrington and then Governor Ogilvie.

Before graduating from DePauw, Dailey took time out for more grass roots work for the GOP. Recruited and funded by Republicans in Washington, Dailey spent the first part of 1963 aiding a liberal Republican win a race for mayor of Baltimore. In the following months, he devoted his efforts to the establishment of college and community GOP groups in southern states where he said his party "hardly existed."

He labeled this his "actually getting into the real world" period. In Mississippi, a slight flap disrupted his presence as a result of his hotel room telephone in Jackson being tapped as part of surveillance by a white citizens group.

"The tap was because I'd come from Washington, and everything from Washington was greatly distrusted in Mississippi in that era," Dailey related. "Something of a tempest was set off when the tap picked up my call to get a date with a cute liberal activist from Mississippi that I'd known in Washington."

After finishing at DePauw, Dailey took a tried-and-true path to the intern program—admission to the University of Illinois as a graduate student in political science. Dispatched by Gove to Springfield, Dailey began his internship in the fall of 1964 doing leg-work for a commission on economic development headed by Senator Arthur R. Gottschalk, a Flossmoor Republican. Research compiled by Dailey was a basis for the legislature's creation the following year of the Illinois Department of Business and Economic Development, a state chamber of commerce operation. Shortly before the end of 1964, on the day the Senate Republican caucus elected Arrington as its new leader, Arrington selected Dailey to be his intern for the rest of Dailey's time in the program.

The interns in Dailey's class were known as Ford Fellows because of the Ford Foundation's financial support for the program in its early years. Later on, state appropriations would cover virtual-ly all costs for the interns along with the salaries of legislative staffers. When Dailey's internship ended after the General Assembly's 1965 spring session, Arrington asked him to stay on as a paid GOP Senate staffer. However, the pay came from Arrington since—as mentioned previously by Buckley, who followed Dailey in joining Arrington as a pioneering professional staffer in 1965—there was no money in the state budget at first for legislative staffing. Dailey and Buckley each received $1,000 a month from Arrington.

Dailey's overall stay with Arrington lasted four years. After Ogilvie was elected governor, Dailey became a key member of his staff with, in Dailey's phrase, "the encouragement and blessing of Arrington."

Down the line, after departing from full-time government service, Dailey went on to find success in the business world while keeping his hand in GOP politics. Always eyeing elective office, he seriously considered running for the Illinois House from his Elmhurst home area in 1966. But, he decided against it, partly because the political winds in DuPage County were not blowing in his favor, and opted instead to remain with Arrington and enter law school at Northwestern University.

"Arrington told me it would be fine if I wanted to run," recalled Dailey, "but he advised me to first get my law degree and make some money so I could be independent, so that I'd not owe anybody anything, be it a GOP county chairman or whomever.

"You're only independent in politics, Arrington stressed to me, when you can tell anybody to go to hell. He was right. I listened to him at the time, and decided not to run."

Dailey eventually realized his dream to run for elective office when the GOP nominated him for state treasurer in 1982. By then, Dailey, law degree in hand, was an established business and civic leader in his new hometown of Peoria and the governor-appointed chairman of the Illinois Health Facilities Authority (which had a major voice over hospital expansion projects in the state). However, he was defeated by his Democratic opponent, James H. Donnewald, a veteran state senator from the Clinton County community of Breese. The two men were not strangers to each other in that Donnewald's first four years in the upper chamber coincided with

Dailey's time as an intern and then staffer for Arrington.

In the years after 1982, the government crowd in Springfield saw less of Dailey (although he remained head of the health facilities authority), but heard regular reports of his increasing emergence as a mover and shaker in the economic revival of Peoria. His endeavors were intertwined with the activities of G. Raymond Becker, a wealthy and prominent Peorian who for a time was Dailey's father-in-law. Along with construction projects and other undertakings, Becker and Dailey expanded a bank they controlled into a major financial catalyst in the Peoria area.

However, word spread in the 1990s of an ongoing investigation of alleged irregularities at the facility, the Community Bank of Greater Peoria. After a time, charges of fiscal improprieties indeed were leveled against Dailey, its former president. Following a plea of guilty in 1998 to several counts of misuse of bank assets, Dailey served two years in a federal prison camp at Oxford, Wisconsin.

Although Dailey hit this pothole in his life long after the death of Arrington, some seized on the Dailey case to resurrect memories of the senator's fondness of his star intern. A few curiously seemed to find it a reason for gloating.

One, conservative activist Thomas F. Roeser, opened a *Sun-Times* column with the following: "'Watch John Dailey. He's going to be somebody some day,' old W. Russell Arrington once said."

Roeser then found it opportune to note that "multimillionaire attorney Arrington...was lionized as godfather of the staff system that revolutionized the Legislature. He started by giving the GOPers smart young men (few women staffers were hired at the beginning). Not to slur by association, but Jim Edgar was one of them." Roeser stretched to further underscore his point by adding, "Arrington was right about the need to watch John P. Dailey."

Well, back in his days as an intern, Dailey was watched. So was Edgar, and so were the other interns—Arrington's disciples and the ones assigned to other legislative leaders—because with few exceptions they brought fresh-faced, idealistic input to an institution struggling for greater relevancy. They were very much a part of the legislative shake-up ordained by Arrington. Their soon proven contribution to a sound lawmaking process clearly justified Arrington's foresight in bringing them in.

And, in not forgetting the hand of Professor Gove in the situation, it should be noted that his desire to improve the quality of the General Assembly entailed more than the tutoring of many of the interns prior to their journeying to Springfield. Gove was front and center in writing elementary texts for Statehouse newcomers, other than interns, wanting an introduction to Illinois lawmaking. He put down on paper valuable tips on the things greenhorns, oftentimes including freshmen legislators, ought to look for in trying to gauge the action.

However, Gove didn't note in his writings, while his friend Arrington still was around, the importance of always being on the watch for a suddenly rapid twitching of the cigar protruding from the mouth of the Senate leader. It was a sure sign of impending excitement—a dead giveaway that somebody or something was going to catch hell.

No, Gove didn't mention the cigar. He left it up to the uninitiated to discover its meaning on their own.

Chapter 15

ᶜ

GOP Strongman

ineteen sixty five. Arrington's debut as Senate leader. The start of an Arrington-engineered make-over of the legislature. The kickoff of the Arrington upheaval.

He was his party's man of the hour, even though some Republicans joined a host of Democrats in bristling under the demanding—bordering on autocratic—nature of his leadership. It was impossible not to recognize, in spite of the mixed-bag record of the 1965 spring session of the new Seventy-fourth General Assembly, that a radically different political sheriff was in town. Arrington wore two guns, and, brother, he was quick on the draw.

Good to his word, Arrington hit the ground running as the legislature convened in January of that year. Actually, he literally blitzed the Statehouse by immediately introducing or announcing the details of his proposed legislation on front burner issues: redrawing of lawmakers' districts; revenue-raising reform; and mandating stricter ethical standards for public officials.

This was a sharp departure from the past, when bills or drafts of bills on serious matters seldom surfaced before the final weeks or days of the then six-month regular sessions. Moreover, Arrington gnawed at the innate culture of the legislature by insisting on more timely committee hearings and longer working hours for the Senate in the early months of the session—normally a period of legislative dalliance. He was a shock to the system.

For the most part, those caught by surprise at Arrington's starting gate militancy were Democrats. They felt justified in exhibiting, at the beginning of 1965, complacent confidence in their discretion to govern Illinois in a manner of their choosing. After all, in the 1964 election, the Illinois electorate did bestow on them pretty much carte blanche to direct the show as they saw fit. The Democratic Party remained in command of the executive branch and handily captured control of the House, leaving only the Senate in Republican hands. The Dems were aware from previous experience that Arrington was not a run-of-the-mill adversary, but they failed to foresee the tenacity he'd apply to his new station as the formal leader of the upper chamber.

As the state's Democrats entered 1965 content to rest on their laurels, they hoped to take time out from political strife to enjoy Kerner's inauguration into his second term as governor and the inaugural festivities in Washington for Democratic President Lyndon B. Johnson, who was successful in the previous November's balloting in holding on to the office he already occupied. The Dems' smug command of the situation just didn't factor into account the pesky Arrington.

Even on Kerner's inauguration day, Arrington stole the governor's thunder by announcing substantive legislative proposals, including one for a state subsidy to improve local police forces. *Chicago's American*, a scrappy underdog among the windy city's highly competitive newspapers, quickly seized on Arrington's burst out of the session's starting blocks to needle the Democrats and egg on the rapidly surfacing antagonism between them and the Senate leader.

"For a party that lost so heavily in the November elections, the Republicans in Springfield have been astonishingly lively—more so, in fact, than the victorious Democrats, who seem to be having some trouble getting their share of the spotlight," editorialized the *American*.

Holding that "this curious situation" largely was due to Arrington and Kerner, the *American* noted that Arrington "has waded into the legislative session with enormous energy, firing off a barrage of spectacular bills and pronouncements; he even jumped the gun…in offering his plan for amending the revenue article of the state constitution." Consequently, it was added, Arrington "has appeared as the principal mover and shaker of the legislature so far." On the other hand, Kerner was scolded by the newspaper for hardly testing the legislative water except for support of a reapportionment bill introduced by Democratic lawmakers.

The *American* did not ignore what it called "some grousing among the Republicans...about Arrington's monopolizing so much of the limelight."

However, the newspaper found such carping "rather petty" in stressing that "Arrington has done a great deal already to build the new 'image' the Republican party obviously needs in Illinois—that of an energetic, hard-driving party that 'proposes, not opposes....'"

As the 1965 session turned out, the *American's* early editorial analysis was prophetic. Arrington never surrendered the limelight that so quickly centered on him. On paper, he ended up reaping only modest success in pushing his expansive proposals for legislation on major fronts. His captaincy of the Senate was blunted time and again by the lopsided Democratic majority in the House. And, if that was not enough of an obstacle, there was the further roadblock of Kerner in the governor's chair.

The tit for tat was that Arrington commanded the scuttling of Democratic-pushed legislation that did not square with his concept of reasonable government. As a matter of fact, nothing of consequence made it through the Senate— irrespective of its sponsorship—without the blessing of Arrington.

Kerner's eventually proposed budget legislation predictably took it on the chin. Refusing to go along with the bulk of Kerner's tax hike requests for generating new revenue, Arrington correspondingly pared down many of the proposed outlays in the governor's spending plan for the next state fiscal period.

Of course, the state funding aspect of the session-long tiff between Arrington and Kerner was nothing new. Since 1961, Kerner's first year in office, every session featured a showdown on state finances between a governor pressing for additional revenue for an expansion of governmental activities and an Arrington laboring to short-circuit Kerner's broadened spending goals on grounds that taxpayers neither needed the new programs nor could afford them. However, the Arrington-Kerner clashes on monetary policy and other pivotal issues in the 1965 session were of more import since the session was Arrington's first as the official GOP Senate leader.

As the weary legislators trudged out of Springfield after the close of the session in the morning hours of July 1, 1965, the most caustic acrimony aimed at Arrington came not from Kerner but from Daley, the state's ultimate Democratic heavyweight and the most political-ly powerful mayor in America.

Arrington thwarted at the session's end Daley's all-out drive for General Assembly approval of a municipal tax package that would have raised an additional $50 million for Chicago needs, mainly the bolstering of the police and fire departments. Other cities also would have benefited. But, Arrington's okay for Daley's push for new rev-enue was contingent on the General Assembly reaching an accord on revised district maps for Senate and House members. When that did-n't happen, Arrington pulled the plug on Daley's proposal.

The courtly mannered Kerner, who disdained political infighting, threw up his hands in disgust at Arrington's savaging of the budget proposed by the governor. Nevertheless, Kerner was typically reserved, in his public reaction to the final appropriations and rev-enue numbers emerging from the session—the components of a budget labeled as Arrington's by Kerner and one, insisted the gover-nor, providing inadequate income for meeting approved expendi-tures.

"This budget…was designed to drain every single penny, so that at the end we wouldn't have a single cent," complained Kerner. "No businessman in his right mind would try to run a business that way."

Daley's response to his rebuff by Arrington was far more scathing. In a press conference after the session's conclusion, a grim mayor read from a printed statement the following:

"The people of Illinois have been dealt a dastardly blow to rep-resentative government by the arrogant Mr. Arrington and his cronies. The courageous police and firemen of Chicago have been given a political answer by the arrogant Arrington and his crew to a city governmental problem of adequate police and firemen. I condemn the duplicity and insincerity of Mr. Arrington and his Republican membership of the Senate."

Harsh words, indeed, even in a climate in which the heat of political battle had yet to subside. In seeking to cast Arrington as a political pariah for Chicago, Daley's rebuke failed to recognize that Arrington gave a green light in the Senate's last hours to the final passage of a $7.3 million pupil transportation appropriation for Chicago's transit authority and to the authorization of a $10 million nonreferendum bond issue for the city's park district.

The acerbity of the mayor's verbal castigation of Arrington was a two-edged sword. Employment of the "arrogant Arrington" appellation was hardly unprecedented, but hearing the satire from the mouth of an angry Daley virtually ensured its codification for public dissemination by Arrington bashers both in and out of Democratic circles.

On the other side of the coin, the personal targeting of Arrington by Daley—who routinely considered it below his political dignity to even acknowledge the names of antagonists—signified the mayor's reluctant acceptance of the full-fledged arrival of Arrington. Without question, Daley's diatribe was a backhanded compliment to Arrington. It amounted to prima facie evidence that the fifty-eight-year-old Arrington, based on his conduct in the 1965 session, had become—for the time being—the most potent Republican in Illinois.

Furthermore, this was a reality not likely to change until the election of another Republican as governor or the appearance of a GOP chief in the House with the forcefulness of Arrington—not a very promising prospect. For a Republican, Arrington was one of a kind. Nobody around could recall, and the memories of some went back a long way, any legislative leader from his party as dominating as Arrington.

Charles Cleveland, a political analyst for the *Chicago Daily News*, took a positive take on Arrington in sizing up the 1965 session that mirrored the opinion of many. Arrington's insistence on GOP unity in the Senate, something not always the case in previous years under the gentler hand of Bidwill, especially impressed Cleveland.

"For the first time in memory," wrote Cleveland, "the Republicans held firm throughout the session, and it was Arrington who kept them in line."

"Nobody else on the Republican side could have been that effective," continued Cleveland. "A combination of orderliness, parliamentary skill and aggressiveness made Arrington unique.

"In many ways, he has the combination of talents that make Mayor Richard J. Daley a complete politician. Indeed, the Senate Democrats found, for the first time, they were facing an opponent with almost dictatorial powers—and, in the long run, they had to surrender."

Numerous downstate scribes—more than a few admittedly inclined to automatically look with favor upon anyone with the guts to give the political behemoth from the north, Daley, a comeuppance—were even more profuse in their praise of Arrington. Joseph Harris of Springfield's GOP-leaning *Illinois State Journal* found Arrington's carrying of the Republican banner nothing short of extraordinary.

"When, in some future year, scholars begin cataloging current Illinois history, they will have to reserve a separate chapter for Senator W. Russell Arrington of Evanston," declared Harris.

"More adjectives have been used to describe the Republican Senate majority leader than have been spent on any other state official of this era, but only one fits him adequately—remarkable."

Harris then proceeded to quite accurately frame the persona of the man who had journeyed a great distance from his modest start in Illinois coal country to the center stage of Illinois public life.

"Arrington, by his very manner, sparks intense feelings in everyone who comes in contact with him—but the feelings are by no means unanimous," the writer pointed out. "His enemies, and they are many and bipartisan, look upon Arrington with a degree of dislike which borders upon hate. His friends, who are growing more numerous, are fiercely loyal. They look upon Arrington as one step removed from a personal Holy Grail, and they its special protectors. Friends and enemies alike hold respect and awe for Arrington, and there are few 'neutrals' where he is concerned."

While not all reporters went as far in lauding Arrington as Harris, every member of the Statehouse press corps recognized that his mercurial personality was terrific for business. His rapid mood swings, fired by that famously hair-trigger temper, ignited conflictive outbursts that made for much livelier reading than the dry recitation of bills passed or defeated.

Arrington's tempo, never short of high gear, prompted some in the Senate press gallery to question whether he'd make it through the session without a third heart attack. Democrats speculated that Arrington would be hard pressed to keep up his self-imposed operating strain without the wheels coming off his largely one-man show. They felt that what they saw as Arrington's unparalleled hubris justified volley after volley of potshots.

As the session entered its last stretch, *State Journal* columnist Kenneth Watson reported that "Arrington is a high strung if brilliant man, and Statehouse Democrats have made no secret of the fact that they expect him to 'crack' when the pressure mounts in the session's closing days."

"On the Senate floor," noted Watson, "there are almost daily signs of an organized effort to keep the short-fused Arrington's temper flaring, and the senator himself complains of this 'vilification of me.'"

Democratic needling of Arrington was nothing new, but it became more penetrating with his elevation to upper chamber boss. The latest Democratic ramrod of Arrington nettling often was Senator Morgan M. Finley, a peppery real estate and insurance businessman who could have been a Mickey Rooney double. Finley also happened to be a neighbor on Bridgeport's South Lowe Avenue of Daley, his political mentor.

Watson, for one, said he couldn't ignore that in "any important debate, Finley can be counted on for a few tart remarks that almost always draw quick and fiery retort from Arrington."

More civil in exchanges with Arrington was his Democratic counterpart in the Senate, Thomas A. McGloon, who was serving his first term as minority leader. McGloon faced the most grievous challenge in the General Assembly, having to mount a counterpoint to Arrington while being handicapped with eight fewer senators in his camp than the thirty-three behind Arrington at the start of the session.

The Democratic leader in the House had easy sailing in compari-

Left to right: Senator Arthur McGloon,
Lt. Governor Samuel Shapiro and Senator Arrington

son to McGloon. He was John P. Touhy, and he was the chamber's speaker because, remember, the commonly named "bed sheet ballot" for House members in the 1964 election had left the Democrats with a majority, 118 to 59, that was beyond the wildest dream of either party.

Touhy, a forty-six-year-old lawyer from Chicago's west side who answered to Jack, emerged from the session with more friends on both sides of the political aisle than any other legislator. Besides running the House smoothly, he made himself a model of fairness in dealing with the body's Republicans because their extraordinarily thin ranks prevented serious challenges to the Democrats' agenda.

McGloon had to cast wishful eyes at his close associate Touhy's go in the chamber across from the Senate on the Capitol's third floor. Like Touhy, McGloon was a Chicago west sider and a product of DePaul University's law school. Both had served in World War II— Touhy in Europe with the army and McGloon with the navy in the Pacific.

Not many of his fellow legislators in uniform during the war had been in harm's way as much as McGloon. As a naval gunfire liaison officer attached to the Marine Corps, McGloon was at the side of Marines leading some of the bloodiest invasions of Japanese-held islands. His bravery under fire at Iwo Jima earned him a Marine general's citation for meritorious service.

It read, in part, that "when his regiment encountered continued and bitter enemy resistance, Lieutenant McGloon worked tirelessly, both day and night, in order to provide and coordinate the best naval gunfire support possible."

McGloon was conditioned for the rigors of Iwo Jima by his earlier participation in the fierce fighting required for the captures of Saipan and Tinian. Remembering Saipan as perhaps the roughest of the island invasions, McGloon believed that he marched "over every single inch of Saipan." He never got out of his mind the night he dodged tracer machine-gun bullets from counterattacking Japanese tanks to summon star shells from offshore ships that lit up the sky to make it possible for the Marines to pinpoint the tanks for destruction.

His encounter with Tinian included one especially pungent recollection that he related in a 1981 memoir for the General Assembly's oral history program, a project of Sangamon State University (later the University of Illinois at Springfield).

"I saw thousands and thousands of dead Marines and dead Japanese," said McGloon. "I learned to eat my meal five feet away from a cadaver. The human body swells up like an animal when it's not picked up right away. It gets very distended, limbs and belly and everything."

Prior to the war, McGloon professed little interest in politics, which was a bit unusual for an Irish Catholic lad in Chicago and especially for one whose father, James C. McGloon, was a Democratic state representative during the World War I years. Although he sometimes passed out political literature, young Thomas McGloon had a dim view of politics as a "heartbreaking game."

Returning to Chicago after the war, McGloon had a change of heart about involvement in public life and began an eight-year period as an assistant public defender. This was followed by four years as an assistant state's attorney in Cook County and then, in 1958, election to the Illinois Senate.

His days of verbal jousting as a prosecutor, McGloon liked to say, prepared him for the argumentative style of debate required of a legislative floor leader. Nevertheless, some never stopped viewing McGloon as too gentlemanly for the frequently nightmarish role of doing linguistic battle with Arrington. Leaving the intentional taunting of Arrington to Finley and others, McGloon maintained a measured composure which ruled out—even during episodes of fireworks on the Senate floor—personal debasement of Republicans.

When Arrington scolded the whole Democratic side for one thing or another, he aimed his remonstrance at McGloon. Knowing that rebuttal in kind fell on deaf ears, McGloon often bit his lip and took the censuring. If comebacks were voiced, the rhetorical skills of Alan Dixon, the assistant Democratic leader, came into play.

On the days, and they did exist, when tempers were under control—and Democratic goading of Arrington was in check—Arrington and McGloon could argue issues in a fashion that revealed the firm grasp of each on the finer points of law.

One individual especially appreciative of unencumbered debates between Arrington and McGloon was Harold A. Katz, an attorney from Glencoe and a freshman Democrat in the House in 1965. Katz, who frequently came across as a quasi academic during an eighteen-year career in the lower chamber, said in a 1988 memoir for the legislature's oral history program that his "fondest memories" as a lawmaker included "those occasions when I would wander into the Senate and hear McGloon and Arrington debate."

As seen by Katz, the two leaders "were men of extraordinary ability. McGloon had a pixieish quality. He knew how to get to Arrington in debate. While we've had great debaters in Illinois, and the Lincoln-Douglas debates come to mind, the most delightful, the ablest debates that I heard in the General Assembly were those between Arrington and McGloon."

When the two matched wits, insisted Katz, "the specifics were not notable. It was the manner and style, the range of the discourse, the wonderful oratory that these encounters developed." To Katz, an Arrington-McGloon debate "was just a great show, better than the movies…in Springfield" to which legislators were given free passes.

Away from the public eye, Arrington and McGloon were not combatants. One who knew this full well was Philip J. Rock, the Chicago Democratic lawyer elected in 1970 to the Senate seat held by McGloon until he became an Illinois appellate court judge.

Rock, whose twenty-two years in the Senate included seven terms as a highly respected president of the body, noted that Arrington and McGloon "were close behind the scene. Actually, they were great personal friends. Senator McGloon held him (Arrington) in high regard."

Quite often, public antagonism between opposing political leaders went out the window when they were off the set, so to speak, or away from the judgmental eyes of reporters. The off-the-court relationship between Arrington and McGloon, aptly underscored by Rock, was more axiomatic than abnormal. The trials of leadership borne by persons such as Arrington and McGloon gave them, to a significant degree, more in common with each other than each had with many of those under his command.

Richard M. Daley, a son of Mayor Richard J. Daley, downplayed the lasting effects of verbal polemics between his father and Arrington, saying the overriding reality was that his father and Arrington "needed each other" to ensure in the late 1960s that the defining issues of the day were addressed.

The younger Daley, responding to questions for this book in February 2004—while himself serving as mayor of Chicago—emphasized that, in hindsight, his father and Arrington buried partisan differences when the chips were down to forge decisions on many crucial matters, such as imposition of a state income tax, that permitted "the people of our city (Chicago) and this state (to) benefit greatly…."

Putting a positive spin on Arrington's interaction with the Mayor Daley of the senator's era was not as doable in the 1965 session as in ones to follow.

On the issue that garnered the most ink, legislative reapportionment, the Daley-led Democrats and Arrington never reached agreement on new maps acceptable to both sides. The intransigence extended to efforts to create revised districts for Illinois congressmen on the one-man, one-vote principle as well as to the realignment of districts for state legislators.

Arrington was loud and clear at the start of the session about the need for the lawmakers to display statesmanship and accomplish within their own ranks the requisite drawing of new districts. However, the attainment of a compromise between the GOP remapping engineered by Arrington and the counterproposals by Democrats never occurred. Along the way, each party repeatedly blew its stack at the other's perceived bullheadedness against coming at least halfway in efforts to reach an accord.

No issue was more important personally for the legislators since, for some, new district lines could spell political survival or death. At the same time, the subject was a snoozer for all but the lawmakers themselves, political science buffs and editorial writers.

The failure of the legislature on reapportionment moved the task of drawing new maps for the Senate and congressmen to the Illinois Supreme Court, where Republican justices were in the majority. The fact that this opened the door for further judicial encroachment into the legislative world was not pleasing to those committed to strict division between the branches of government. As for House districts, responsibility for their revision fell to a bipartisan commission to be appointed by Kerner. A similar panel deadlocked in 1963, leading to the following year's expensive and confusing election of House members at large. In event the next commission also flunked its assignment, a repeat of the 1964 bed sheet balloting for House members was likely in 1966.

As with reapportionment, Arrington jumped the gun on another of his top priorities—reform of revenue raising—by pushing what he wanted on the matter before legislators were even in their seats. Arrington, already an old war-horse on this dry but unavoidable subject, now wanted the General Assembly to approve a multi-point submission to voters in which they would designate what they'd like to see in a revision of the state constitution's Revenue Article.

The Arrington approach would have let the electorate say yes or no to major policy options for the future raising of public dollars. The choices included whether or not to permit a flat-rate income levy, to authorize the legislature to impose a graduated income tax, to ban any state income tax period, to establish for taxation purposes the classification of real property and to similarly sanction the classification of personal property. Notwithstanding his historical aversion to enactment of an Illinois income tax, Arrington felt the time was long overdue for new citizen input on the issue.

Predictably, much of the sharpest debate during the session swirled first around Arrington's revenue plan and then on differing proposals on the subject subsequently put forward. Finally, as the session neared an end, enough Republicans and Democrats came together to provide the two-thirds majority necessary in each chamber for submission of a Revenue Article amendment to voters in the 1966 general election. More than a few hailed this as the most striking achievement of the session. If so, Arrington deserved credit for providing much of the impetus for it to happen. However, the wording of the proposed amendment was significantly different from that sought by Arrington, leaving him less than enamored with parts of the proposal and skeptical of its chances for voter ratification.

Most eye-catching about the submission was its authorization for the General Assembly to enact a flat-rate income tax of 3 percent on individuals and corporations. This could be increased to a maximum of 6 percent with voter approval. If an income tax was levied, all personal property taxes—collected so unevenly as to constitute a joke—would be abolished within four years. In addition, the proceeds from at least the first 1 percent of the income tax, if instituted, would be distributed to local governments to replace revenue from the personal property tax. Too, the proposed amendment would make it possible to take the sales tax off food and drugs, a supposedly appealing aspect to lower income folks spending a higher percentage of their money for food than wealthier people.

Arrington also got the ball rolling right away on consideration of legislative action to improve the ethical standards of lawmakers and discourage conflicts of interest. A package introduced by Arrington included a resolution requiring disclosure by a legislator of a possible conflict of interest during deliberation on a bill to a commission of seven members, six of whom would have been lawmakers. The plan lacked teeth, though, because of an absence of provisions for enforcement and penalties. His package also had measures spelling out an ethics code for state employees and providing for the naming of a board to police it.

The Democrats chimed in on the subject with their own proposals, including one creating a board on legislative ethics to be dominated by laymen, not members of the club. That measure, pushed by House Dems, did stipulate penalties for offending legislators. However, the many hours devoted to discussion of these initiatives came to naught, as all the proposals went down the drain in the session's final days when tempers and rivalries became overheated.

The goose egg on ethics legislation was at least mildly surprising in view of the lingering aftereffects from Paul Simon's 1964 magazine article on Illinois legislative corruption—and also because of a tempest sparked late in the 1965 session by the disclosure of mysterious tape recordings which allegedly revealed lobbyists conversing about the bribery of legislators to kill proposed legislation not wanted by the currency exchange industry. Names of a number of legislators were said to be mentioned on the recordings.

Although the incident failed to help bring about passage of ethics legislation, it did spur formal inquiries by commissions in each chamber designed to get to the bottom of the matter and recommend, if needed, remedial action. The probes, which stretched out for many months, were largely exercises in wheel spinning as legal wrangling and other roadblocks prolonged the suspense, but generated few answers. In fact, a lot of the interest remained centered on the circumstances of the taping itself, which certainly had touches of a spy tale.

The generally accepted version was that the lobbyists' conversation occurred in a room that was bugged by an unknown person or persons in Springfield's Leland Hotel. A columnist for *Chicago's American* subsequently was tipped off to the existence of the recordings in a supposedly anonymous letter. Acting on information in the letter, the writer reportedly found the tapes in a locker in the Chicago Greyhound bus station. The newspaper then printed excerpts from a transcript of the recordings, igniting the uproar.

As for the masterminding of the bugging, the most prevalent

guess was that it was the work of George Mahin, the top gun of the Chicago-based Better Government Association. Corruption fighter Mahin, who made the privately funded BGA an anathema to much of the state's political establishment, never admitted such a role, though.

Back on the main issue—the contents of the tapes themselves. It was ironic that the House Legislative Ethics Commission, the lower chamber panel investigating the recordings, found them so garbled as to be virtually unintelligible when legal proceedings holding up access to the tapes finally were resolved. The legislators on the commission, after getting their hands on the recordings some eighteen months after the bugging, concluded that the tapes they received were copies, and poor ones at that. Without the original tapes, it was held, far-reaching findings by the commission were not possible.

The muddled inconclusiveness of the affair was expected all along by cynics convinced that conundrums surrounding Illinois legislators usually wound up to be unfinished puzzles. Do not forget, they never failed to mention, the riddle of Clem Graver.

Graver was a Republican state representative from Chicago who disappeared shortly before the end of the legislature's 1953 spring session. He never was found. Graver was abducted by several men after putting his car in a garage near his home, as his wife looked on from a second-floor window. She said they dragged her husband to a waiting auto and sped away. It was assumed, at first, that Graver was kidnapped for ransom, but the family never got a call. Numerous detectives looked into Graver's interests in trucking firms and other businesses and even into his alleged friendships with Chicago hoods, but a motive for the abduction was not pinned down. While the fruitless search for Graver through the years took many strange turns, his disappearance remained great feedstock for those holding that the sometimes inexplicable world of the General Assembly only further sullied its image.

The revelation of the recordings did its part in adding a long-standing contribution to the dubious side of General Assembly lore. More immediately, it cast something of a shadow over the 1965 session, a cloud that encouraged attention to perceived shortcomings—such as the absence of ethics legislation and the doomed remap efforts—while obscuring positives.

Still, there certainly were numerous developments that should have gotten more play.

Legislative leaders worked out of the limelight with Kerner to pave the way for a statewide system of junior colleges, an important expansion of higher education. Legislation to improve the state's program on food inspection was passed. Illinois' pioneering Family Court Act was revised and updated. The month for the state's primary election was moved from April to June, an action to shorten the general election campaign season and to hopefully increase the national importance of Illinois primaries. By holding them closer to national conventions, it was thought, Illinois primaries could be make-or-break occasions for some presidential aspirants.

An arsenal of crime-fighting measures received a green light. A number of them were intended specifically to strengthen the hand of law enforcement in fighting organized crime. One anticrime bill that didn't pass would have legalized wire tapping, even though Sheriff Ogilvie of Cook County and Chicago Police Superintendent O. W. Wilson considered it vital to law enforcement.

Nobody could take more satisfaction with the legislature's favorable response to most of the crime bills than Arrington, a main sponsor through the years of legislation sought by the Chicago Crime Commission. His pride in the passage of the anticrime measures was not daunted by the subsequent veto by Kerner of much of the package on constitutional and other grounds.

On the drier, but still quite noteworthy side of things, the 1965 meeting of the seventy-fourth legislature turned out to be a springboard for a full-blown review—with an eye toward retooling—of much of Illinois government itself. Before going home, the lawmakers signed off on the establishment of three commissions to formally address widespread concerns that key parts of the state's governing machinery no longer were up to snuff for the times.

One, the Illinois Constitutional Study Commission, was empowered to analyze all provisions—some of them ridiculously antiquated—in the state's basic charter. Following that, the panel was to recommend to the General Assembly the most feasible method of updating the then ninety-five-year-old constitution. From the start, betting was heavy that the commission would recommend the calling of a state constitutional convention as the only way to bring about sufficient reform of the document.

The Commission on State Government-Illinois was created to recommend an overhaul of the executive branch. Its wide breadth of responsibility made it only the third panel of its kind in Illinois since 1900. Named to chair it was Jack F. Isakoff, a government professor at Southern Illinois University and an old hand on the technicalities of state government. This commission was affectionately known by its acronym, COSGI.

However, the most recognized acronym belonged to the third newly created commission. It was COOGA, which stood for the Commission on the Organization of the General Assembly. COOGA constituted, as far as anybody knew, an unprecedented initiative for a systematic study to modernize the state's legislative branch. The undertaking was long overdue in the minds of political reformers— a featured one being Arrington in this case—who believed that the legislature could not continue to labor under a bad light.

To put it simply, the launching of these commissions represented a three-front offensive to generate changes that would make Illinoisans proud of state government.

Arrington was in the vanguard of support for all three, and he guaranteed that their approval in the Senate was virtually automatic. His voice was among the loudest crying out for years for a sweeping update of the Illinois Constitution. His legislative career was marked by many efforts to refashion programs of executive branch agencies to meet changing priorities. And, of course, betterment of the General Assembly had become a motivating passion of his life.

Arrington was not the chairman of COOGA, but was an ex officio member by virtue of his legislative office (as was Speaker Touhy). The chairman was Representative Katz, who sponsored the House measure setting up the commission. According to form, it should have been called the Katz Commission, and many did so. But, Arrington was insistent on calling it COOGA for reasons that may have included his hesitancy to give a first-term Democratic lawmaker significant name recognition on a cause championed for such a long time by the senator.

Katz, who like Arrington hailed from the North Shore, proved to be a meticulous leader of a commission that took its mandate seriously and would find many of its recommendations adopted in the legislature. Along the way, Katz—a diplomat to begin with—went overboard to accommodate input from Arrington, as well as Touhy and McGloon. With Arrington especially, Katz was quite aware of the senator's years of toil in laying a foundation for the commission. Too, Katz recognized the danger to the commission's chance of progress should Arrington became dissatisfied at any juncture with the operation of the panel.

However, Arrington was not about to let himself, or anybody else, become a barrier to the success of COOGA.

In 1978, William L. Day, the editor emeritus of *Illinois Issues* magazine, concluded in a look back at COOGA that its legacy was nothing short of converting the legislature from a reactive to an initiating body. COOGA contributed greatly, Day emphasized, to a revised framework that let the General Assembly manage its business better and, in the process, become much more of an originator of—and fighter for—its own conceived programs.

Katz justifiably got his due from Day. But Day stressed that Katz had two major things working in his favor in the launching of COOGA. The first was that one positive result of the bed sheet ballot election of House members brought many new and reform-minded individuals into the House, if only for the 1965 session. Secondly, noted Day, Katz was blessed with backing "for the idea of streamlining the legislature by one of the most remarkable men of our time to sit in the Illinois Senate, W. Russell Arrington...."

For the record, Arrington did help push through the legislature a bill introduced by Republican Senator Harris W. Fawell of Naperville that sought to do just about the same thing as Katz's bill creating COOGA. Following tradition, Kerner signed the measure sponsored by his fellow Democrat, Katz. Subsequently, Fawell, a Capitol newspersons' favorite who was much less conservative than most on his side of the Senate, became vice chairman of COOGA.

The reformist image of COOGA also was bolstered by the selection as its secretary of Representative Marjorie Pebworth, a first termer in the lower chamber and a blue-ribbon gal par excellence. A resident of the Cook County village of Riverdale and married to a Sears, Roebuck & Co. executive, Pebworth was a onetime high school librarian who had served as president of the League of Women Voters of Illinois.

Fortuitously, Pebworth also became chairperson of the constitutional study commission, which was set up by legislation she sponsored. An appreciable amount of what COOGA would propose was tied to constitutional change. And, the road toward that change was paved by her commission.

While the advent of the three commissions was heralded by folks wanting a big-time shake-up in Illinois government, the creation of the panels hardly made the headlines at the end of the 1965 session. The banners were reserved for the spicier topics and for the paramount personalities supplying the spice.

Enter Arrington. As if Charles Cleveland wasn't already sufficiently extolling the performance of Arrington, Cleveland was joined by fellow *Daily News* writer Raymond R. Coffey in a postsession assessment that declared Arrington's commanding presence left little to the imagination.

Joining others in labeling Arrington the Senate's "new super strongman," the two wrote that "there can be no question that Arrington, for all practical purposes, was, all alone, the State Senate this year." They repeated the frequent observation that Arrington "got both Republicans and Democrats angry at him," but stressed that "there was no question that he was running the show."

True, said Democrats, Arrington ran the show. But, they contended, its rating was far from five-star because of Arrington's obstinate refusal, in their eyes, to permit serious consideration of civil rights legislation and measures dealing with other domestic issues. The criticism on the civil rights front—mainly over Senate Republicans' refusal to let House-passed bills combating housing discrimination out of committee—stuck in Arrington's craw. It would have a bearing on the future. The more routine denunciation that he automatically turned thumbs down on most of Kerner's increased tax and spending proposals, as well as on many Democratic pet projects, was dismissed by Arrington as anticipated partisan rhetoric.

He took with a grain of salt the newsletter accusation of Democratic Representative Abner Mikva that Arrington's "underlying notion of government is clearly wrong and in large part accounts for the decline and decay of state government in Illinois and throughout the country."

Mikva's newsletter, reprinted in East St. Louis' *Metro-East Journal* and other places, questioned whether it was "not too much to ask that the State Senate become a part of the twentieth century."

Arrington was actually amused when Daniel M. Pierce, a freshman Democrat in the House from Highland Park, cheerily passed out what he dubbed "the Arrington button" late in the session. The kicker was that the button was worn under a lapel and only could be displayed by a flip of the lapel. When turned out, the button was seen by onlookers to carry only one word: "No."

No buttons were necessary to propagate Arrington's take on the session. Numerous members of the press did it for him. In addition to Coffey and Cleveland, there were ones like veteran George Tagge, the *Chicago Tribune's* political editor since 1943. Arrington's management of the Senate, estimated Tagge, did more than anything else to recoup some of the spirit that the Illinois GOP lost in its terrible showing in the 1964 election.

In fighting "Mayor Daley's forces to a standstill," penned Tagge, Arrington "was a man of both fire and ice. He appeared cool and feverish at the same time as he directed the battle from his party's only remaining fortress."

Arrington's orchestration of the Senate was a lesson in control. His steerage was as sure-handed as the domineering direction of John Ford or Howard Hawks in the making of a Hollywood movie. The Senate had become an Arrington production.

Still, control was a necessary first but not last step for Arrington. He needed to put his new domain—his fiefdom—to better use. Yes, the Senate was his oyster. Now he wanted to get more out of it. He was on the right path, but he wasn't there yet.

Chapter 16

❦

1967—No Longer Bridesmaids

Finally, he crossed home plate. Or, more accurately, the General Assembly did. Arrington's drive to move the legislature from the passenger's seat to the driver's seat in Illinois governance crossed the goal line in the initial session in 1967 of the new Seventy-fifth General Assembly. Bridesmaids no longer, the lawmakers emerged front and center in the scheme of things.

In the later words of Arrington, "We really ran the state…we began to make the legislature look like something."

A tip-off to the new order was spelled out quite clearly in the introductory wording to *Building a Better Illinois*, a precedent-setting booklet laying out beforehand and in great detail the GOP's intended legislative program for 1967

It was an Arrington-choreographed manifesto, and its most revealing paragraph stated:

"Today one must not serve in the General Assembly as a mere rubber stamp for the Governor. Nor would he want one. The people of Illinois have cogently shown in recent elections that they want three branches of government—not one. We in the Legislature are duty-bound to be separate and independent. We must initiate our own legislative programs. We must debate their merits within the context of our constituents and the common good of the State. And then we must approve them or retain them for further study."

Paging through the booklet after the six-month session concluded, it was apparent that the GOP had a high batting average in the

number of objectives achieved out of the many initiatives proposed—covering a spectrum ranging from governmental ethics legislation to crime-combating measures. Faced with hampering circumstances in 1967 that were absent in 1965, Democratic legislators
had little choice but to go along with the Republicans on so many
topics. Governor Kerner, likewise, found himself boxed in by a mil-
itantly rejuvenated GOP.

As in the 1965 session, Arrington was again the legislature's man
on horseback. However, the role was much more satisfying this time.

In truth, the whole two-year life of the Seventy-fifth General
Assembly (covering 1968 as well as 1967) was a prodigious time for
Arrington, a period offering an opportunity for showcasing of the legislature beyond anything that was remembered. For Arrington personally, he was the biennium's undisputed king of the hill in a manner not
possible before 1967 and not to be repeated in such a clear-cut fashion after 1968—when the political dynamics were different.

The Arrington visible in the 1967-1968 biennium certainly had to
contribute quite a bit to the esteem in which the senator was held by
David Kenney, a longtime political science professor at Southern
Illinois University.

Categorizing Arrington as "an unusual legislative leader" in a letter to this writer, Kenney said he found the man from Evanston to be
"intellectually brilliant, hard-nosed in the best sense, capable of
playing hardball with the best, and truly a statesman in seeking goals
that were eminently in the public interest."

"To me," concluded Kenney, "he (Arrington) stood head and
shoulders above all of the other legislators."

If Arrington's rule of the roost was as imperial during 1967-1968
as some suggested, he did suffer one political jolt that rocked him to
the bone and gave the biennium's first session its most dramatic
moments. The incident erupted near the end of the session, sorely
threatening the Arrington mystique and leaving him, temporarily at
least, as a legislative emperor with no clothes.

More on that to come.

Overall, though, the session in the first half of 1967 was a positive watershed for Arrington. To understand what partially made this

Senator W. Russell Arrington

possible, one had to look back at several developments between the end of the 1965 session and the start of 1967.

The reapportionment standoff that vexed the windup of the 1965 session was resolved. Before the end of August 1965, a little short of two months after the session's conclusion, justices of the Illinois Supreme Court were joined by federal judges in approving a redistricting of the Senate that closely approached the "one man, one vote" ideal of the United States Supreme Court. Under the new map, thirty of the upper chamber's fifty-eight districts covered Cook County (twenty-one in Chicago and nine in the city's suburbs) and the remaining twenty-eight applied to the rest of the state.

Arrington had no quarrel with the realignment, which reduced the size of his district and renumbered it. Now designated the First District, an enumeration he coveted, its revised territory included Evanston and New Trier townships, half of Northfield township and a small part of Niles township. The new district was cut to be another politically sure bet for Arrington, which was convenient for him since all the Senate seats were on the ballot in the ensuing 1966 election. It was no wonder that Arrington was in a fine temperament as he departed with son Michael for a tour of European capitals after the judges finished the Senate remap.

Following the approval of Senate redistricting, the state's highest tribunal and federal jurists proceeded to also reapportion Illinois' congressional districts. And—to the surprise of many—the bipartisan commission named by Kerner to revise House districts got the job done shortly before the end of 1965, thereby avoiding another bed sheet ballot for electing lower chamber members in 1966.

Both Democrats and Republicans were optimistic about their chances under the new Senate map of winning the majority of seats in the 1966 voting. As for the GOP's prospects, Arrington believed that the drive to retain control of the body needed to be more high-powered. Stimulating greater Republican oomph boiled down to a great extent to the raising of more money for the candidates. Arrington needed to break new ground again.

Never before, in Arrington's words, "had anyone, the party or anyone else, given any money for the Senate members. Everyone had to do it on his own."

So, after the adjournment of the 1965 session Arrington spearheaded a political fund-raising dinner in Chicago's Conrad Hilton Hotel—in spite of his lack of enthusiasm for such things—to raise dollars for funneling to GOP Senate candidates facing serious opposition. "We sent letters to all the friends of Republicans and the lobbyists…and started to sell tickets," Arrington said. Even though the time had yet to arrive in Illinois when political contributions had to be publicly disclosed, little secret was made of the fact that the $100-a-plate dinner brought in about $185,000. Arrington could not help but be proud of the event, which he quickly turned into an annual affair

In fact, that initial dinner went so well that Arrington assumed he was going to be commended when William Fetridge, his old friend from Evanston Young Republican Club days, asked him to lunch after the dinner. Fetridge was, after all, the headliner of the United Republican Fund, which while raising dough for party candidates had never, according to Arrington, given to GOP senators. But, the lunch wasn't what Arrington expected.

"It made me damn mad," Arrington related, "to find out at that lunch that the objective was to ask me to give $20,000 from our dinner proceeds to the United Republican Fund. That got to me, and I made it clear there was not going to be any money given to the fund. That money was going to be used to provide funds for our senators."

The dinner's take, disbursed at the direction of Arrington, apparently was put to good use. The general election in November 1966 did more than leave the GOP in command of the Senate. Its majority was increased by five seats, giving Republicans a lead of 38 to 20 over Democrats and boosting Arrington into an even stronger catbird seat.

On the personal front, Arrington easily held onto his own seat. In the primary in June 1966, he disposed of a challenge from Robert J. Salberg, a Wilmette salesman and political novice. Arrington's general election opponent, State Representative John A. Kennedy, a Winnetka Democrat and founder of an electronics firm, also was

handily defeated. (Soon after the general election, Republican senators unanimously approved the retention of Arrington as their leader
in the upcoming biennium.)

The election produced other good news for Republicans with
Charles Percy's successful bid to oust Democrat Paul Douglas from
the United States Senate he held since 1948 and Ray Page's winning
campaign for reelection as Illinois superintendent of public instruction. Too, not to be overlooked—even though hardly noticed downstate—was Richard Ogilvie's elevation in the election from Cook
County sheriff to president of the county's governing board of commissioners, a post seldom held by a Republican. The brightest result
for Illinois Democrats was the victory by State Representative Adlai
E. Stevenson III over a fellow House member, Republican Harris
Rowe of Jacksonville, in the race for state treasurer.

On another note, sufficient votes were not recorded for approval
of the proposed amendment to the Revenue Article of the Illinois
Constitution that was submitted to the electorate as a result of
General Assembly action back in 1965. As feared by Arrington and
others, the amendment—which would have permitted far-reaching
revisions in revenue raising by state and local governments—was
doomed to defeat because of its controversial authorization for the
legislature to impose a state income tax.

However, in respect to the running of Illinois, the major outcome
of the 1966 balloting was the Republicans' recapture of the Illinois
House. It wasn't even close. The final seat count in favor of the GOP,
99 to 78, left Democrats stunned and dispirited. Many of them contended privately that their party's poor showing in 1966 was a backlash in many parts of the state against the growing Vietnam War, the
increasing demonstrations in the civil rights movement and the
domestic policies of President Johnson's administration.

Nevertheless, while Democrats looked within themselves to
address their sudden slide with Illinois voters, the return of the
House to the Republican fold boded well for Arrington more than
any politician. This was the key development between 1965 and the
start of 1967 that put him on his legislative apex. A Democratic-dom-
inated House, always ready to blunt his Senate actions, was no more.

He was now clearly on a par with Kerner. Actually, he was on more than equal footing with the Democratic governor, prompting Kerner partisans to grouse privately that the governor would have to grovel more than ever before at Arrington's feet to get anything he wanted legislatively. Some said with exasperation that Arrington might as well be governor. McGloon and Touhy were even telling folks that they fully expected Arrington to run for governor in 1968.

Arrington himself was mum on such speculation—at least to those not part of his inner circle. He did allow, as the lawmakers convened for business at the beginning of 1967, that he considered his health to be no hindrance to anything in his political future. His past heart attacks were exactly that—part of his past, he insisted. The onus was not on him, he asserted, but on others to summon up the energy needed to keep up with the heavy legislative work load he envisioned for the first session of 1967.

At the same time, Arrington exercised caution—in spite of his dominating role—not to slight his new GOP counterpart in the House, Ralph Tyler Smith.

The return to control of the House by Republicans relegated Touhy to minority leader and opened the door to the election of the first Republican speaker since John W. Lewis Jr. of Marshall held the post in the early 1960s. Lewis, whose years in the legislature went back to 1941, was still in the House and wanted to return to the presiding officer's podium. However, the speakership went to Smith, a fifty-one-year-old lawyer first elected to the lower chamber in 1954. His election to the post was assured when most of the GOP representatives from Cook County threw their support behind him—even though Smith resided in Alton, the Mississippi River city in southwestern Illinois that Arrington's parents were living in when Arrington was born.

Smith was a bit of a political anomaly because his district covered a Democratic industrial area in the western part of Madison County. But, his hold on his seat was ensured by the cumulative voting system that guaranteed representation for the minority party in the election of three representatives from each House district (a procedure discarded as a result of the electorate's approval in 1980 of the so-called Cutback Amendment to the Illinois Constitution).

There were more than a few Norman Rockwell touches in Smith's background. Born in Granite City, he received a bachelor of arts degree from Illinois College in 1937 and graduated with honors from law school at Washington University in St. Louis in 1940. While there, he held a forty-hour-a-week job as desk clerk and bookkeeper at the YMCA in Granite City. Serving as a navy officer in World War II, he commanded a gunboat in the Pacific during the last part of the war. After his release from active duty, Smith, a Presbyterian, moved to Alton and began to practice law.

One thing Smith had not commanded was the spotlight during his House years. Espousing positions that avoided both liberal and conservative extremes, Smith was associated mainly with nuts-and-bolts legislation—measures dealing with highways and traffic safety, along with revenue and appropriation bills. "I like to think," he used to say, "I know what it takes to run Illinois." In political jargon, he was a good legislative mechanic though he never displayed any of the political dynamism of Arrington.

Smith's ascension to the top of the House obviously invited immediate comparisons with Arrington. How, it was asked, could Smith begin to coexist on a par with Arrington? Their personalities were markedly in contrast: Smith's being so outwardly restrained and the other's being everything but that. And wasn't Smith really just a beneficiary of a statewide Republican resurgence that in many ways had been stoked by the forcefulness of Arrington?

The prophecy was clear enough to the soothsayers: Smith was bound to be grossly overshadowed by Arrington, sparking GOP disunity between the two chambers and, consequently, hurdles to the Republicans' legislative progressions.

But it didn't happen.

Arrington was a paragon of patience in dealing with Smith, conspicuously turning off around Smith the up-and-down currents of the Arrington persona so unnerving to Democrats and some of his fellow Republican senators. In short, Arrington went to great length to avoid upstaging the new speaker.

Once the inaugural 1967 session got under way, Arrington includ-

ed Smith in the numerous press conferences he called to promote
GOP agenda items. Smith was not as schooled as Arrington in dealing with the fourth estate, but Arrington did not take advantage of
those occasions to portray his far greater track record in leadership
and in addressing big picture issues. Veteran observers hadn't foreseen the low-key Arrington who appeared with Smith.

Downstate House Republicans concluded early in the session
that their fears of the speaker being dominated by Arrington apparently were not to materialize. If some had any criticism of Smith, it
was that he seemed subject to undue influence by House
Republicans from Chicago, led by House majority leader William E.
Pollack, a Chicagoan.

Nevertheless, Smith got good grades as he presided in sonorous
tones over the lower chamber. It couldn't have been easy, but his grip
on the House reins did not waver as he wielded the gavel through
boiling debates on open housing, tax increase measures and other
controversies and Democratic filibustering. Predictably, his performance catapulted him into the select group of Republican leaders mentioned as possible candidates for the party's nomination for governor
the following year.

Arrington's silence on any interest he might have entertained
about the office did not inhibit him from one cogent observation.
When Frank Maier of the *Chicago Daily News* asked him whether
the 1967 record of the General Assembly would be crucial to the
GOP's hopes of capturing the governor's office in 1968, Arrington
quickly replied:

"You bet your life. The Republican Party in Illinois will prosper
or falter on what we do…."

The Republican legislators did not blow it. The degree to which
a party's legislative record possibly affected the party's candidate for
governor may have been only in the eyes of a beholder. However, if
the next GOP nominee for governor wanted to draw upon the party's
legislative performance in 1967 for sustenance, there was much to
choose from.

The session covering the first six months of 1967 was remembered
as one in which lawmakers signed off on asking voters to decide on

the calling of a constitutional convention, approved another submission to voters seeking approval of a billion-dollar bond issue to fight air and water pollution, took a major step toward the regulation of firearms, passed legislation seeking to reduce abuses in the extension of consumer credit, worked out revisions in the state mental health code to greater protect individuals' civil rights in commitments to institutions and finally gave a green light to codes of ethics for all three governmental branches—legislative, executive and judicial.

Although Kerner again failed to obtain the additional revenue-generating package he wanted, Arrington and Smith passed a new revenue program that they insisted was sufficient to finance broadened state services. Their biggest new revenue producer was a hike from 4 to 5 cents on a dollar in the state sales tax. Part of the added money went to municipalities. Other levy hikes passed were a 1-cent per gallon increase in the motor fuel assessment, a 2-cent a pack jump in the state cigarette tax and a modest increase in the corporation franchise tax.

The Republican majorities in each chamber made their voices heard loudly on anticrime legislation, as always a top GOP priority. Besides the action on gun control, the party's lawmakers spearheaded passage of measures aimed at curbing looting during riots, providing stronger penalties for armed crimes of violence, upping the funds and expanding the curriculum for the state's local police training program, setting minimum salaries for local police officers and firemen and hiking the state police ranks to 1,400 persons from 1,100. All of these bills were signed by Kerner, who was on record in support of some of them during the session.

On the other hand, one GOP-backed measure to combat crime that ignited heated debate before being passed was vetoed by the governor on constitutional grounds. It would have authorized law enforcement officers to stop and search a person in public places in Illinois if the officers suspected that the individual had committed or was about to commit a felony. However, Kerner—a longtime opponent of so-called stop-and-frisk legislation—nixed the bill on a ground that it departed from traditional constitutional safeguards against unreasonable searches and seizures.

The gun control legislation was a milestone in the increasingly vociferous drive to bring about some degree of accountability in the state in the sale and possession of firearms. Kerner and some other Chicago Democrats wanted the General Assembly to require registration of all handguns sold to the public as well as licensing of the owners by local police authorities. But, sportsmen's groups and gun enthusiasts saw those undertakings as infringements on an individual's right to bear arms.

Enter Arrington.

Believing issues surrounding the proliferation of guns were too volatile to be ignored, Arrington introduced middle-ground legislation requiring Illinois residents to obtain a permit—a firearm owner's identification card—from the state's Department of Public Safety before buying or possessing firearms or ammunition. In doing so, he had support from the Illinois State Rifle Association, the Chicago Crime Commission and certain other contingents. They felt that registration of owners of weapons instead of the guns themselves was the most workable and acceptable approach to addressing the trafficking of firearms.

Arrington's proposed legislation was not part of the package of crime-fighting measures recommended for passage in *Building a Better Illinois*, the GOP legislative mandate for 1967. His move on the matter did not endear him to a number of Republicans and Democrats south of the Chicago area, especially from southern Illinois, who opposed any restrictive legislation pertaining to firearms. To many rural Illinoisans, even a somewhat modest regulatory proposal like Arrington's was a political hot potato.

Typical of those recognizing this was Representative Ben C. Blades, a Fairfield Republican and former state trooper, who said the legislation "has a good intention in seeking to keep guns out of the hands of criminals and others who shouldn't have them. But it won't do the job."

Nevertheless, Arrington pushed through the Senate what became known as his compromise proposal—earning in the process nods of approval from editorial writers and liberal groups openly acknowledging that, without the intervention of Arrington, nothing on gun control was likely to pass. Smith followed by successfully ushering

Arrington's program through the House. The legislation then was approved by Kerner, who conceded that half a loaf was better than no loaf in dealing with gun control.

While the attachment of Arrington's name to sponsorship of the firearm owners' registration law was not anticipated, his lead role on so many other developments of consequence during the session was foreseen. Few measures of import for Illinoisans passed without the Arrington imprimatur, meaning that either his name was on them or he was instrumental in orchestrating their passage.

As one of many examples, Arrington was the sponsor of the formal resolution approved by the General Assembly that called on voters to decide in the following year's election whether they wanted a state constitutional convention to be held. The Illinois Constitution study commission set up by the legislature in 1965 did conclude as predicted that wholesale revision of the charter through a convention offered the only possibility for adequate revision. For years, Arrington was among those convinced that a full-scale convention was needed to address numerous outdated sections of the then ninety-seven-year-old document.

Arrington also was on board in 1967 in support of the bulk of the recommendations coming out of the Commission on the Organization of the General Assembly, another outgrowth of the 1965 session. Of course, many of the steps for a legislative overhaul deemed necessary by the panel (the Katz commission to some and COOGA to others, including Arrington) had been urged for some time by Arrington.

To his credit, Representative Katz, the commission chairman, had not strayed from his diplomatic determination from the start to accord Arrington and his views the broadest latitude as the panel fulfilled its mandate. As a result, Arrington proceeded without hesitation to implement in the Senate by fiat in 1967 a number of the alterations sought by the commission for streamlining of General Assembly operations. The bipartisan harmony on the subject buttressed Democrat Katz in making similar headway in the House.

Action was not delayed on COOGA's most significant proposition—that the General Assembly increase its relevancy by meeting annually instead of every two years, another longtime Arrington objective.

A few hours before the legislature concluded the session covering the first six months of 1967, the Senate voted along party lines to adopt an Arrington resolution recalling the General Assembly back into session on September 11, 1967, to react to gubernatorial vetoes of bills enacted earlier in the year and to consider certain other matters. The House went on to concur in the action. At the same time, Arrington let it be known that he intended to also have the legislature back in session in 1968 to address timely issues. All of this was ground breaking activity, key steps in Arrington's long contemplated game plan for revolution of the legislature.

Under the then existing Illinois Constitution of 1870, the General Assembly was required to convene early in each odd-numbered year. The document was vague on adjournment. Nevertheless, midnight on the last day of June in the odd-numbered years was the traditional adjournment time, and the legislators normally adjourned sine die —meaning without designating a day on which to assemble again. Lawmakers did sometimes meet for short periods between the biennial six-month sessions, but the meetings resulted from calls by the governor instead of by legislative leaders.

State voters were asked in the 1964 election if they wanted to amend the constitution to provide for annual sessions, but the proposal was rejected. Subsequently, Illinois Attorney General William G. Clark, a Democrat, held that the General Assembly could have annual sessions merely by adjourning until a specific date instead of sine die.

Arrington's leadership on the tradition-shattering move by the legislature to call itself back into session at a time of its own choosing was, for him, a capstone of the first session in 1967. The Senate Democrats were not in favor of returning to Springfield so soon, but they knew that on this subject and many others at this juncture they were up against a legislative powerhouse on an unprecedented roll.

Few upper chamber Democrats would have taken issue privately with a July 5, 1967, editorial in the *Daily News* that called the just-completed session a piece of work by Arrington.

Expressing a view coming out of many other newspaper typewriters, the *Daily News* declared that "the 1967 Legislature was 'Arrington's session,' meaning that the whole shooting-match bears the imprint of the imperious majority leader of the Senate...."

"As you look back," the editorial continued, "this session composes into a rather respectable monument to its principal boss, even though some sizable chips were knocked off it along the way."

The paper did not ignore Smith in praising the session's output, even though a contrast between the speaker and Arrington was underlined. "Smith's tactics in the House were radically different from Arrington's," noted the *Daily News*. "Where Arrington knocked heads, Smith rubbed backs. But the two, in spite of differences, were an effective team...."

Although Arrington bent over backward to combat the casting of Smith as a second fiddle when they appeared together before the press, a backseat for the speaker in the media spotlight was inevitable. The intense preoccupation of the press with Arrington, so evident in the stormy 1965 General Assembly session, reached a peak in 1967.

By this stage, most of Arrington's life was being carried out in a fishbowl anyway. He made few moves that escaped the attention of reporters and broadcasters. This was hardly unexpected since his political career was receiving the bulk of his time and energy. He still maintained his law office in Chicago, but his private practice consisted mainly of legal services for Combined Insurance.

The relationship between Arrington and the press was, in the barest sense, a very symbiotic one. Extremely so.

The senator and the media—the segment of it covering Illinois public life—were two dissimilar entities existing in a more or less intimate association of mutual benefit. This did not mean that they were enamored with each other, nor did it imply anything to the contrary. It did mean that Arrington and the fourth estate each needed the other to sustain the main reason of each for being.

As pointed out earlier, journalists covering Illinois government recognized long before Arrington became Senate leader that he was good for business. However, the characteristics that made this so became just more accentuated after he began calling the shots.

Namely: his rapid-fire proposals for the governing of the state;

his tell-it-like-it-was manner, straight from the gut without hesitation regardless of where the chips might land; the temper with the explosiveness of nitro; and his ready accessibility to questioners, on or off the Senate floor. Arrington was a fountainhead of news and, in turn, a money-maker for those who made a living reporting it.

The quid pro quo was that press coverage was a necessity for Arrington to achieve the political dynamism that had become the major goal of his life. Without publicity, his advocacy of a public betterment agenda and what many saw as an accompanying self-aggrandizement along the way were going nowhere.

Norton Kay, the press secretary for Governor Dan Walker in the 1970s, hit the nail on the head. When Walker, a little known Democrat commenced a walk the length of Illinois to first call attention to his gubernatorial candidacy, Kay said that press coverage of the undertaking was the key to its success. As Kay put it, "If the press didn't report that Dan was walking, then we weren't walking."

Arrington entertained no qualm about his need for media coverage. At the same time, word persisted that he retained a healthy skepticism of reporters, or certain ones at least. As king of the hill, he naturally found more demands on his time for interviews. Turndowns of requests almost never happened, but some coming to see him felt less than comfortable in his presence.

Dorothy Storck of *Chicago's American* felt a twinge of unease when she visited Arrington in his law office for a profile in early 1967 that sought to go beyond the normal political stuff.

She opened her story after the interview by writing that it was "a little like going into the principal's office. There is this strange feeling of guilt—but you can't quite remember what it is you've done wrong." She did find Arrington courteous, she said, but in an "almost courtly...steel-encased way."

"But," she quickly tacked on, "he isn't overly fond of reporters. They have, he says, misquoted him too often."

Perhaps as a reflection of this mistrust, Storck noted that a "young assistant named Don or Tom" was enlisted to take notes on everything transpiring in the interview. The note taker had to be either Donald Tolva or Tom Corcoran. Tolva, a graduate of the law school at Loyola University in Chicago, had progressed by that time from being a legislative intern to a full-time GOP Senate staffer under Arrington. Corcoran, who was raised on his family's farm near Ottawa, Illinois, and who graduated from the University of Notre Dame, joined the Republican Senate staff after working for a number of the party's victorious state Senate candidates in the 1966 election.

As Storck probed for personal insight into Arrington while Tolva or Corcoran took notes, she found, as she went on to write, "the most powerful politician in the legislature…hasn't time for small talk."

"There is no idle chatter," noted her article.

In spite of that finding, Storck did not strike out in trying to bring out a softer side of Arrington. He admitted to having given up cigarettes completely at the urging of son Michael and, in view of his heart attacks, he revealed that he wore a metal tag around his neck to inform persons about the medication to give him in event he had another one. He even complied with a request by Storck to see the tag.

"Surprisingly," she related in her piece, "he unbuttons his white shirt to search inside against his bare chest for the tag. He can't find it right away, and—surprisingly again—he grins like a kid about to produce his prize aggie."

The writer was caught off guard by the grin, which didn't fit her picture of Arrington.

"It isn't often that Arrington grins," Storck concluded. "That is a fairly uncontrolled thing to do—grin. And everything about Arrington suggests complete control. His words do not tumble out. They come measured with a slight—and controlled—intonation that is not quite a lisp.

"His hands do not fidget. And his eyes gaze through beige-rimmed bifocals with disconcerting steadiness."

Reporters in the Statehouse—the ones who followed Arrington the most—saw him in much the same vein. They found him as programmed in answering their questions as he was in orchestrating the business of the Senate. There were no complaints about the availability of Arrington. It was that symbiosis. His understanding of the role of the press in the scheme of things—and particularly in his scheme of things—could not be overstated.

Yet, the scribes sensed detachment in dealing with Arrington. It went beyond getting the message about his impatience for chitchat. They detected a standoffishness in Arrington, a person they had no choice but to accord rapt attention when the legislature was in session. They got only so close, but no closer. They were kept at arm's length.

While journalistic purists would have frowned on a cozy relationship between Arrington and the press as a disincentive to objective coverage, the reality was that most of the Illinois politicians benefiting from consistently favorable publicity courted the press unabashedly. They were frequent visitors to the smoky Statehouse pressroom on the Capitol's third floor, and they did not hesitate to sidle up to the bar with reporters at wee hour watering holes. They figured—quite on target—that it was simply blarney about reporters still writing critical stories about officials with whom they socialized.

Arrington was not known, contrary to some of his fellow pols, to lavish praise on or pen congratulatory notes to reporters lauding his actions. Likewise, he refrained from making the mistake of some in his shoes who openly screamed about the appearance of articles critical of them.

As an aide in close proximity to Arrington, John Dailey observed that his boss did on occasion "talk back" in private to columnists who sought to take him to task. Arrington was careful, Dailey said, "to not attack a story itself, the opinions being expressed," but would "attack only factual inaccuracies." A columnist stung by such Arrington criticism "might feel discredited," added Dailey, leaving the writer often angry and likely "to strike at Arrington again."

Nevertheless, emphasized Dailey, "Arrington really didn't care because he was so confident that he didn't have to kowtow to anybody."

Where the press was concerned, Dailey simply felt that Arrington "really didn't look outside for approval or acceptance. He was not insecure. He was comfortable in his own skin. He knew who he was because he was a self-made man, not just financially but in the kind of person he was, the kind he wanted to be."

Arrington avoided playing favorites among the press. He was not a secretive tipster, meaning he didn't pull a certain reporter off to the side to give him or her an early lead on soon-to-break legislative developments or reveal to the scribe some unsavory activity that ought to be investigated. Pragmatism was one reason. The Chicago newspaper world still was dominated by four major and very competitive dailies at the time. To get caught being partial to one in the news-gathering game was an invitation to hostile treatment from the others.

The pressroom was an enclave unto itself in the Statehouse. Some officials were too paranoid about the media to even set foot in the lair of the fourth estate. Arrington was certainly not one of them. He too was among the leading news makers who never ended visits to the pressroom without at least poking his head into the cramped working cubicle of each Chicago daily. Also, unlike some other notable personages from the Chicago area, he was not oblivious of the desks of downstate newspapers—often dubbed the pygmy press—or the wire services. The stops by a figure like Arrington as he made his way through the pressroom were observed closely by the news hounds.

When the legislature was in session, the pressroom was a loose assemblage of roughly thirty radio, television and newspaper reporters and photographers. The number dropped considerably when lawmakers were not around. During those periods, the press corps still included the Statehouse bureau chiefs for the Chicago dailies and the individuals manning the bureaus of the principal St. Louis papers, the *Post-Dispatch* and *Globe-Democrat*. Statehouse correspondents for the *Copley News Service* and the *Chamberlain-Loftus News Service* remained on hand, as did the Statehouse reporters and columnists for the *Illinois State Journal* and the *Illinois State Register* (the two Springfield dailies that were merged into one paper, the *State Journal-Register*, in 1974). In addition, the wires—the *Associated Press* and *United Press International*—each were staffed year-round by a bureau chief and one or two additional folks. The presence of broadcasters was thin when legislators were out of town—although a few stayed close to the scene, like highly respected Bill Miller, who pioneered radio coverage of Illinois government through news feeds to stations around the state.

A respectable portion of the most thorough detailing of legislative doings was carried out by reporters from downstate papers who called the pressroom home mainly during sessions. Correspondents like leprechaunish William O'Connell of the *Peoria Journal Star* or steady Edward Nash of the *Waukegan News-Sun*. A decent share of the major disclosures of official wrongdoing also was attributable to downstate scribes. This became quite apparent in the final years of the 1960s when papers such as the *Alton Evening Telegraph* dispatched to the Statehouse staffers with strong investigative skills (like Edward T. Pound).

On the whole, though, the tempo of the pressroom was set by the Chicago dailies and their Capitol bureaus. And, it could be a crazy pace indeed. It was inevitable that the rough-and-ready world of journalism in Illinois' largest city, where the big dailies competed in cutthroat fashion, spilled over into the Statehouse pressroom. No quarter was shown as each of their bureaus scrambled to outdo the others, whether in scoring a beat on a news story or in uncovering dirt on politicians.

The overriding importance of what the Chicago reporters were writing was visible to all making early morning rounds in Springfield on legislative days. The daily sight of Chicago morning papers the *Tribune* and the *Sun-Times* at the State House Inn breakfast table of Arrington and his crew was typical of the scene in other Springfield hotels and Statehouse offices. The hands of more than a few of the potentates trembled as they hastily turned inside the papers to see what the leading political writers, the *Tribune's* George Tagge and John Dreiske of the *Sun-Times*, were saying about them.

Later each day, runners or secretaries for Statehouse bigwigs anxiously waited at the Capitol newsstand for the arrival of the afternoon or "pm" newspapers. The one grabbed most quickly was the *Daily News*, a depository of well-crafted writing and the hard-bitten output of Mike Royko.

Chicago's most widely read columnist, Royko famously went to bat for everyday working types by sticking pins in the high and mighty with sarcasm, satire, poignancy and flat-out humor. His targets primarily were politicians, especially Daley and lesser denizens of Chicago's Democratic machine. Royko's visits to Springfield may have been infrequent, but his impact on Statehouse discourse and imagery was heavy.

In a broader sense, Royko personified the boisterousness of Chicago journalism so immortalized in the play, *The Front Page*, by Ben Hecht and Charles MacArthur. Many of the raucous traits it portrayed remained visible in the old *City News Bureau of Chicago*, which still was going strong in the 1960s as a training ground for young reporters as it fed police, fire and other news stories to the papers and radio and television stations in the city. Before joining the *Daily News*, Royko was a night editor for the *City News Bureau*. More than one Chicago reporter covering Springfield in Arrington's time practiced tricks of the trade perfected at the bureau.

While every word under the byline of Tagge, Dreiske or Royko might impact a politician's career, the reporting by those running the day in and day out operations of the pressroom bureaus also could not be ignored. They were the front liners who covered the basics of Illinois government, and they had to be cultivated or at least handled gingerly. Arrington assumed this responsibility for himself—although never doing so in a condescending fashion. Many major officials, leading off with Kerner, relied on emissaries in dealing with the working press. The governor often seemed uneasy at press conferences, but he had a skilled spokesman in Christopher Vlahoplus, who left the *UPI* bureau in Springfield to join Kerner's staff.

A very interesting collection of individuals staffed the pressroom bureaus as Arrington rose to news-making prominence in the 1960s. For the *Sun-Times*, there was young Morton Kondracke, who went on to gain stature as a journalist in the nation's capital, and persnickety Burnell Heinecke, who pushed for details in his stories that many officials were hesitant to disclose. The *American's* man, Malden Jones, excitedly approached Statehouse coverage with a full-speed-ahead demeanor. The direct counterpart in the pressroom for this writer, who manned the *Post-Dispatch* bureau, was the Globe-Democrat's Marion (Hap) Lynes, a gentlemanly old schooler. The most colorful of the bureau persons, by many lengths, was cherubic Henry Hanson of the *Daily News*. Hanson mixed drinking and fine writing with a generous dollop of mischievous puck. His intrusive antics to land exclusive stories sometimes entangled him in the damnedest imbroglios with officials, but he was impossible not to like.

The bureau chief engendering the highest respect in the Statehouse world was Robert P. Howard of the *Tribune*. No journalist was more of a Capitol fixture than Howard, unless it be Charles N. Whalen, the mild-mannered *AP* bureau head who'd covered Illinois government for more than a quarter of a century before Arrington came to power. Howard had more dimensions than most of his pressroom contemporaries. A historian, he went on to become president of the Illinois State Historical Society and the author of a definitive history of the state, as well as a book on Illinois governors.

A factor in the popularity of Howard was that, in sticking to straight news reporting, he avoided doing the investigative probing that left unfavorable tastes in the minds of those targeted. When an unsavory situation in Springfield required reportorial sleuthing, the editors of the *Tribune*— Illinois' largest daily newspaper—sent crack gumshoe reporters from the home office to handle the task. This was a savvy way in that, as an upshot, Howard remained in good stead with all sources in covering the regular news.

As stalwarts of the pressroom establishment, Howard, Whalen and a few others did not find it easy to countenance the radically changing climate of Statehouse reporting in the late 1960s when the first of a wave of stinging muckrakers—hell bent on exposing corruption in Illinois public life— burst onto the scene. The older hands lamented the transformation of the pressroom from a largely cozy nest of congeniality for some elected officeholders and bureaucrats into a hotbed of distrust of officialdom.

The changing tide affected Arrington little on the personal front. He'd never used the pressroom for socializing in the first place, and he was to remain untouched by the growing disclosures of wrongdoing that were tarnishing the reputations of numerous top Illinois officials as the 1960s neared an end.

Arrington may not have generated a warm and fuzzy rapport with members of the Statehouse press corps, but it was rather remarkable that they virtually all viewed him as above suspicion in the ferreting out of official corruption. Arrington was one subject the pressroom veterans and newer arrivals agreed on. His hands were clean of any crumbs from the state's fiscal cookie jar.

As the 1967 spring session entered its climactic weeks, the entire media crowd also was of a mind that Arrington was omnipotent in his influence over his fellow Senate Republicans and in his dealings with Illinois Republicans in general. Standing up to Arrington within the GOP had seemingly become out of the question.

Imagine the shock, then, at the stunning rebuke of Arrington by his own seatmates in what was easily the session's most dramatic episode. Unfolding with about two weeks remaining before adjournment, it left Arrington's hold on power hanging by a thread. Arrington suddenly knew the awful feeling of being an emperor with no clothes.

Chapter 17

ℭ

Leadership on the Brink

*T*here never was any question about the really hot-button issue before Illinois lawmakers in their 1967 spring session. It was the passion-ridden pursuit of open occupancy legislation. Looming unsettlingly over the session, freedom of residency spurred a surefire wedge debate that dominated legislative consciousness—whether some in the chambers wanted to admit it or not.

Blacks in the General Assembly—and their number included a few firebrands—were under a gun to get the legislature off the dime in the confrontation of segregated housing. The civil rights movement was crystallizing on the issue in the legislature. Keeping it under wrap after interminable festering beneath the skin of the General Assembly was no longer in the cards.

The 1960s were, after all, about change. However, to a considerable extent, the General Assembly had been immune to the pressures generated by the societal upheaval imploding the country. The Statehouse had been a relatively safe cocoon from the riptides of rebellions in the outside world—the challenge by the early wave of baby boomers to the political establishment's espousal of the Vietnam War and the strident refusal by blacks to accept any longer the denial of certain rights.

The nonviolent side of the civil rights campaign, initiatives like peaceful lunch counter sit-ins, teach-ins, love-ins and such, reached its heyday in the early 1960s. In the latter years of the decade, though, nonviolent protest was stuttering, and violent eruptions in

Los Angeles, Harlem and other places were taking center stage. Activists had been energized greatly in the political spectrum by the passage by Congress and signing by President Johnson of the Civil Rights Act of 1964. By 1967, many of them found it hard to swallow that commensurate political action in Illinois had so languished.

Voluntary and involuntary restrictions on blacks obtaining housing in parts of Chicago, its suburbs and many sizable downstate cities were an especially frustrating sore point for blacks and liberal Democrats laboring for years to bring civil rights issues to the serious attention of the General Assembly. While recognizing that statutes probably wouldn't alter attitudes, they felt, nevertheless, that legislative remedies could counter the orchestrations of some in the real estate, insurance and mortgage lending industries that contributed to so-called redlining—the perpetuation of housing discrimination through the withholding of home-loan funds or insurance in respect to situations considered poor economic risks.

Thus, goaded by irritable constituents no longer patient with foot-dragging in Springfield, the small contingent of blacks in the House (under fifteen in the 177-seat body), utilized filibustering and other real or threatened tactics of disruption in 1967 to prevent the chamber from turning its back on open housing bills.

As a result, the blacks—quarterbacked by Chicago Democrat Harold Washington, a future mayor of the city—succeeded with strong Democratic backing and assistance from a handful of Republicans in pushing more than one measure on the controversial subject out of the House. Indeed, the helpful Republicans may have been few in number, but they were front and center in the charge for passage.

For instance, Representative Noble W. Lee, a Chicago Republican and dean of the John Marshall Law School in his city, sponsored one of the approved bills, a measure he called "the simplest and most straightforward open occupancy law you can pass."

It simply provided for the Illinois criminal code to be amended to prohibit a person from refusing to "sell, lease or rent real property for the purpose of residential occupancy thereof solely because of race, creed, color, national origin or ancestry." Violation would have been a misdemeanor.

The success of open housing proposals in the House was not unexpected. Nor was the fate of the issue in the Senate.

However, it was the nature of the upper chamber's reaction to open occupancy bills, whether originating in the Senate or coming from the House, that produced hard-boiled drama—the bare-knuckle stuff that journalists cannot seem to get enough of. Still, again, there was little suspense hanging over the outcome in the Senate. All around could have written the script ahead of time. One remarkable twist, though, caught about everybody flat-footed. The individual who pulled it off was lucky to escape with his political skin intact.

Almost to a man, the GOP majority in the Senate (Chicago Democrat Esther Saperstein was the only woman in the body in 1967) opposed open occupancy legislation. Those Republicans who might have had second thoughts about their stance against such legislation were kept in line on the issue by a coterie of their seatmates particularly steadfast in their opposition to fair housing measures.

Heading the circle of unyielding opponents was the small band of Republican senators from Chicago itself—men like John J. Lanigan and Joseph J. Krasowski—and a number of the Republicans representing Chicago's largely white suburbs.

Just as blacks and some of the other Democrats were prodded by their constituents to win a breakthrough on open occupancy legislation, Lanigan, Krasowski and their suburban allies were under pressure from many white residents in their districts to block any such advance.

The opposition was based on a gnawing fear that the stability of largely Caucasian neighborhoods in Chicago and many of its suburbs would be disrupted by an overnight influx of blacks and other minorities as a result of freedom of residency legislation. Chief among the concerns was that such legislation would open a wide door to so-called blockbusting. This was the word for an unscrupulous scheme in which profiteers induced home owners to sell quickly, and usually at a loss, by stressing a likelihood of depressed property values as a result of threatened minority encroachment. In turn, the homes were resold at inflated prices.

As Lanigan and other anti-open housing Republicans stood their ground in the Senate in what they perceived as the defense of the sanctity of their home neighborhoods or towns, they came under heavy fire from critics inside and outside of the chamber for allegedly undercutting the hopes and aspirations of blacks fighting for quality of life improvements. At the worst, Lanigan and the others were branded as outright racists.

More than one Democrat joining in the criticism of the fair housing opponents harbored private reservations about the potential impacts of the proposed legislation. However, these Democrats were covered in backing their party's line in support of the legislation because of the virtual certainty that the almost total GOP opposition meant the legislation had little or no chance of getting out of the upper chamber.

The solidarity of the GOP on the issue prompted some in the Statehouse press crowd—most of whom were more than subtly sympathetic to open housing advocates—to categorize the leading Senate Republicans in opposition as members of a murderers' row against fair housing bills. Some of these Republicans occupied seats on the Committee on Registration and Miscellany, to which all open occupancy bills were assigned through an arrangement deemed necessary by Senate Republicans for maintaining political equilibrium within their party's caucus.

The makeup of the eight-member GOP majority on the committee ensured its burial ground role for freedom of residence bills. The chairman was attorney Frank M. Ozinga of the south Chicago suburb of Evergreen Park, a traditional conservative known affectionately to his colleagues as "the stubborn Dutchman." The vice chairman was Chicago lawyer Albert E. Bennett. Lanigan, a thirty-two-year-old public accountant at the time, and his hard-nosed friend Krasowski, nicknamed "K-25" after the number of his district, were on the panel. The other four Republicans were Chicagoan Walter Duda, a teacher and school counselor; realtor Arthur R. Swanson of Chicago; Karl Berning of Deerfield, a former Lake County treasurer; and Howard R. Mohr of Forest Park, owner of a fuel oil company. The automatic thumbs-down from these eight to all fair housing measures certainly justified their designation by media folks as a murderers' row on the issue.

The committee's four Democrats, led by Fred Smith, had no more chance than Don Quixote in his unrealistic attack on a windmill of advancing any open occupancy bill out of the panel. It mattered not that one of the four, Richard H. Newhouse, a University of Chicago law graduate, argued eloquently for passage of such legislation. Along with Smith, Newhouse was among the Senate's four black Democrats.

Previews of the initial session of 1967 hardly predicted that Ozinga's panel would be a headliner, but the committee's hearings in the old, ornate judicial chamber on the Statehouse's second floor became spectacles when open housing bills were on the docket. On those occasions, people on both sides of the housing issue joined all reporters and broadcasters in the building in jamming into every inch of the room long before panel members entered to take their seats. Subsequently, as witnesses were questioned, a stern Ozinga frequently had to rap his gavel for order when catcallers in the audience threatened to get out of hand. It was great theater for the news business.

As the leader of the Senate, Arrington had acquiesced to the process in the body for considering open residency measures by signing off on the graveyard role of the Ozinga committee as a pragmatic step toward the maintenance of the unity on his side that was essential for many other issues.

And yet, as the session moved on, there were rumblings about Arrington. Signs indicated early on that he was not completely at ease with his party's rigid stonewalling in the Senate on an issue commanding a lot of attention. The signs took on meat in mid May, about a month and a half before the intended adjournment of the session, when Arrington backed a move to exempt open housing bills introduced in the Senate from a deadline for Senate committee action on measures originating in the chamber. This didn't sit well with those wanting fair housing bills killed with dispatch.

Then, a week later, Arrington personally delivered to the registration and miscellany panel a modestly worded proposal for the fostering of open housing that he'd worked up himself. GOP opponents of any statutory language on the subject still were not overtly incensed with Arrington, figuring he was making a token move to counter the charges of racial bigotry increasingly being hurled at Senate Republicans. They knew, too, that the Ozinga committee was not likely to give any special consideration to the Arrington initiative simply because of his legislative potency. In fact, Ozinga had pointedly informed Arrington of such.

For the opponents, the Ozinga panel was always their ace in the hole in the Senate.

Thus, and predictably so in what most observers assumed to be a preordained script, Ozinga's committee formally refused with one month remaining in the session to give a green light to any of the Senate-introduced fair housing bills before it. Arrington's proposal was tossed aside when it was offered as an amendment to a bill submitted by Senator Cecil A. Partee, a black attorney from Chicago.

Considered the main bill on open occupancy introduced in the Senate, Partee's proposal would have prohibited a property owner or his agent from discriminating in the sale or rental of property on the basis of race or creed.

But, before voting on the Partee bill, the committee refused to adopt Arrington-proposed changes in the measure that would have greatly rewritten it. Arrington's amendment would have banned racial discrimination by real estate brokers, salespersons and others in property transactions. However, the right of a property owner to sell or lease real estate he or she occupied as a residence would not have been subject to the law under Arrington's wording. After rejecting the Arrington amendment, the committee voted along party lines, 8 to 4, against a favorable recommendation on the Partee measure.

For all practical purposes, the registration committee's blockage of all Senate bills on fair housing should have signaled the end of any further serious consideration of the issue in the session set to conclude at the end of June 1967. The committee still would have before it legislation on the subject from the House (such as the Noble Lee measure), but its burial by the Senate panel was viewed as automatic. Correspondingly, any new move by Arrington to intervene in the matter was hardly thought to be likely.

That's when the most amazing episode of the session—a scenario darn near shocking in most minds—transfixed the Statehouse for several days in the middle of June as a result of an Arrington thunderbolt out of the blue. Arrington was not done, not by a long shot.

Without any advance notice, he orchestrated an unorthodox maneuver to bring an open housing bill to the floor of the Senate for the first time. He did it by getting the body's Public Welfare Committee to vote to amend a minor public aid bill before it (a measure already passed by the House) with language that turned the bill into proposed freedom of residency legislation. Then, by the same vote of 8 to 7, the committee recommended the revised measure's passage.

For this to happen, three of the panel's ten Republicans joined with Paul Simon, Newhouse, Smith and the committee's other two Democrats to give the bill a green light. The GOP trio were the panel chairman, Naperville's Harris Fawell; Jack T. Knuepfer of Elmhurst; and Edward McBroom of Kankakee. Fawell and Knuepfer were known to be open to moderate fair housing proposals, but the conservative-minded McBroom's yes vote was unexpected.

Nevertheless, in explaining his position in committee, McBroom told caught-off-guard reporters that "it has been well known this session that Senator Arrington has favored a reasonable and workable bill on this problem."

Although the bill amended with Arrington's language wasn't as far-reaching as the most ardent fair housing backers desired, Arrington told the welfare panel that it was, as McBroom felt, a "reasonable approach" that could be accepted by persons in various walks of life.

The altered measure would have outlawed racial discrimination by persons in the sale or rental of any real estate or housing accommodation. However, it did not cover owner-occupied homes and owner-occupied apartment buildings containing ten or fewer household units. Too, condominiums and commonly named cooperative apartments were exempted.

Mild as his proposal seemed to some, Arrington's quick-strike move to bypass routine notification of his own caucus of his intention and to turn to a committee normally out of the loop on this

Left to right: Senator Cecil Partee, Lt. Governor Paul Simon,
Senator Arthur McGloon, Reverend Jesse Jackson,
Senator Arrington and Senator Charles Chew

explosive issue unleashed a hellish backlash from his Republican seatmates—the bulk of whom most emphatically did not favor any legislative action on open residency. To most of them, Arrington's stratagem was a sneak attack.

Lanigan, at any other time a supporter and admirer of Arrington, couldn't contain his anger over the unannounced maneuvering by Arrington to get the bill before the whole Senate. Equating the steps taken to bring this about with the "tactics used at Pearl Harbor," Lanigan added that "unfortunately, they are the tactics of my own leader."

Senator Robert W. Mitchler of Oswego, a Republican stalwart, chimed in, "Our leadership has violated our confidence by dropping this bombshell suddenly in our laps." But, he cautioned, Arrington and those aiding his effort "are certainly out of order this time if they expect us to rubber stamp this thing."

The acrimony of Mitchler and many others on his side of the aisle would be thrown in Arrington's face during a five-hour caucus of the GOP senators prior to the Senate's consideration of the public welfare committee's decisions on behalf of fair housing legislation.

Arrington was hardly a newcomer to being the main topic of the Statehouse buzz, but it was never before for being berated in a confab with his fellow Republican senators. The caucus was, as always, a closed-door affair, but the Capitol crowd had a pretty strong inkling of what was transpiring.

Some of those always mingling in the Statehouse when the General Assembly was in session were surmising, as the caucus went on and on, that the GOPers were in the process of demoting Arrington from his leadership post. Talk of other legislative matters went out the window as the fate of Arrington was conjectured by the well-dressed lobbyists stationed outside the doors of the third floor's two chambers.

Put on hold for the moment was the incessant deal-making by the varied interests congregating on the third floor balcony under the magnificent dome of the Statehouse. The normally cacophonous back-and-forth surrendered to a strange hush along the storied brass rail riding the parapet circling the balcony. That rail, with its elaborate lampposts, was a polestar of Illinois legislative legends and lore.

Why, many asked, did Arrington put himself in this position? Why would he risk ostracism within his own party ranks on an issue of bread-and-butter importance only to Democrats? Why?

There had to be more to it, most observers reasoned, than a move to simply show that not all Republicans were insensitive to the social inequities of segregated housing. Arrington already had made that point earlier in the session in a far less drastic fashion; one that didn't put his command of the Senate on the line. So, it was assumed, more had to be involved for Arrington to push the envelope on his leadership to such an extreme. A personal motive had to exist for Arrington to pull off something that he'd never countenance from any other Republican or Democrat in the chamber.

One guess was that Arrington was smarting privately from being painted as an intolerant obstacle for civil rights campaigners. Political memories were conveniently short on some things, but everlasting on others. As noted earlier, Arrington was quickly deprived of credit by civil rights advocates for his major role in the passage of 1961 legislation setting up the Illinois Fair Employment Practices Commission to counter discrimination in workplaces. To do this, he had gone against the grain on the GOP side of the Senate.

Arrington also had espoused, prior to 1967, the enactment of freedom of residency legislation, as long as it did not take effect until also approved by voters in a statewide referendum.

Other examples of moderation by Arrington on social issues through the years were there for all to see. But, they were overshadowed by certain lingering criticism of Arrington going back to the days—prior to the establishment through Arrington legislation of the Illinois Department of Public Aid—of his spearheading of highly-publicized legislative investigations of corruption in the state's public assistance programs. Accusations that Arrington had little concern for poor blacks and impoverished whites, primary recipients of public aid, refused to fade away. The aspersion was akin to a sore festering beneath the political surface of Arrington—under skin very thin to begin with.

If any individual had insight into Arrington's mind-set during the open housing showdown he ignited in 1967, it was John Dailey, a constant presence then at the senator's side. Dailey felt it important to try to put the matter into perspective in discussing Arrington with this writer on an icy day in February 2003 at Lake Geneva, Wisconsin.

Not to be forgotten, Dailey initially pointed out, was that Evanston was a biracial city, one with an identifiable black middle class. As one of the few Republican senators with an appreciable minority population in his district, the pragmatic side of Arrington sufficiently prompted him to not ignore the fair housing issue.

There was more to Arrington's thinking, though, Dailey stressed.

"When other GOP senators were asking him (Arrington) why he was doing this," said Dailey, "he replied that it was the right thing to do."

Arrington was not a crusader in the normal lexicon of politics, Dailey continued, "and he was against forced integration. However, he was for freedom of opportunity, and he believed that persons shouldn't be discriminated against living in a place if they could afford to live there. Arrington didn't take on an issue unless he had satisfied himself that the issue was right. And on this one, he did see discrimination in housing, as well as in other aspects of society."

As for the proposed legislation Arrington herded out of the public welfare panel, Dailey said that "he knew, practically speaking, that the bill wouldn't really do much. But, he wanted it passed as a symbol. He also thought that the bill, if approved, would go a long way to counter the social unrest so visible at the time."

"Another factor in Arrington's mind, in his political mind," added Dailey, "was that the open occupancy issue was dividing our party. So, in undertaking what he did, Arrington was attempting to defuse the issue politically. Yet, that consideration should not overshadow the fact that he was there to address issues and try to solve problems. And, I want to repeat, he did see this issue as a real problem."

Furthermore, in response to suggestions that Arrington went too far in forcing his GOP colleagues to face a Senate floor vote on open housing at that particular juncture, Dailey replied: "He was great at brinksmanship. He was skilled at going to the brink. This did scare many of his own Republican senators, who were chicken to do so. But, Arrington usually knew exactly what he was doing."

This time, though, the brinksmanship blew up in his face as far as his political brethren were concerned.

Since written records were not made of matters broached in caucuses, no transcript existed of what was said during the extraordinarily long one of the GOP senators beginning in the morning of June 16, 1967. Bits and pieces coming to light in the days afterward left no doubt, though, that Arrington was subjected to the most severe dressing down of his political career. As the rest of the Capitol remained on tenterhooks, Arrington was eating humble pie inside the room sealed off for the caucus.

Actually, the whole day was out of kilter for him from its start.

The night before, Arrington and his staff were guests at a dinner at Springfield's Illini Country Club hosted by the University of Illinois trustees. Since the event lasted into the late evening hours,

Arrington took the unusual step of canceling the regularly scheduled breakfast meeting for him and his staff early the next morning. He was not aware that, while he and his crew dined, other Republican senators were spreading the word that a GOP caucus would convene earlier than usual in the morning and that Arrington would not be running the show. Moreover, nobody left word for Arrington about the plan.

It didn't take long for Arrington to suspect something was amiss when he arrived at his Statehouse office the morning of June 16. His recollection of the occasion was crystal clear when he proceeded in the next decade to tape the memoirs of his life.

"As I reached my office about five minutes before eight (o'clock)," he recalled, "there didn't seem to be anybody on the Senate floor" or anywhere else to be seen.

"I thought that a little odd," he continued, "so I thought I better look around and see what was happening. Just by chance, I decided to go down to the (Statehouse) mezzanine to see where in hell everyone was. I found out pretty quickly what was going on."

Discovering his troops already assembled in caucus without him, Arrington still moved to "take the gavel" to run the meeting. However, the mallet was in the hands of Paul W. Broyles of Mount Vernon, a member of the Senate since 1945 and a leading archetype of the Republican-style Bourbons long paramount in the chamber. Broyles, no fan of Arrington, was not about to surrender the gavel to his leader.

"Senator," Arrington quoted Broyles as saying, "it is not necessary for you to take the gavel. I'll run the meeting."

Sensing that any quibbling was out of the question, Arrington sheepishly retreated to a seat—fully aware at this point that he was about to pay a price for his fair housing bill schematism.

As related by Arrington, "They just started to raise hell with me about that bill. I let them talk as much as they wanted to. As a matter of fact, they talked for five hours, and for those five hours they just gave me hell. They threatened to revoke my leadership. They just talked, talked, talked. Fortunately, I didn't say anything. It was also good that I had gone to the bathroom before entering the room, because if I had left that meeting at any second they would have thrown me out."

Hardly any of his seatmates gave Arrington a pass, with some airing long pent-up grievances on specific issues and others simply voicing to his face their annoyances over his dictatorial manner of leading.

Some reproved him mildly, like the courtly attorney from Carbondale, John G. Gilbert; the gentleman farmer from Carthage, Clifford B. Latherow; and the even-tempered lawyer from Freeport, Everett E. Laughlin. More acerbic in getting irritations with Arrington off their chests were folks such as jurists G. William Horsley of Springfield; Egbert B. Groen of Pekin; and excitable Dennis J. Collins of DeKalb. Another not mincing words was Hudson Sours, the Peoria attorney so well schooled in the classics that he often quoted from Latin in taking antagonists to task.

Arrington himself "especially remembered," he recounted, the input from Tom Merritt, an insurance and real estate businessman from the eastern Illinois town of Hoopeston.

"Tommy Merritt made an impassioned speech against my (open occupancy) bill. Yet, he cried while he was giving me hell. He had tears in his eyes as he said he regretted that I had made the stand that I had. Nevertheless, he stated that he still was going to support me as president pro tem."

When finally permitted to speak near the end of the marathon conclave, Arrington sought to remind those gathered that he'd informed them sometime before that he intended to seek passage of fair housing legislation in the session. "I also reminded them," he related, "that they had said they didn't care what I did because the effort wouldn't go anyplace in any event."

As tempers cooled, and the meeting was winding up, it was apparent that the majority on hand sided with Merritt in not wanting a replacement for Arrington. With this being the case, Arrington requested permission to leave the room before the others.

"When I knew that they still supported me, even though they didn't like it," he said, "I asked that they stay at the meeting a little longer while I go up to the third floor and announce to the hundreds of people waiting there what was the outcome. I went up and told the crowd the Senate still was going to be in session that day, and that the bill was going to be called. Doing this showed I still was the leader."

Nevertheless, Arrington added in his memoirs, "a lobbyist friend of mine told me later that everybody had been watching the meeting room to see if steam or smoke was coming out—a sign that the pope was being dethroned for a new president pro tem." The press, said Arrington, "really thought I was doomed—and for some time so did I."

When the other Republican senators finally emerged from the caucus room, most wore grim expressions and none would comment on what had transpired. Broyles simply said any statements had to come from Arrington.

After Arrington revealed that his bill would be called, Democratic senators expressed optimism that at least thirty votes, the minimum number needed for passage in the upper chamber, could be obtained for the measure. This meant that, after factoring in the certain Democratic yes votes, eleven Republicans still would have had to back the bill for approval.

Arrington had voiced hope the previous day, after he'd maneuvered to get his open housing bill out of committee, that as many as ten Republicans would support his move on the Senate floor. However, the hostile climate of the caucus quickly was exhibited in the Senate after it convened on the heels of the caucus and turned its attention to Arrington's initiative.

The climactic moments came when the GOP majority prevailed in a vote, 32 to 21 (with five senators not voting), not to concur in (accept) the public welfare committee's favorable recommendation on Arrington's measure.

Only two Republicans, Fawell and Knuepfer, joined Arrington in voting with the Democratic minority to accept the committee decision. The third Republican who joined Fawell and Knuepfer in voting to get the bill out of the public welfare panel, McBroom, dropped support for the measure on the Senate floor. At the head of the parliamentary maneuvering designed to block the bill's passage was none other than one of Arrington's two assistant leaders, Joseph Peterson.

He was readily assisted by Everett (Nubby) Peters of St. Joseph, a staunch Republican Bourbon looking to stick it to Arrington since his unceremonious dumping from his coveted spot in the leadership of the Illinois Budgetary Commission.

In sharply rebuking its leader and turning down his mild proposal for open occupancy legislation, the Republican majority opened itself up to a continuation of the scathing condemnation on fair housing that Arrington wanted so badly to fend off.

Most senators had not even gotten out of their seats in the seconds following the session's adjournment before Alan Dixon let fly that "he (Arrington) had the necessary votes, but the reactionary guys worked the moderate Republicans over so brutally in the caucus that the support was killed."

"The occasion," charged the Democrats' assistant leader, "turned out to be a great gain for prejudice, bigotry and hatred."

As for Arrington, he retired quickly to his office after Lieutenant Governor Samuel Shapiro, the Senate's presiding officer, gaveled the session to a close. It was there that this writer, seeking comment, found Arrington a short while later. He was slumped in his chair, unusually subdued and alone—except for the presence of his gatekeeper, Dee Bastas.

Asked why he risked his party standing on an issue almost totally identified with Democrats in the state, Arrington softly answered with a reply that was mirrored by John Dailey when he was questioned about the matter some thirty-six years afterward.

Housing discrimination, Arrington said, was "a social problem that forced me to do what I did."

Acknowledging that his proposed legislation only would have begun to address the problem, Arrington held nevertheless that his approach was "a reasonable beginning to determine if the solution could be through law."

"I know some didn't like my proposal because they thought it was too weak," the senator went on. "But, the others had proposals that never could pass. I had to sit and wait until they failed. But, I knew all along that I'd try."

Arrington voiced a belief that "for a while" he thought "I could really do it." Although saying that he felt he "had the votes" on the floor for passage when he pushed his language out of the committee, he then added that his optimism waned when "the agitated feelings of some of the others caused my votes to wiggle, and they couldn't go along with me."

As for the caucus that portended defeat for his effort, Arrington noted only that "in those five hours we got a lot of matters ironed out, and my people now understand my position better."

He had a final word for Democrats too.

"I'm happy that those on the other side saw my sincerity also…they see now how hard it is to achieve this thing."

Taking on such a challenge did not enhance Arrington or his party politically. Other Democrats dutifully took up the Dixon cudgel and further beat the GOP over the head for perceived racial bias. The episode did nothing to elevate Arrington personally with most of his fellow Republicans. There were exceptions, though, like Jacksonville's Harris Rowe, the Morgan County GOP leader and the party's unsuccessful candidate for state treasurer the year before.

In a letter to Arrington several days after his failed coup, Rowe wrote that he could not "resist the temptation to write you and commend you for the stand you took on a fair housing bill. It sounds as though all kinds of hell broke loose, but, for what it is worth, I am convinced that you were on the right side of the issue, and that the Republican Party would be a great deal better off if the Senate had approved your bill.

"I simply wanted to commend you for your stand. Having traveled the statewide route, I can vouch for the fact that this is a monkey that the Democrats have put on our backs, and this was our opportunity to get it off."

Donald Rumsfeld, who then represented Arrington's home area in Congress, echoed Rowe in a letter to Arrington shortly after the end of the session.

Stating that he thought Arrington "did the right thing with respect to fair housing," Republican Rumsfeld added that since "I'm sure you caught a lot of hell, I thought I'd let you know that many feel your efforts were wise."

Arrington was cited by some editorial writers and other media types for courage in his abortive effort to get an open occupancy bill passed. However, a number of the most visible civil rights activists were noticeably muted or even silent on Arrington's action, substantiating a belief in many quarters that the housing issue entailed a major political caveat—namely, that no Republican was to get any credit on the issue.

In the period from 1968 to 1972, when he was assigned to Blessed Sacrament Catholic Church in Springfield, Father Frank Westhoff was a visible protagonist in the Statehouse for open housing legislation and other civil rights causes. Westhoff had taken some classes taught in Chicago by Saul Alinsky, an organizer of community groups seeking to give a greater voice to the poor and downtrodden. Westhoff's attempt to employ in the Capitol some of Alinsky's confrontational tactics angered few persons more than the Senate's GOP Bourbons.

"I was considered political poison by the Republican senators," Westhoff recalled in a 2003 interview in a Springfield restaurant. "They just didn't want to be seen with me."

"I knew Russell Arrington was Mr. General Assembly, and that he was all powerful," continued the priest. "I'd written him letters on the open housing issue, but he'd never responded to any of them. In those letters, I chastised Senate Republicans for their opposition views on the issue."

Finally, at some point after Paul Simon became lieutenant governor in 1969, he took Westhoff to meet certain individuals in the Statehouse. One was Arrington. Coming face to face with Arrington outside a hearing room, Westhoff never forgot Arrington's only words after the introduction by Simon.

"You are a big pill to swallow," Arrington told the priest.

To this, Westhoff replied: "Sir, when you're sick, you need big medicine."

Westhoff was referring, as he noted in the interview years later, to the GOP's stance on open occupancy. Westhoff also acknowledged in the interview that, at the time of his brief exchange with Arrington, he either was unaware of or had forgotten about Arrington's push for a fair housing bill in 1967.

The fear among many Arrington followers that he lost all around in the 1967 episode had to be fueled by another pummeling of their man by John Dreiske. The *Chicago Sun-Times* scribe seemed to conclude in a column June 19, 1967, that the proceeding sounded a death knell for Arrington's leadership.

After granting that "it did take guts to do what he (Arrington) did," Dreiske went on in the rest of his piece with an excoriation of Arrington so caustic that it virtually condemned him to political exile.

In Dreiske's words, the whole happening was a "tragic misplay" in which Arrington played "footsie in a deal with Democrats kept secret from his own colleagues"—thereby leaving the senator "without a place in his party's future political councils." Claiming that only a politician with "an all-powerful deity complex" could blunder so blatantly, the columnist equated the rebuke of Arrington in the GOP caucus and on the Senate floor with "a public shaming of the doughty, acerbic little fashion plate that embarrassed even the onlookers who dislike him profoundly."

Consequently, to make sure readers did not miss his point, Dreiske insisted that the episode "stripped him (Arrington) of all but a nominal chunk of political power and influence. His leadership in the Senate has become token. His leadership anywhere else has disappeared like fair weather friends."

No question, Dreiske wound up, "the rule of the Republican Senate majority ceases to be a dictatorship, and becomes a regency of the sort that usually transforms the official ruler into a figurehead."

It wouldn't take long to see that such a dreary prognosis for Arrington was overkill. Soon enough, he'd be more than a little justified, if he did such a thing, in satirizing Dreiske and a few others of like mind by paraphrasing Mark Twain's famous comment that "the reports of my death are greatly exaggerated."

For those who kept score, the General Assembly did send to Kerner out of that 1967 session a bill that gave freedom of residency advocates a taste of what they wanted. The measure, sponsored by Representative Gerald W. Shea, a Riverside Democrat, sought to prohibit blockbusting in Illinois. The legislation, which the governor signed, stipulated that it was unlawful to solicit the sale, lease or listing of any residential property by contending that the value of the property was slipping because of the entry into the neighborhood of a person or persons of a particular race, religion or national ancestry.

In addition, by the end of that year, at least twenty-six municipalities in the state had passed fair housing ordinances. Seventeen took the action after the heated row over Arrington's initiative. The ordinances varied from token measures setting out little more than a statement of municipal policy to strong language ones providing wide coverage and strict enforcement against individuals refusing to sell or rent housing to blacks and members of other minority groups.

Ivan R. Levin, the downstate director of the Illinois Commission on Human Relations, pointed out that "generally, of course, adoption of an ordinance in itself doesn't put much of a dent in segregated housing. Many are convinced nothing significant can happen in this field without state level action."

Nevertheless, added Levin, "Many of these local leaders waited for the General Assembly to act. But, in view of what happened, they now must feel they have a better understanding of the need for this kind of legislation than do others who are not local officials."

One of the twenty-six cities with a fair housing ordinance on the books was Evanston, Arrington's hometown.

Chapter 18

ℭ

Entering New Territory—A Ground-Breaking Session

It ended a little after midnight on Thursday, October 19—the abbreviated but unprecedented second session of the General Assembly in 1967, the one breaking new ground because it was convened by the legislature's leaders acting on their own.

Officially, the meeting was a reconvening of the session covering the first six months of the year. Before that session ended, it was determined at the insistence of Arrington (with House Speaker Ralph Smith in tow) that the lawmakers would reassemble in Springfield September 11.

Bringing the legislators back to Springfield in this fashion was novel because the General Assembly traditionally ended its regular six-month session each biennium by adjourning without specifying a definite time for reassembling. The legislature had met between its regular sessions at the direction of the governor, but not on its own initiative.

The main reason given for the reconvening was to consider overrides of vetoes by Kerner of certain bills passed earlier in the year. Arrington knew, though, that odds against any overrides were heavy because of political realities. The Republican majority was not large enough in either chamber to muster, without Democratic help, the two-thirds vote needed to overturn a veto. And, McGloon and Touhy had served notice they would oppose efforts to upset vetoes and embarrass Governor Kerner, their fellow Democrat.

Factually speaking, only three gubernatorial vetoes had been overturned in Illinois since 1870, the last in 1936. This was not a siz-

*Left to right: Representative William E. Pollock, Senator Arthur
McGloon, Representative John Touhy, Representative Raymond E.
Anderson, Governor Otto Kerner, Senator Arrington, (unknown)*

able number in that, from 1870 through 1965, Illinois governors had
vetoed 2,678 bills.

The more realistic motive for summoning the legislators back to
their Statehouse desks was to help advance the long-harbored goal of
Arrington to increase the importance of the General Assembly in
daily governance of the state. Moving to dump the age-old impression of the legislature as "out of sight, out of mind" was just one
more thumbing of the nose by Arrington at Illinois tradition.

Many legislators, especially ones with full-time jobs separate
from their political careers, were disgruntled before, during and after
the reconvened session. To some, the whole exercise was a waste of
time. In addition, a number of Democrats charged that their minorities were being cast as unwilling straight men and the public as an
unnecessary bill payer for a play intended primarily to illustrate the
power of essentially one individual, Arrington.

Nonetheless, a number of his colleagues nodded heads in agreement when Arrington told reporters in the session's aftermath that
"regardless of the attitude of some, we've definitely achieved as a fact
the desirability of keeping the General Assembly alive the year-round."

McGloon was among those eyeing the reconvening with suspicion, but he grudgingly conceded afterward that "in time, with the working out of the obstacles, this process can be used successfully to correct mistakes we make in the regular sessions." Confident of having a pretty good idea of the Arrington game plan for the General Assembly, McGloon hardly doubted that there'd be plenty of future opportunities to work out kinks in the functioning of the now continuous session.

The next round already was ensured when the legislators reacting to the orchestration of Arrington—consented before ending the first reconvened session to reassemble March 4, 1968. Furthermore, Arrington predicted that future segments of the continuous session, functioning smoother on the experience gained in the initial effort, could "let us become more adventuresome on the issues to be considered."

Introduction of measures on most controversial matters was forbidden in the first reconvened session, which covered eight legislative days in the period from September 11 to October 19. The restriction was a primary reason a number saw the session as a waste of time. To them, it was folly to return the legislators to Springfield and then not permit consideration of main issues.

The brief session's record was certainly scanty. Attempts to override Kerner vetoes predictably failed in both houses. Only two bills were passed. One was aimed at curbing pollution in Lake Michigan.

The other repealed several controversial amendments to the Illinois inheritance tax law that were approved by the legislature in the regular six-month session earlier in the year. The amendments provided that life insurance proceeds would have been subject to the tax for the first time, and that the full value of property held in joint tenancy would be used in determining the tax instead of half the value of such property. The changes were repealed because of belated concerns that the broadened tax base was unfair to persons least able to afford it, such as widows and dependent children.

The action on the inheritance tax was cited by Arrington as "a first sterling example of where this legislature was able to dedicate itself immediately to a newly created problem. If we had not come right back in session, the matter would not have been considered until early in

1969. By then, it would have been extremely difficult to repeal."

One hard-to-miss aspect of the reconvened meeting was that the rigid grip on the flow of business by Arrington countered a lingering impression that his fair housing escapade near the end of the year's regular session had crippled his authority as Senate leader. McGloon acknowledged as much when he chatted off the cuff with observers, not long before the renewed session's windup, at the small stand on the Statehouse's third floor that served hot dogs and soft drinks to Capitol workers and visitors.

The Senate minority chief conceded that Arrington seemed unstoppable in his determination to keep the legislature in an unending session at the beck and call of its leaders. Correspondingly, he added, this in effect would pave the way for Arrington to achieve his goal of having the General Assembly in annual sessions instead of just the six-month meetings every other year.

But, cautioned McGloon within earshot of several reporters, such an increased work load would create "an extreme hardship on many members who have to be away from home this much over the biennium." If nothing else, he suggested, unending sessions would necessitate an increase in the then $9,000-a-year salary of legislators.

Not long afterward, Arrington crossed the path of these same reporters as they were leaving the Statehouse to traipse the short walk along East Capitol Avenue to the office of Western Union, where their stories of the day's legislative activity would be telegraphed to the home offices of their newspapers.

Informed of McGloon's comments a bit earlier up by the hot dog stand, Arrington remarked that the unending session was going to be a fact of life irrespective of a legislative pay raise.

The lawmakers "are given $9,000 a year, and they should do something to earn it," Arrington made clear. "The cooperation may not be quite what we want yet, but this thing is going to continue."

Chapter 19

C

Here, There, Everywhere

*F*ollowing one of his numerous press conferences in 1967, Arrington was striding down the hallway behind the Senate chamber with Donald Tolva and Dick Dunn when he suddenly turned to Tolva and asked, "What's the status of the flags?"

Tolva and Dunn, two of the bright Arrington disciples, would each serve in the future as a chief of staff for Arrington. At that moment, though, Tolva was working as a member of the GOP Senate staff, and Dunn was a Ford Fellow intern assigned to Arrington. The flag question caught both by surprise—especially Tolva, to whom it was addressed.

Hearing no reply to his query, Arrington looked at Tolva again and snapped, "Is this a matter of first impression with you?" For Tolva, a person normally attentive to the most minute details, it apparently was a matter of "first impression."

"Don was flabbergasted," Dunn recalled years later. "Even though Arrington quickly cooled down, Don wasted no time getting on the phone to John Dailey to find out if he knew what he (Arrington) wanted. And, it turned out that it was Dailey who'd been asked by Arrington to get flags of the United States and the state of Illinois to stand by his desk. John said Arrington wanted the flags because he was being photographed so often."

Well, that answered the question of what Arrington was talking about, but Tolva still was perplexed. Where could he find the flags at the drop of a dime to stave off further impatience by his demanding boss? The intern at Tolva's side came to his rescue.

"I told Don I'd have the flags within an hour," said Dunn, whose father at the time was a commanding general in the Illinois National Guard.

Hightailing it out of the Capitol and across Monroe Street to the State Armory, a fortress-like building resembling a giant mausoleum, Dunn requested and received an immediate audience with General Harold R. Patton, the assistant adjutant general of Illinois.

"I told him (Patton) that Senator Arrington was mad about not having flags," related Dunn. "He said to take the two flags (American and Illinois) standing by his own desk, and I did. He had an army enlisted man carry the flags over to the Statehouse and set them up in Arrington's office." Tolva was very relieved.

The placement of the national and state flags along or behind the desk of an Illinois public official was more than a decorative step. It symbolized that the individual had risen to exalted status in the political world—either in the view of the public or in his or her own eyes. Normally, the flags stood only by the desk of the governor or another elective statewide officer. Rank and file legislators seldom were pictured with flags in the background, nor were most of their leaders. A few did, though, soar far enough out of the legislative maelstrom to leadership respectability to justify flags. One certainly in Arrington's time—besides Arrington himself—was Paul Powell. In the decades remaining in the twentieth century after the Arrington era, a case for flags could be made for House Speaker Michael Madigan, as well as two presidents of the Senate—first Democrat Philip Rock and then James (Pate) Philip, the longtime DuPage County Republican leader.

Coincidentally or not, the appearance of the flags in Arrington's rather unpretentious office in the northeast section of the Capitol's third floor occurred during a period of heightened speculation over the possibility of his running for governor in the 1968 election.

As 1967 moved along, and with a good deal of Statehouse life being dominated by Arrington's command of the legislative scene, many other politicians and columnists seemed to almost assume that

Arrington would be in the upcoming gubernatorial contest. Given the general expectation that Governor Kerner would seek election to a third term in 1968, Arrington's unending opposition to Kerner on so many issues was taken by some pundits to be posturing by the senator for an electoral challenge to Kerner. To them, this was Arrington's ultimate goal in the conduct of his role.

Arrington himself, at least for a while in 1967, continued to be coy on the subject.

Few Illinois political figures attaining a certain magnitude ever denied entertaining, at some point, a dream of occupying the state's highest elective office. To have their names bandied about in shoptalk about the governorship was supreme gratification. Arrington would have been, and should have been, disappointed if he hadn't been depicted as gubernatorial material.

As 1967 progressed, his public stance on any aspiration to be governor was to demur on the matter—to deflect questions with evasive replies of wait and see. This was standard stuff, but in the case of Arrington somewhat disconcerting considering his normal propensity for straight talk that left no doubt of what he wanted and where he intended to go.

The truth of it, as gleaned from those close to him at that juncture, was that Arrington certainly could picture himself in the governor's chair. Furthermore, he was confident that he had the governmental knowledge and political fortitude to be a strong and independent governor, much like his friend William Stratton. His ego being what it was, Arrington basked in the columns painting him as the Illinois GOP strongman who could have his party's nomination for governor for the asking.

But, it was not to be.

Upon reflection, it was easy to compile reasons militating against an Arrington candidacy for governor. Foremost, he did not have the necessary fire in the belly for the challenge, the willingness of some to lay everything on the line—including personal resources—to win the office. Frankly, the governorship was not the coveted pot of gold at the foot of Arrington's rainbow. His two heart attacks were another impediment. Even though Arrington usually brushed aside, with a back-of-the-hand swipe, questions from reporters about his health, his inner circle recognized that concern about his heart condition would come into play—and legitimately so—in the arduous under-taking of a gubernatorial campaign.

In addition to the rigorous demands on one physically in a statewide race, the temperament of a candidate could not be ignored. Arrington bred anxieties on that score too. His impatience with mediocrity, his quicksilver temper and his penchant for shoot-ing from the hip were not advisable characteristics for a statewide candidate.

Arrington's disposition was brought up by Paul Simon in his inclusion of the senator in a listing by Simon of the most influential Illinois politicians during his years of public service. The ranking was included in *Incredible Illinois*, a book by Illinois author Bill Nunes that came out twenty-five years after Arrington's death.

In it, Simon described Arrington as "a real leader" with a "great mind" who would have been governor or a United States senator "but for a somewhat prickly personality." "Diplomacy," added Simon, "was not his strength."

One quite likely reason Illinoisans never saw an Arrington race for governor was that campaigning was far from his first love in pol-itics. Facing few heavyweight opponents in his legislative races through the years, Arrington had not been compelled—at least in the view of other Illinois politicians—to build a reputation as a vigorous campaigner. Folks back on Arrington's political home field knew him to be a strong campaigner when any occasion demanded it, but the big margins of his victories projected an image of a person used to electoral cakewalks.

Then there was that "certain something" called charisma. Since John Kennedy gained the White House, people had come to expect an amalgam of charm and attractiveness in major candidates, traits adding up to political sex appeal. Arrington looked every bit of his sixty-one years in 1967, an appearance deemed distinguished by his followers but far from telegenic in the minds of political promoters acutely aware of the rapidly increasing importance of television in campaigns.

Arrington's fathering of the movement of young staffers into the General Assembly did not dissuade some from questioning whether he would be the right kind of candidate for capitalizing on the growing presence of youthful activists in campaigns. However, one who knew better on this count was James Bagley, an active Democrat in the late 1960s when he was a political science student at private North Park College in Chicago. His college days came to mind when Bagley contemplated Arrington many years afterward in Indian Wells, California, where he lived after leaving a law practice in Chicago to produce movies.

"Most campuses were very liberal at the time, but North Park was conservative and populated with a lot of young Republicans," said Bagley. "They'd participate with young Republicans from other colleges at active conventions, sometimes at the Edgewater Beach Hotel in Chicago. Arrington would speak at these rallies. I can tell you that he was their god, their Republican god. These people took their politics seriously, and they were inspired by Arrington."

Many young Republicans did hustle around the state in support of their party's nominee for governor in 1968. The candidate wasn't Arrington, but Richard Ogilvie.

It was not until the sun was setting on 1967 that the Arrington crowd finally knew for sure that its boss was not throwing his hat into the gubernatorial ring. Even Arrington insiders were among those for whom the suspense had become palpable while he hemmed and hawed through the year about seeking the governorship. Ultimately, in deciding not to do it, Arrington was perceived by Tolva to be burdened by another consideration in addition to the health and other factors weighing against a run.

"Russ was uncharacteristically unsure of himself on this one, not sure that he could win and not sure how he would handle defeat," surmised Tolva.

In the event Arrington had gone for governor, the likelihood of GOP primary opposition from the gubernatorial-eyeing Ogilvie would have been negligible. That was the strong impression coming out of a private meeting between the two in the period before Ogilvie's formal announcement of his candidacy for governor in

December 1967.

Tolva and Dailey were with Arrington in his law office when Ogilvie, then in his first year as Cook County Board president, came in for the memorable chat. Tolva never forgot Ogilvie sinking into the soft couch and being informed by the senator, who was sitting at his desk, that he, Arrington, would not be running for governor. "This was a meeting to clear the air," remembered Tolva, "because it was assumed that Ogilvie wanted to run for governor, but probably would not have done so if Arrington had intended to run. So, Arrington was giving Ogilvie an open door to go for governor."

Beyond removing himself as a possible roadblock to Ogilvie's bid for governor, Arrington also signified to Ogilvie that he would favor his candidacy in an expected contest for the GOP gubernatorial nomination in the primary election in June 1968. House Speaker Smith already was solidly on board for Ogilvie and had accepted a role as downstate manager of a likely Ogilvie campaign.

Unlike Smith, Arrington insisted that his backing of Ogilvie be low-keyed at least through the primary stage so as to not overly antagonize his fellow senator, Arthur Gottschalk, who himself was attempting to round up support for the Republican nomination for governor. Consequently, it was predictable that Arrington would hit the ceiling when Ogilvie partisans moved in following weeks to emblazon publicly the support by Arrington for their man. Arrington's pique didn't endure, but a few pundits sought to magnify the matter by depicting it as a sign of early friction between Arrington and Ogilvie.

Actually, in a departure from the norm, Arrington appeared unusually free of political tension as 1968 dawned. With the uncertainty of his flirtation with the governorship out of the way, he seemed to be ever more firmly seated at the top of his own political game—orchestrating a commanding role for the General Assembly. His rebound from the humbling setback of his open housing initiative, coupled with his successful push for the ground-breaking session back in the previous fall, left Arrington as a legislative emperor again fully clothed.

Nineteen sixty-eight would become one of the twentieth century's more pivotal years. Not many Americans survived it without their lives or souls being altered by stupendous events happening so frequently they nearly became commonplace. The Tet Offensive in Vietnam. The capture of the USS Pueblo by North Korea. President Johnson's disclosure that he wouldn't be a candidate for reelection. The assassinations of Martin Luther King Jr. and Robert Kennedy. The episodes went on and on, culminating in August with the disastrous Democratic National Convention in Chicago.

For Democrats in Illinois and the rest of the country, the convention was a nightmare. Their frustration soared as they watched the ripping apart of their party by raging Vietnam War protesters. Chicago, the Democratic mecca, was under siege. The smoke finally cleared, but the world was slow to forget the rampaging dissidents, the counterattacking Chicago police, the National Guardsmen and the federal troops. Even Illinois' die-hard Demos realized their party was in a state of desperation going into the final months of the state and national election campaigns.

They could only look back longingly at the beginning of the year. Their outlook had been so much rosier then because it was anticipated that Johnson would seek to retain the White House and that the still seemingly popular Kerner planned to run for another term as governor.

For Arrington personally, 1968 started on the right foot when he and Ruth announced the engagement of their daughter Patricia to Robert J. Smythe, a onetime resident of Park Ridge, Illinois, then involved in business in Toledo, Ohio.

Arrington was pleased in that he had enjoyed a friendship with John Smythe, the father of Robert, since their undergraduate days together at the University of Illinois. Patricia and Robert had met at the University of Michigan, where she was a student for three years and from which he'd received degrees in business administration. In January 1968, Patricia was working in New York City at the Columbia University College of Physicians and Surgeons. The wedding took place that same year on April 20 at her church, St. Mark's Episcopal in Evanston.

Two years earlier, Patricia's brother Michael had married Janie

Senator W. Russell Arrington and son Michael B. Arrington

Watson, a cheerleader at Evanston Township High School when Michael played football there. The late 1960s were years of increased bonding between Michael and his father. In the years after his high school days, Michael channeled the toughness he'd shown on the football field into the Marine Corps, where his three-year stint included rigorous airborne and scuba diving training with the First Force Reconnaissance Company of the First Marine Division. Later, he pursued studies that would lead to a bachelor of arts degree in political science from the University of Illinois at Chicago.

Although Michael got a bird's-eye view of his father's Statehouse role when he worked on his staff during the regular six-month session of 1967, there always had been, and still remained, a determination by Michael to be his own man. He could have remained in his father's retinue or landed some cushy public position with the help of his father. But, Michael wanted to chart his own course.

Seeking to carve out his own niche, he handled public affairs for the Union League Club for a spell and then became executive director of the South Loop Improvement Project, an undertaking of businessmen to upgrade the section of downtown Chicago south of Van Buren Street. He held that position when he made an unsuccessful bid for elective office in 1969, losing a race for an aldermanic seat in Evanston. The loss was ironic in that his father's first try for elective office back in 1941 was for an Evanston aldermanic seat, and it was not successful. Like his father, Michael felt afterward that losing the aldermanic election was the best thing that could have happened for his career.

Before 1969 was over, though, Michael made a move that was clearly to propel him out of his father's shadow. In August of that year, Michael founded—in spite of his father's initial skepticism about its chance for success—the Arrington Travel Center. Starting from scratch, he would steer the Chicago-based venture during the next three decades into a highly successful business employing more than 500 persons, generating some $225 million in annual sales and serving a wide variety of major corporations and professional firms around the globe.

The undertaking would become the largest single-stockholder travel agency in the United States, and that lone stockholder was

Michael. On the personal side, Trudi Robertson, the Arrington Travel office manager, became Michael's second wife in 1971 (his marriage to Janie ended in divorce in 1969). In July 1998, Michael sold his agency to Navigant International, a worldwide travel corporation. By then, the son had demonstrated that his father was not the only Arrington to have a Midas touch in private enterprise.

But, back to the start of 1968. Illinois public life in the first weeks was quiescent, belying the political upheaval that would mark much of the rest of the year. It was the calm before the storm. Even Arrington settled into a rather placid routine.

One anticipated development early in the year was the installation of Arrington for another term as chairman of the board of the Robert R. McCormick Chicago Boys Club. For years, the 3,000-member club on North Sheridan Road was a recipient of a considerable amount of Arrington's time, energy and resources.

More than in other periods, Arrington was able to comply with the steady flow of requests to appear here and there. For instance, he participated in a conference in St. Louis, sponsored by the United States Chamber of Commerce, on modernizing state and local governments—obviously one of his pet interests. He found hours to accept some of the unending invitations to talk on college campuses. He was the principal speaker at a ground-breaking ceremony for a new residence hall and student center at Kendall College in Evanston, and he journeyed to DeKalb to address classes at Northern Illinois University.

In the world of Arrington, though, even mundane undertakings sometimes didn't end up being mundane. His visit to the Northern campus was spiced by his receipt of a ticket for a parking violation. The slight triggered a letter afterward to Arrington from James Wilson of the university's political science department.

Sending a copy of the ticket with the letter, Wilson wrote that "the enclosed item (the violation notice) can be listed as a souvenir of your visit. We have had a great deal of fun at the expense of the university police. It does, as you would admit, take a lot of guts to ticket a Cadillac with license plate number one."

Arrington did provide a bit of an early year surprise for his fellow Republicans when he told a GOP leadership gathering at

Rockford that passage of a state income tax and approval of an open occupancy law were inevitable in Illinois. His prophecy was echoed at the meeting by Ralph Smith.

The prediction, especially on the tax, generated scowls from many on hand who noted the traditional opposition by most Republicans, and a good number of Democrats, to enactment of a state income levy. Arrington did qualify his forecast by stating that Illinois still was "not ready yet" for an income tax, but he added that the state was running out of alternatives for raising the amount of money needed to meet its spiraling fiscal responsibilities.

However, talk of the income tax prediction at the Republican get-together soon was relegated to a back burner by a much greater political surprise. On February 7, 1968, Kerner caught both political friends and foes off guard by announcing that he would not seek reelection as governor. Declining to go into great detail on his decision, he said little more than he had chosen "not to run" for personal reasons that took into account "the well being of my family in light of the extraordinary demands on the governor."

Few matters could rank higher on the Richter scale of Illinois politics than a sudden declaration by a sitting governor—one seen as still potent with the electorate—against running again. The chain reaction to such a development might go pretty far down the line, bringing new candidates to the fore and scrambling an election year outlook. In other words, the bets were quickly off on an election that all at once was far less predictable than many thought was the case before Kerner's announcement.

The prospect for victory by the Republican nominee for governor took an immediate turn upward. This automatically increased the glare of the public spotlight on Ogilvie, who generally was viewed as the front-runner for the nomination. It also couldn't help but bode well, at least to some degree, for GOP aspirants for other statewide offices or perhaps certain General Assembly seats.

Democrats were in no way lacking in formidable possibilities for their gubernatorial candidate. Three of their incumbent state officers were mentioned right away as likely contenders: Treasurer Adlai E. Stevenson III; Auditor of Public Accounts Michael Howlett; and

Attorney General William Clark. The name of R. Sargent Shriver, head of the federal antipoverty program, also was thrown into the mix. Shriver was a Maryland aristocrat who'd formerly lived in Chicago when he ran the Merchandise Mart, a holding of his father-in-law, Joseph P. Kennedy. Actually, Shriver was most mentioned as the possible Democratic opponent for United States Senator Everett M. Dirksen of Illinois, a Republican whose seat also was on the ballot in 1968. Whatever, with names like Stevenson and Shriver available for the ballot, the Democrats' chance for a glamour-studded state ticket was quite plausible.

One thing hard to miss was that speculation about the Dem candidate for governor pretty much ignored Lieutenant Governor Samuel Shapiro, who seldom was even a blip on Illinois' political radar screen. In spite of being in his eighth year in the state's second highest office, Shapiro simply was viewed as not aggressive enough to effectively head the state ticket.

However, Shapiro had enjoyed a close rapport with Kerner and, more importantly, was extremely loyal to his friend Mayor Daley, the dominant as ever party boss in the state. And, of course, the state ticket would be dictated by Daley through the party's so-called slate-making process, a rigidly scripted proceeding behind closed doors in which Daley's candidate selections were rubber-stamped by party officials. In the primary elections that followed the slatings, Democratic voters were expected to simply endorse the candidates already dictated by Daley.

The slating exercise in 1968 was carried out three weeks after Kerner revealed he'd not be a candidate again for governor. When the secret proceeding concluded, an anxious Illinois political world was informed that Shapiro and Clark would head the Democratic ticket. Shapiro was backed for governor and Clark for the race against Dirksen. Howlett was tabbed for reelection to the office he held, but neither Stevenson nor Shriver was slated for anything.

Since professional politicians in Illinois see the governorship as crucial for real power in the state and a United States Senate seat as far less important in the equation, reaction to the slate focused on Shapiro. Republicans already buoyed by Kerner's bowing out could not contain their joy at the belief that Shapiro was far from the Democrats' strongest choice for governor. Numerous Democrats, especially away from Chicago, were dismayed because they privately shared the feeling of many in the GOP about Shapiro.

Fearful Democrats took a measure of solace in the likelihood that Shapiro would enter the general election campaign as the incumbent governor. This assumption resulted from the expectation, which had picked up considerable steam since Kerner's announcement, that he would resign from the governorship not too far in the future to accept a federal judgeship.

The rest of the Democratic ticket was a mixed bag. Secretary of State Powell was endorsed for reelection, and Francis Lorenz, director of the Illinois Department of Public Works and Buildings, got the nod for attorney general. New ground was broken with the slating of Fannie Jones, an East St. Louis school teacher, for nomination for clerk of the Supreme Court. Jones was believed to be the first black ever slated for a statewide office by one of the two major political parties in Illinois.

Analysts weren't quite sure what to make of the slate-making choice for the lieutenant governor nomination. It went to Paul Simon. The state senator wanted endorsement for the race against Dirksen. But some Democratic leaders expressed reservation that he might not be strong enough statewide to take on Dirksen. Too, some felt that his desire to run for the United States Senate was undercut by his independent stands on many issues during his legislative career.

More than a few Simon adherents were skeptical about their man running for lieutenant governor. They feared the timing was not right in view of the perception of Shapiro as a weak choice for governor. They were quite aware that a candidate for lieutenant governor never had won when his party's nominee for governor was defeated. Too, the running mate tandem of Shapiro and Simon had the ring of an all-Jewish duo, which, if true, would have departed from the general aim of Illinois Democrats to put together ethnically balanced tickets.

Of the two, only Shapiro was Jewish (Simon, as noted earlier, was a Lutheran minister's son). Shapiro's climb up the ladder of success was one of those feel-good stories that Americans loved to read about.

In truth, there were numerous parallels between Arrington and Shapiro, an affable, somewhat retiring individual a year younger than Arrington.

Like Arrington, Samuel Harvey Shapiro—who was born in a Baltic village in Estonia—emerged from an early life of modest circumstances. A roly-poly man whom many affectionately called "Mister Sam," the lieutenant governor was a son of a shoe cobbler in Kankakee. A public high school product, as was Arrington, Shapiro graduated from law school at the University of Illinois a year before Arrington did. Although his parents would have made necessary sacrifices for his education, Shapiro paid most of the cost for his university years out of his own pocket, using money he earned, in part, playing a violin in dance orchestras.

In 1946, Shapiro was elected to the Illinois House, two years after Arrington was elected to his first term in the body. Shapiro served in the chamber for fourteen years before being backed by Daley and other Democratic leaders for a successful bid for lieutenant governor in the 1960 election. Their thinking was that a downstater was needed to run for "light governor" to provide geographic balance for a ticket to be headed by gubernatorial candidate Kerner, a Chicagoan.

Those with political memories recalled few if any clashes of consequence between Arrington and Shapiro in the years between 1946 and 1955, when they were in the House at the same time. Later, in the Senate, a respectful decorum existed between the pair as Shapiro fulfilled his state constitutionally mandated role as presiding officer over the chamber, and Arrington served as its majority leader. Arrington clearly ran the show, dictating every aspect of the conduct of business. Yet, Shapiro retained his dignity by diplomatically wielding the gavel in a fashion that assured the minority Democrats of a voice while not affronting the ruling Republicans.

As a legislator, Shapiro had been recognized widely for his ongoing efforts to improve the lot of patients in the state's mental health institutions. He built an aboveboard reputation while seldom swerving on votes from the Democratic line decreed by the party's Chicago machine.

In something of an understatement, he was quoted more than

once as saying he "always tried to stay with the (Democratic) organization when at all possible." For campaign purposes, Republicans cast Shapiro as a Daley lackey—just like they always pictured Kerner. The put-down, which was certain to be leveled at Shapiro in Chicago's suburbs and downstate, smacked of a political boilerplate.

On the plus side for Shapiro, the expectation that he'd be running for governor as an incumbent became reality in May 1968 when Kerner resigned from the governorship to become a judge of the United States appellate court in Chicago. The resignation was the first by an Illinois governor since Shelby M. Cullom left the office in 1883 for a seat in the United States Senate.

One of Kerner's first acts in his new role was to administer the oath of the office of governor to Shapiro, the state's sixth lieutenant governor to reach the governorship. The last one before Shapiro was John H. Stelle of McLeansboro, who became the chief executive after Governor Henry Horner died in October 1940. Shapiro was the state's first Jewish governor since Horner.

An upshot of Shapiro's elevation to governor was an addition of more icing to Arrington's political cake. It prompted joking by Democrats—maybe only half in jest—that new Governor Shapiro better take care not to leave the state. If he did, or if the governor's office was to become vacant for any reason, Arrington as Senate president pro tempore was next in the line of succession to move into the governor's chair. Arrington was in a phrase Democrats found politically scary—a heartbeat away from the governorship.

Shapiro's first phone call after sitting down in the governor's office went to Arrington, inviting him to drop in for a chat. Arrington did so, and the two conversed for a half hour. Afterward, Arrington called it "a pleasant visit" that was a solid first step toward combating frequent Arrington criticism that the governor's office usually failed to communicate with him.

Arrington also emphasized that he assured Shapiro, in event the governor traveled outside Illinois, that "there would be no effort on my part to disturb things. I would consider myself only a ministerial officer. It would be inane and stupid of me to do anything dramatic."

But Arrington's immediate move into the fancy office of the lieutenant governor shortly after it was vacated by Shapiro led to drama in the never-ending soap opera world of the Statehouse. Before the year was out, even many of his loyalists conceded it had the earmarks of a public relations faux pas.

The office, located along the hall behind the Senate chamber, was a far cry from the cramped space a few steps to the east that Arrington had occupied. The lieutenant governor's office was a commodious suite consisting of two high-ceilinged rooms with a private washroom, fireplace, thick carpeting and ornate trimmings.

The quick grab of Shapiro's former office, which Arrington himself called "taking possession," caught everybody off guard, including the senator's aides. Since the only entity with a possible say on the matter was an obscure panel known as the Senate chamber maintenance commission that was dominated by Arrington, the decision was essentially his alone. However, most assumed that Arrington would voluntarily move out of the suite after a new lieutenant governor was elected in the coming November.

Relocation of Arrington's command post gave Statehouse wags something to talk about for a few days besides the election picture. The General Assembly itself did little early in 1968 to divert attention from the electoral jockeying.

The first reconvening of the legislature in the year occurred as scheduled March 4, but the meeting lasted only one day. Arrington and Smith collaborated to allow unlimited introductions of bills and resolutions in both chambers, but put off any further activity until the lawmakers came back to Springfield July 15, the next date set by the GOP leaders for a reconvening in the now continuous session.

Arrington generated the only real news coming out of the March get-together. Over the heated objections of Democrats, he pushed a resolution through the Senate that altered the body's rules governing the power of standing committees. The resolution extended to the periods between sessions the authority of the panels to conduct investigations, call witnesses and, Arrington insisted, even issue subpoenas if necessary during inquiries. Giving the committees investigative power when the legislature was not in session, Arrington explained, was one more step toward day-to-day involvement by lawmakers in Illinois public life.

The complaint of Democrats was that the expanded power would permit the Republican-controlled committees to heckle or even disrupt the operations of Democratic-run governmental units, mainly in Cook County. They cited the resolution as one more example of Arrington abusing his power by rewriting Senate rules to run roughshod over the minority party.

Any claim along this line drew a mild chuckle from Pate Philip in the days after his stint as Senate leader.

"You had to remember that Arrington had a super majority," recalled Philip. "He ran the Senate in a strong fashion, and that included the interpreting of the rules. When the Democrats would yell that he was bending or just openly violating the rules, he'd pick up the rules book, throw it at them and say: 'Here's your rules book. But, I am the rules.'"

Within a few days of the passage of the investigation broadening resolution, Arrington did announce that the Senate Committee on Municipal Corporations would launch immediately a probe of corruption in Chicago's building department. Democrats charged that it was the kind of political inquisition they had predicted. However, the inquiry came on the heels of a long investigation by the *Chicago Tribune*, assisted by the Better Government Association, revealing serious irregularities in the city's building code enforcement agency that hampered efforts to rid Chicago of slums.

In respect to the General Assembly as a whole, picking July 15 as the next day for it to convene was based on political expediency. By then, the June 11 primary election would be history and, according to past experience, the state would be in a temporary electoral lull before lawmakers and other candidates on the ballot entered the heated months prior to the general election. Arrington and Smith particularly didn't want the General Assembly detracting attention from the primary since virtually all of its competitive races were in the GOP.

One of the Republican primary contests forced Arrington to walk a political tightrope. In that race, two of his Senate seatmates were among three aspirants for the GOP nomination for state auditor. One was William C. Harris of downstate Pontiac and the other Terrel E. Clarke of the Chicago suburb of Western Springs. The third contender was Mayor Wes Olson of Quincy. The prominence of Harris had escalated when Arrington anointed him to join Coulson as a majority whip in the upper chamber following the sudden death of Joseph Peterson the previous August. However, even though Harris now was part of Arrington's leadership team, a number of Arrington aides felt closer to Clarke—who like Harris was in the insurance business.

Another Republican senator, Donald D. Carpentier of East Moline, was running against Wilmette attorney Brian B. Duff for the GOP nomination for secretary of state. Carpentier was a son of longtime Secretary of State Charles F. Carpentier, who died in office in 1964.

Arrington did get a break from fence-sitting when Gottschalk dropped his bid for the Republican nomination for governor before the primary. This permitted Arrington to openly give Ogilvie unconditional backing for the nomination—support that no longer had to be muted as when Gottschalk was a contender.

Ogilvie still faced primary opposition from three other men wanting the nomination. The strongest opponent was Peoria industrialist John H. Altorfer, the unsuccessful GOP candidate for lieutenant governor in 1964. The others were former Governor Stratton and lawyer S. Thomas Sutton of Wayne. Sutton's candidacy was a limited one based mainly on his outspoken opposition to racial integration. Not supporting Stratton was difficult for Arrington and other old friends of the former governor, but it was recognized that he was too far beyond his political prime for his candidacy to be taken seriously.

As was widely expected, Ogilvie was victorious in the June primary. But, Altorfer made it closer than predicted. Had it not been for Ogilvie's huge lead in Cook County, Altorfer well may have upset the onetime sheriff since he outpolled Ogilvie in the rest of the state. Overall, Ogilvie led Altorfer statewide, 335,727 to 288,904, giving Ogilvie a winning vote margin of 46,823. Stratton and Sutton finished far back.

In spite of Ogilvie's narrower-than-anticipated plurality, he entered the general election campaign favored to defeat Shapiro.

Ogilvie was not the only member of the state GOP ticket looking like a winner in the upcoming November balloting. Dirksen was heavily favored to retain his United States Senate seat against William Clark, and many predicted Winnetka businessman Robert A. Dwyer, the party's lieutenant governor nominee, would beat Paul Simon. Former Illinois Treasurer William Scott appeared formidable as the Republican candidate for attorney general, and Justin Taft, an administrative aide to the sheriff of Sangamon County, seemed solid as the party's candidate for Supreme Court clerk.

The perhaps two weakest links in the ticket were Arrington scat-mates Harris and Carpentier. Harris whipped Clarke and Olson in the primary contest for the GOP nomination for state auditor, but faced a tough November foe in the office's incumbent Democrat, Howlett. And Carpentier survived his primary race only to enter the general election as an underdog in bidding to unseat Secretary of State Powell.

Support for the GOP ticket emerging from the primary was not the only catalyst for Arrington's election-year energy. Since he was not on the ballot for reelection in 1968, he had the time to be in the front row of those crusading for voter approval at the November election of the call for an Illinois constitutional convention. In addition, Arrington had become chairman of a national group of Republican state legislators backing Richard Nixon for the Republican nomination for president.

Nixon's standing among Illinois Republicans was high, thanks in no small measure to the support of Arrington and many of the state's other party bigwigs. It tended to dwarf the sentiment of some in both the moderate contingent and dwindling liberal wing of the Illinois party for New York Governor Nelson A. Rockefeller, a GOP moderate who launched the most serious but ultimately unsuccessful challenge to Nixon for the party's presidential nomination. In backing Nixon, Arrington attempted—without success—to get him to tab Illinois' junior United States Senator, the far from conservative Charles Percy, as his running mate for vice president. To Arrington, a Nixon-Percy combo would have appealed to enough of the political spectrum to be nearly unbeatable.

Arrington's affinity for Nixon entailed more than met the eye of outside observers. The two were very well acquainted, not just politically but also in a social context. Arrington business associate Clement Stone ranked near the apex, if not at the top, of Nixon political contributors. In tandem with this, Arrington and Ruth found themselves easily gravitating into warm and personal settings with Nixon, Stone and their wives. Nixon's obvious respect for Arrington would be reflected by certain undertakings in which Nixon, as president, would get Arrington engaged.

The backing of Nixon by the likes of Arrington, Dirksen and Ogilvie paid off for the former vice president when he received support from the bulk of the Illinois delegates to the GOP national convention in Miami Beach in August. All in all, the convention and its nomination of Nixon for the presidency was a genteel tea party in comparison to the riotous nominating convention of the Democrats that was soon to follow in Chicago.

Arrington usually avoided national party conventions, but did show up in Miami Beach in 1968 in. the company of Stone. Unlike Stone, Arrington was not a delegate. Calling himself "a relaxed observer," Arrington watched most of the proceedings on televisions in the suites that he and Stone maintained at both the Marco Polo hotel, the Illinois delegation's base, and the Hilton Plaza hotel, Nixon's campaign headquarters. For Arrington, the event was an unusual outing in that he was seen only sporadically and said even less.

"I got a lot of sun, and I swam in the ocean," he remembered. Indeed, the most memorable of several newspaper photos of Arrington during the convention was a *Sun-Times* shot of the swimsuit-clad senator standing in the surf on the beach of the Marco Polo. Most likely, the warm water of the Atlantic was a welcome respite for him after the conclusion of the recently reconvened session of the General Assembly.

Arrington and Shapiro had played the leading roles in the two-week meeting that began July 15. The session was a hectic affair in which a number of major issues were confronted. Simultaneously, the lawmakers continued to try to work out kinks in their still new repertoire of repeated get-togethers at the call of the leaders in addition to the normal six-month sessions every other year.

Sensing ahead of time that the session was likely to fray nerves, McGloon dispatched a gracious letter to Arrington on July 2 that congratulated him on his upcoming sixty-second birthday July 4 and, in addition, sought to remind Arrington that there were other things in life maybe more important than the legislature. McGloon's sincere concern for the health of his friend across the Senate aisle was conveyed in his gentle admonition to Arrington to "stay away from firecrackers, keep the blood pressure down, and enjoy your birthday," the first of "many, many more to come." As for days ahead, McGloon urged with his tongue in cheek that they "be tranquil, peaceful, satisfying and meaningful."

McGloon, above all, knew this was wishful thinking. Everyone else, too, recognized that the reconvened session was laden with political overtones promising anything but tranquility.

Shapiro had much at stake because the session presented a unique opportunity for him to increase voters' familiarity with his leadership skills and, thus, perhaps improve his chance in the general election. The design of Democrats to promote Shapiro included an address by the new governor to a joint session of the General Assembly on crime fighting. Since Ogilvie was denied exposure in the legislative session, it fell to Arrington to carry the GOP banner.

In Shapiro, Arrington had a different type of political adversary than he'd had in Kerner. While Kerner was often uptight and defensive, Shapiro traipsed the corridors of power in a nonchalant manner with a trademark smile on his face. Some opponents were disarmed by the ever-present smile, while others were confounded or even irritated by it. Shapiro as governor certainly was a different kind of animal for Arrington to deal with, especially since his demeanor cast him in the eyes of many—including a bevy of media folks—as a nice guy contrast to the normally high-strung senator.

Bipartisanship did prevail on one principal issue during the session as Shapiro and Arrington's side agreed on the passage of legislation to permit the borrowing of up to $60 million in motor fuel tax funds for use as general revenue in an effort to avert a state fiscal crisis. There also were votes on both sides for legislation—backed by Shapiro and cosponsored by Arrington—guaranteeing access to fire insurance for slum property owners, a move considered necessary in view of the ongoing upheaval in Illinois' inner cities.

The partisan cooperation dissipated, though, on the hardly new but hot button issue of the day, the controversial proposal to authorize law enforcement officers to stop and search persons in public places. Nineteen sixty-seven was not the first time in the 1960s that stop-and-frisk legislation, pushed primarily by Republicans, was passed. Each bill was vetoed by Kerner, who never backed down from seeing the proposed legislation as a breach of citizens' constitutional rights. Arrington, incensed over Kerner's position, moved in the reconvened session to override the veto of the 1967 measure.

However, the effort failed in the Senate when Arrington and his troops couldn't overcome unanimous Democratic opposition to obtain the needed two-thirds majority vote for an override. At the same time, Shapiro had the gall—as Arrington saw it—to call for approval of a stop-and-frisk bill in his address to the two houses. Shapiro said that rising rates in street crimes and other criminal activities in the state necessitated the passage of some kind of legislation on the subject. At the same time, Shapiro maintained that his proposal satisfied United States Supreme Court decisions holding street searches permissible under certain conditions.

Shapiro went even further on the anticrime front, asking the lawmakers to sanction the registration of all firearms in Illinois and doubling of the state police to 3,000 officers. Clearly, his proposals were intended to blunt a major campaign theme of Ogilvie. The Republican was thought to be making headway by insisting that a prime issue in the 1968 election was his allegation of inadequate governmental response to riots and soaring crime rates.

The governor knew that Republicans would shoot down his calls for registration of guns and a big hike in state cops because the GOP couldn't let Shapiro capture momentum on crime control, a cause traditionally more associated with Republicans. However, Arrington had to rethink his initial opposition to Shapiro's stop-and-frisk measure after Kerner's veto of the 1967 Republican bill on the subject was upheld. If he didn't back off his opposition, Arrington could have looked petty politically since he himself had worked hard for a law on the matter and also because many of his party's senators wanted such a statute irrespective of its sponsorship.

Consequently, he did not block Senate passage of a Democratic-introduced measure on the issue that was amended to include some stipulations sought by the GOP. The compromise bill was then approved by the House and signed into law by Shapiro after the lawmakers went home.

Under the new statute, which both parties intended to use to gain political mileage, a policeman was authorized to stop a person in a public place for a period described as reasonable when the officer "infers from the circumstances" that the person has committed or is about to commit a crime. When the questioning officer further suspected that he or another individual was in danger of attack, he could search the detained person for weapons. If a weapon was discovered, the officer could take it until the end of questioning. Subsequently, he had to either return the weapon, if lawfully possessed, or arrest the detainee.

Black leaders and civil libertarians continued to frown on the law in contending that it could be used by police to harass members of minority groups. That argument usually was enough to persuade many Illinois Democrats from supporting such a law; however, political expediency dictated that an exception to the normal Democratic stance had to be made at this particular time. Too, Shapiro repeatedly stressed that the law conformed to the limitations on street searches set out by the Supreme Court.

Shapiro also signed several other anticrime bills coming out of the reconvened session, including one sponsored by Senate Republicans that provided specific authority for municipalities to appoint and utilize auxiliary policemen on a restricted basis.

The abbreviated session saw passage by the House of another open occupancy bill that went to its death in the Senate. However, the upper chamber did sign off on a House-approved measure giving cities clear legal power to enact fair housing ordinances. Although more and more towns in the state were enacting these ordinances on their own, the legislature never had sanctioned the local actions. By doing so, the General Assembly was thought by freedom of residency proponents to have provided a defense against possible court actions aimed at invalidating the municipal ordinances.

The July session was the last reconvening scheduled for the seemingly never-to-end Seventy-fifth General Assembly. With the work load heavier than originally anticipated, the normal legislative pace gave way in the two weeks to a more hurried timetable. Truncated hearings and minimal debate accompanied some proposals that would have been objects of prolonged oratory and deliberation in a more regular session. The rapidity of the proceedings understandably produced confusion.

This was quite noticeable at one stage in the Senate, when Arrington was absent for several days while substituting as governor in the absence of Shapiro. During those hours when Arrington was not in the chamber orchestrating business, a breakdown in decorum prompted a Democratic senator from Chicago, Robert E. Cherry, to frustratingly declare to his colleagues, "If anyone here is confused, it's because he's been listening."

Orderliness hardly ever went out the window when Arrington was present in the chamber. Statehouse visitors couldn't help but be struck by the contrast between the Senate and the House, where the noisily flitting around the floor by the more numerous members might rival the pandemonium of a stock exchange. Even youngsters noticed the difference.

When two of Tom Corcoran's kids, Camilla and Evan, came to the Capitol to see the legislature in action, they were ushered into the House gallery as well as the Senate's. Afterward, Corcoran asked the youngsters whether they "preferred watching daddy at work in the Senate or going over to see the House."

"Their quick reply," related Corcoran, "was that the Senate was boring but the House was fun, a lot more fun."

From a political viewpoint, the July 1968 session was a draw as both parties reaped enough mileage on issues to cover their election-year flanks. The rancor habitually marking Arrington's bouts with Kerner was largely absent in his jousting with Shapiro, who appeared to go out of his way to take into consideration, even countenance if necessary, the always potential explosiveness of Arrington.

On his part, Arrington proclaimed the session to be the final successful test of the legislative experiment he was so instrumental in engineering—the continual operation of the General Assembly at the direction of its leaders. Although some Democratic legislators (and more than a few Republicans) still dragged their feet at the idea, they realized along with everyone else on the scene that no more years would pass without the two chambers convening at least once. Annual sessions had arrived, and nobody was more responsible for this new world than Arrington.

As future developments were to illustrate, the July session was the last one in which Arrington was the undisputed Republican ring-master. Monumental legislative challenges still lay ahead for the man, but the election November 5, 1968, was to alter his standing at the top of Illinois government. After the legislators' summer sojourn in Springfield that year, Arrington disappeared from front pages until late in the year. When he did reappear in headlines, it was the sort of publicity he could have done without.

The November election did not produce the complete Republican sweep in Illinois that some had forecast. However, in the eyes of national analysts, the outcome did return Illinois to the list of traditionally GOP Midwestern states. Presidential race winner Nixon prevailed in the state over his Democratic opponent, Vice President Hubert H. Humphrey, and Dirksen was elected to another term in the United States Senate. Ogilvie topped Shapiro in the gubernatorial contest; Scott captured the attorney general's office; and Justin Taft got the voters' nod for Illinois Supreme Court clerk.

As for the new General Assembly opening for business in January 1969, the election left the GOP with a lopsided lead in the Senate, 38 to 20, and the House still in Republican control, 95 to 82.

The GOP comeback in statewide offices was tempered somewhat by the successful campaigns of Powell and Howlett to retain their posts, secretary of state and state auditor respectively. However, the most noteworthy result of the balloting was the highly unexpected victory of Simon over Robert Dwyer in the contest for lieutenant governor. Never before had Illinoisans elected a Republican governor and a Democratic lieutenant governor at the same time, or vice versa.

Although Powell and Howlett were previously proven strong candidates across the state, their victories were far from sure bets because of seething internal friction among Illinois Democrats in the months before the election. The success of Simon was even more of a long shot since he was running statewide for the first time.

Unlike Powell and Howlett, Simon had maintained a close relationship with Illinois Treasurer Stevenson and other Democrats whose dissatisfaction with Daley's domination of the party surfaced publicly in the wake of the party's national convention in his city. The mayor's much-discussed role at the convention, most conspicuously the bloody police crackdown he ordered on undisciplined demonstrators, was alleged by critics to have given Daley and his party a black eye.

Many of those angered by Daley, including an untold number normally in the Democratic column, threatened to vent their protest by voting against Shapiro and perhaps others on the Democratic ticket. Shapiro was singled out as the most vulnerable because his allegiance to Daley through the years was the subject of much of the campaign criticism leveled at the incumbent governor. As the outcome showed, many of the state's 5,676,131 registered voters who supported some candidates on the Democratic ticket like Powell, Howlett and Simon did not, in fact, go along with Shapiro.

Even though the Republican tide in Illinois did not develop to the extent many predicted, Shapiro's defeat by Ogilvie returned the GOP to the control of Illinois government for the first time since 1960— the year of Kerner's first election as governor.

When Ogilvie was recovering from the destruction of part of his face by an exploding German shell in France during the final months of World War II, the thought of someday capturing Illinois' highest office was probably the farthest thing from his mind. The reconstruction of his visage was the reason for his usually staid expression, which was in sharp contrast to Shapiro's perpetual smile in the gubernatorial contest.

By the time of his race with Shapiro, Ogilvie—then a forty-five-year-old attorney living in the Cook County village of Northfield— had come a great distance. After serving time as a federal prosecutor in Chicago during which he'd successfully pursued notorious gangland chief Tony (Big Tuna) Accardo, Ogilvie sought elective office to fight what he termed the abuses of the Daley machine. His victory in the race for sheriff of Cook in 1962 helped spur the GOP on a path to renewed political vigor in Chicago's suburbs. In 1966, he ousted a Daley-allied Democrat from the presidency of the county's board of commissioners. His drive for governor two years later was cast in part as a quest to eliminate machine politics in Springfield, a reference to the conventional GOP charge that Democratic governors were minions of the Chicago mayor.

Ogilvie was in many ways a most appropriate candidate for governor in 1968. In continuing to depict himself as an angry young man crusading against political bossism, he stood to benefit from the unrest in Democratic ranks over Daley's leadership. The topsy-turviness in American life, spurred by widening civil strife, amply justified the stress in his campaign on a need for greater law and order. His pragmatic, business-first composure appeared to resonate favorably with many.

In the end, Ogilvie's victory margin over Shapiro—127,794 votes, or 51.2 percent of the total cast for governor—was not very broad. Nevertheless, the fact of Shapiro's defeat by even that amount made Simon's plurality over Dwyer in the neighborhood of 100,000 to be nothing short of remarkable. In searching for an explanation of the Shapiro-Simon vote disparity, some suggested that anti-Jewish sentiment may have factored into the situation in parts of Illinois. A more convincing reason, though, was the apparently strong appeal by Simon to independents and some Republicans, in addition to traditional Democrats.

The election produced a field day for Statehouse hangers-on. Talk centered initially on the awkwardness which was likely to fester with a Republican governor and Democratic lieutenant governor. At the same time, the grapevine was awash with speculation about the forthcoming relationship between Ogilvie, the new Republican topkick under the Capitol dome, and Arrington, a person not accustomed to sharing the GOP limelight.

Also taken into account was the upcoming interaction between Simon and Arrington in that the new lieutenant governor would be presiding over the Senate. Only a month after the election, the two did bump into each other. The confrontation itself wasn't much more than a fender bender with Arrington easily prevailing. However, the senator paid for the victory with a bruised image.

The encounter was not over a vital issue or anything else affecting the well-being of even a single state resident. It revolved around office space, and who got what. One would have thought a governmental crisis was at hand the way the press jumped on the matter.

Arrington should have known he was asking for trouble when he revealed his intention to remain in the suite normally occupied by the lieutenant governor—the space he had seized after Shapiro left for the governor's office. Simon had expected to routinely move into the suite that Statehouse historians said had been designated by tradition for the lieutenant governor since 1878.

Simon didn't like it, but he knew his mild objection to Arrington's apparent assertion of squatter's rights was whistling in the wind. The Senate and the assorted offices in the vicinity behind the chamber were Arrington's fiefdom, and nothing short of the National Guard was about to evict Arrington from his latest abode. Simon would have to settle for the much smaller office complex, close by, that Arrington formerly had occupied. Although it was recently remodeled at the direction of Arrington, Simon would be operating out of what many saw as postage-stamp space hardly dignified enough for the state's second highest elected official.

Arrington's stated reason for keeping the larger office was that he had a bigger staff and more work to handle than the lieutenant governor. He tried to deflect attention from the resultant flap by talking up the GOP's rebound in the election and stressing the importance of the electorate's approval in the balloting of the call for the first state constitutional convention in nearly half a century. Arrington took justified pride in the vote for a convention in that he'd advocated another con-con for years and sponsored the General Assembly resolution that put the successful proposal for the call on the 1968 ballot. The senator also urged the press to explore the reasons for voters' rejection in the election of the proposed $1 billion state bond issue for financing the preservation of natural resources.

But, he wasn't going to get off the hook. Intrepid journalists, individuals usually relegated to a small desk with a typewriter in a cubbyhole, couldn't bypass this golden opportunity to prick the ego of one of the high and mighty. Many took their cue from Royko— the curmudgeonly scribe, a son of a barkeeper, who often was the first to find Arrington a juicy target.

Royko compared Arrington's occupation of the lieutenant governor's office to a sit-in, the name for the frequent action of civil rightists to remain in the seats or on the floor of an establishment as a means of organized protest. "The shocking thing" about Arrington having the "gall" to sit in, Royko noted satirically in his *Daily News* column, was that he "isn't a student, a hippie or even an anarchist.

"He is the majority leader of the Illinois state Senate, a Republican, a millionaire from Evanston, a lawyer, a conservative. And he is no kid That just shows how widespread the disrespect for law and order is in our society. For a long time, only poor, young blacks were sitting in. Now a rich, old gray is doing it."

If Arrington wanted his new fancy digs that badly, Royko concluded, "let him work for it. If he had any ambition, he'd run for lieutenant governor. In our society, even a millionaire white Anglo-Saxon Protestant Republican from Evanston can aspire to that high office." Of course, Arrington was not exactly an "Anglo-Saxon Protestant," but Royko was not about to let complete accuracy get in the way of the point he sought to make.

As other pencil lads followed suit with their own jabs at Arrington on the subject, Simon refrained from piling it on with any negative quotes for attribution. As a practical matter, no figure in the Statehouse was closer to the press corps than Simon. It had more to do than with his openness when answering questions. Simon himself was a member of the club. After he no longer was running his chain of small newspapers in Illinois, he still considered himself an active journalist by mixing the authorship of books and columns with his duties as a public official. Any even perceived slight of the man almost always was countered automatically by reporters on their own initiative. Prompting by Simon was not necessary.

In a discussion with this writer in 1994, Simon—then a United States senator— went so far as to suggest that the usurpation of the lieutenant governor's office represented "a power play by Arrington, a man to whom things like big offices, big cars and diamond rings meant a lot." But, he added, Arrington had "the jurisdiction to determine" who occupied the office. Far more important, Simon insisted, was his view, echoed by so many others, that Arrington did more than any other person in modern Illinois political life to "upgrade the legislative process."

Simon's mind-set about Arrington hadn't wavered by the time of this writer's final interview with him not long before his death in 2003. The meeting took place at Carbondale, where Simon had established the Public Policy Institute at Southern Illinois University after retiring from the Senate in 1996.

As he saw it, Simon emphasized, the uproar over the lieutenant governor's office never was "anything heavy enough to really fight over. It just wasn't a life and death matter for me, but it didn't turn out to be a good public relations move on his (Arrington's) part. The office was, I always guessed, a kind of symbol for him"

Anyway, as Gene Callahan, Simon's right-hand aide noted, "Paul always said that great things happen in small offices. And, he was serious about it."

In looking back during that last interview, Simon indicated that Arrington figured uniquely in the memories of his Statehouse days. There was even a personal sidebar to their relationship. Simon's first wife, the former Jeanne Hurley, who died in 2000, had been a Democratic state representative from Wilmette, part of Arrington's North Shore backyard, during Arrington's early years in the Senate.

More than anything, Arrington was "kind of above it all," Simon said, "meaning that, among his attributes, he was the intellectual superior of all of them (Republican senators). He just had such a great mind." Like others, Simon marveled at Arrington's "lack of tolerance for fools…an impatience that led him to tell off the guys on both sides that were not so bright or just not doing their job."

"My impression was that he was driven more than almost anybody else," Simon continued, "and I tied much of that to him having some feeling that he had to prove himself because of his father's coal mining background around Gillespie. I knew he had to make a success of himself the hard way, and that this was behind his attitude on some social issues that others could do it if he could."

After Simon as lieutenant governor moved into the gavel-in-hand post on the Senate podium in the 1969 session, and Arrington continued as GOP majority leader, clashes between them were anticipated. Simon would indeed be on the receiving end during tense hours of more than one Arrington tongue-lashing. However, Simon absorbed them in stride, rationalizing in his words that "they came with the territory."

"We didn't have any encounters that lasted beyond the moment," he explained. "I realized he had the basic power in the chamber, and I could see that he made sure the place was run the way it should have been. At the same time, I didn't knuckle under to him. If you refused to knuckle under, you got his respect. He obviously had mine."

Many watchers found the juxtaposition of Arrington and Simon to be a stitch. Here was Arrington, the man with the volcanic personality, standing by his red leather chair on the GOP's east side of the chamber, cigar in hand, methodical in his insistence on orderly proceedings, not beyond warmth for fleeting seconds but more inclined to impose his will with a red-faced abruptness that could cow even the most stouthearted.

Simon was not intimidated. However, judging by his appearance, one imagined that he might be. More than two decades younger than Arrington, Simon still exuded the apple-pie image of righteousness that accompanied his arrival in the Statehouse fourteen years earlier. With the face of a bespectacled choirboy and his trademark bow tie, Simon could have come off to those who didn't know better as a timid eccentric likely to wilt before Arrington. But, there was a tough-mindedness about Simon reflected by a surprisingly deep voice—a vocal tone that hardly ever revealed anger or frustration as he moderated the business of the Senate. Simon was a paragon of temperance in holding forth with Arrington.

The composure of Simon was virtually impregnable. His character was such that profanity also was out of the question. Callahan never heard Simon utter anything stronger than "by George" when he was displeased. The Simon staff was truly stunned when Richard J. Durbin, a Springfield lawyer serving Simon as Senate parliamentarian, once claimed that he'd actually heard his boss say "damn." Durbin, later a member of Congress and then a United States senator, insisted that Simon mouthed the word in a fit of exasperation as he slammed the gavel down with a bang during a fractious debate.

Simon's respect for Arrington didn't translate into endearment for the senator. The prickly personality that Simon felt to be an impediment to any Arrington gubernatorial candidacy prompted a feeling, remarked Simon, that "Arrington was not a guy that I'd want to have dinner with every night."

Nevertheless, the two regularly conferred off the stage on the bills to be called on given days as well as on the intended disposition of other items on the Senate calendar. Arrington's crew members trusted Simon's procedural fairness. A number also held Callahan in high esteem, especially newer arrivals who welcomed his willingness to share his institutional knowledge of the Statehouse.

Callahan, the administrative assistant and press secretary for Simon, wrote a must-read column for the *Illinois State Register* that related insights into Capitol doings not found elsewhere. He left the newspaper in 1967 to work for the Kerner-Shapiro administration, and he joined Simon's staff in 1969. In spite of his Democratic allegiance, he found much in Arrington to admire, especially his work ethic.

"I always liked guys who worked hard, and Arrington stood at the top of the list," stated Callahan. "There were so many things about him you couldn't forget, like the way he showed real leadership on the fair housing issue…a stand that almost got him bounced from his top spot.

"When I was writing my column, Arrington got a lot of my attention. There were times I praised him, and occasions when I blistered him. Unlike some, he never whined about the negative times. He wasn't in that category, and I had to respect him for it."

However, most unforgettable about Arrington, according to Callahan, was "that very forceful personality...the strongest by a long shot in the Senate in that period."

That forcefulness—the power of Arrington to bend unwilling individuals to do his bidding—faced its stiffest test in his legislative life in the session covering the first six months of 1969. It was the session that taxpayers wouldn't forget.

Chapter 20

℃

1969—A Session Extraordinaire

*T*he question was destined to become part of the political lore of Illinois. A deadly serious Arrington posed it to Governor Ogilvie.

"What fool in the legislature do you think you are going to get to sponsor the bill?" he asked.

The answer from a sober-faced Ogilvie became just as famous.

"You, Russ."

The exchange, brief and to the point, occurred during a meeting between the governor and Republican legislative leaders prior to Ogilvie's presentation to the General Assembly of his first proposed state budget on April 1, 1969. The governor was confirming to his listeners something that was widely rumored. Yes, it was true that his April Fools' Day message would be political dynamite because he intended to call for passage of a state income tax.

Silence gripped the air after Ogilvie told Arrington he wanted him to introduce the tax legislation. All eyes were fixed on the Senate leader, who'd skillfully maneuvered to keep the land mine issue of state income tax enactment at bay for years. Although he'd come to believe that an Illinois income levy was inevitable, he still was holding that the right time politically for its passage lay in an undesignated future year.

After being put on the spot by Ogilvie, Arrington finally responded, reminding all present that he'd championed opposition to a state income tax throughout his legislative career.

Then he looked at Ogilvie and added, "But, if in your judgment, Governor, it's that time, then I'll sponsor it." You could have heard a pin drop.

After Ogilvie made public his desire for an income levy, Arrington told questioners—among many surprised that he'd agreed to sponsor it—that he intended "to live up to my responsibility as a legislative leader. We may have to resolve ourselves into a position to do things we may not want to do."

Nevertheless, the Arrington uttering those words was visibly sullen. For several days after his consent to the governor's request, Arrington moved around sluggishly in a seeming state of moroseness. Several aides recalled him saying that he was sick to his stomach. Arrington never had shirked heavy issues in the past, but the onus to obtain passage of an income tax put a burden on his shoulders far beyond anything he'd undertaken.

So much was at stake.

Hand wringing over the state's morass of fiscal troubles had dominated the atmosphere since the new Seventy-sixth General Assembly opened its first session—a regular six-month one—back on January 8. (Prior to the convening, the old Seventy-fifth General Assembly met that day for one final hour to vote to hike the annual pay of legislators to $12,000 from $9,000.)

Most leaders of both parties conceded that Illinois' recurring money problems could not be solved by the current tax system—a patchwork widely viewed as unfair to many taxpayers and inadequate for meeting the state's needs.

In a last written communication to the legislature, outgoing Governor Shapiro warned that "Illinois will live from crisis to crisis" unless an answer was found to the state's revenue predicament. Shapiro said it was imperative that the new General Assembly provide a long-term solution if Illinoisans were no longer to be "denied an equitable tax structure as well as the manifold services and improvements that they have a right to expect from their government." As a backdrop to Shapiro's message, more and more individuals and groups were voicing support for an income tax as the only way to go.

Ogilvie himself followed up on Shapiro's admonition by telling

Senator Arrington and Governor Richard B. Ogilvie

lawmakers in an appearance before them in a joint session, some three weeks after his inauguration, that the state was teetering "on the brink of bankruptcy." He declared that he had no alternative but to seek increased revenue, but he did not specify what he had in mind.

On the other side of the coin, the great political danger inherent in approval of a state income tax was just as widely recognized.

Ogilvie emphasized in addressing the legislators that solution of the monetary plight required, among other things, "support and leadership from both parties and from all concerned citizens." But, the reality of the matter was that the responsibility for leading the charge for fiscal health fell to the party in control of state government, and in 1969 that party was the GOP. If pushing for the income levy had been an easy political pill to swallow, the tax would have gone on the books years earlier.

When Republican senators were briefed by Arrington on Ogilvie's income tax plan during the morning of April 1, several hours before the governor openly outlined his budget message in an appearance before all the lawmakers, the response was quite chilly. As if going for the tax wasn't difficult enough, they felt his proposed starting rate was exorbitant. Few could believe that Ogilvie was asking for imposition of a fixed-rate tax of 4 percent on the incomes of individuals and corporations, nor that he also wanted at the same time new or higher levies on tobacco products, alcoholic beverages, rented equipment and certain consumer services. He did refrain from seeking a sales tax hike, but he still was advocating the most drastic tax increase program by an Illinois chief executive in years. Without the increased revenue, Ogilvie stressed, he'd have no chance to implement the wide number of new or revised programs and initiatives he had in mind for a broad scale renovation of Illinois government.

In the wake of the budget message, many people began to take a closer look at Ogilvie and the magnitude of everything he wanted to do. Head scratching was especially noticeable downstate, where the new governor was mainly viewed as a law-and-order fellow. Now a new question was being asked. Was he really a Republican?

Standard-bearers of the party in those days were not exactly identified with big-time tax and spend programs, or with initiatives leading inevitably to larger government. Such subjects normally were in the domain of Democrats.

It was easy to see that Ogilvie, in moving to get an income tax passed as early as possible in his term (he did not face reelection until 1972), was picking the most politically safe time to do so. Also, some surmised that the governor called for a higher income tax rate than expected in an effort to establish a bargaining position for the political battle to be triggered by his proposal. Based on the reaction by many in the GOP to the Ogilvie income tax, a number of Democratic votes almost certainly would be required if an income tax measure of any significance were to pass.

The drive for the income tax outweighed all other Illinois political developments in 1969. This was really saying something in that this would be the year in which the General Assembly—by going along with just about all of Ogilvie's reorganization proposals—did much to change the face of Illinois government. Nineteen sixty-nine also was a year of greater than usual extracurricular activity in the state's public arena: election of delegates to the Illinois Constitutional Convention; enmeshment of the Illinois Supreme Court in scandal; and, to boot, even charges of wrongdoing on contracts at the traditionally wholesome Illinois State Fair.

All events transpiring in the whirlwind year, as important as they seemed at the time, would fade in the memories of most Illinoisans—with the exception of the income tax. The political fallout from its approval buttressed the old adage that nothing lingers more in the mind of voters than pocketbook issues. Arrington certainly had paid homage to this saying—made it a staple of his Republicanism—prior to the arrival of Ogilvie.

His agreement to sponsor the income tax legislation, the ultimate affront to Arrington's long-honed sensitivity to tax hikes, was taken as the definitive answer to the question of whether the Statehouse was big enough for both him and Ogilvie. Arrington's deference to Ogilvie on his tax plan confounded many who'd expected Arrington to become a contradictory factor for Ogilvie after his move into the governor's chair.

Charles Nicodemus, the *Chicago Daily News* political editor, was in a majority at the dawn of 1969 when he predicted that Ogilvie "seems certain to find Arrington one of his greatest blessings and biggest burdens."

The blessing part, wrote Nicodemus, came from Arrington—the "most talented and respected, cantankerous and unloved member" of the legislature—being "a hard-working, dynamic leader without peer in either house."

"Equally important, he is a fierce, effective crusader for the prerogatives, prestige and power of the legislature in general and the Senate in particular," Nicodemus added. The crusading characteristic, as much as Arrington's "abrasive personality," opined the writer, seemed "destined to bring him into eventual conflict" with Ogilvie.

Nicodemus did not miss the obvious in a comparison of the senator and the pipe-smoking governor, who was short like his longstanding friend Arrington but much heavier.

First off, the two were likened by the reporter as "strong-minded, stubborn men with sometimes explosive tempers." Each was depicted as a political conservative tempered by pragmatism—with Arrington's surfacing mainly through a liberal bent on social issues.

Differences between the pair were found by Nicodemus to be much sharper.

"In style," he penned, "Ogilvie tends more toward the taciturn side, a competent speechmaker but no eloquent turner of phrases. He listens well to counsel, choosing the best from his aides' offerings. Arrington, in contrast, usually appears to take advice from no one.

"And he is probably the General Assembly's fiercest debater, an articulate, innovative lawmaker whose rapier-quick wit and devastating sarcasm can shred an opponent on either side of the aisle.

"Ogilvie is a steady, head-down, push-straight-ahead plodder, who usually minds his tongue in public no matter what his inner thoughts. Arrington, in contrast, is mercurial."

Those trying to detect signs of early conflict between Ogilvie and Arrington pointed to the circulation at the start of 1969 of a booklet setting out a comprehensive GOP legislative program for the year. Brought out by Arrington and Smith, but authored mainly by Arrington, the document was similar to the one Arrington distributed at the start of the first session in 1967.

This time, though, it was pointed out that GOP legislators were pushing their own program when the governorship was in the hands of their party, unlike 1967, and when the new governor had a legislative platform of his own. However, Ogilvie quickly diffused any potential friction in the matter by saying that he "had no objections" to the GOP lawmakers' action. Furthermore, a lot of what Arrington's document proposed did parallel Ogilvie's goals, such as creation of a new agency to centralize control over the state's adult and youth correctional facilities and a switch from biennial to annual budgeting for the state.

Since the governor and Arrington were on the same page in so much of what they felt was needed for state government improvement, perhaps the trickiest concern to face the new Republican omnipotence was whether Ogilvie or Arrington received credit—or, in at least one case, blame—for the forthcoming upheaval. The odds appeared to favor Ogilvie because he had the bully pulpit of the governor's office, with all of the prestige and high visibility accompanying it.

In the end, the primary recognition for the incredible output of the six-month session of 1969 was steered to Ogilvie. The governor sought it, earned it and got it. Arrington, far beyond any other legislator, made it possible. His Statehouse prowess was never on better display. Still, he played second fiddle to Ogilvie. If there was any way for it to be otherwise, Arrington did not cash in on it. Hard as it was for some to fathom, the Arrington ego was put on ice.

The income tax, the centerpiece of everything enacted in 1969, was indelibly linked to Ogilvie. It was his baby in the eyes of the public, and efforts by himself and others in the GOP to give Democrats part of the credit for its passage were not successful. They wanted no such thing, which was understandable after witnessing the political fate of Ogilvie in his run for a second term.

Therefore, a year before his death in 1979, irony was not absent when Arrington seemed to belatedly feel regret that he didn't get more credit for the passage of the income levy. In the dictation of his memoirs in 1978, Arrington took something of an exception to a *Chicago Tribune* columnist's labeling of Ogilvie as the father of the Illinois income tax.

"I suppose he (the columnist) is right," said Arrington, "but it was my bill that introduced the income tax, and it was my work that got the bill passed. I'm not real happy that we had to impose an income tax, but for him to say that he (Ogilvie) is the father of the tax is stretching the point quite a bit."

Added Arrington: "There was no question that the state needed the money. The state would have been bankrupt if the bill had not passed."

The measure proposing the income tax was Senate Bill 1150, a number not to be forgotten by state fiscal junkies. Introduced by Arrington, he was joined in its sponsorship by the two assistant GOP leaders, Coulson and William Harris, and a Democrat, James P. Loukas of Chicago, who was on the way to becoming a political ally of the Republican governor.

Arrington choreographed every step in the politically excruciating drama required to get SB 1150 out of the Senate. The role of

Harris in getting this done could not be overlooked, though. Instead of the somewhat reserved Coulson, Arrington turned to Harris, a legislative spark plug if there ever was one, to serve as the floor manager for rounding up votes for the tax.

Harris, an individual always shooting for the stars, scurried around to his own drumbeat. A son of a Pontiac funeral home owner, his desire to be a navy pilot in World War II was blocked by color blindness. Nevertheless, he was the top performer in his training class of naval enlistees, and by the time he emerged from the navy in 1945 following service in a South Pacific war zone, he'd risen to the rank of chief petty officer.

Returning to his hometown after the war, he married country school teacher Jeanne Turck, worked as a mortician, tried his hand at cattle farming and then became an insurance sales agent. Needing yet another outlet for his enthusiastic energy, he ran successfully for the Illinois House in 1954. After six years in the body, he was elected to the Senate in 1960.

As with most of the influential legislators, Harris was well schooled on state finances. He was the last of the potent chairmen of the freewheeling Illinois Budgetary Commission, the legislative panel ticketed for extinction when Ogilvie moved rapidly and forcefully to make the executive branch the king in Illinois' budget-setting process. Harris was a vociferous opponent of any state indebtedness, regardless of the purpose for which it was incurred. For this reason alone, Harris readily agreed to lend a vigorous hand to the drive for passage of the income tax.

Arrington couldn't have made a better choice than Harris for assistance in the arm-twisting for the levy. The upbeat nature of the chunky redhead, who still sported an old-fashioned 1950s crew cut, didn't appear to be dimmed by his losing candidacy for state auditor in 1968. He was well liked by most Democrats in the Senate, as well as by his fellow Republicans. He'd emerged in the minds of many as a likely successor to Arrington as Senate GOP leader, if and when Arrington departed the Statehouse. Of course, nobody envisioned Harris going for the position while Arrington was still in the saddle, but, then again, nothing in politics was carved in granite.

The cast of leading players in the fight for the income tax included Clyde Choate. Calling Choate, the minority whip in the House, a firebrand on the subject was not stretching it.

Choate's day in the sun on the tinderbox issue was instigated by the proposed rates in Ogilvie's proposal. Disappointment was evident in some quarters that a flat-rate income levy was sought instead of a graduated or so-called progressive type. The nod went to a flat-rate imposition primarily because of Illinois constitutional language that had been used earlier in the century as an obstacle to consideration of a graduated income tax.

However, Ogilvie's intent to tax the incomes of both individuals and corporations at the same flat rate of 4 percent triggered debate too inflamed to be ignored. Numerous Democrats long had held that they'd frown on a flat-rate income levy that hit individuals as hard as corporations. In the Senate, McGloon did voice reservation about the Ogilvie plan—but not stridently. McGloon was very aware that his boss, Daley, would be interacting with the governor to bring about Democratic support for the tax, which the mayor did not oppose since part of its proceeds would go to local governments.

Choate, a twenty-three-year veteran in the House from the deep southern Illinois town of Anna, was not as subtle about his indignation over the Ogilvie proposal. His position was clear from an income tax bill he'd introduced—a measure that would have taxed corporations at 5 percent of their income and individuals at only 2 percent.

The ire of Choate, not to be ignored since he received allegiance from a number of downstate Democrats, boiled over after the Senate Revenue Committee recommended in early June 1969 that SB 1150 be approved. The measure escaped the panel only after the rate of the tax was reduced to 3 percent from 4 percent for both corporations and individuals on a motion by Arrington. He said he took the action after concluding that he could not obtain sufficient GOP support for the higher rate wanted by Ogilvie. Arrington's move hardly put an end, though, to the brouhaha over the proposed levy.

Most upsetting to Choate, and those of a similar mind, was that Arrington's amending of the uniform 3 percent rate of imposition into the bill reflected more than his concern over garnering Republican senators' votes. In doing what he did, Arrington also was acquiescing to a deal between Daley and Ogilvie intended to make the tax more palatable to Democrats. The 3 percent rate, it apparently was assumed by the mayor, governor and Arrington, would make legislators of all shades feel safer in voting for an income tax. The problem was that too many lawmakers in each party still were not in step with the big boys on this one.

Open rebellion erupted. Not among the Daley-dominated Democrats from Chicago, but from downstate House Democrats led by Choate. Why, asked the insurgents, did thirty-seven of the forty-one states then with an income tax assess individuals and corporations at different rates if that was not the thing to do?

Putting muscle into his defiance of the deal between Ogilvie and Daley (and sanctioned by Arrington), Choate launched a filibuster and threatened to tie up the House with parliamentary moves if the protest of the downstate Democrats was not heeded. The warning had to be taken seriously because Choate was backed by most of the thirty-five House Democrats from outside Cook County. The GOP majority in the lower chamber, itself divided on the income levy proposal, was not likely to produce enough votes for passage without significant Democratic help. Thus, besides already having their hands full with many of the Senate Bourbons, Arrington and other income tax backers had to reckon with Choate and his followers in the House.

Choate, one of fourteen children in a Depression-poor family of a farmer-miner and his wife, had made a name for himself before his arrival in the House in 1947. He entered politics after becoming a hero for repeated gallantry in World War II, climaxed by his incredible courage during an encounter in France on October 25, 1944. When a tank destroyer commanded by army sergeant Choate was set ablaze by German fire that day, he risked death to save the lives of his men by maneuvering alone to destroy a Mark IV tank of the enemy and drive back German infantry. It was for that bravery that he received the Congressional Medal of Honor, which was personally presented to him by President Truman.

Early on in the House, Choate became savvy at horse trading on behalf of the lower region of Illinois and numerous other interests. His ally much of the time was fellow southern Illinoisan Paul Powell. Sometimes Powell and Choate brought home the bacon for their territory with tactics viewed as more devious than on the up and up. Their defenders countered that the two often had to scheme unmercifully, employing every wile they could muster, in order to play ball with or sometimes even con the more numerous Chicago area legislators. Only through such machinations could southern Illinois remain competitive in the legislative process. However, many righteous folks could not see that.

Urban political sophisticates forced to barter with Choate found him more than a little countrified. Still, they had to watch what they said about him since he was a genuine American hero still in his political prime in 1969.

As for any aspersions about his legislative maneuvering, Choate cast them aside in depicting himself as an advocate of little people. It was this cloak that he wore in crusading to ensure that individuals were not taxed at the same rate as corporations.

By the middle of June, with the session set to run only two more weeks, Choate had brought enough legislators to his corner to get the mighty Daley, if not yet Ogilvie, to cave. The mayor sent word to Springfield that he'd changed his mind, that he also would insist on an income levy with a higher rate for corporations than individuals. Ogilvie wouldn't budge, though, insisting on a uniform rate for all concerned.

A problem for Ogilvie, however, was that his fight was as much with Republican lawmakers as Democrats. He knew Arrington was struggling to get enough votes in the Senate to pass SB 1150 with its identical taxation rate of 3 percent for individuals and corporations. Too many of the troops either remained hesitant to vote for any levy on incomes or recognized that Democrats like Choate were making it politically unacceptable to back an income levy without a lower rate for individuals.

Only a handful of GOP senators had given a green light to the income tax. One was the plainspoken lawyer from Carbondale, John Gilbert, who held that both the state and Chicago desperately needed the added revenue from the levy. Gilbert remarked that in his mind "any thinking person in the legislature who was not playing partisan politics or worrying about his own election realized that." But, more ink was given to Bourbon snorters like Hudson Sours who was passionate in his thinking that Republican legislators who agreed to an income tax were putting their heads on a political chopping block.

John W. McCarter, Ogilvie's budget director, was taken aback by the hostility of some toward the tax when he went into Senate GOP caucuses at the direction of the governor to answer questions about the proposed levy. McCarter was impressed with the forbearance of Arrington in striving to maintain a measure of control in what McCarter called "those wild, wild sessions."

As McCarter remembered, there were a certain number of downstate Republican solons who, "in spite of their adamant opposition to the income tax, had been cajoled or bullied into support of it, or at least, you know, fainthearted support of it, by Arrington or Coulson or Bill Harris. As for others, you could see Arrington working this patient strategy of holding people in line by keeping them talking and trying to find some common ground."

Since the ball game on the income tax question was in the Senate, final rounds of hectic maneuvering dominated the hours leading up to the Senate vote on the proposed levy the night of June 27. In the middle of it all were Ogilvie and his two top strategists, Jeremiah Marsh, the governor's special counsel, and former Chicago newspaperman Thomas Drennan, Ogilvie's cleverish political advisor.

At the culminating juncture, the governor parked Arrington, Smith and their top lieutenants in his office, and he installed McGloon and House Democratic chief Touhy in the nearby smaller office of Brian Whalen, Ogilvie's young right hand man who held the title of deputy governor. Ogilvie then moved back and forth, from one office to another, conveying proposals and counterproposals.

Begrudgingly, Ogilvie finally had given up securing an income tax with the same rate for individuals and corporations. He threw in the towel after the Democrats refused to bend from their Choate-induced position and after Arrington and Smith concluded that there was absolutely no hope of obtaining enough GOP votes to pass a bill with a 3 percent rate for both individuals and corporations. Consequently, out of those climactic hours of negotiation prior to the Senate balloting emerged the compromise legislative package that would have such major repercussions.

SB 1150 was amended under the accord to impose a levy of 2.5 percent on the adjusted gross income of individuals and a 4 percent tax on the earnings of corporations. In a further step considered essential for Chicago Democratic votes, the compromise provided for one-twelfth of the revenue from the tax to be rebated to local governments in the form of block grants to help school districts, reduce property taxes or to be used for other goals.

The compromise package also allowed municipalities and counties to receive a greater share of the proceeds from the state sales tax, another concession to Daley. Additional pieces of the revenue-raising package included a jump in the state levy on gross receipts from the renting or leasing of hotel rooms and hikes in the so-called sin taxes, the state levies on cigarettes, beer and other alcoholic beverages. Another result of the compromise was a go-ahead for approval of Ogilvie's ambitious program for upgrading highways. Along with upping the state motor fuel tax and vehicle registration fees, the program featured as its main event the setting up of a trust authority authorized to issue $2 billion in bonds to finance road construction and repairs.

Grandiose was the only word to describe a revenue-generating package with so many tax hikes. Understandably so, many Republican senators still felt hard pressed to support the package, especially ones from downstate areas where reelection was not as automatic as it was for Chicago Democrats tied to Daley's machine.

Encouraging to proponents of the compromise was that it fit the expectations of numerous governmental reformists. Too, enter the army of newspaper editorialists beating a drum for the income tax from day one. All of them had provided a resonant cheering section for Arrington as he pursued the hardest legislative sell of his life. Even at the windup, though, his steamrolling remained suspect because of a hard-to-bury assumption that he was duplicitous in sacrificing his long aversion to increased taxation for fealty to Ogilvie.

In the end, there were a few votes to spare as SB 1150 was

approved in the Senate, 35 to 22. Twenty-one of the thirty-eight Republicans voted for it, and fourteen Democrats, all from Chicago, said yes. The GOP no voters were spearheaded by flag bearers for the old guard—people like Sours, Broyles, Groen, Deerfield's Karl Berning and newspaper publisher John W. Carroll of Park Ridge. More than one Republican voting in the affirmative said they probably were signing their political death warrant. More than one turned out to be prophetic.

Compared to its ordeal in the Senate, SB 1150 was expected to move smoothly through the House. Unlike the Senate with its huge Republican majority, GOP control of the House by a lesser 95-to-82 margin meant that many more Democratic votes were available, if needed, for the income levy. Furthermore, GOP opposition to the tax in the House did not appear to be as fierce as in the upper chamber.

The job of guiding the measure through the predictable histrionics on the House floor fell to Edward Madigan, a toned down but firm-handed Republican from Lincoln. He would go on to earn considerable respect as a ten-term congressman from central Illinois and then as secretary of agriculture in the administration of President George H. W. Bush.

The House vote came during the evening of June 30, a few hours before the end of the session. The bill passed, 91 to 73, with sixty-nine Republicans and twenty-two Democrats in support. The negative voters included Choate, who'd tried unsuccessfully in the House to amend the measure so as to further cut the rate for individuals from 2.5 percent to 2 percent—the level for individuals he sought in his income tax bill that failed to pass.

A signal of what was to come was illustrated by a bit of Democratic sleight of hand with the House vote. Numerous Democrats voted yes on the electronic tallying board while the voting was in progress, but switched to no just before the final count was recorded when it became obvious that their votes weren't needed for passage. Consequently, the recorded vote made it look as if backing for the income levy came mainly from Republicans. This was the beginning of Democratic moves—largely destined to pay off—seeking to exonerate the party from any share of the blame for taxpayers' unhappiness with the income tax.

Ogilvie wasted no time in signing SB 1150 on July 1. He invited Democratic legislative leaders to join their GOP counterparts at a ceremony in his office. But, the Democrats stayed away. As an upshot, photographic coverage of the event showed only Arrington, Harris and Smith standing behind Ogilvie as he displayed his signature on the income tax measure. The absence of smiles from the legislators' faces didn't deter many seasoned Republicans from cringing at the thought of the picture's likely impact in future campaigns.

At the insistence of Arrington, the legislature did take one noteworthy action to soften public anger over the income tax by voting to submit to the electorate in 1970 a proposed state constitutional amendment that would eliminate the detested personal property tax on individuals. Not hard to predict, voters ratified the amendment.

In retrospect, the opening session of the Seventy-sixth General Assembly in 1969 was a watershed for the governance of Illinois. The new governor asked for what seemed like the world, and the legislators—still under the thumb of Arrington—gave him the bulk of his wish list.

Business leaders and other GOP stalwarts could only watch in disbelief as Ogilvie maneuvered with Arrington and other Republican legislative leaders to obtain approval of programs so large in their concepts and costs that the governor's Democratic predecessors looked like pikers. More than massive tax and spending was involved. An overhaul of government structure was undertaken. For initiatives not completed this first year under Ogilvie, groundwork was laid for their implementation in succeeding years.

It was hard to know where to begin in summarizing the changes wrought by the GOP in 1969's six-month session. Besides the gigantic highway improvement program, the legislature approved an unparalleled increase in the level of state aid to public schools. The desire of Ogilvie and Arrington's posse to reorganize the penal system did result in legislative ratification of the division of the Illinois Department of Public Safety into two new departments, one primarily administering the state's corrections institutions and the other coordinating various state law enforcement activities.

A lot of attention was showered on one new operation in the fresh law enforcement agency. The official name of the operation was the Illinois Bureau of Investigation, but it quickly became known as the state's Little FBI. Its establishment sparked comments ranging from those feeling that unbridled organized crime in Illinois merited such an entity to those contending that Ogilvie was not sufficiently aware of police state tendencies in some of his programs.

Municipalities and counties were expected to get a boost from the legislature's okay of Ogilvie's request for creation of a new Department of Local Government Affairs. It was mandated to assist local units in budgetary and other complex matters, as well as to serve as a clearinghouse for state and federal programs and grants available to local officials.

Not to be overlooked was Ogilvie's takeover of the direction of state spending through his creation of the Bureau of the Budget as an arm of his office. The wresting of the basic budget-making function from the General Assembly, accompanied by a move from biennial to yearly budgeting, was a momentous development. It made the governor, more than ever, the chief figure in the control of Illinois' purse strings and, consequently, in the government of the state— from the major agencies to nickel-and-dime offices. Nothing else did more to ensure that Ogilvie left the governorship a considerably more authoritative office than he found it.

Arrington's support of Ogilvie's thrust to make the legislature more of a reactive than originating factor in the budget process struck some as a departure from his endless crusade to buttress the sovereignty of the General Assembly. A few went further, asserting it was a clear example of something they thought they'd never see— Arrington subjugating himself to another governmental person. Even though Ogilvie was a governor from his own party, the submissive-ness was so out of character for Arrington. When the matter was raised with him, Arrington replied that he stood foremost for good government and that the putting together of a proposed state budget should have been a priority role for the governor all along.

The governor may have been the cover boy of the session, but Arrington always was in the news. A leading example of his name being affixed to more than the income tax was the long-sought approval of legislation designed to shed light on money dispensed by lobbyists. This development had a Rabelaisian touch in view of a book that was not kind to the senator.

Arrington was the chief sponsor of legislation—consisting of a pair of bills, signed by Ogilvie—that required Illinois lobbyists for the first time to disclose some of the dollars they spent to promote or oppose measures before the General Assembly or a constitutional convention. The measures came under the heading of unfinished business since Arrington noted that lobbyists weren't covered in 1967 when the legislature approved regulations on the conduct of lawmakers themselves, members of the executive branch of Illinois government and the judiciary.

Besides calling for disclosure of their expenditures, the measures required lobbyists to describe the legislation in which they were interested. Violators of the statutes were subject to a fine and imprisonment. Critics argued that exemptions in the revelation requirement were too broad to permit the obtaining of an accurate picture of the amounts dished out to influence legislative actions. Nevertheless, the bills provided for much stronger regulation of lobbyists than an old registration law, which was widely criticized as being too weak to be taken seriously.

Arrington's spearheading of the legislation was sardonic in the opinion of some because he was repeatedly criticized through inference in a 1968 book, *Fat-Cat Lobbyists Make Your Laws*, by a former Republican senator, Robert R. Canfield of Rockford. He obviously had little love for Arrington or lobbyists, some of whom—regarded as members of the "third house"—were better known than the persons they sought to influence.

Canfield, defeated five years earlier in a campaign for state attorney general, repeatedly implied that Arrington coddled business lobbyists who funneled cash to GOP coffers. Especially egregious, Canfield contended, was Arrington's protection of the insurance industry against unfavorable legislation. This happened to be the industry, Canfield reminded readers, that "aided him (Arrington) in growing from a man of ordinary means to one of considerable wealth."

Declaring that "the well-organized insurance lobby actually sits closer to the Illinois legislature throne than any other such group," Canfield wrote sarcastically that it was "difficult to say how the insurance lobby got headquarters in the office of the president pro tem of the Senate while the truckers' lobby was moved two doors down the hall to another office facing the Senate floor, and the very aggressive and expanding nursing-home lobby took its place in an office adjoining the president pro tem's office on the other side. Other lobbying contingents took their places in state offices surrounding the Senate floor, with larger and better accommodations than the senators were provided."

While no offices near the Senate floor, or anywhere else in the Statehouse, were assigned to lobbyists, some legislators privately praised the book as on target in its depiction of the correlation between some lawmakers and lobbyists. Others called it unfair and full of innuendoes—a hatchet job by a Republican with an apparently sour grapes attitude toward his party. Even those defending the book noticed that it gave scant if any attention to the open use of Democratic legislators' offices by unions and other Democratic-leaning groups, as well as their infusion of big dollars into Democratic campaigns.

Among other Arrington hallmarks in the six-month session, he joined with House Democrat Harold Katz of Glencoe to lead a successful push for legislation providing for the nonpartisan election of delegates to the voter-approved state constitutional convention. This caught the attention of the *Wilmette Life*, which applauded the decision to go the nonpartisan route as "a major victory for some of the North Shore's leading political figures as well as the public at large."

"It took political courage," editorialized the newspaper, "to support the nonpartisan proposal because the legislature is so notoriously partisan. Many old-timers in both parties look askance at any such attempt to limit their influence in the development of a new state constitution. Those who backed the (nonpartisan) effort from the start had to rise above these internal party pressures."

The electoral process for convention delegates—two to be elected from each of the fifty-eight state senatorial districts—consisted of a primary September 23, 1969, and a general election the following November 18. The convention itself was set to open December 8. Arrington received encouragement from many quarters (but not many editorial pages) to run for a delegate seat, and he initially filed petitions to do so.

However, he withdrew his candidacy after two justices of the Illinois Supreme Court raised doubts via a minority but strong opinion about the constitutionality of legislators serving as convention delegates. Arrington said it was vital to the success of con-con that no legal shadow threaten it.

The *Sun-Times* gave Arrington high marks for "his unselfish decision to withdraw as a candidate," and the *Daily News* followed suit in spite of its acknowledgment that Arrington "has been a powerful force in the battle to get a constitutional convention, and deserves full credit for shepherding con con to this point." Arrington still would play, the *Daily News* added, "an important and continuing role as an expert adviser to the convention."

Arrington was hopeful, even optimistic, that the election of delegates and convening of the convention would garner broad public attention. After all, a rewriting of the state's fundamental governing charter—dry as it might appear to many an ordinary Joe—had profound implications for the gut of Illinois government. No person's interests could be divorced from the revisions, if approved by voters.

Whether a delegate or not, Arrington considered the coming of the convention at long last a personal accomplishment. He felt the same about his appointment earlier in the year by his friend, President Nixon, to a prestigious national panel, the Advisory Commission on Intergovernmental Relations. Arrington was one of three state legislators named to the body, whose twenty-six members also included governors, congressmen and mayors, as well as private citizens and federal and county officials. The commission had a wide-ranging mandate to recommend major policy changes in the allocation of responsibilities and revenues among all levels of government.

For Arrington, it was a dream assignment, an opening to exercise his voice at the highest level for strengthening the role of the states in American governance.

Arrington also was trying to take comfort in the favorable recognition by many newspapers and political progressives—both in and out of Illinois—of the state's extensive governmental revamping in 1969. Ogilvie got most of the national ink, with some suggesting that he so vividly embodied a new wave of enlightened leadership as to make himself a future possibility for the White House. Not all ignored the presence of Arrington.

The *Los Angeles Times*, in a piece authored by D. J. R. Bruckner, pinpointed Arrington as the most obvious of "some very strong-willed GOP leaders" on the Springfield scene when Ogilvie arrived.

To Bruckner, Arrington was "a wasp-tongued, enormously efficient man whose ego is only a little smaller than the formidable mind which has kept him on top of everyone else in the legislature." He seemed to imply that one of Ogilvie's triumphs was the harnessing of Arrington's energy and political skill to the will of the new governor.

Forget not, stressed Bruckner, that prior to Ogilvie, in years when the Democrats held the governorship, "Arrington used to work out his own legislative programs and push them against those of the administration, often successfully. In all party affairs, he was the leader."

Bruckner joined the list of those believing the passage of the income tax earned Ogilvie his greatest respect. Therein, though, lurked the political quicksand for the governor and his party. Soundings from every corner of the state revealed angry resentment by many rank-and-filers at the new imposition. They were not in the mood to be appeased by the promises of good things to come from the levy. Unknown to most people at the time, apparently including Ogilvie himself, were polls taken by Thomas Drennan that showed Ogilvie to have fallen into an incredibly deep political abyss because of his income tax push.

The ongoing Democratic ploy to coat Ogilvie and the GOP with liability for the income tax was pursued through the partisan bickering that colored a five-day reconvened session in October, the last meeting of the General Assembly in 1969. The session's main action was approval of a $40 million appropriation to cover refunds due taxpayers from the new income levy, another reminder that the tax was on the books.

As if the income tax wasn't enough to rile many Illinoisans, the populace was irked further in 1969 by several government scandals. One besmirched the apple-pie image of the state fair, where an investigation by the *Tribune* and Better Government Association triggered disclosures of mismanagement at the fair—including irregularities in the handling of concession contracts. Ogilvie got wind of the inquiry before its completion, and set machinery in motion for the state police and federal agents to also probe the matter. By so doing, he precluded his administration from any accusation of negligence in case the investigating proved fruitful, which it did.

For his part, Arrington directed the Legislative Audit Commission to examine fiscal records of recent fairs, including the one in 1969, to determine areas where legislation might be proposed to combat shady practices.

Another scandal during the year was of far greater magnitude. It brought disrepute to the Illinois Supreme Court, the panel of dark-robed justices of lofty authority closeted in their judicial temple just east of the Statehouse.

Charges of corruption in the state's highest tribunal by a self-styled court reformer and aggressive investigation of the allegations by newspapers started the rolling of a ball that led to the resignations of two of the court's seven members, Chief Justice Roy J. Solfisburg Jr. and Justice Ray I. Klingbiel. A special commission, appointed in a follow-up by the Supreme Court itself to further probe the charges, requested the resignations after concluding that the two judges clearly were guilty of impropriety in the court's handling of a 1967 case involving Theodore J. Isaacs, a former state revenue director under Governor Kerner.

Solfisburg and Klingbiel were said to have violated judicial canons of ethics by receiving, through middlemen, stock in the Civic Center Bank and Trust Co. of Chicago right before or during the time the court was considering a case involving Isaacs, an officer and general counsel for the bank. The commission determined that Isaacs was connected with the shares reaching the justices. Subsequently, Klingbiel wrote an opinion of the court that upheld a lower court's dismissal of criminal conflict of interest charges against Isaacs. Those charges grew out of a disclosure that Isaacs owned part of a Chicago envelope company that sold more than $1 million in envelopes to the state when Kerner was governor. (Isaacs was the Kerner confidant who orchestrated the irregular racing stock deals involving Kerner during his governorship that resulted in Kerner's federal indictment and imprisonment after leaving the governor's office.)

The Supreme Court and state fair scandals were not the only unsavory situations tarnishing the character of Illinois government during Ogilvie's years in office. The next to arouse great public indignation broke at the end of 1970. However, well before its eruption, many Illinoisans—mainly because of the Supreme Court disgrace—were already dismayed over both the ethical decay of their government and the moral failings of those entrusted to operate it.

The ax from such public dissatisfaction almost always fell on the party in power—the party of Ogilvie and Arrington at this juncture. An unease in GOP circles as 1969 neared an end was increasingly visible among the party's legislators, a number of whom just could not shake a foreboding of doom largely as a result of the income tax approval.

Sensing the trepidation, Arrington donned the persona of a coach in a pepper-upper letter to Republican senators November 17, 1969.

"I cannot emphasize too strongly my belief that the road to reelection for all of us is paved with an aggressive defense of the total legislative package we enacted," he wrote. "There is no need for apologies or lame excuses for the income tax. We will win next year with a united party vigorously defending our Governor and our program."

After listing increased school aid funding and other legislative accomplishments "certain to be popular with the voters," Arrington underlined the importance of reminding constituents "again and again that none of the accomplishments would have been possible unless we also had the courage to restructure and make more equitable the revenue programs necessary to fund the services the public wants."

Having the letter in hand was helpful. But many of the recipients weren't too sure they'd be sleeping any better at night.

Chapter 21

℃

The End of the Run

*A*mericans inclined to rhapsodize about the past almost always remember things to be better than they were. Viewed through rose-colored glasses, the 1970s were happy days, just like the decade's hit television show with that name—the one featuring the Fonz and those other delightful characters. After struggling to survive the bucking bronco ride of the 1960s, many folks were quite content with the decade of hip-hugging bell-bottoms, platform shoes, the Twiggy look, Laverne and Shirley, the romance of *Love Story*, the pet rock craze, the country's Bicentennial gala, mysterious skyjacker D. B. Cooper's leap to fame, the hypnotic rhythm of disco, Billy Beer, the first VCRs and happy face buttons.

But, much in the 1970s was unsettling: the scorch of Watergate driving Nixon from the presidency; the humbling end for America in the Vietnam War; the horror of Attica; the Jonestown suicides; and the assassination attempts on President Gerald Ford. Troubles like these undercut national confidence by leaving people conflicted, even harboring fear.

Journalist David Halberstam, author of a book chronicling the 1950s, said that the era of the 1970s, like the decade he had written about, "wasn't as wonderful as it seemed to be."

The reality was that self-doubt colored the stability of America in the '70s. A malaise oozed through the social fabric as an unusual combination of inflation and recession only bolstered the loss of faith in the judgment and integrity of the national leadership.

In Illinois, the decade debuted with a Republican Party down slide—a slip that couldn't be blamed on the Washington scene since it began in 1970, well before the crass Watergate burglary in 1972 that led to the fall of Nixon. A return to prominence by the Illinois GOP would have to wait until 1976, when Republican James R. Thompson parlayed a corruption-fighting record as United States attorney in Chicago into election as governor.

The unfortunate thing for the party in Illinois in 1970 was that it suffered from its own success. The Republican revolution that originated in the ballot box in 1968 had accomplished too much too soon. By the end of 1970, the party was in a hole in Illinois that was only going to get deeper.

Ogilvie, the catalyst for the Republican slippage, eventually was granted the iconic status of a martyr for having the courage to sacrifice his political appeal by calling for and getting approval of the income tax. It was prudent by then for Democrats to echo others in acknowledging that Illinois government never would have escaped an impossible fiscal straitjacket without the added revenue from the income levy.

But while governor, Ogilvie entertained no illusion about public reaction to the income tax. At the time of its passage, he had taken Brian Whalen, his staff chief, to lunch at Springfield's Illini Country Club and told him: "I am now the most unpopular person in Illinois. It will be a tough road on this, but we'll do our best." Burdened mainly by the negative baggage of the income tax, he went on to lose his bid for reelection in 1972 to Democrat Dan Walker, a maverick in his party who was a sparkling campaigner.

The first electoral backlash for Illinois Republicans came in 1970 in the wake of the income tax. The levy certainly weighed on voters' minds, and there was more for the GOP to worry about. The Democrats put up sterling candidates—namely Adlai Stevenson III, Alan Dixon and a refreshing newcomer, Michael J. Bakalis—for the major offices on the ballot. By comparison, their Republican opponents turned out to be lacking.

Stevenson, the state treasurer, defeated Ralph Smith for the United States Senate seat that had been held by Republican Everett Dirksen. After the death of Dirksen in September 1969, Ogilvie

Left to right: General Robert E. Wood, U.S. Senator Everett M. Dirksen
of Illinois, (unknown), Senator Arthur R. Gottschalk
and Senator Arrington

named Smith, then Illinois House speaker, as his replacement. The selection was ripe for second-guessing because of GOP fears that Smith was not formidable enough to hold the seat. In the 1970 balloting, voters were to elect the person to serve out the rest of Dirksen's final term, which did not expire until 1974.

Backed by the now Ogilvie-dominated machinery of the state GOP, Smith survived a 1970 primary election challenge from William H. Rentschler, a Republican businessman from Lake Forest. However, the general election was a veritable slugfest of extreme rhetorical insults, and Smith couldn't overcome the favorable name recognition and other strong aspects of the Stevenson candidacy. Stevenson already was a proven statewide vote-getter, and for once, in Stevenson, it was the Democratic candidate who had the best and brightest young faces in the supporting cast. (Thomas J. Wagner, his closest aide, and Lawrence Hansen were fine examples.)

The rain of barbs coloring the Stevenson-Smith race even extended to Clement Stone. Arrington's wealthy business associate was chairman of Illinois Citizens for Smith, and Democrats took delight in claiming that Stone was out to buy a Smith victory. Stone himself provoked the talk by saying that, through outright contributions and loan guarantees, he probably was responsible for at least $1 million in assistance for Smith and certain other Republican candidates in the state.

With a month to go before the general election, and smelling victory, Democratic workers merrily parodied Stone at their state party convention in Chicago. To the tune of "Oh, My Darling Clementine," they sang: "Oh, your dollars, all your money, oh, my darling Clement Stone." The wording was not as nice when they teed off on Stone in back rooms.

Stevenson clobbered Smith, but Dixon's triumph was not by as large a margin. Dixon, moving to end his stellar state legislative career with a successful run for statewide office, defeated the less than charismatic Edmund Kucharski in the contest for the Illinois treasurer's office being vacated by Stevenson. This was particularly stinging for Ogilvie and his party. Kucharski, the treasurer of Cook County and also the county's Republican chairman, couldn't have been closer to Ogilvie. (When Ogilvie was sheriff of Cook, Kucharski was his undersheriff.)

Notwithstanding the Democratic trend in many parts of Illinois, the outcome of the other statewide race was still a major surprise. Republican Ray Page, the state superintendent of public instruction for eight years, was upset in his bid for reelection by Bakalis. Page's reputation was not bolstered by press criticism of some of his office's purchasing procedures and of his maintenance of a flower fund stoked by contributions from his employees. However, Bakalis, a thirty-two-year-old American history professor and assistant dean at Northern Illinois University, was a political unknown. When Daley persisted in his desire to slate him to run against Page, many dismissed Bakalis—a son of a Chicago wholesale baker who'd emigrated to this country from Greece—as a throwaway candidate. Consequently, his victory understandably was viewed in some places as a rare feel-good story in Illinois politics.

The defeats of Smith, Kucharski and Page left Republicans feeling anything but good. However, the 1970 election's most depressing result for the GOP was the politically unthinkable loss by the party of control of the Illinois Senate. The only outcome preventing the election from being a complete disaster for the GOP was its retention of the majority in the House, if only by a thin margin of 90 to 87.

In the last hours before the general election, *Chicago Tribune* reporter John Elmer hardly stood alone in his thinking when he wrote that "most prognosticators…give the Democrats no chance to capture the Senate" where "it would take a miracle for the Democrats to take over." Arrington expressed confidence to questioners that a Democratic gain in the Senate, if any, would not exceed one or two seats.

Hardly anybody in the Statehouse could remember when the Senate was not a Republican bastion. Since the election of 1940, the party had occupied a majority of the seats in the upper chamber. During that thirty-year period, the GOP plurality was almost always decisive. Arrington and the bulk of his Republican seatmates did not know what it was like to kowtow to Democratic shot calling in the Senate.

Officially, nine seats in the Senate held by Republicans were captured by Democrats in the general election, leaving each party twenty-nine. However, in the case of a tie, the initial expectation was that Lieutenant Governor Simon, the chamber's presiding officer, would cast a vote for president pro tempore under his constitutionally-granted authority to vote "when the Senate is equally divided." Of course, Simon's vote was assured for the Democratic senators' nominee for the leadership post.

As it happened, when the new Senate organized in January 1971, Chicago Democrat Cecil Partee became the first Democratic president pro tem in three decades and the first-ever black in the post. Partee was elected by a 29 to 28 count, with all Democrats voting for him and one Republican refusing to join his colleagues in supporting Arrington. That Republican did not vote under a designed GOP strategy to let Partee win without Simon being allowed to cast a tie-breaking vote. To have let Simon vote, Republican senators felt, would have undercut their stubborn refusal to acknowledge the legality of Simon voting to end ties.

Arrington himself cruised to reelection in 1970, the last year he'd be a candidate for public office. Two trial lawyers, Henry T. Synek of Winnetka and John C. Mullen of Wilmette, competed in the primary for the Democratic nomination against Arrington in the general election. Synek, a previously unsuccessful candidate for the Illinois House, defeated Mullen, but lost as expected to Arrington in the final balloting for the Senate's First District seat.

The biggest setback in the election for Senate Republicans came in Chicago, where Lanigan, Krasowski and the other four GOP incumbents from the city were ousted by Democratic challengers. In each race, the Republicans faced a reenergized Democratic machine seeking to reassert its muscle in mainly white neighborhoods where it had somewhat slipped in the 1960s. Predictably, the Democrats brought up the income tax again and again, irrespective of whether all of the Chicago Republicans had voted for it. Lanigan for one did support it, leaving no doubt in his mind that this was a principal reason for his defeat.

In a broader sense, GOP senators who went down, and some of those who narrowly survived, felt they quite likely had acquiesced too readily in giving Ogilvie virtually all of his numerous and far-reaching requests for governmental change in 1969 and, to a lesser extent, in 1970. Some also didn't hide dissatisfaction with Arrington, whom they felt had sacrificed their best interests in making sure that so much of what Ogilvie wanted got through the legislature.

When the lawmakers gathered in Springfield at the end of March to begin their 1970 spring session under the new annual meeting format, many in the GOP fervently prayed for a respite from more headline-grabbing program initiatives—most notably ones requiring added taxes. Some welcomed the simultaneous proceedings of the constitutional convention, also in Springfield, which they hoped might attract some of the capital press coverage normally reserved for the General Assembly.

The convention did siphon some of the media attention, but its often sleep-inducing business wasn't capable of diverting the spotlight from legislative fireworks explosive enough to not disappoint those who lived for political name-calling. Interestingly, though, the most significant outgrowth of the legislators' presence off and on in Springfield to the end of June lacked much of the normal partisan acrimony. That development was the passage of legislation, proposed by Ogilvie, that completely overhauled the state structure and statutes for fighting air and water pollution.

At the center of the revision were two new entities, the Environmental Protection Agency for detecting despoilers of Illinois' natural resources and the Pollution Control Board for prosecuting them. Conservation and environmental groups said the new setup placed Illinois in the forefront of the fight against polluters, even though some aspects of the enforcement programs were watered down to satisfy industrial critics. Even with that, manufacturers wary that the legislation in its final form still threatened their operations asked Senate Republicans to block it. However, it passed out of the upper chamber, as in the House, with bipartisan backing.

Ogilvie's success on the antipollution front was not matched in his other major legislative pursuits in 1970. Downstate Republicans in both houses left him hanging in at least two major confrontations that angered them. One was the governor's support of state aid for Catholic and other private schools, a proposal that aroused religious antagonism while failing to pass. Opponents contended that Ogilvie was demonstrating political favoritism here for his home base of Cook County, a place loaded with Catholic voters and parochial schools.

The other imbroglio surrounded a state assistance program for mass transit recommended by the governor. His call, at one stage, for another increase in the state gasoline levy to provide dollars for the undertaking especially ticked off many GOP lawmakers who protested that voters already were up in arms over the income tax imposed a year earlier. Republicans away from the greater Chicago area added testily that the mass transit initiative, which died, basically was intended to bolster the fiscally troubled Chicago Transit Authority.

The impasses over the parochial aid and CTA proposals reflected a marked breakdown of rapport between Ogilvie and many legislators of his party. It also rekindled vestiges of the old standoffishness between Chicago and downstate. Caught in the middle on these matters were Arrington and Ralph Smith's replacement as House speaker, Jack E. Walker, a journeyman Republican from Lansing. Each conveyed to his party members what the governor wanted, but neither did so with the forcefulness so exhibited by Arrington the year before.

When Ogilvie finally was convinced to withdraw his motor fuel tax hike proposal, he joined a move to permit the mass transit aid to come from borrowed motor fuel tax receipts. But, GOP senators from south of Chicago still wouldn't go for that approach without the accompanying passage of a bill authorizing the CTA board to call a referendum on levying a property tax for that system. Democrats balked at the referendum, and a few Republicans also refused to support it.

After the referendum proposal and the mass transit assistance program died in the Senate in the last hours before the General Assembly left the Statehouse for the final time until late in 1970, Ogilvie confirmed that he'd asked Arrington during the concluding moments of Senate floor action to discard the referendum bill. Arrington refused because a number in his caucus told him his leadership would fall into limbo if he tried to comply with Ogilvie's request. The governor's magic wand in dealing with Republican legislators had lost its spell.

As the mass transit issue more and more dominated the General Assembly's spring scene, the accompanying political invective became increasingly rancorous. Daley and his lieutenants harangued Ogilvie to a great extent, and Arrington to a lesser degree, for failing to muster sufficient GOP support for a rescue of the CTA, whether through a statewide tax hike or sizable state subsidy. Arrington countered that the put-downs weren't relevant to political reality, but only intended to inflame Chicagoans' perception of a built-in bias against their city by a number in the GOP. The bottom line of the Democrats' polemics was to weaken further the appeal of certain Republican legislative candidates in the general election, Arrington speculated. Unluckily for the GOP, his suspicion turned out to be accurate.

In spite of the legislative collapse on the subject, Arrington realized that the CTA's financial ailments were only part of a chaotic morass ensnaring all segments of mass transit in the Chicago area.

Consequently, in the fall of 1970, he urged the drafting of legislation creating a mass transit authority responsible for the overall planning and coordinated operation of all public and private bus and rail commuter systems in the heavily populated northeastern corner of Illinois. As he saw it, consideration of the legislation would be a General Assembly priority in 1971. While conceding the vast technical challenges to be met in merging management of all the separate operations, Arrington said he was in agreement with others that a unified mass transit network for the Chicago area under a regional authority—a new superagency—was inevitable.

A few more years were to pass before the legislature worked through the complexities involved in providing for the establishment—subject to Chicago area voter ratification—of a regional transit authority for the northeastern part of the state. In the years after the authority was approved and conducting business, its operation was lauded by many as one of the finest examples of a cohesive urban transportation system in the nation.

Political bickering persisted to the time the new authority was up and running, but, in 2004, Richard M. Daley preferred to look back on its creation as a hallmark of cooperation at the start of the 1970s between his father, the first Mayor Daley, and Arrington. In his written comments for this book, submitted when he was Chicago's chief executive, the younger Daley said that Arrington's laying of groundwork for the regional agency was a case of the senator again "working across political lines" with Daley's father to ensure in the end that what was best for the Chicago area was secured.

It was a prime example, Daley maintained, of what he meant when he said his father and Arrington "needed each other."

However, there was no public sugarcoating of Arrington's relationship with the first Mayor Daley and other Democrats when the senator remained in play. The contentiousness was not above nitpicking. The legislators barely had settled into their seats at the start of 1970's spring session before they were sent home for a two-week "vacation." The break was decreed by Arrington because he'd consented to spend a good part of the two weeks in Hawaii with Clement Stone.

Stone wanted Arrington to participate in a convention of Combined Insurance's top salespersons. While in Honolulu, a place quite familiar to Arrington through past trips for business and pleasure, he also intended to touch base with friends in the Hawaii legislature. None of this impressed Chicagoan Paul F. Elward, a Daley Democrat in the House and frequent sniper at Arrington.

He suggested that taxpayers were jilted by the lawmakers' exodus from Springfield so soon after convening. But, he asserted, such "unfortunate" things happen when the General Assembly "too often marches to the drumbeat of one man—Senator Arrington."

The enduring closeness of Arrington and Stone was a red flag to Democrats, and they considered it fair game for potshots, however frivolous. One only could guess how far Democrats might have gone if they'd known that Arrington briefly was piqued by Stone in the months before their outing in Hawaii.

Arrington's irritation was an offshoot of a public tempest late in 1969 over a revelation that a new home for Delyte W. Morris, the highly regarded president of Southern Illinois University, was being built on the Carbondale campus for what state officials and others viewed as the outlandish cost of $900,000. The construction was proceeding at the same time the Ogilvie administration was striving to combat what it regarded as decades of lavish spending by higher education. Furthermore, it was charged that SIU violated state law and the policy of the Illinois Board of Higher Education by starting the project without the approval of the board.

A firsthand account of the situation was furnished to Arrington by Senate staffer Thomas Easterly after he learned details of it while visiting his former home base of Carbondale. Arrington reacted, recalled Easterly, by "immediately hitting the ceiling...feeling this was a breach of public trust."

Arrington thought the matter was ripe for an investigation by the Legislative Audit Commission; he readied the process for it to happen. Suddenly, though, in a dramatic move, Stone attempted to defuse the uproar through a $1 million gift of stock—accepted by the SIU trustees—to cover the cost of the house. Announcement of Stone's generosity caught Arrington off guard. He hit the ceiling again, this time over Stone.

"The intervention of Stone infuriated the senator," said Arrington assistant Richard W. Carlson. "He wanted the audit commission to go into the question of the fiscal responsibility of all involved, and he didn't want Stone's action to perhaps take Morris and the SIU people off the hook."

Carlson related a vivid memory of "Arrington sitting with some of us, chewing hard on his cigar, and saying, 'I told Clem to leave the politics to me.'"

The controversy wound up costing Morris much of his authority and prestige. The end of his long presidency came in 1970, just one more chapter in the fade-out that year of some leading people and things in Illinois public life.

A far more significant development in the passing of the old order in 1970 was the electorate's decision late in the year to accept the product of the Sixth Illinois Constitutional Convention, thereby triggering the passing into oblivion of the state's 1870 constitution.

Delegates to the convention completed work on a proposed new governing charter in early September 1970, nine months after the convention convened. This gave supporters, including most of the state's leading officials, more than three months to campaign for voter acceptance of the document at a ratification referendum the following December 15. By a vote of 1,122,425 to 838,168, it was approved.

Compared to the one it replaced, the Constitution of 1970 was much more geared toward meeting some of the governmental, social, environmental and other problems of the state's more than 11 million residents. Yet, it was not a drastic overhaul. The convention's product was characterized by Samuel W. Witwer, a Kenilworth attorney who served as convention president, as "neither reactionary nor radical...neither regressive nor visionary. It is practical."

In a nutshell, the new charter was designed to provide a more equitable tax structure, ensure greater racial equality and foster new relationships between state and local governments. It incorporated in its bill of rights a guarantee against discrimination on the basis of race or creed in employment and in the sale or rental of property—longtime goals of Arrington that had angered many in the GOP, most noticeably his unsuccessful move for open housing legislation in 1967.

The bill of rights also was expanded to include an assurance of freedom from unreasonable eavesdropping as well as from other invasions of privacy. The right of individuals to keep and bear arms was included—a testament to the clout of the gun lobby at the convention. Encompassed were substantial provisions for home rule intended to reverse the old doctrine that made local governments relatively helpless creatures of the state. Broad powers on taxing, borrowing and regulating were authorized for the first time for cities of more than 25,000 and counties with an elected chief executive officer. Everybody recognized that this segment was a major bonus for Chicago, enough in itself to have locked in the necessary support of Daley for the document.

One of society's growing priorities was reflected by a new article on the environment. It specified that each person had a right to healthful surroundings as well as a duty to provide for such.

The constitution's many other new provisions included: replacement of the state auditor of public accounts with a comptroller; elimination of the elected state superintendent of public instruction in favor of a chief state education officer named by a new Illinois board of education; establishment of a new board to supervise election code administration throughout the state; insertion of a new finance article spelling out budgeting and accounting procedures constructed to permit better management of taxpayers' dollars; and appointment by the legislature of a new auditor general to examine all aspects of state finances.

As the charter was pieced together by the delegates, the state's two top Republicans, Ogilvie and Arrington, maintained low profiles. Many delegates believed that the two not only were seldom seen around the convention, but also were little heard from. It was true that they infrequently surfaced at the convention, believing that by staying away they couldn't be accused of trying to steamroll delegates on issues. However, each kept tabs on the proceedings through staffers dispatched to the scene, and, on some matters, made sure that trusted delegates were aware of their positions.

Arrington formally addressed the delegates at least once when he appeared before them in the historic House chamber in the renovated Old State Capitol in downtown Springfield. He called for giving the General Assembly broad power to investigate courts and impeach judges. He got part of what he wanted in that the new document more narrowly defined the previous impeachment language by specifically giving the House power to conduct investigations into possible causes for impeachment of executive and judicial officers. The trial of an individual impeached by the House still would be conducted in the Senate.

Arrington, long an outspoken proponent of revenue reform, surprised the delegates by asking them to avoid major changes to the revenue article. Only minimal revision was needed, he held, because of the Illinois Supreme Court's upholding of the validity of the 1969 income tax legislation. His position was pretty much heeded, although misgiving persisted among some that the article lacked flexibility for the future. A concern was its prohibition of a graduated income tax, a potential problem in the long run for the so-called little guys.

After the convention ended, Ogilvie campaigned vigorously for voter adoption of the new charter. However, Arrington remained low-keyed during the drive, even sometimes telling crowds at events for Republican Senate candidates that he had not made up his mind on the proposed constitution. Persons in Arrington's circle said he certainly wanted the document ratified, but maybe feared that too much visible support on his part might make him a lightning rod for critics. Ironically, one of the most up-front opponents of adoption was young delegate John Alexander, one of the convention's three vice presidents and a person who felt the convention's output fell far short of what was needed for the betterment of Illinois. This was the same John Alexander who'd been an Arrington staff intern.

The approval of a new constitution, an Arrington goal for seemingly forever, should have given him pause for great satisfaction. The victory was bittersweet, though, occurring at a time when Arrington's world appeared to be imploding.

Although still reeling from the GOP's calamitous Senate losses in the general election, Arrington nevertheless spearheaded a stab at still gaining something important politically when the two chambers reconvened for a brief meeting in the second week after the balloting. The undertaking, a political long shot, failed.

Arrington's objective was to achieve legislative reapportionment of Illinois House, Senate and congressional districts before the expiration of the outgoing Seventy-sixth General Assembly. He and other Republicans felt that the realignment couldn't wait until 1971, when the new legislature to be seated almost surely would have a Democratic-controlled Senate. However, the initiative was stymied by successsful parliamentary moves by suddenly rejuvenated Democrats and a signal from Ogilvie that he'd not approve any redistricting bills passed by the departing legislature. To do so, he noted, would be poor public policy because the General Assembly then included a number of lame-duck members.

On the heels of this disappointment, Arrington faced a more personal challenge. William Harris announced that he was running against Arrington for the Senate GOP leadership post in the new Seventy-seventh General Assembly being seated in the coming January.

Harris' candidacy had the ring of a palace uprising in that he was one of two assistant Republican leaders in the upper chamber, a position he held by the grace of Arrington. Nevetheless, Harris professed to have sufficient backing for his quest from GOP solons tired of Arrington's autocratic manner and his willingness to do the bidding of Ogilvie—whose ambitious programs, remember, were blamed by many Senate Republicans for the party's downfall in the chamber.

The move by Harris naturally got Arrington's dander up; he posited himself to stand fast. Arrington loyalists quickly reminded all concerned that Harris showed, in working for the income tax and other Ogilvie propositions, that he himself was a stalwart of the governor. The acknowledged popularity of Harris with numerous Democratic senators, intended to be a selling point for Harris' candidacy, was not exactly a desirable thing for the GOP leader in the soon to be evenly divided Senate, Arrington people added. Arrington benefited the most, though, from calling in a lot of the political IOUs that he'd accumulated from so many Republican senators.

Early signs of possible success by the Harris coup had dimmed considerably by the time the GOP senators caucused in early December on the leadership contest. When the private session broke up, Arrington emerged as the winner. Some still couldn't believe that Harris had the temerity in the first place to mount the challenge.

Without doubt, the episode still was on the minds of William Harris and his wife Jeanne when they sat down with this writer in the summer of 2003 in a restaurant at Pontiac, their hometown. Harris was ill at the time and barely able to speak (he died a year and a half later), but Jeanne communicated for both of them.

"We always were asked how Bill could have been so blunt as to challenge Arrington," she said. "Well, he (Bill) didn't turn out to have the votes, and, of course, Arrington won. That left Bill a political nobody for a while. He was no longer in leadership. In fact, if there was a 'lower Slovobia' in Illinois politics, Bill was in it."

Her husband's failure to unseat Arrington, she stressed, "left us very convinced that Russ Arrington was the last of a kind—an all-powerful individual."

Yet, she added, "Bill just learned so much from Arrington, mainly on how to run the ship. He never stopped respecting Arrington, even after losing to him."

Following Harris' defeat, Arrington replaced him in the Senate GOP leadership team with Terrel Clarke, the senator from Western Springs who unsuccessfully ran against Harris for the Republican nomination for state auditor in 1968. Harris bounced back politically later on, serving as president of the Senate from 1973 to 1975 and as its Republican minority leader from 1975 to 1977. (Under the Constitution of 1970, the majority leader in the Senate presided over the body instead of the lieutenant governor, and was titled president of the Senate instead of president pro tempore.)

Another turnabout for Arrington as a result of the GOP's loss of a Senate majority was his surrender of the lieutenant governor's office suite to Simon, who by then was halfway through his term as lieutenant governor. The retreat kicked up little of the ballyhoo that greeted Arrington's takeover of the suite two years before.

Arrington's aides sought to downplay the departure, but Gene Callahan—never one to shun good-natured political mischief—made sure the pressroom was alerted to the vacating so that it could be noted and photographed for posterity. The situation was just too good for Simon man Callahan to pass up.

"I never gave a second thought to telling the reporters about it," remembered Callahan with a wry grin. "Some of Arrington's people were supposedly pretty upset that it was getting attention, but I never heard that Arrington himself had any complaints about the press showing up."

After finally getting into the lieutenant governor's office complex, Callahan recalled one thing in particular that caught his eye. "We found a phone identified by a slip of paper stuck to it that said 'Clem's line,'" he said. "We assumed it was a private line to Clement Stone…which we thought was most unusual."

The abdication of the large quarters couldn't have been more symptomatic of the end of a Statehouse era dominated by Arrrington. Even those not enamored by him felt the Senate was never out of kilter with him in charge. The well-ordering he'd brought to the chamber faced reconstitution in 1971. There was much angst among Arringtonites over whether he could keep in play the objectives and ideals he stood for in Illinois government.

Actually, 1971 opened with the Capitol in an uproar over another matter. The public and the media were in a tizzy over a disclosure right before the end of 1970 that Secretary of State Paul Powell, who died in October of that year, left an $800,000 cash hoard, a large sum at the time. Everybody was asking where the dough came from. It was a mystery promising to cause a big stink.

Arrington hated to see this, as the Powell affair was sure to give Illinois officialdom another black eye. He also harbored chagrin for the memory of Powell as a person, believing that the impact of the money stash would diminish the legislative accomplishments of a legendary Democratic lawmaker. Arrington liked Powell and, more importantly, highly respected him for his mastery of the legislative process and willingness to bury partisan differences on certain issues if the welfare of the citizenry was to be served. At the same time,

Arrington did not doubt that Powell had taken bribes and brokered deals as a former House power broker in order to feather his own nest.

Nevertheless, the excitement over Powell was not preoccupying Arrington's attention as 1971 commenced. Here, in the final innings of his political life, he suddenly was behind the eight ball. Lord knows, he hadn't anticipated facing such a predicament.

Chapter 22

℃

Knockdown Punch

*I*t was the second Sunday in January 1971. Robert Cahill and Robert Albritton, key Arrington assistants on the GOP Senate staff based in Chicago, were to ferry Arrington from the big city to Springfield that day, just as various Arrington aides had been doing for years. After the two—driving the senator's latest black Cadillac—picked up their boss, they assumed he'd waste little time discussing the General Assembly business awaiting him in the state capital.

Before the subject was broached, though, Albritton courteously asked Arrington how he was feeling. The answer was not something the two assistants wanted to hear.

"He told us he'd had a problem during the night," recalled Albritton. "He said he'd gotten up to go to the bathroom and that his leg had collapsed, causing him to fall."

"Are you okay now?" Albritton inquired of Arrington.

"His reply," said Albritton, "was that his leg was still numb."

Arrington's words immediately triggered an alarm bell, Albritton related during a telephone interview in early 2005 from his home in Oxford, Mississippi, where the Alabama native then was a political science professor at the University of Mississippi.

"We knew his history of heart attacks, of course," said Albritton. "Everyone around him was aware of them. So that was a concern."

Consequently, Albritton continued, "We told him, 'Senator, we think we should stop and get that checked out before we go to Springfield.' He didn't argue with us."

*Left to right: U.S. Senator Charles H. Percy, Senator Arrington
and (unknown)*

After a brief visit to Arrington's law office to grab some toiletries, the two drove him to Billings Hospital at the University of Chicago complex. They escorted him to the emergency room. Moments later, he was seated in a wheelchair, taken to a regular room and placed in bed. Cahill and Albritton intended to stay with him, but he insisted they proceed to Springfield and, in Albritton's words, "tell people there that something had come up and that he'd not be coming down right away." Except for one or two persons, Arrington did not want the two aides to tell anyone he'd been admitted to a hospital. Arriving in Springfield, Cahill and Albritton complied with his request.

"When we left him, he was still in good spirits," added Albritton. "And, he was quite lucid."

Later however, Albritton and Cahill learned, along with the rest of the Illinois political world, that Arrington subsequently suffered a massive stroke at Billings, one that left him partially paralyzed and unable to walk, talk or write. Even though Arrington's health always was surrounded by question marks, Albritton still called the disabling stroke—an outgrowth of a vascular blockage in the troubled leg—an "unbelievable development."

Arrington insiders at first sought to publicly downplay the seriousness of the situation, saying they expected the sixty-four-year-old senator to recover quickly and reappear in Springfield in a short while. However, before many days had elapsed, those in the know confirmed rumors that Arrington's absence from the Capitol most likely would continue through the remainder of the whole six months scheduled for the first session of the Seventy-seventh General Assembly. The legislature had convened January 6, a few days before Arrington entered Billings.

In the final minutes preceding the convening, Arrington had helped quarterback the passage of a bill by the dying Seventy-sixth General Assembly that provided a substantial pay boost for legislators from $12,000 annually to $17,500. Putting his muscle behind the measure, quickly signed by Ogilvie, was his last meaningful action as Senate majority leader.

With the Seventy-seventh General Assembly now up and running, many of the persons trying to adapt to Arrington's empty chair in the Senate could only guess at the severity of both his speech impairment and paralysis of one side of his body. Still, most Republican senators insisted that Arrington remain, at least in name, the minority leader in the chamber   his new, if not exactly coveted, title as a result of the 1970 election.

Nevertheless, the GOP Senate staff in Springfield realized, in the aftermath of the stroke and with an uncommunicative Arrington lying in a Chicago hospital bed, that it would be impossible to prevent the emergence of a Republican leadership vacuum in the upper chamber. The staffers, unwavering Arrington loyalists, also recognized that supporters of William Harris' recently failed bid to unseat Arrington as GOP Senate leader were likely to push for Harris to fill the vacuum. A gain of the driver's seat by Harris, the aides knew, would not be favored by Arrington.

A consensus was reached without delay by Arrington-aligned

senators and key staffers that Terrel Clarke, anointed a few weeks earlier by Arrington to be an assistant leader of Senate Republicans, was the best person to direct GOP senators in the absence of Arrington. Sensing the urgency of the matter, Arrington's crew tracked down Clarke in Florida, where he was vacationing, and asked him to return to Springfield as soon as possible.

Clarke heeded the summons and was on a plane within hours for Lambert airport at St. Louis. Waiting for him there, with Arrington's Cadillac, were staffers Jim Edgar, Richard W. Carlson and H. Thomas Schwertfeger. On the drive to Springfield, Clarke (called "Tec" because of the initials of his name, Terrel E. Clarke), was briefed by Edgar on policy matters he now needed to grasp in greater detail than before.

By the time the Cadillac reached Springfield, Clarke had been given a crash course on the nuances of dealing with new legislative chieftains Cecil Partee and W. Robert Blair. Democrat Partee now led a true Democratic majority in the Senate as president pro tem because the absence of Arrington handed Partee's party a one-vote advantage. Republican Representative Blair, a Park Forest attorney and realty company president, was the newly elected speaker of the House, where the GOP retained a slim majority. Although it was impossible to fill Arrington's shoes, Clarke handled his expanded role with increasing capability as the session progressed.

The first months of the Seventy-seventh General Assembly actually were abnormal in that the lawmakers for once were relegated to second billing in the Statehouse. The center of attention remained the unanswered questions about the source or sources of Powell's cache of $800,000, most of which was said to have been discovered in shoe boxes hidden in the suite of the late secretary of state at Springfield's St. Nicholas Hotel.

An army of reporters and investigators swamped the Capitol and other spots tied to Powell in a frantic search for information to unravel the mystery of the dough. Many leads were followed, but none led to definite conclusions as to where the money came from. Arrington's guess that Powell, a man tight as a drum, simply had not spent many of the dollars garnered from bribes, political contributions and mandatory donations from his office's employees remained as credible a supposition as any other.

One clear outgrowth of the probes of Powell's financial dealings was a cloud cast over many of his political cronies, most of them Democrats. For one thing, the inquiries confirmed the often rumored ties, through stock or other holdings, between many of Illinois' leading politicians and the state-regulated horse racing industry. In many cases, the interests of the politicos were well hidden or cleverly camouflaged. Some involved were legislators, the fact that would have left Arrington most dejected had he been on the scene in early 1971.

But, he wasn't. If one had been able to get a look at him at Billings Hospital, it would have been difficult to believe that he'd ever again make it into the Statehouse.

In his memoirs, Arrington expressed gratitude for the care he received at Billings under the direction of his attending physician, the well-regarded Dr. Joseph B. Kirsner. But, family members and others privy to the situation recognized that Arrington required extensive therapy of a nature that was not available at Billings. One of these persons was Leonard Lavin, Arrington's longtime business and social acquaintance.

In retrospect, Lavin felt that he had been a catalyst for Arrington's move to a setting more appropriate for his condition. As Lavin told it, he observed, during a visit to Arrington at Billings, that "he couldn't walk or talk. The doctors had given up on being able to do anything more for him there, and they were deciding to send him home."

At that point, Lavin continued, "I asked Russ to blink his eyes if he could hear me. He did. I next told Russ that if he'd like to try the rehabilitation necessary for him, he'd have to be moved to another place. I asked him to blink twice if he wanted to try that. He did. Then, I proceeded to call a friend, a doctor at an institute."

The doctor called by Lavin was Dr. Henry B. Betts, who at the time was medical director of the Rehabilitation Institute of Chicago. Dr. Betts, who later became president of the institute, was a renowned physiatrist—a physician specializing in physical medicine and rehabilitation.

When Lavin contacted Dr. Betts, he said that the doctor "told me at first that 'we'd love to help, but no room is available.' However, I emphasized to Dr. Betts what a wonderful man Russ was, and that he really needed help. Dr. Betts replied that he'd see what he could do. Then, he called me and said he'd taken a beauty parlor at the institute and would make it into a small suite for Russ. And, that's where Russ went."

The move from Billings to the institute came at the end of February 1971 at a time when the institute was housed in an old warehouse along Ohio Street. The facility was anything but luxurious. Arrington thought the atmosphere was awful, even though he did come to understand that a special effort had been made to provide a single room for him.

Arrington did not receive this room, explained Dr. Betts, "because of his rank." The doctor acknowledged, however, that upon being "made aware of his (Arrington's) political importance," Arrington got the single "because he was going to have a lot of visitors."

Dr. Betts added that Arrington did not receive "any care that would not have gone to anybody else. The same care goes to rich and poor alike."

Nevertheless, Dr. Betts noted that he took Arrington under his "personal wing" because he was "a patient that certainly did need a lot of attention."

It didn't take very long, though, for Dr. Betts to see that Arrington was determined "to do whatever he could do to come back." Although pointing out that Arrington was "not lucid or intellectually reliable when he first came in," Dr. Betts stressed in a 2004 interview in his Chicago office that Arrington became "an exemplary patient" once "his mind returned enough for him to know what was going on."

"He took advantage of every part of the treatment," Dr. Betts remembered. "He put in many extra hours of speech therapy, and he showed exceptional drive in his physical therapy. He didn't want to waste any time. He never had a slump where he became discouraged and I had to pull him out of it. He was a self-starter who stayed accelerated. He knew he had to do every bit of work we put before him.

He was determined to talk again, to walk again, to do things for himself. I'd be hard pressed to think of another patient more highly motivated than Senator Arrington."

"By God," declared Dr. Betts, "he was going to get well."

Chapter 23

Ɛ

Fighting Back from the Canvas

Very few thought they'd see him return, let alone walk into the Senate chamber. But Arrington did exactly that on October 12, 1971.

Nine months after the stroke that sent him to the mat—a knockdown blow that threatened to leave him a hopeless invalid—Arrington slowly and carefully, bolstered by an ebony cane and a brace on his right leg, entered his old lair to triumphant applause from his fellow senators and the clicking and grinding of television and news cameras.

Normal decorum was abandoned as Democrats welcomed him back with the same gusto as Republicans.

"God bless you, Senator Arrington," intoned Democratic leader Cecil Partee, determined not to be outdone by other well-wishers.

Even stone-faced reporters put objectivity aside to join the line-up of those greeting Arrington as a returning hero. Some hardly disguised the feeling in stories filed afterward.

"A special measure of style has returned to the General Assembly," wrote Tony Fuller of the *Chicago Daily News*. The absence of "the Republican grandee from Evanston," continued Fuller, "caused the Senate to flounder about, taking days to do work it would otherwise accomplish in an afternoon.

"And the immaculately tailored, syntactically flawless, urbane Arrington style has been missed in a chamber where fraternity-type pranks and traveling salesman jokes are still in vogue."

Going further, some scribes held that the presence of Arrington punctured for the moment the gloom in the chamber caused by public dismay over the ongoing disclosures of windfalls for major political figures from secret financial dealings—ethically questionable if not illicit—between themselves and the horse racing crowd. And, of course, an uncomfortable number with the largest portfolios of racing stocks were legislators.

Arrington had no connection to the messy situation, or, for that matter, to any other scandalous wrongdoing during his time. Staying clean was a badge of honor, embellished all the more by his visibility as the state's most prominent legislator for so many years. His return to the Senate floor provided some reinforcement—if only temporarily—for the face of integrity the Senate was expected to wear.

Compared to the fireball of the past, the Arrington that hobbled into the largely forgettable fall session of the Seventy-seventh General Assembly was greatly toned down. Not that all had changed. Seated in his chair, he still puffed on hefty cigars, and frequently was seen swiping errant ashes off the legs of his pin-striped suits. His partial speech impediment resulting from the stroke meant his days of unrivaled oration were over. However, he had no trouble barking out his votes on issues, or in getting across what was on his mind in measured conversations.

His participation in the abbreviated session led to speculation that he apparently had no intention of leaving the legislature. However, the thought was put to rest by a press release, handed out by Arrington aides after the session, which announced that he would not seek reelection to the Senate in 1972.

A typical retirement announcement for an Illinois official almost always declared that a distinguished career was coming to an end. In Arrington's case, the words were true. The press release language that Arrington's departure would conclude "one of the longest and most prestigious careers in Illinois legislative history" triggered no argument.

It was telling that, out of all that could have been highlighted, the release emphasized that Arrington pushed to revitalize the General

Assembly to "counter the growing power of the federal government."

"The only way to fight big government in Washington," Arrington was quoted as saying, "is to have effective government on the state level." The release added that Arrington strove to advance "the cause of the states" while acting as a wheelhorse in organizations such as the National Conference of State Legislative Leaders (which he helped establish).

As Mark Q. Rhoads summed it up, Arrington used his influence in the NCSLL and related groups to cement his stature as "one of the architects of the modern state legislature, not just in Illinois but in many states." Rhoads, an assistant to Arrington in the dusk of his legislative career and later a Republican member of the Senate from Western Springs, was around Arrington enough in 1971 and 1972 to appreciate what Rhoads called the senator's "remarkable progress toward recovery" from the stroke.

The significant extent of Arrington's comeback from his apoplexy—albeit a struggle without end—was a story of courage and, as Dr. Betts couched it, utter determination.

His recuperation permitted much more than his return to the Statehouse—where his presence in the post-stroke period sometimes amounted to little more than cameo appearances. As the 1970s moved on, Arrington was able to savor many of the pleasures of life, even more so in some respects than in his full-blown legislative years when the great investment of his time in public and professional pursuits often limited his partaking of routine amenities. Now, longer hours were available for dinner engagements, family get-togethers and other social occasions, as well as various events— some of which were held in his honor.

Arrington also managed to remain involved in his leadership roles with the McCormick Boys Club, the American Foundation of Religion and Psychiatry, the Mental Health Association of Chicago, the Illinois Masonic Hospital and other entities.

Through it all, though, his therapy remained a top priority the rest of his life.

In the early period of his recovery, he took heart from the example of stage and film actress Patricia Neal, who had suffered a series of massive strokes in 1966 that left her paralyzed and unable to speak. Fighting back, her recovery had progressed far enough two years after the strokes to permit her to appear in a film and win nomination for an Academy Award. If Senate aide Robert Albritton remembered it right, Arrington made contact with Neal. "He latched on to her as an inspiration," said Albritton, "believing that if she could do it, he could do it."

Arrington's stay at the rehab institute had lasted four months. After that, he moved to an apartment in Chicago's north side Astor Towers, where he lived until late in 1973. From there, he relocated to an apartment in the building at 1550 North Lake Shore Drive facing Lake Michigan, a move arranged by his son Michael. It remained his residence until his death. At first, Arrington rented his apartment, which consisted of two units on the twenty-fifth floor overlooking the lake. Later, he purchased his living area when the building was converted into condominiums.

The requisites for recovery from the stroke had precluded a return by Arrington to his Edgemere house. Although he still saw Ruth with regularity, they were never to live together again after the stroke. About the time Arrington was moving from the Astor apartment to Lake Shore Drive, Ruth, a heavy smoker, underwent an operation for lung cancer. She tried to follow a rigorous program to recover from the operation, but the disease was so advanced that there really was no hope. She died at the age of sixty-six on October 24, 1973, in the Edgemere home, where she had continued to reside. She and Arrington were married forty-one years.

The death of Ruth did not bring an end to female companionship for Arrington as the 1970s moved along. He frequently had a woman at his side at public events or when dining at one of his favorite hotel restaurants or Chicago steak houses frequented by political notables. One such individual off and on was Jean Howard, a bright acquaintance well known in certain civic circles.

Paul N. Goodson, who served two stints as Arrington's live-in aide during the '70s, remembered evenings when Arrington and Howard dined at his place or hers, and then squared off in gin rummy or hashed over issues of the day. Jean "thought she was good thera-py for him by challenging him," said Goodson. "She'd intentionally rile him up…argue with him. She'd call and talk to Dr. Betts about what she could do to help him."

A woman frequently on Arrington's arm in the latter part of the decade was Elizabeth Lee Hague, a widow who at the time ran an advertising agency in Chicago. Elizabeth, a classy redhead when she was introduced to Arrington at his request, didn't hesitate to frame their relationship when she was contacted by telephone a quarter of a century later at her home in Bradenton, Florida. By then, she was the wife of Lewis G. Kearns, a retired investment firm executive.

"Russ and I had what you would call a wholesome love affair," Elizabeth said. "It was a gentle relationship in which we had so much fun together. Actually, we were perfect together because we had so many similarities, like the appreciation both of us had for the social graces."

Being squired by Arrington could have a heady side, Elizabeth found out, as she rubbed shoulders with President Gerald Ford on an occasion or two and Chicago Mayor Jane Byrne more than once. There also were, of course, the very tony affairs at the mansion of Clem and Jessie Stone. However, more rewarding, in her opinion, were dinners at which she brought her family together with Arrington's.

"Russ truly savored these times," Elizabeth said, "because he really wanted to see normal settings in which everybody in our two families was present. I don't think there is any way to overemphasize how important Pat, Mike and the grandchildren were to him in those last years."

Still, most evenings she and Russ ate alone. The routine often entailed, she noted, "Paul (Goodson) picking me up at my office and taking me to his (Arrington's) Lake Shore place. We'd then maybe have a drink, which might be followed by a salad, stone crabs and pistachio ice cream, which he knew I loved. After that, we'd watch and discuss television news, catch up on Chicago politics and some-times end up playing cards."

Still, no person was more familiar than Goodson with Arrington's

*Senator Arrington and Governor Dan Walker (next to Arrington
in center of photo) receiving honorary Doctor of Letters degrees
at Lincoln College in 1973*

daily regimen in the final stage of his life. Goodson, one of six children of an Indiana dairy farmer, left teaching at an elementary school to live and work with Arrington from 1972 to 1974. After a return to the classroom, he rejoined Arrington in 1978 and remained in his service until Arrington's death. Goodson reminisced about his last period with Arrington in a 2004 interview at the Chicago law firm where he then was employed.

He had his own private living area in Arrington's condo because he was at the former senator's beck and call from Sunday afternoon through Friday afternoon of every week. Most days went the same. When Arrington awoke about 6 a.m., Goodson had a breakfast of orange juice, cereal, toast and coffee awaiting him. And the morning's *Chicago Tribune* always was spread out on the big dining table.

Returning to his bedroom after breakfast, Arrington used his cane to pull out the sleeves of the suit and shirt he wanted to wear, and Goodson took them out of the closet. Arrington showered and shaved himself, but Goodson helped him dress. By that point, Estelle Richards, another Arrington employee, usually had arrived to tend to the condo during the day.

Departing his residence with most of the morning remaining, Arrington was driven by Goodson to either his law office or, on days when therapy was scheduled, to the rehab institute or Northwestern Memorial Hospital. They traveled in Arrington's recognizable Cadillac, which Chicago police—aware of its owner—never ticketed for its sometimes illegal parking. Goodson noticed that Arrington still kept, but no longer used, the old green convertible he'd lovingly driven in tooling around Springfield in days gone by.

Even on days of therapy, Arrington still made it to his law office. There, he huddled as always with Marion Meyers (Marion Belland before her marriage to Les Meyers), the woman who'd run the place for what seemed like forever. In truth, she'd been the biggest constant in his life outside of his family and perhaps Clem Stone. She was privy to everything about him, and loyal to the core.

Fetching lunch for Arrington and Marion was usually another Goodson chore, although it seldom included more than cottage cheese and Jell-O. Nineteen seventy-eight was the year in which Arrington—at the suggestion of doctors as part of his therapy—dictated his memoirs into a recorder. Most was done during these visits to his office, with Marion at his side as much as possible. She herself was seriously ill with cancer at that juncture.

Goodson found Marion fascinating, saying that "B" (as she was called) was "never out of the Arrington picture…he relied on her for everything." Aware that she was an eye-catching blonde for many years, Goodson found believable one story about her. "I was told," he related, that many years earlier a drugstore in downtown Chicago advertised a cigarette brand on a billboard that featured an attractive woman. "And so the story went," he said, "that woman was none other than her (Marion)."

Days with Arrington afforded Goodson little lax time. He accompanied Arrington to meetings of boards on which he remained active, including those of Combined Insurance and Alberto-Culver. He ushered Arrington to evening banquets and other dinner engagements, where his duties even encompassed making sure that Arrington's meat was cut for him (something he could not do).

One occasion that greatly showcased Arrington's extensive

recovery from the stroke occurred May 2, 1978, at the Conrad Hilton Hotel. Arrington labeled it "the event of my life" in his memoirs. The proceeding was a dinner of the McCormick Boys Club in honor of Arrington. The affair was chaired by Peer Pedersen and emceed by Hugh Hill, the Chicago TV newsman who, like Arrington, had come a long way from his days as a youngster in Gillespie. The attendees were a virtual who's who of public life in Illinois. Three distinguished guests, former governors Ogilvie, Shapiro and Walker, extolled the virtues of Arrington in special comments. The evening's finale called for a response by Arrington—and he delivered it with flying colors.

Arrington had spoken in public since the stroke, but not on such a grand occasion. He fretted ahead of time over whether he was sufficiently recovered to address this particular assemblage; he was leaning against it on the eve of the dinner.

However, as he recounted in his memoirs, "I decided at the last minute I was going to speak. Had I not done it, I don't know what it would have done to me internally. It (probably) would have ruined my self-confidence…it would have been disastrous (for me) not to have done it."

Fortunately, he added, "people thought it turned out very well. As a matter of fact, several persons called me and said they were very happy that I talked."

One individual at the dinner especially appreciative of what he witnessed was Dr. Betts.

"Since I'd known him (Arrington) when he couldn't talk at all," he related, "I sat there thinking 'just look at that' when he walked across the room in the hotel and gave a speech that was quite elegant. It was dramatic, and I was moved by it."

Arrington continued to appear—and sometimes speak—at public events in the months that followed, a number of them to aid organizations or causes he supported. However, the occurrence that stood out in many minds remained the May 1978 dinner for him at the Conrad Hilton. It certainly was one of the first things his peers remembered when his life came to an end October 4, 1979.

Most Chicagoans' attention that day centered on the scheduled arrival in the city that evening of Pope John Paul II and on the mass he was to celebrate the next day in Grant Park. Goodson wasn't thinking about the Pope, though.

Something seemed to be wrong. The morning of that day, exactly three months after his seventy-third birthday, Arrington didn't emerge from his bedroom at the normal time. Nor had he summoned Goodson to his bedside (Paul never entered the bedroom until called in by Arrington). After Estelle Richards arrived at the condo, and still with no word from Arrington, Goodson and Estelle decided to lean close to his bedroom door. They heard only what sounded faintly like water running in the sink of the bathroom off the bedroom.

Getting an uneasy feeling, Goodson asked in a loud voice if Arrington needed assistance. Hearing no reply, Goodson determined to investigate. Entering the bedroom, he observed Arrington sitting in a chair at his bathroom vanity, slumped over the sink. "Obviously," said Goodson, "he (Arrington) was not alive."

Arrington "had a habit, often before coming out in the morning, of sitting down at the sink or vanity and running water to clean his dentures. He was in the act of doing this, since the water was still running, when he died."

Believing Michael Arrington to be out of town, Goodson immediately called the office of Pedersen, the person the Arrington family most entrusted in such a situation. Police also were notified. After Pedersen was alerted to the matter by his office, he rushed to the Arrington condo. Police already had shown up.

"A policeman asked me to identify the body," said Pedersen, "and I did so. It was, to say the least, a very sobering experience." Arrington's death certificate would note that he died of a "coronary occlusion."

Michael Arrington was away at the time, as Goodson suspected. He was in Stockholm dealing with business when his wife, Trudi, notified him of his father's death. Michael quickly returned to Chicago, aware he had work to do in arranging a funeral service befitting a person with the stature of his father.

Chapter 24

ɸ

The Legacy

he life of Arrington embodied the American dream. His personification of the eternal tale of a poor boy who made good was driven home in eloquent eulogies by Governor James Thompson, United States Senator Charles Percy and Clement Stone at a memorial service for Arrington four days after his death. The theme also was underscored by the Reverend Harold Blake Walker, the minister emeritus of the First Presbyterian Church of Evanston, who officiated at the heavily attended service at the John L. Hebblethwaite Funeral Home in Evanston.

At least two of the speakers, Stone and Percy, had themselves emerged from very modest beginnings to achieve great success. Therefore, Stone felt he was on sound ground in stressing that detrimental conditions in one's early years need not deter a person from reaching for and grasping life's golden rings. All should take heart from the example of Arrington, he implored.

It was true, Stone said, that Arrington "was the son of an Irish coal miner and knew poverty as a boy." But, to those "who are poor" and "have a lot of disadvantages," emphasized Stone, "the opportunities are here, just as numerous as they were back in the days" when Arrington worked his way through school and made something of himself.

To Stone, an individual's philosophy, particularly if he or she truly lived it, was "perhaps more important" than the person's biography.

"Russ did live his philosophy," said Stone, "a philosophy that any young man born of poor parentage and living in this great land of America could, if he were motivated to do so, render a great service to the future."

The remarks of Percy were geared to Arrington's grandchildren: Steven Russell Smythe and David Arrington Smythe (sons of Patricia and Robert Smythe during their twenty-year marriage) and Jennifer Lorraine Arrington, a daughter of Michael and Trudi. (Another grandson, Patrick Browne Arrington, was born in the years after Senator Arrington's death to Michael and Trudi.)

In the words of Percy, Arrington "inspired every member of his family, and I trust that he shall always be an inspiration to his grandchildren. He loved them, just as he loved all of us."

Percy, in his thirteenth year in the Senate at the time, expressed hope that the grandkids would someday appreciate what a "remarkable, great American their grandfather was."

Percy also emphasized that Arrington "certainly had a great feeling for God, he had a feeling for his Maker, he had a feeling that we should fear God in a way that expresses our love for God, but we should fear no man; and I know of no man that had less fear of his fellowman than Russell Arrington."

Although a fiercely loyal Republican, Arrington was said by Percy to be a firm believer in the two-party system—so much so that he "never looked upon his party as restricting his thinking or putting him in a mold that he had to adhere to."

Percy surprised none of the political leaders and dignitaries from other walks of Chicago life at the service when he suggested that Arrington's business acumen provided strong footing for responsible politics. Percy, a onetime industrialist, stated that, above all else, Arrington's strongest suit was government finance. Arrington recognized that "unless something is soundly conceived financially, it is built on sand," Percy pointed out, leading to his conviction that "state government must be structured on a solid rock of conservative fiscal responsibility."

Labeling Arrington "the dean of Illinois politics," Thompson— then in his third year as governor—pronounced that "no person in

Arrington family members Ruth, Mike, Pat and Russ

the history of Illinois politics, of any time, of either party, in any branch of government, ever had the profound impact on the legislative branch as did Russ Arrington."

Just as important, underscored Thompson, Arrington was a pragmatist who "believed in using politics and government to get things done—to solve people's problems, even if he didn't always agree with all of the solutions…a unique hallmark of Russ Arrington."

An obvious example, noted Thompson, was Arrington's sponsorship and push to passage of the state income tax legislation in 1969.

"It was not a popular fight. He was not personally persuaded that it was the right way to go, but he knew that something had to be done to give state government in Illinois a solid financial footing and to enable it to keep the promises that government explicitly, as well as implicitly, makes to its people to provide a civilized, decent, orderly society and to help those who cannot help themselves. Those are the…premises of government…(they) cannot be done without resources."

After his burial beside Ruth in Memorial Park Cemetery in

Skokie, plaudits for Arrington continued to rain. Their gist usually mirrored what Neil Mehler, the *Chicago Tribune* political editor, had written six years before Arrington's death but after his legislative career was over.

In a few paragraphs, Mehler painted a word-picture of Arrington that well could have been his political epitaph, albeit a long one.

Arrington, wrote Mehler, "was a tough-minded egotist who led that band of (Republican) conservatives down a path they often didn't want to travel and into an era of professionalism that has left an indelible mark on the General Assembly.

"Arrington, as majority leader, put research teeth into the Senate. He hired a staff of professionals to do his homework for him, gave staff aides to his Republican committee chairmen, and printed a program of goals for the GOP majority in the Senate, even if his colleagues didn't agree with all of them.

"He was not loved by any means—but he was damn well respected. He would bring his troops into his office for a party caucus and, using Knute Rockne locker room inspirational techniques laced with profanity, tell them where they were going. If they didn't like it, they could fight him, but that's where he was taking them.

"He outworked everyone. He used guile, emotionalism and four-letter words to mold the Senate into a more professional body. He was flexible where his troops were often doctrinaire. He had his bright young aides get the facts and the figures to support his positions."

Arrington thought, concluded Mehler, "a leader should lead."

Leadership sometimes meant putting rigid partisanship aside, something Arrington did on more than on a few occasions. A person who saw this in Arrington was former Governor Dan Walker, a Democrat who took office at the start of 1973. Arrington was gone from the legislature by then, but he and Walker were together on occasion. One time was May 19, 1973, when Arrington and Walker each received an honorary doctor of letters degree from Lincoln College in Lincoln, Illinois. Actually, Walker became acquainted with Arrington years before he became governor when Walker went to Springfield as a leader of the Chicago Crime Commission to push for commission bills being sponsored by Arrington.

"He (Arrington) took me by the hand, and helped me navigate the legislative process," Walker recollected during a 2004 interview at the former governor's home in Escondido, California. "He even coached me on my committee testimony. And, the bills passed."

During Arrington's years at the Senate helm, Walker said, "he did what was necessary for the welfare of Illinoisans on matters of importance. He was a statesman, a status reached by very few legislators. When the chips were down, he rose above partisanship."

"During my time as governor," Walker lamented, "I regretted that there was no Arrington in the opposite party in the Senate. I could have talked with him about state issues. Our discussions would not have had to be dominated by politics. For that reason alone, Arrington was most unusual."

As so often happens in the world, Arrington did not live to hear the ultimate sobriquet attached to his name by some of those who followed him in the pantheon of Illinois politics. Put simply, they called him the father of the modern General Assembly.

Those were the exact words of Michael Madigan in his interview with this writer in 2003, when he was speaker of the Illinois House and a person destined for a place in the state's political history. "No doubt," he said, "Senator Arrington is the father of the modern General Assembly."

Mayor Richard M. Daley, in his comments for this book, altered the description only slightly in saying that Arrington —in spite of his often strained relationship with Daley's father, the initial Chicago Mayor Daley—was "known as the father of the modern legislature."

Former Senate President Philip Rock echoed this assessment, and went on to add that "he (Arrington) made it clear to governors that we (the legislative branch) were equal to the executive branch— irrespective of politics."

In considering the always sensitive relationship between governors and legislators, Arrington was alive and getting better every day when he received an unexpected letter February 15, 1973, from Paul Simon. It was a gracious communication in view of the many turns in the long comings and goings between the two men.

"There is no question," wrote Simon, "that you have contributed more to the well-being of the people of the state than most who have served as governor of our state."

Arrington's response to this tribute was not recorded.

However, he surely was pleased.

Interviews

❧

rimary interviews for the book were conducted with the following individuals in the period between December 2002 and February 2005. Elected state and federal officials are identified as such with their current or former titles at the time of the interviews.

Robert B. Albritton, John Alexander, Michael Arrington, James Bagley, Denysia (Dee) Bastas, Dr. Henry B. Betts, former Illinois House Speaker W. Robert Blair, H. Dickson Buckley, Gene Callahan, Richard W. Carlson, former Illinois Congressman Tom Corcoran, William R. Coulson, John P. Dailey, former United States Senator Alan J. Dixon, Richard E. Dunn, Thomas A. Easterly, former Governor Jim Edgar, Wallace Gair, Paul N. Goodson, former Illinois Senate President William C. Harris and wife Jeanne, Hugh Hill, Elizabeth Lee Kearns, former State Senator John J. Lanigan, Leonard Lavin, Illinois House Speaker Michael J. Madigan, Barbara Edwards Mehlenbeck, former Illinois Comptroller Dawn Clark Netsch, Arthur C. Niemann, Peer Pedersen, former Illinois Senate President James (Pate) Philip, former Illinois Congressman John E. Porter, Linda Relias, former State Senator Mark Q. Rhoads, former Illinois Senate President Philip J. Rock, former Illinois Congressman Daniel D. Rostenkowski, Walter Roth, former United States Senator Paul Simon, Patricia Arrington Smythe, Mrs. William G. (Shirley) Stratton, Donald E. Tolva, former Governor Dan Walker and the Reverend Frank Westhoff.

*(Unknown), Vice President Hubert Humphrey (in center)
and Senator Arrington*

In addition, Mayor Richard M. Daley of Chicago, Southern Illinois University professor emeritus of political science David Kenney and Secretary of Defense Donald H. Rumsfeld submitted written comments for the book.

Select Bibliography

Anton, Thomas J. *The Politics of State Expenditure in Illinois.*
Urbana: Univ. of Illinois Press, 1966.

Barnhart, Bill, and Gene Schlickman. *Kerner: The Conflict of
Intangible Rights.* Urbana: Univ. of Illinois Press, 1999.

Canfield, Robert R. *Fat-Cat Lobbyists Make Your Laws.*
New York: Vantage Press, 1968.

Casey, Robert J., and W. A. S. Douglas. *The Midwesterner: The
Story of Dwight H. Green.* Chicago: Wilcox & Follett Co., 1948.

Cohen, Adam, and Elizabeth Taylor. *American Pharaoh: Mayor
Richard J. Daley.* Boston: Little, Brown and Company, 2000.

Gertz, Elmer, and Joseph P. Pisciotte. *Charter for a New Age: An
Inside View of the Sixth Illinois Constitutional Convention.*
Urbana: Univ. of Illinois Press, 1980.

Gilbert, John G. *Memoir.* Springfield: Sangamon State Univ., Oral
History Office, 1985.

Gove, Samuel K., and James D. Nowlan. *Illinois Politics and
Government.* Lincoln: Univ. of Nebraska Press, 1996.

Hartley, Robert E. *Paul Powell of Illinois: A Lifelong Democrat.*
Carbondale: Southern Illinois Univ. Press, 1999.

Howard, Robert P. *The Illinois Governors: Mostly Good and
Competent Men,* 2d ed. Revised and updated by Peggy Boyer Long

U.S. Senator Howard Baker of Tennessee and Senator Arrington

and Mike Lawrence. Springfield: Univ. of Illinois at Springfield, Institute for Public Affairs, 1999.

Improving the State Legislature: A Report of the Illinois Commission on the Organization of the General Assembly. Urbana: Univ. of Illinois Press, 1967.

Katz, Harold A. *Memoir,* 2 vols. Springfield: Sangamon State Univ., Oral History Office, 1988.

Kenney, David. *A Political Passage: The Career of Stratton of Illinois.* Carbondale: Southern Illinois Univ. Press, 1990.

Kilian, Michael, Connie Fletcher and F. Richard Ciccone. *Who Runs Chicago?* New York: St. Martin's Press, 1979.

Manaster, Kenneth A. *Illinois Justice.* Chicago: Univ. of Chicago Press, 2001.

Martin, John Bartlow. *Adlai Stevenson of Illinois.* New York: Doubleday, 1976.

McCarter, John W., Jr. *Memoir.* Springfield: Sangamon State Univ., Oral History Office, 1984.

McCarthy, Robert W. *Memoir,* 2 vols. Springfield: Sangamon State Univ., Oral History Office, 1983.

McGloon, Thomas A. *Memoir,* 2 vols. Springfield: Sangamon State Univ., Oral History Office, 1981.

Murray, David. *Charles Percy of Illinois.* New York: Harper & Row, Publishers, 1968.

O'Neill, William L. *Coming Apart: An Informal History of America in the 1960's.* New York: Quadrangle Books, 1971.

Parkhurst, John C. *Memoir,* 2 vols. Springfield: Sangamon State Univ., Oral History Office, 1984.

Pensoneau, Taylor. *Governor Richard Ogilvie: In the Interest of the State.* Carbondale: Southern Illinois Univ. Press, 1997.

Pensoneau, Taylor, and Bob Ellis. *Dan Walker: The Glory and the Tragedy.* Evansville, Ind.: Smith-Collins, 1993.

Royko, Mike. *Boss: Richard J. Daley of Chicago.* New York: E. P. Dutton & Co., 1971.

Simon, Paul. *P. S. The Autobiography of Paul Simon.* Chicago: Bonus Books, 1999.

Thiem, George. *The Hodge Scandal.* New York: St. Martin's Press, 1963.

Van Der Slik, Jack R., and Kent D. Redfield. *Lawmaking in Illinois.* Springfield: Sangamon State Univ., Office of Public Affairs Communication, 1986.

Index